Arabic as
One Language

Related Works from Georgetown University Press

The Teaching of Arabic as a Foreign Language: Issues and Directions
Mahmoud Al-Batal, editor

Teaching and Learning Arabic as a Foreign Language: A Guide for Teachers
Karin Ryding, foreword by Roger Allen

Arabic Language and Linguistics
Reem Bassiouney and E. Graham Katz, editors

Al-ᶜArabiyya: Journal of the American Association of Teachers of Arabic

Arabic as One Language

Integrating Dialect in the Arabic Language Curriculum

Mahmoud Al-Batal, Editor

Georgetown University Press / Washington, DC

The publisher is not responsible for third-party websites or their content. URL links were active at time of publication.

Library of Congress Cataloging-in-Publication Data

Names: Al-Batal, Mahmoud, editor.
Title: Arabic as One Language : Integrating Dialect in the Arabic Language
    Curriculum / Mahmoud al-Batal, editor.
Description: Washington, DC : Georgetown University Press, 2017. | Includes
    bibliographical references and index.
Identifiers: LCCN 2017007580 (print) | LCCN 2017010313 (ebook) | ISBN
    9781626165038 (hc : alk. paper) | ISBN 9781626165045 (pb : alk. paper) |
    ISBN 9781626165052 (eb)
Subjects: LCSH: Arabic language--Study and teaching. | Arabic
    language--Spoken Arabic. | Arabic language--Dialects.
Classification: LCC PJ6066 .A69 2017 (print) | LCC PJ6066 (ebook) | DDC
    492.7/80071--dc23
LC record available at https://lccn.loc.gov/2017007580

♾ This book is printed on acid-free paper meeting the requirements of the American National Standard for Permanence in Paper for Printed Library Materials.

19 18   9 8 7 6 5 4 3 2   First printing

Printed in the United States of America

Cover design by Martha Madrid

To teachers and students of Arabic everywhere
in the hope that this work
will contribute to richer teaching and learning experiences
and deeper appreciation of its beautiful mosaic

Contents

Preface

The question of the relationship between *al-fuṣḥā* "formal literary Arabic" and *al-ᶜāmmiyya* "colloquial Arabic" and their place in teaching and learning has occupied Arab intellectuals and education specialists at least since the early days of Arab Nahḍa "awakening" in the nineteenth century. The issue has been and continues to be debated vigorously because it is complex and laden with ideology. The sociolinguistic maxim "When we talk about language, we are also talking about something else" points us toward the ways in which the question of Arabic touches on politics, religion, and cultural identity. Current pedagogical practice throughout the Arabic-speaking world makes *al-fuṣḥā* the sole focus of curricula intended for native speakers of Arabic, while *al-ᶜāmmiyya*, the means of daily communication, is not admitted into the curriculum.

The field of teaching Arabic as a Foreign Language (TAFL) in the United States and elsewhere in the world has largely upheld this practice and developed its own vision of *al-fuṣḥā* that came to be known as Modern Standard Arabic (MSA). The sole attention to MSA worked well at a time when the learning of Arabic in the West was perceived of as an academic pursuit focused on deciphering and translating texts with very little attention to the speaking skill—especially because this coincided with an Arab public sphere that was largely censored and linguistically corrected. This pedagogical practice drew justification from Charles Ferguson's "diglossia" in 1959 that presented *al-fuṣḥā* as the "high" prestigious variety of language and *al-ᶜāmmiyya* as the "low" variety.

This single-minded attention to MSA in the TAFL curricula continued until the 1980s, when new concepts, approaches, and practices emerged in foreign language education. The communicative approach to language teaching and the proficiency movement promoted sociolinguistic and pragmatic competencies along with contexts, functions, and authentic language. These trends continued to evolve in the 1990s with a new emphasis on developing cultural knowledge and intercultural communication in language curricula. These developments presented teachers of Arabic with the challenge of designing curricula that are communicative- and proficiency-based in a language variety that is not used in interpersonal communication. Gradually the status of MSA as the only form of Arabic we teach our students came into question, and we began to hear calls to introduce dialects to the Arabic curriculum in order to bring the curriculum in line with communicative approaches. Large programs introduced dialect courses at the upper levels; however, these courses remained separate from the core Arabic curriculum that continued to privilege MSA.

The new millennium accentuated and accelerated these challenges, as the United States saw an unprecedented growth of interest in the study of Arabic and in study abroad in the Arab world. The high level of demand for Arabic created the opportunity for the development and publication of new textbooks, two of which integrate MSA and dialect, yet also underscored the fact that the exclusive focus on MSA and the almost complete exclusion of the dialect from the curriculum at the lower levels of instruction was not preparing students for real communication or intercultural communication.

Despite these developments, however, the integration of dialect into the teaching of Arabic remains the practice of a minority of programs in the United States. Opposition to integration is often attributed to care for the well-being of the students, on the basis that it would cause confusion, or because teachers fear they might teach students a dialect for which they have no use. This book presents research from a variety of programs demonstrating that the difficulty of learning two varieties of a language is far outweighed by the benefit of skills gained and that dialect is important in building linguistic and sociocultural skills no matter which dialect is taught. (More data and evidence is available than could fit in the book; additional data, as noted in each chapter, is provided on this book's product page on the Georgetown University Press website.) What is left after that is language ideology: the deep-seated beliefs that many educated speakers of Arabic share about what constitutes "proper" or "correct" language and the equally deep feelings about the link between *al-fuṣḥā* and Islam. But these ideologies cannot constitute the main guiding principles for the profession of TAFL.

The main aim of the present volume is to shift the debate on dialect integration in the field of Arabic from the realm of ideology to that of pedagogy. It does so by providing Arabic teachers and curriculum designers with insights and experiences of Arabic programs in the United States and abroad that have integrated dialects into their curricula. These insights are based on actual program models, classroom practices, and students' output, augmented by student and teacher perspectives gathered through surveys and interviews.

This book is aimed at present and future teachers of Arabic as a foreign/second language, program directors and coordinators, and students interested in learning more about how Arabic can be studied and taught. The book may also be of interest to specialists in foreign language education interested in understanding the current dynamics of the Arabic field and its future trajectories.

The book includes sixteen chapters that deal with a wide variety of issues related to integration. The chapters are written by instructors who teach in Arabic programs in the United States, the United Kingdom, Italy, and the United Arab Emirates and who have implemented integration in their own teaching. The book is organized in four sections described below.

Part 1: Dialect Integration: A New Frontier for Arabic

Section 1 includes five chapters and provides general background to the issue of integration as a new frontier for the field of Arabic. In chapter 1, Mahmoud Al-Batal presents a vision of "Arabic as One," in which dialect and MSA are conceived as one language, integrated and coexisting in the classroom from the onset. He then argues why this vision should replace what he calls the "firewall of separation" between MSA and the dialects, noting the increased presence of spoken Arabic in the public sphere across the Arab world, the changing needs of Arabic learners, and the new trends in language pedagogy. Al-Batal discusses six current models of integration that demonstrate the flexibility that institutions have in implementing an integrated approach that addresses their particular goals and contexts. In the "Arabic as One" vision, he argues, lies a fuller understanding of the Arabic language and a richer appreciation of the intricacies of Arab cultures.

In chapter 2, Munther Younes synthesizes his long experience exploring how to integrate dialect and MSA. Should the two registers be integrated simultaneously? Should they be introduced in the same course or through separate tracks? Taking the Arabic program at Cornell as a case study, Younes argues that MSA and dialect are one in the same communication system with complimentary roles and, as such, should be given an equal weight in curriculum development. By navigating the reader through examples of specific activities that engage both the written and oral proficiencies, the author illustrates a program based on shared elements of dialect and MSA, particularly at the early stages of instruction.

In chapter 3, Kirk Belnap provides the history and development of dialect integration at Brigham Young University (BYU), explaining how the desire to provide students with the skills to communicate in both informal and formal contexts became the foundation of BYU's program. Analyzing data gathered from BYU students who studied abroad, the author highlights the ability of the program to teach and students to learn and function in Arabic in MSA and multiple dialects. Furthermore, he demonstrates how proficiency in one dialect increases students' enthusiasm for proficiency in other registers of the language, including MSA. Belnap argues that dialect integration is worth any initial confusion experienced by either instructors or students in order to develop superior proficiency in Arabic.

In chapter 4, Jonathan Featherstone analyzes the reasons for a lack of institutional practice of the integrated approach, specifically in the United Kingdom. He introduces a teacher-training program based on the concept of integration at the University of Edinburgh as a way of addressing the fears, worries, and, confusion associated with integration in the minds of many Arabic teachers. This training program aids instructors in deconstructing and reconstructing their perceptions of Arabic in the hopes of helping them better understand the relationship between MSA and the dialects. The program also helps the teachers develop both the creative tools required to teach an integrated curriculum and the empathy needed to understand the learning process for students under this approach.

In chapter 5, Elizabeth Huntley provides a comprehensive background to the question of integration in the field of Arabic and discusses the arguments that are presented for and against integration. She also compares the reactions of students learning under the integrated approach in a beginning-level course at the University of Michigan to those studying dialect and MSA simultaneously while abroad. Huntley underscores the importance of implementing an integrated curriculum from the very start in order to mitigate possible confusion among students on the various differences in dialect and MSA.

Part 2: Curricular Models and Approaches to Integration

Part 2 is composed of four chapters that document the curricular models and approaches to integration that have been developed at major programs in the United States and abroad. In chapter 6, Manuela Giolfo and Federico Salvaggio use the Common European Framework of Reference for Languages (CEF) and information and communications technology (ICT) as models to develop a task-based curriculum that seeks to place equal but separate emphasis on MSA and the dialects in an integrated approach. By separating Arabic into four basic skills and then further into two subcategories of reading and writing versus listening and speaking, the authors develop a method for monitoring appropriate student use of dialect and MSA across the various levels of language proficiency. The authors then demonstrate, through ICT, a method for determining the linguistic output for each of the separate skills based on tasks completed by students. They conclude that the appropriate use of dialect and MSA is possible in an integrated approach, and they demonstrate a method for accurately assessing student proficiency in both registers across the four skills.

In chapter 7, Emma Trentman demonstrates a way to address integration through a genre-based curriculum. Theoretically based on the systemic functional linguistics definition of text and genre, Trentman develops a beginning-level Arabic curriculum at the University of New Mexico structured around "Can-Do" statements. The use of Can-Do statements, such as "I can talk about jobs and careers," as a basis for the curriculum creates a way to incorporate contexts for appropriate usage of dialect and MSA in a natural fashion. The author advocates the use of genre-based pedagogies to address both how to integrate dialect and MSA in an Arabic language program and how to create sociolinguistic awareness among students.

In chapter 8, Mike Turner introduces a program for integrating the teaching of Moroccan Arabic dialect materials into a first-year Arabic course that uses the *Al-Kitaab* textbook series. He describes the increasing urgency of developing materials for teaching Moroccan in the integrated classroom, propelled by recent changes in the TAFL field, and outlines the principles that should inform this task. A key component of the author's proposal is an independent online Moroccan Arabic Supplement, already prototyped and implemented in a first-year Arabic course, which provides task-based activities and supporting audio-visual materials in Moroccan on par with the materials currently available in the textbook for Egyptian and Levantine. The chapter explains the design and editorial decisions that were made while preparing the supplement.

In chapter 9, Sonia Shiri and Charles Joukhadar present the integration model used by the Arabic Flagship Program at the University of Arizona, which designates a time for MSA and a separate time for dialect in the same Arabic course. The authors identify the importance of minimizing mixing between the two registers for students learning dialect and MSA simultaneously. They argue that, by heightening students' ability to "notice" and differentiate between the two varieties early on, students maintain the awareness that dialect and MSA are separate registers and, consequently, develop a sociolinguistically appropriate proficiency. Instructors play a major role in maintaining this separation and in fact act as the guiding force that strengthens the strategy of "noticing" among students. Their study argues for the possibility of achieving proficiency in an integrated classroom while maintaining a sociolinguistic distinction between the two varieties.

Part 3: Integration and Skill Development

Part 3 of this volume includes three chapters, each of which focuses on the effect of integration on overall skill development in Arabic skill with special attention paid to student output. In chapter 10, Lama Nassif seeks to categorize the phases of integration as exhibited in the spoken output of students at the elementary, intermediate, and advanced levels. A secondary goal of her study is to determine to what extent learners are successful in developing sociolinguistic competence in the two registers. By analyzing student production of verbs, negation markers, and conjunctions, Nassif codifies the features of speech in integrated instruction, identifies the systematic patterns in student speech production, and determines the degree of success of the integrated approach to develop sociolinguistic awareness among students. Nassif substantiates the success of integration by demonstrating the development of a rich linguistic awareness and repertoire that prepares students well for real-life use of the language.

In chapter 11, Thomas Leddy-Cecere maintains the focus on students' spoken output by analyzing student output as a product of the various dialect and MSA input the students have received through integration. Leddy-Cecere's study uncovers the existence of natural linguistic processes that appear and reappear among students studying the two registers simultaneously and examines the extent to which these processes are predictable and can help in determining pedagogical outcomes of integration. Through class observation and student interviews, the author lays out four developmental stages exhibited by students progressing through the Arabic program at the University of Texas at beginning through advanced levels. The study reveals an identifiable and predictable trajectory for the developmental phases of dialect among students in this curriculum, which in turn offers an important insight into further pedagogical assessment and curricular design for current and future implementation of the integrated approach.

In chapter 12, Greg Ebner and Jeff Watson challenge the notion that MSA will suffer when adopting an integrated approach. The authors argue that integration is capable of supporting an equal and strong focus on MSA and dialect simultaneously and demonstrate that there is no statistically significant decrease in MSA proficiency because of this integration. Through the analysis of test scores from West Point's Arabic students, the authors compare the achieved proficiencies of students who are studying only MSA to those focusing on MSA and a dialect and show that test results were statistically similar for students before and after integration. They argue that students are up to the challenge of developing the skills to navigate both registers.

Part 4: Learners' and Teachers' Attitudes and Perspectives

Part 4 includes four chapters that aim to bring student and teachers' perspectives to the discussion. In chapter 13, Martin Isleem investigates student and instructor perspectives on the integration of dialect and MSA. He analyzes attitudes of both groups toward an integrated curriculum and investigates whether students' learning orientations and instructors' teaching orientations are in line with one another. Isleem argues that the instructors' attitudes toward colloquial Arabic and MSA directly affect student motivation and outcomes in both registers. This study provides evidence that the two groups have positive views toward the integration of dialect in the curriculum. However, the study notes the existence of a gap between student and instructor motivations to integrate and preferences for actual implementation in the classroom. The amount of time that students want devoted to colloquial dialect in the curriculum is higher than the time actually devoted by instructors in the classroom. The chapter concludes that, while there is overall support for integration, more effort is needed on the part of programs to better align instructors' perceptions with students' needs and perspectives.

In chapter 14, Mahmoud Al-Batal and Christian Glakas contribute more evidence to the ongoing discussion on student perception toward the teaching of dialect along with MSA. Reporting the results of a survey of 184 students of Arabic at the University of Texas at Austin, the authors analyze student perceptions of the linguistic and nonlinguistic benefits of integration. The authors argue that, together with the results of previous surveys, their study points toward a larger trend among students of Arabic who feel that learning the dialect and MSA simultaneously is realistic and necessary in order to reach their desired proficiency in the language, cultural understanding, social connections, and professional preparation.

In chapter 15, Mai Zaki and Jeremy Palmer focus on a recent change in student language learning needs that reflects an increased desire to communicate effectively with native speakers and connect with the larger Arab culture. It is through this lens that the authors assess the success of an integrated approach to meet these needs at the American University in Sharjah. By analyzing the results of pre- and postsemester student surveys, journals, and dialect activities, the authors explore techniques for creating a curriculum that places equal emphasis on MSA and the dialect and lessens the confusion between the two varieties. The authors conclude that integration supports students' motivation to communicate with native speakers and help them capture the cultural nuances of the language.

In chapter 16, Caroline Najour provides insights on teachers' speech in an integrated classroom and discusses how instructors navigate an integrated classroom in terms of code switching between the two registers. The author reveals emerging patterns, strategies, and triggers of code switching used by instructors while they move along the MSA-dialect continuum. Najour also analyzes the role of the instructor in the integrated classroom in creating a supportive environment that welcomes the integration of different dialects and MSA among students. The spontaneous shifts between dialect and MSA by teachers in an integrated approach, Najour argues, expose students to the linguistic reality of the Arabic-speaking world and prepare students for more successful interactions with native speakers.

This book is accompanied by a website that provides extended data and detailed examples intended to supplement the content of some chapters. Reference to these web materials is made in the notes section at the end of relevant chapters.

The pedagogical issues related to integration are complex and require concerted effort on the part of teachers and curriculum developers to address them. This book hopes to advance our ability to develop programs that embrace variety and incorporate it in well-thought-out and planned curricula. This is our best hope to help our students develop the complex skills they need to understand and engage the wonderfully diverse Arabic-speaking reality.

Acknowledgments

Like all edited volumes, this book represents a collective rather than an individual effort. I owe a great debt of gratitude to all those who brought it to fruition. First and foremost, and on behalf of all the authors in the volume, I want to thank the students of Arabic who, knowingly or unknowingly, have significantly contributed to this volume. The various chapters in the book are based on student-generated data, whether it is their language output, attitudes, and perspectives or their classroom performance. This provides further evidence of the fact that we teachers learn a great deal from our students and that they are the real impetus for innovation and change. To all our students we extend a heartfelt *alf shukr* for continuing to be such amazing and inspiring teachers.

I want also to thank the colleagues who have shared with us here their valuable perspectives on theoretical and practical aspects of integration in Arabic. The expertise that is reflected in the various chapters is immense and will undoubtedly propel the Arabic field forward toward curricula that are more reflective of learners' needs and the new realities of Arabic language and culture.

Cameron Ford provided tremendous assistance during the various phases of the project. Her efficiency, punctuality, and attention to myriad details during all phases of the review process have been invaluable, and for this I am truly grateful. I would also like to thank James Stratton for the additional editorial help he provided while preparing the book manuscript.

Hope LeGro, assistant director of Georgetown University Press (GUP) and director of Georgetown Languages at GUP, played a significant role in grasping the vision of this project and supporting it from the early stages. This volume would not have materialized without her constant encouragement, feedback, and guidance. Glenn Saltzman, Editorial, Design, and Production Manager at GUP, and her team provided outstanding support to all contributors throughout the production process. We extend to all of them our heartfelt thanks.

I am deeply indebted to Kristen Brustad for continuing to be a great source of inspiration in my life and for helping me realize and appreciate the oneness of Arabic through its varieties. I owe her much beyond what words could express.

مع خالص الشكر والامتنان لكم جميعاً !

PART 1

Dialect Integration

A New Frontier for Arabic

Dialect Integration in the Arabic Foreign Language Curriculum

Vision, Rationale, and Models

MAHMOUD AL-BATAL

The American University of Beirut

THE QUESTION of how to approach the sociolinguistic situation in Arabic pedagogically and how to handle the complex reality of Standard Arabic and the dialects in teaching Arabic as a foreign/second language poses an existential question that has occupied Arabic teachers and curriculum developers for a long time. This question was one pondered by Cornelius Van Dyck, an American missionary and translator of the Bible into Arabic who lived in Lebanon and wrote in an essay in 1892:[1] "Beginners often ask, 'shall I learn the classic or the vulgar Arabic first?' The proper reply to this question is, 'learn both together.' Get your phrases in the common dialect so as to be able to use them without appearing pedantic, but learn the correct, classical expression at the same time, if there be a difference" (Van Dyck 1892, 3).

Van Dyck's words resonate today as the field of Arabic continues to face the complex and constantly evolving sociolinguistic realities of Arabic in the curriculum and the classroom. Over the past thirty years, teachers of Arabic in the United States have offered a variety of models for the "Arabic" they want to present to their students and the relationship they want to project between Modern Standard Arabic (MSA) and the multiple dialects spoken throughout the Arab countries (see Al-Batal 1992; Alosh 1991, 1997; Nicola 1990; Palmer 2007; Parkinson 1985; Ryding 1991; Wilmsen 2006; Younes 2015). While some Arabic programs have decided to incorporate the teaching of the dialect with MSA within the same course, most programs have opted for an approach that focuses on MSA primarily or exclusively. In such programs, exposure to an Arabic dialect takes place outside these MSA courses either in separate courses offered at the higher levels of instruction or at overseas programs.

However, while exclusive privileging of MSA continues to dominate the Arabic teaching profession in the United States, integration of a dialect alongside MSA in the Arabic curriculum has gained significant momentum in the past twenty years as more programs are making a concerted effort to create a niche for dialect in the Arabic curriculum. A multitude of factors have brought about this change (which we discuss later in this chapter), which is contributing to new curricular approaches and practices that are reflected throughout the various chapters of the present volume. Integration is a complex issue because of the ideological and cultural issues underlying it and because of the questions about authenticity of communication that would be raised if it were left out. Despite these challenges, however, debate in the field seems to be shifting from whether dialect integration should at all be carried out within the Arabic curriculum to how it can best be implemented in a manner consistent with communicative demands and learners' needs.

The present volume situates itself within this new debate, offering a range of perspectives on how to integrate. This chapter frames the various perspectives on integration presented throughout this volume in three parts. The first part discusses the MSA–dialect separation vision that has dominated the field and proposes an alternate vision of "Arabic as One," on which the concept of integration is based. The second part presents arguments in support of this vision, and the third part provides a description of six models of integration that are currently applied within educational institutions in the United States and that are consistent with the "Arabic as one" vision.

A Tale of Two Visions

The teaching of Arabic in the United States has evolved in tandem with many developments, among them foreign policy concerns, developments in foreign language education, methods of teaching Arabic in the Arab world, and challenges of teaching languages with widely varying dialects. These forces have shaped the visions that drive many of the curricular decisions made within Arabic programs across the United States. The predominant vision in the twentieth century has been one of a "firewall of separation." Only recently has an alternative vision—that of "Arabic as One"—emerged.

The Firewall of Separation Vision

In most K–12 and college-level programs in the United States, "Arabic" refers solely to MSA, as reflected in course titles (e.g., Elementary MSA, Intermediate MSA). Whether or not it is the intention of the program administrators, such titles serve to signal a rigid separation between MSA and the dialects in these programs. This separation is based on a polarized, bidimensional model that draws its rationale from the diglossia theory (articulated by Ferguson 1959) and its portrayal of formal Arabic (MSA in this case) as a "high" variety of Arabic compared to the "low" variety represented by the dialects. This model also draws its rationale from the widely held view in the Arab world that *al-fuṣḥā* (MSA) is the superior form of Arabic and that it alone should be an object of study. This view is anchored in the belief among many native speakers of Arabic that the dialect is the vulgar language of the street and that it has no connection to literary or cultured expression (Maktabī 1991). It is also shaped by the belief that calls to promote the dialects in education have emanated from imperialist and orientalist schemes aimed at distancing Arabs from each other and from their heritage (Saʿīd 1963; Al-Ḍāmin 1986). The past few years have seen a rise in the number of conferences, programs, and articles across the Arabic-speaking world whose stated goal is to defend Arabic (meaning *al-fuṣḥā*) and protect it from two prominent dangers it faces: foreign languages and the dialects (Muḥammad 2007; Al-Banna 2011; Ḥiwār al-ʿArab 2013). The separation view is also shaped by the perception that the Arabic dialects are, to a greater or lesser degree, mutually incomprehensible (Maktabī 1991). *Al-fuṣḥā*, according to this view, is what unites the Arabs politically and culturally and makes it possible for them to communicate. Thus, it should be the sole focus of any teaching and learning of Arabic within the Arab world or without.

This vision of Arabic has long dominated both the philosophy and practices of the vast majority of Arabic programs worldwide and created a pedagogical "firewall" whose aim is to keep *al-fuṣḥā* and the dialects separated, as illustrated in figure 1.1.

According to this vision and the practices connected to it, the dialect is entirely kept out of the classroom, and teachers speak always in MSA and use materials that are exclusively in MSA. Munther Younes (2015) provides a detailed discussion of the reasons why programs opt to focus exclusively on MSA and refuse to integrate any dialect elements in the Arabic classroom. Such reasons include the fear of causing confusion among students and the lack of consensus in the field on which Arabic dialect to teach alongside MSA. A common argument that is made by teachers who hold such views is that instruction should focus on MSA while the students are in the United

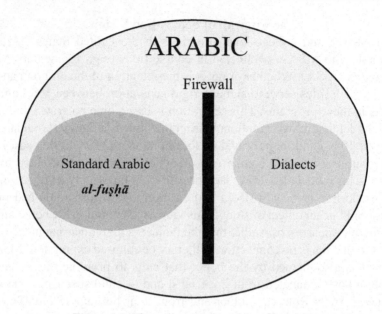

Figure 1.1 Firewall separation vision of Arabic

States. If students travel to an Arabic-speaking country, then they can learn the dialect of that country. In this view, teachers avoid causing their students confusion and at the same time avoid making a choice for which dialect to teach. Most importantly, they keep their students' Arabic "free and clear" of any possible dialect influence.

This firewall vision of Arabic is problematic on many fronts. The separation it creates is artificial and stands in sharp contrast with the linguistic reality across the Arab world, where MSA and the dialects coexist harmoniously and interact and intersect constantly in a wide variety of spheres. To deprive students of the knowledge of Arabic dialect is to deprive them of the chance to learn how to communicate naturally with the majority of Arabic speakers who do not feel comfortable interacting in *al-fuṣḥā*. Moreover, it limits students' ability to learn about many social aspects of Arab cultures. In addition, the proficiency model it claims to represent for the speaking skill is faulty, as explained by Peter Heath (1990). The way in which Arabic dialects are currently isolated from MSA in the Arabic curriculum serves to reinforce the perception that they are different languages and grossly distorts the reality in which the dialects are integrated with MSA in the lives of Arabic speakers everywhere.

The "Arabic as One" Vision

In contrast to the firewall separation vision of Arabic, we propose here an alternative vision based on the belief that varieties of Arabic do not represent separate isolated entities but are part of one language system called "Arabic."

Figure 1.2 illustrates this vision and presents Arabic as a multidimensional entity that is made up of various components that include Standard Arabic (*al-fuṣḥā*), the principal dialect of any Arabic speaker (or learner), and the other Arabic dialects to which all Arabic speakers are increasingly exposed.

Unlike the "firewall" representation of Arabic, the present figure shows that the various components of the language coexist with each other and are constantly interacting with each other. This vision of Arabic is anchored in the belief that all these components have legitimacy within the Arabic language system and that they belong in any Arabic classroom that claims to be teaching Arabic within an authentic communicative framework. Each component fulfills certain functions and tasks and is equally important to the overall construct of "Arabic." Moreover, Arabic has no inherent hierarchical structure in which one variety is more important than another or one dialect is more "Arabic" than another. This vision does not perceive of any firewalls separating these components from each other. Nor does it believe that any one component of Arabic could pose a threat to the other components

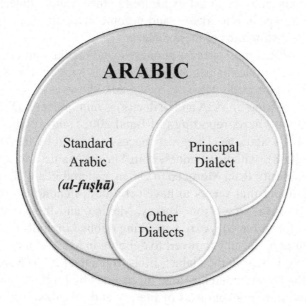

Figure 1.2 Arabic as one language vision

because all of them are symbiotically connected to each other. The best way to appreciate the relationship among these various components is not to approach each one separately in a piecemeal fashion but to approach them holistically to allow learners from the earliest levels of instruction to develop awareness of the synergies that exist among these various components. In doing so, learners learn to deal with one Arabic rather than separate "Arabics."

Rationale for the "Arabic as One" Vision

The vision of "Arabic as One" draws its rationale from the following four imperatives:

It reflects the new changing realities of Arabic. Over the past three decades, the relationship between MSA and the various Arabic dialects has undergone a significant evolution spurred by the proliferation of technology, social media, and satellite channels throughout the Arab world. This evolution has helped the dialects expand into public spheres that had previously been the sole domain of MSA and promoted further interaction between MSA and the dialects, on the one hand, and among the various dialects, on the other. Because of modern technologies, Arabic speakers worldwide now enjoy remarkable opportunities to get exposure to other Arabic dialects—in addition to further exposure to MSA—and become more attuned to the sounds, vocabulary, and structures of these dialects.

By means of text messages on phones, social media, and interactions on chat rooms, the Arabic dialects have emerged as a medium of communication in writing alongside MSA. In news talk shows and in TV and radio programs, the mixing of MSA and dialect(s) is omnipresent. Dialect use has made its way into news reporting (Al-Batal 2002) and weather broadcasts in some Arab TV stations. The great success achieved by the Turkish soap opera *Nūr* (2008), which was dubbed in Syrian Arabic and achieved tremendous popularity from Morocco to Oman, ushered in a widespread trend of dialect dubbing that seems to have set a new standard in the industry. Foreign soap operas (e.g., from Turkey, Mexico, and India) that had been traditionally dubbed in MSA are now being dubbed in dialects. Reacting to a recent attempt by Disney to revert to dubbing in MSA of its *Frozen* movie after years of dubbing in the dialect, Elias Muhanna (2014) wrote that such reversal "reflects, rather, an ideology propagated by linguistic purists in the region, rooted in many centuries of literary and religious history. . . . The age of the Arabic vernacular is here; someone just needs to tell the talking snowman."

Dialects are increasingly used in writing street advertisements and TV commercials. This used to be a realm reserved for MSA, but now dialects throughout the Arab world are becoming the standard for advertisement both in oral and written communication. Thanks to the media, Arabic dialects are also interacting with each other at levels unwitnessed before. On Arabic TV programs such as *Aḥlā Ṣōt* (*The Voice*), *Man Sa-yarbaḥ al-Milyōn?* (*Who Wants to Be a Millionaire?*), and *Arab Idol*, all of which have widespread popularity throughout the region, participants from various Arab countries use their dialects to communicate with each other. Moreover, a recent trend has emerged in TV series aired during the month of Ramadan in which we see actors and actresses from different Arab countries speaking their own dialects in their roles in these series. Such programs represent new realities in interdialect communication and provide strong evidence that speakers of Arabic can and do understand each other when they speak in their own dialects—with various degrees of leveling—without the need to resort to MSA.

In the sphere of literature, which has traditionally been dominated by MSA, colloquial is being used as a medium of expression alongside MSA in narration and dialogues in a growing number of new novels in countries such as Egypt, Lebanon, and Morocco.[2] The same phenomenon can be observed in modern Arab rap music, where some young Arab hip-hop artists are using a mix of MSA and dialect as a new medium of artistic expression.[3]

These new realities in the modern Arab world underscore the fact that the dialects have gained much prominence in the public sphere and that new modes and levels of MSA–dialect and interdialectal interaction are constantly emerging. Approaching Arabic as one language and integrating dialect in the Arabic classroom enables Arabic programs to reflect these new realities and allow learners to understand and appreciate the dynamics that exist among the different varieties of Arabic. Maintaining the firewall separation represents a great disservice to Arabic learners and will produce unidimensional learners who have difficulty functioning in the increasingly multidimensional universe of Arabic.

It is more consistent with new trends in language pedagogy. Approaching Arabic as one language and creating space for the dialect within the Arabic curriculum would help us develop curricula that are more in tandem with new approaches to language pedagogy, whether they are proficiency-based, task-based, or content-based. Back in the 1990s, the advent of the Communicative Approach and the Proficiency movement—with the former's focus on sociolinguistic competence and pragmatics and the latter's on functions, contexts, and authentic texts—presented the field of Arabic language teaching with questions of how the curriculum could be reconfigured in a way that could develop the kind of proficiency that reflects authentic texts and contexts. The new approaches to language teaching and learning have challenged teachers to rethink the way they perceive of Arabic and teach it in their classes. Recent focus on task-based and content-based instruction gives yet more reasons to incorporate dialect in the instruction. For communicative tasks that are completely performed in a dialect in the real world, how can we introduce the task and train the students to perform it in an Arabic variety that is not consistent with the task? Similarly, undertaking content-based instruction at the higher levels will necessarily include video materials in mixed forms of Arabic. How could a nonintegrated approach to Arabic prepare students to deal with these contexts in their Arabic courses?

While a small number of programs have responded to these challenges by incorporating dialect in teaching, most Arabic programs have opted for proficiency-based curricula that maintained the firewall separation between MSA and the dialects. As a result, proficiency-based approaches to Arabic instruction and assessment continued what Karin Ryding (2006) describes as "reverse privileging of MSA."

Another positive development toward developing an integrated approach to Arabic has been the publication of the American Council on the Teaching of Foreign Language (ACTFL) Language Standards in 2006, which provide a new curricular framework for the teaching of world languages with a focus on communication and culture. While the standards remain focused on K–12, they nevertheless provide strong support for incorporating dialect within the Arabic curriculum. In the preamble to the Arabic standards, we find the following statement that reflects the spirit of the "Arabic as One" vision: "An essential part of knowing Arabic is knowing both the *fusHa* and one or more *cammiyas*, and mastering how, when, and to what extent to mix them, either by introducing colloquialisms into *fusHa* or by bringing *fusHa* structures into *cammiya*" (NSFLEP 2006, 116). True proficiency in Arabic and genuine implementation of the five Cs of the language standards cannot be realized through a compartmentalized vision of Arabic. Dialect integration is a must if the field wants to develop curricula that are based on authentic language use and are truly reflective of innovative approaches to language pedagogy.

It promotes the learning of culture and intercultural competence. A curriculum based on "Arabic as One" that integrates dialect is more conducive to helping students develop a broader and deeper understanding of Arab culture. The last two decades have witnessed increased attention to culture and ways to integrate culture within the language curriculum in order to help learners develop intercultural competence (see, for example, Byram, Gribkova, and Starkey 2002; Fantini and Tirmizi 2006; Lustig and Koester 2006). The focus on culture and intercultural competence as an important goal of language learning has presented teachers of Arabic with yet more challenging questions. How can the teaching of culture be accomplished without exposing students to the Arabic dialects that carry tremendous cultural content? Can the exclusive focus on MSA in teaching help learners develop well-rounded cultural understanding? Should dealing with culture be postponed until students travel to study in the Arab world, taking into consideration that only a small fraction of them do so? Should the study of culture focus on literature and readings about culture or should it also reflect the pragmatics of language as they are manifested in real-life interpersonal interactions?

In two recent studies on students of Arabic in programs abroad, Sonia Shiri (2013, 2015) underscores the connection that exists between the learning of culture and the learning of dialect. She points out that students who study abroad in the Arab world recognize the importance of learning any dialect, regardless of their own regional focus, in order to gain overall communicative and intercultural competence. Similarly, Corinne Stokes (2016) asserts that an intercultural approach to Arabic requires the integration of multiple registers in the classroom.

The focus of the World Language Standards on culture as one of the five Cs of language makes it incumbent upon the Arabic field to reexamine its approach to culture and the language varieties that convey this culture. In a world that is increasingly multicultural, diverse, and multidimensional, Arabic programs cannot expose students to a culture that is unidimensional in terms of the linguistic variety it reflects. Nor can they afford to hold the position that full knowledge of the culture lies somewhere else outside the classroom. There is much cultural knowledge that needs to be developed, and this needs to begin on the first day of class in an environment that embraces all forms of cultural expression in Arabic.

It responds to student needs and interests. Integrating dialect within Arabic as a Foreign Language (FL) curricula represents the most adequate response to learner needs as they have been analyzed in recent research. In a survey of students studying Arabic in the United States, Kirk Belnap (2006) reports that the following are the top three reasons why students study Arabic: (1) interacting with people who speak Arabic, (2) traveling to the Arab world, and (3) developing better understanding of Arab culture. In a different survey, Ghassan Husseinali (2006) arrives at the same results, identifying the top three reasons as follows: (1) conversing with Arabs, (2) travel, and (3) understanding world cultures.

These surveys demonstrate unequivocally that the clear majority of students studying Arabic are first and foremost interested in conversing with speakers of Arabic both in the United States and abroad and in learning about Arab culture. Such needs cannot be fulfilled if we continue to carry on with "business as usual" and follow an Arabic curriculum that is based on MSA as the sole medium of communication and cultural understanding. The goal of preparing students to converse with speakers of Arabic cannot be fulfilled through a curriculum that focuses on MSA alone. Speaking in Arabic involves using a dialect and mixing it with MSA, depending on the context and task. Students need to be prepared to converse in Arabic that sounds natural and real. Incorporating dialect in the curriculum will not lessen students' knowledge of MSA. More dialect does not lessen the MSA input because of the overwhelming percentage of shared forms in all varieties of the language. The studies by Nassif and by Ebner and Watson in this volume show that exposing students to an Arabic dialect alongside MSA will not result in lower proficiency in Arabic. To the contrary, it will produce learners who are well rounded and equipped to deal with "one Arabic" in its various varieties.

Integrating dialect in the Arabic curriculum from the early stages of instruction will also help prepare students adequately for travel and study-abroad experiences. We can see this post-2001, when, simultaneous with the unprecedented increase in Arabic enrollments in the United States in the post-2001 era, there was a huge increase in interest for study abroad in various Arabic-speaking countries. However, many of the students who participated in the study-abroad programs were not adequately prepared to function because many of them had studied only MSA and were not aware that the MSA they had studied in the United States was not used in daily communication (Palmer 2007; Shiri 2013).

What makes the situation more complex is the fact that many Arabic programs in the Arab world also subscribe to the vision of firewall separation between MSA and the dialect and provide little, if any, training in the dialect. The dialect training is usually done in separate classes so as to prevent any possible mixing of the dialect and MSA. The position of many Arabic study-abroad programs was outlined in an Open Doors report. This report, which focused on a workshop held in Morocco to discuss study abroad in the Arab world and was prepared by the Institute of International Education (IIE 2006), observed that

workshop participants had different perspectives on whether MSA or dialect learning should be the priority in study abroad programs. Several

Arabic linguists in the group emphasized that knowledge of MSA is the only solid foundation upon which Arabic competency can be built; others argued that dialects are more essential for foreigners. But many participants agreed that study abroad programs should seek to expose participants to dialects as much and as soon as possible and to integrate MSA and dialect instruction. (Bhandari and Chow 2008)

Arabic teachers and program administrators must take a careful look at Arabic programs abroad and consider the extent to which these programs serve students' needs and interests. Voices from Arabic students throughout this volume call for integration of dialects in the curriculum. They see value in it culturally, linguistically, and professionally and are asking us as teachers to align our priorities with theirs.

Models of Integration

Based on the model presented above, the question then becomes, how can we position these different varieties of Arabic within the curriculum and how can we create a "one Arabic" curriculum that integrates dialect? There is no one answer to this question, as a number of models with different profiles and philosophies have been developed at American institutions. In order to gather comparable information on the various approaches to integration, we asked six of these programs (Cornell University, Brigham Young University, Western Michigan University, University of Arizona, University of Texas at Austin, and the Defense Language Institute Foreign Language Center) to respond to the following questions:

1. How many years of Arabic do you offer in your program? How many hours do students meet in each of these years?
2. How is integration applied in each of these years?
3. What variety do the teachers speak in class? Is this consistent across the years of instruction?
4. Do you correct students if they use a colloquial word in MSA-based activity and vice versa?
5. How do you approach the writing skill? Do you correct the students if they use colloquial in their writing?

The following is a brief description of these models based on the questions listed above.[4]

The Cornell University Model

The Cornell model of integration is one of the oldest in the United States.[5] The core language program at Cornell provides a language sequence of three years and two additional courses (Modern Arabic Literature and Current Events in the Arabic Media) for students who have completed Advanced Arabic.[6] Elementary Arabic meets five hours per week; Intermediate and Advanced, four hours a week; and the other courses, three hours per week. The program uses the ᶜArabiyyat al-Naas textbook series, which reflects the Cornell program's approach to teaching Arabic.

The guiding principle for integration within the Cornell program is to reflect the Arabic linguistic situation as it really is: spontaneous conversation in colloquial language and reading, writing, and formal scripted speech in MSA. Readings are presented in MSA but discussed in the dialect. The percentage of MSA increases with the rise in the level of the course: this means that in the third year, students have more exposure to MSA, spoken and written, than they do in the first year.

The Cornell program follows two principles that govern teachers' talk in class. The first is that the classroom should be as conducive to successful learning as possible. This means that both the teacher and the students need to be comfortable and the classroom environment stress free. The second is that language should be used as a means of real communication, not of performance. For many Arabic teachers who have received their training in Arabic departments in the Arab world, the use of MSA is a performance. Reading and writing MSA is natural and comes easily to educated Arabs just as speaking in the colloquial comes naturally to them. Teachers, of course, differ, with some preferring to use more MSA in speaking than others. The program does not set rules about how much of one or how little of the other to use. The main goals are to create a classroom environment that is conducive to effective learning and using the language for communication without being subjected to the pressure to converse in a variety that lacks authenticity.

The approach to writing and corrective feedback depends on the level and the goal of any given activity. In general, the program focuses on communication and successful delivery of the message first and moves toward more accuracy as the student moves up on the proficiency scale. This applies to both linguistic and sociolinguistic errors in the use of the wrong language variety. While the use of the negative particle mish "not" is permitted in first-year written compositions, it is considered to be an error to be corrected in a third-year written composition. By the same token, when students join the Cornell program and use the MSA verb dhahabtu "I went" in speaking, since that is what they learned in high school, the program accepts it initially but the students are gradually steered toward the sociolinguistically normative patterns of usage.

The Brigham Young University Model

The Brigham Young University (BYU) "core" Arabic program is a two year program that meets five hours per week.[7] The program doesn't offer a third year on campus, but students go abroad for the fall semester, where they take sixteen credit hours of Arabic, which is equivalent to two years of regular study at the upper level. Students return with speaking proficiency in the Advanced range on the ACTFL scale (2012). After the study-abroad program, all students have the option of taking advanced-level courses (such as a course on Arabic literature or advanced Levantine Arabic). Most of these courses are two credit hours and meet twice a week. Most returning students take more than one class, with majors enrolled in three.

During the first three weeks of Elementary Arabic, students learn to converse in Levantine while they learn the Arabic script as homework. Later, more class time is devoted to MSA. On average, approximately equal attention is given to Levantine and MSA during the first year. In the second year, the focus is approximately 75 percent on MSA, and during study abroad a third of the students' time is on Jordanian (an hour of class and two hours of out-of-class speaking, either with a tutor or out on the street). Most of the advanced-level courses focus on MSA, but informal discussion is often mixed.

As for the dialect variety used, the BYU program typically introduces Levantine Arabic, but teachers bring in their native dialects as well. Currently there is an Egyptian adjunct who often speaks Egyptian in informal discussion in the debate and current events classes.

The program does not focus on correcting mixing, and a lot of natural mixing takes place in informal conversation. However, if an activity is supposed to be focused on MSA or Levantine, teachers draw attention to the appropriate word by modeling the sentence as it should be.

The BYU first-semester syllabus acknowledges that mixing is natural and that it will take time for the student to develop a feel for when to use what. The program considers communication to be the top priority; accuracy is an important part of advanced-level formal communication. In terms of teachers' talk, there is wide variation, but the program tries to be encouraging and raise consciousness gently.

The Western Michigan University Model

Western Michigan University (WMU) offers a three-year sequence in Arabic.[8] The first semester is all dialect, and MSA is introduced in the second semester half way through the course (with focus on reading and listening). The second and third years integrate MSA and the dialect: MSA reading activities accompanied by dialogues and conversation in the dialect.

The WMU Arabic program encourages students to study one dialect only and aims to have all students start and finish with the same dialect. The program focuses primarily on the Egyptian dialect, but when a Levantine speaker is available to provide instruction, students are introduced to Levantine, maintaining the goal of retaining one dialect throughout. This allows a cohort to go through the three years with the same dialect. If there are students with interest in a dialect that is not offered, they are given the choice to work with a tutor on their desired dialect.

The program follows a gradient approach to error correction. In the first two semesters, when students use dialect words in writing, teachers do not deduct points for that, but they point it out. Lexical borrowings from MSA into the dialect are acceptable. In the advanced levels, students have either to maintain separation of MSA and the dialect or to mix them the way native speakers do. In the third year and the translation course, no colloquial is permitted in MSA writing, and at the more advanced levels, students are corrected if they use dialect in their essays.

The University of Arizona Model

The University of Arizona Arabic program offers five years of Arabic instruction.[9] During the first three years, students meet for five hours per week, and fourth- and fifth-year courses meet for three hours per week each. In addition, the program offers dedicated Egyptian, Levantine, and Moroccan dialect courses each for three hours/week. The program also offers optional weekly conversation tables for MSA, Levantine, Egyptian, and Moroccan Arabic.

In the first month of the first year, students spend half of their time on dialect learning (speaking) and the second half on MSA (reading and writing). Thereafter and through the third year, they attend four hours of class for MSA (reading/writing, listening/speaking) and one for dialect per week (speaking). Fourth- and fifth-year students attend the conversation tables for dialect.

Teachers speak MSA in the MSA portion of the program and dialect in the dialect classes in the lower levels, and they code-switch when working with materials at the higher levels that involve Educated Spoken Arabic. In short, teachers model the form of Arabic that is the focus of the class. Students are mostly aware of the differences between MSA and dialect and are expected to stay within one or the other variety without extensive mixing. When they mix, they either self-correct spontaneously or they are asked to self-correct by the instructor. Minor levels of mixing are not corrected.

Students typically do not mix MSA and dialect in writing. They are encouraged to use dialect and MSA in texting and other technology-mediated informal communication and to use MSA in essays or blogs. In the rare cases when they use dialect in an MSA essay, they are asked to self-correct to the relevant variety unless they are switching to dialect on purpose for a particular effect, in which case the mixing is integral to their piece and therefore intentional.

The University of Texas, Austin Model

The University of Texas, Austin (UT) Arabic program offers a three-year language sequence that comprises the core language and culture program. The first and second year offer six hours per week, and the third year, five hours per week. After the third year, students can choose from a variety of three hours per week of content-based courses in Arabic. All UT Arabic courses are described as "Arabic" not "Modern Standard Arabic," as is the practice within many Arabic programs. This decision was made to reflect the program's vision that Arabic is to be presented as one language and that students are to learn Arabic with the "flavor" the dialect provides. Students are exposed to language input in both MSA and a dialect from the first day of instruction and throughout the program. There is not a single course in which there is no dialect input. The program uses the *Al-Kitaab* textbook series in which vocabulary items are presented in different colors to reflect MSA, Levantine, Egyptian, and, recently, Moroccan Dārija. In the first-year sections, the flavor of the Arabic offered within each section depends on the instructor. Each class works primarily with one dialect and MSA, and all students are encouraged when studying vocabulary in the book to choose one vocabulary item (from the MSA and the class dialect options provided) and use it as their "active" form and learn the other form for recognition.

As students move to the second semester, they may find themselves in a class that focuses on a different flavor of Arabic. Students are encouraged to use whatever forms they prefer in communicating with other students, to continue to use what they learned in their previous class, and to share their knowledge with their peers. Teachers are open to any form of Arabic and welcome any and all varieties of Arabic in class. Mixing of MSA and dialects is permitted, as the focus at this stage is primarily on communication. As a result, one may be in a second semester class and hear these forms of the interrogative for "what?" إيه؟, ماذا؟, شنو؟ , شو؟ in the same classroom. While students are expected to master only one form of the vocabulary they learn, they are exposed to other forms in a way that reflects the way Arabic is actually used. Communication is not impeded because there is much shared among the varieties of Arabic. The concept of "Arabic as One" is constantly reflected in the language used by the teacher and students in the classroom.

Teachers at UT speak Arabic in a way that features a mix of MSA and dialect based on the activity/topic at hand and the context. The program's goal is to create an environment that reflects the way Arabic is used today. Mixing between MSA and a dialect, on the one hand, and between dialects as we see among Arabs living outside their dialect homes, on the other, is quite common in many regions of the Arab world, and the UT program wants students of Arabic to experience this even before they travel. The ability to understand and respond in some form to mixed language is becoming a requirement for students to access the enormous Arabic materials available on the internet and social media outlets.

In terms of writing, students in the first semester tend to use some dialect words in their writing, especially commonly used words and vocabulary for which they do not yet know an MSA version. Teachers do not correct them for doing this because the focus here is on communicating the message. In the second semester, students become more aware of the fact that most writing is done in MSA, and their writing shows increased use of MSA words and structures. If some colloquial words are used, they are not usually corrected if the meaning is successfully conveyed.

The Defense Language Institute Foreign Language Center Model

Although the Defense Language Institute Foreign Language Center (DLIFLC) Arabic program is different from the university programs listed here, it does feature integration.[10] The Defense Language Institute was one of the first in the country to offer a program in the late 1950s that provided simultaneous exposure to MSA and a dialect (Al-Batal 1992).

At present, the DLIFLC offers an Arabic program that provides instruction for sixty-four weeks with six to seven class hours per day. DLIFLC teaches MSA and a number of dialects that are mixed with MSA: the Iraqi dialect started in 2009; Levantine, 2011; Egyptian, 2013; and Sudanese, July 2015. The dialects are taught from the very first day of class.[11]

The instructors concentrate on teaching students to speak in the dialect and then introduce MSA for reading and writing. The program offers one hour of MSA (reading) and focus on form per day in the first semester, and this increases to two hours in the second semester and up to three hours in the third semester. Speaking is always in dialect. Even in the reading MSA hour, the discussion is always in dialect. At the higher levels, the reading (MSA) and listening (dialect) have many words in common. All synonyms of a word are accepted. If the course is in dialect, then MSA is accepted. No correction is done, but feedback is always provided and appreciated. There is no focus on writing.

Conclusion

These models demonstrate the variety of approaches to integration based on programmatic contexts and learning outcomes. They demonstrate that Arabic programs can find different ways to integrate, but the decision must first be made to perceive MSA and the dialects as part of one Arabic and to accept that they both have legitimacy in the classroom. These models also show that programs can adopt different approaches to deal with mixing MSA and the dialects. While programs must define their own pedagogical approaches to mixing, and find ways to help students develop their ability to mix, we need to remember that the ability to mix appropriately will improve gradually as students are exposed to more meaningful input and as they receive feedback from their teachers. An interesting study by Thomas Leddy-Cecere in the present volume identifies systematic patterns in mixing and suggests that mixing is not to be seen as a random process. We need to rethink what to expect when students mix and at what level students can master mixing in a manner similar to that of native speakers. The fact that students mix incorrectly should not be blamed on integration; it should be seen as a natural phase of the student's evolving interlanguage. Incorrect mixing is comparable to incorrect use of grammatical structures: the gap between comprehension and production is not a sign of failure or fossilization but rather will gradually lessen with time and practice. Like all aspects of language acquisition, feedback and encouragement from the teacher and the belief in the students' ability to master this skill will help students learn to mix naturally.

Despite the different approaches to integration and the different ways of implementing it, all these programs share the conviction that it is the responsibility of the Arabic program to empower learners to communicate in a way that approximates what takes place in the real world of Arabic, and to equip them with the ability to comprehend variation, apply it, and—most importantly—appreciate it. These programs also recognize that this responsibility begins on day one with the commitment to exposing students to language variation, and it should not be postponed to upper-level courses or relegated to programs in the Arab world. The competencies involved in recognizing and navigating the reality of Arabic as a living and lived language must be part of the learning outcomes for every level of instruction.

References

Al-Banna, Rajab. 2011. "Taḥdhīr: Al-Lugha al-ᶜArabiyya fī Khaṭar." *Masress.* https://www.masress.com/october/119448.

Al-Batal, Mahmoud. 1992. "Diglossia Proficiency: The Need for an Alternative Approach to Teaching." In *The Arabic Language in America*, edited by Aleya Rouchdy, 284–304. Detroit: Wayne State University Press.

———. 2002. "Identity and Language Tension in Lebanon: The Arabic of Local News at LBCI." In *Language Contact and Language Conflict: Variations on a Sociolinguistic Theme*, edited by Aleya Rouchdy, 91–115. London: Routledge Curzon Press.

Al-Ḍāmin, Ḥātim Ṣāliḥ. 1986. "Al-ᶜĀmmiyya wa al-Faṣīḥa." In *al-Lugha al-ᶜArabiyya wa al-Waᶜy al-Qawmi*, 2nd ed., 219–25. Beirut: Markaz Dirāsāt al-Waḥda al-ᶜArabiyya.

Alosh, Mahdi. 1991. "Arabic Diglossia and Its Impact on Teaching Arabic as a Foreign Language." In *International Perspectives on Foreign Language Teaching: ACTFL Review of Foreign Language Education*, edited by Gerard Ervin, 121–37. Lincolnwood, IL: National Textbook Company.

———. 1997. *Learner, Text, and Context in Foreign Language Acquisition: An Arabic Perspective.* Columbus: Ohio State University National Foreign Language Resource Center.

American Council on the Teaching of Foreign Language (ACTFL). 2012. "ACTFL Proficiency Guidelines 2012: Speaking." American Council on the Teaching of Foreign Languages. https://www.actfl.org/publications/guidelines-and-manuals/actfl-proficiency-guidelines-2012/english/speaking.

Belnap, R. Kirk. 2006. "A Profile of Students of Arabic in US Universities." In *Handbook for Arabic Language Teaching Professionals in the 21st Century*, edited by Kassem M. Wahba, Zeinab A. Taha, and Liz England, 169–78. Mahwah, NJ: Lawrence Erlbaum.

Bhandari, Rajika, and Patricia Chow. 2008. *Open Doors Report on International Educational Exchange.* New York: Institute of International Education.

Byram, Michael, Bella Gribkova, and Hugh Starkey. 2002. "Developing the Intercultural Dimension in Language Teaching." Strasbourg: Council of Europe.

Fantini, Alvino, and Aqeel Tirmizi. 2006. "Exploring and Assessing Intercultural Competence." *World Learning Publications*, Paper 1. http://digitalcollections.sit.edu/worldlearning_publications/1.

Ferguson, Charles. 1959. "Diglossia." *Word* 15: 325–40.

Ḥalabi, ᶜAfīfa. 2012. *Mish Muhimm*, 2nd ed. Beirut: Asameena.

Heath, Peter. 1990. "Proficiency in Arabic Language Learning: Some Reflections on Basic Goals." *Al-ᶜArabiyya* 23: 31–48.

Ḥiwār al-ᶜArab. 2013. "Al-Lugha al-ᶜArabiyya fī Khaṭar." *Al-Arabiya*, June 28. http://www.alarabiya.net/ar/programs/arab-conversation/2013/06/28/%D8%AD%D9%88%D8%A7%D8%B1-%D8%A7%D9%84%D8%B9%D8%B1%D8%A8-%D8%A7%D9%84%D9%84%D8%BA%D8%A9-%D8%A7%D9%84%D8

%B9%D8%B1%D8%A8%D9%8A%D8%A9-%D9%81%D9%8A
-%D8%AE%D8%B7%D8%B1.html.
Husseinali, Ghassan. 2006. "Who Is Studying Arabic and Why? A Survey of Arabic
Students' Orientations at a Major University." *Foreign Language Annals* 39:
395–412.
Institute of International Education (IIE). 2016. "Middle East and North Africa
(MENA)." *Institute of International Education.* http://www.iie.org/Our-Global
-Reach/Middle-East-and-North-Africa.
Lustig, Myron W., and Jolene Koester. 2006. *Intercultural Competence: Interper-
sonal Communication Across Cultures*, 5th ed. Boston: Pearson.
Maktabī, Nadhīr M. 1991. *Al-Fuṣḥā fī Muwājahat al-Taḥaddiyāt*. Beirut: Dār al-
Bashā'ir al-Islāmiyya.
Muḥammad, Sīdī. 2007. "Al-Lugha al-ᶜArabiyya fī Khaṭar am fī Taṭawwur?" *Al
Jazeera* (May 21). http://www.aljazeera.net/news/cultureandart/2007/5/21/%
D8%A7%D9%84%D9%84%D8%BA%D8%A9-%D8%A7%D9%84%D8%
B9%D8%B1%D8%A8%D9%8A%D8%A9-%D9%81%D9%8A
-%D8%AE%D8%B7%D8%B1-%D8%A3%D9%85-%D9%81%D9%8A
-%D8%AA%D8%B7%D9%88%D8%B1.
Muhanna, Elias. 2014. "Translating 'Frozen' into Arabic." *New Yorker*, May 30.
http://www.newyorker.com/books/page-turner/translating-frozen-into
-arabic.
National Standards in Foreign Language Education Project (NSFLEP). 2006. *Stan-
dards for Foreign Language Learning in the 21st Century*, 3rd ed. Lawrence,
KS: Allen Press.
Nicola, Michel. 1990. "Starting Arabic with Dialect." In *Diglossic Tension: Teaching
Arabic for Communication*, edited by Agius A. Dionisisu, 42–45. Leeds: Folia
Scholastica.
Palmer, Jeremy. 2007. "Arabic Diglossia: Teaching Only the Standard Variety Is a
Disservice to Students." *Arizona Working Papers in SLA and Teaching* 14:
111–22. http://slat.arizona.edu/sites/default/files/page/awp14palmer.pdf.
Parkinson, Dilworth. 1985. "Proficiency to Do What? Developing Proficiency in
Students of Modern Standard Arabic." *Al-ᶜArabiyya* 18: 11–44.
Ryding, Karin C. 1991. "Proficiency Despite Diglossia: A New Approach for Arabic."
Modern Language Journal 75: 212–18.
———. 2006. "Teaching Arabic in the United States." In *Handbook for Arabic Lan-
guage Teaching Professionals in the 21st Century*, edited by Kassem M. Wahba,
Zeinab A. Taha, and Liz England, 13–20. Mahwah, NJ: Lawrence Erlbaum.
Saᶜīd, Naffūsa Zakariyyā. 1963. *Tārīkh al-Daᶜwa ilā al-ᶜĀmmiyya wa Āthāruhā fī
Miṣr.* Alexandria, Egypt: Dār Nashr al-Thaqāfa.
Shiri, Sonia. 2013. "Learners' Attitudes Toward Regional Dialects and Destination
Preferences in Study Abroad." *Foreign Language Annals* 46: 565–87.
———. 2015. "Intercultural Communicative Competence Development during and
after Language Study Abroad: Insights from Arabic." *Foreign Language Annals*
48: 541–69.

Stokes, Corinne. 2016. "Teaching Culture in the Arabic as a Foreign Language Classroom." Unpublished PhD diss., University of Texas at Austin.

Van Dyck, Cornelius. 1892. *Suggestions to Beginners in the Study of Arabic*. Beirut: Near East School of Theology. Special Collections. Archive Box 7, 679.

Wilmsen, David. 2006. "What Is Communicative Arabic?" In *Handbook for Arabic Language Teaching Professionals*, edited by Kassem M. Wahba, Zeinab A. Taha, and Liz England, 125–38. Mahwah, NJ: Lawrence Erlbaum.

Younes, Munther. 2015. *The Integrated Approach to Arabic Instruction*. London: Routledge.

Notes

1. I am indebted to Anthony Edwards for providing me with this quote.

2. Examples of novels that use the dialect include Egyptian Khālid al-Khamīsi's *Tāksi* (2007) and Aḥmad Al-ᶜĀydi's ᶜ*an takūna* ᶜ*Abbās al-*ᶜ*Abd* (2003), and use of the dialect in dialogues can be seen in novels by the Lebanese novelists Elias Khouri and ᶜAlawiyya Sobḥ. A recent publication titled *Mish Muhimm* by ᶜAfīfa Ḥalabi (2012) features pages written in Lebanese colloquial written side by side with MSA. The authors describe the book as نصوص بالعربي الفصيح وبالعربي المريح (Texts in eloquent Arabic and comfortable Arabic).

3. For an example, listen to this song by the group al-Rās: https://soundcloud.com/el-rass-the-head/manyakhaf.

4. Much of the wording used in the following section reflects the language used by the people who provided me with their program description.

5. Information on the Cornell program was provided by Professor Munther Younes via email communication.

6. Cornell also offers additional courses taught in Arabic. These include a first-year course called Arabic for Native Speakers, where students who can speak an Arabic dialect learn to read and write the language, and two courses at the second-year (intermediate) level called Arabic through Film, and Arabic Grammar and Writing.

7. Information on the BYU program was provided by Professor Kirk Belnap via email communication.

8. Information on the WMU program was provided by Professor Mustafa Mughazy via email communication.

9. Information on the Arizona program was provided by Professor Sonia Shiri via email communication.

10. Information on the DLIFLC program was provided by Natela A. Cutter, DLIFLC public affairs chief, via email communication.

11. There are also some Arabic courses at DLIFLC that are offered entirely in MSA, with no dialects introduced.

2

To Separate or to Integrate, That Is the Question

The Cornell Arabic Program Model

MUNTHER YOUNES

Cornell University

IN SPITE OF some remaining pockets of resistance to introducing the col-loquial in the Arabic-as-a-foreign-language (AFL) classroom, there has been an unmistakable trend in the past quarter century toward recognizing its importance to the foreign learner and introducing it as part of the Arabic curriculum (Belnap 2006; Husseinali 2006; Palmer 2007; Shiri 2013; Wilm-sen 2006).

In a survey of the professional and institutional profiles and attitudes of college-level teachers of Arabic in the United States, Mahmoud Abdalla and Mahmoud Al-Batal report a "wide acceptance of the principle [of integrating] colloquial Arabic in instruction" among Arabic teachers, where the majority "(over 65%) strongly agree or agree that training in a dialect should start at the early stages of instruction." They add, "These figures reflect a noticeable change in the Arabic field, which has, for a long period of time, mainly focused on the teaching of MSA [Modern Standard Arabic] at the lower lev-els of instruction despite the fact that colloquial is the variety used to perform all functions related to the ACTFL [American Council for the Teaching of Foreign Languages] Novice and Intermediate levels" (2011–12, 16).

Abdalla and Al-Batal see a "disconnect" between the teachers' attitudes toward integrating the colloquial in the first two years of instruction and the fact that "the majority of programs incorporate colloquial Arabic to a small extent or not at all. [There exists] a contradiction between the beliefs of the teachers . . . and the actual teaching practice" (2011–12, 16).

This "disconnect" could be the result of a lack of a consensus in the profession on the issue of colloquial incorporation and the absence of a clear path for actual implementation. Disagreement generally revolves around two related issues: which colloquial to incorporate and when and how it should be incorporated. Since there is no standard colloquial variety and since we cannot be certain in many cases with which Arabic speakers our students are likely to be interacting, how can we decide which variety to introduce? Even if we knew which variety to introduce, should it be introduced before, after, or simultaneously with *al-fuṣḥā* (Standard Arabic)? If introduced simultaneously, should the two be introduced in the same course or in two separate tracks?

In this chapter, I address the second issue: when and how to incorporate the colloquial in the Arabic program. The issue of which colloquial to introduce is an open question whose answer depends on the location of a program, its staffing, funding, prominence of the colloquial variety, or some other factor. For more on this, the reader is referred to Ryding (2013), Abdalla and Al-Batal (2011–12), and Younes (2015), and to references there. I will use the Arabic program at Cornell University as the model of what I believe to be a fully integrated Arabic program where the colloquial and *al-fuṣḥā* are introduced simultaneously from the beginning of the Arabic course and used side by side throughout such a course.

Cornell's Fully Integrated Arabic Program

The Arabic program at Cornell adopted what can be described as an integrated approach (IA) to Arabic instruction in 1990 and has followed it since then. Integration is reflected in the instructional materials and instructional activities inside and outside of the classroom. The instructional materials represented by the textbook series *ᶜArabiyyat al-Naas*, part 1 (Younes, Weatherspoon, and Foster 2014), part 2 (Younes and al-Masri 2014), and part 3 (Younes and Chami 2014) and the instructional practices based on them reflect the typical patterns of linguistic behavior in the Arab world and not the exceptional cases. The typical patterns mean the use of *al-fuṣḥā* for reading, writing, and scripted speech and the use of *al-ᶜāmmiyya*, or colloquial Arabic, for spontaneous conversation and discussion, while the "exceptional cases" refer to the use of each variety where the other one is normally used. So in the three volumes, reading and writing activities are presented and conducted in *al-fuṣḥā* while conversation and discussion, even discussion of *al-fuṣḥā* materials, is conducted in *al-ᶜāmmiyya*. In the following paragraphs, I offer a description and rationale of the IA as well as its actual implementation in the classroom and in instructional materials and the challenges that accompany all of these.

Key Features of the Cornell Integrated Program

In this section I present what I consider to be the main features of the integrated Arabic Program at Cornell University.

Reflecting Arabic Sociolinguistic Realities

The basic philosophy of the IA at Cornell is that the AFL classroom and instructional materials are a true reflection of the Arabic sociolinguistic situation. As is well known, native speakers of Arabic use *al-ᶜāmmiyya* for ordinary conversation and *al-fuṣḥā* for reading, writing, and scripted speech. The first key feature, then, is that ordinary conversation is conducted in *al-ᶜāmmiyya* while reading, writing, and scripted speech are treated as the realm of *al-fuṣḥā*.

One Communication System, Not Two

An important feature of the Arabic sociolinguistic situation is that *al-fuṣḥā* and *al-ᶜāmmiyya* are two sides of one communication system. The relationship between the two is radically different from the relationship between English and Spanish, for example, or even between closely related languages such as French and Spanish. As elements of *al-fuṣḥā*, the language variety used in education in Arabic-speaking countries, are integrated into the educated Arabic speaker's linguistic repertoire, the gap between the two varieties is diminished and the transition from one variety to the other is generally spontaneous and effortless. On the other hand, while similarities and correspondences abound between French and Spanish, there are enough phonological, morphological, and syntactic differences to set them apart as two different languages that are not mutually unintelligible, unlike *al-ᶜāmmiyya* and *al-fuṣḥā*.

The Complementary Roles of the Two Varieties

An important feature of the Arabic sociolinguistic situation is that the two varieties, *al-ᶜāmmiyya* and *al-fuṣḥā*, complement each other. The set of functions requiring the use of *al-fuṣḥā* is typically different from that requiring the use of *al-ᶜāmmiyya*.

Ferguson's study of Arabic diglossia (1959) describes the distinct functions of each variety in great detail. In spite of the commonly expressed reservations about Ferguson's analysis and the existence of numerous counterexamples, the basic pattern of linguistic behavior among Arabic speakers still holds. For example, a dialogue between a traveler and a passport control employee at an airport in an Arabic-speaking country takes place in al-ᶜāmmiyya, but writing an entry in a diary describing that experience generally requires al-fuṣḥā. As Badawi wrote in 1973 (150), a university professor reads his lecture notes in al-fuṣḥā but discusses the contents of his lecture in al-ᶜāmmiyya, a practice that is as widespread today as it was then. For the purposes of the present study and as has already been mentioned, the general pattern of usage is that al-ᶜāmmiyya is used for ordinary conversation while al-fuṣḥā for reading, writing, and scripted speech.

In theory, much of the linguistic material can be presented in either al-fuṣḥā or in al-ᶜāmmiyya. For example, the same story can be told in either al-ᶜāmmiyya or al-fuṣḥā. But in al-ᶜāmmiyya it is typically told orally, and in al-fuṣḥā it is told in writing. The reverse would be an exception. Complementarity lies here in the choice of the medium in which the language material is presented. It should be emphasized, however, that because we are dealing with a living language actively used by tens of millions of people, the situation is in a constant state of change, and the boundaries are not always clearly delineated.

Building on Shared Elements

The second major feature of the IA is that it takes advantage of the fact that the two varieties of the language form one system of communication in which the overwhelming majority of linguistic elements are identical. Rather than focusing on differences, which are considered the minority and which can often be handled by regular rules, the IA focuses on what is common to the two varieties.

To illustrate, in the selection and composition of materials for the ᶜArabiyyat al-Naas textbooks (Younes, Weatherspoon, and Foster 2014; Younes and al-Masri 2014; Younes and Chami 2014), the authors made a conscious attempt to avoid using those vocabulary items and grammatical structures that are found in one variety but not in the other, particularly at the early stages of instruction. In the case of al-fuṣḥā reading passages, for example, the case and mood systems (ʾiᶜrāb) and the use of لم and ليس for negation were avoided as much as possible. In terms of vocabulary, such al-fuṣḥā words as šāhada-yušāhid "to watch" and ṭahā-yaṭhū "to cook" were avoided in favor of the shared words tafarraj-yatafarraj (or tfarraj-yitfarraj) and ṭabakh-yaṭbukh, respectively.

On the al-ᶜāmmiyya side, localized sounds, words, and structures were avoided in favor of more common standard or "educated" forms. For example, in some rural Palestinian Arabic dialects, the q and k of al-fuṣḥā are represented by k and č, respectively, as follows:

Table 2.1 Sample pronunciation of words in *al-fuṣḥā* and rural Palestinian Arabic (RPA)

Al-fuṣḥā	RPA	Meaning
qalb	*kalib*	heart
kalb	*čalib*	dog

In the textbooks, such rural Palestinian Arabic forms were avoided in favor of the more standard spoken forms *qalb* (or *ʾalb*) "heart" and *kalb* "dog." Another example from the same dialect is the verb *baka-yibka* "to be," which was avoided, and *kān-yakūn* was used instead. A third example is the greeting *kēf ḥālak* "How are you?" common to both *al-fuṣḥā* and *al-ʿāmmiyya*, which is introduced long before the *al-ʿāmmiyya*-only *kēfak*.

The result is that entire phrases and sentences appear almost identical in the two varieties. Consider, for example, the following sentence taken from a reading passage in *ʿArabiyyat al-Naas*, part 1 (Younes, Weatherspoon, and Foster 2014, 178).

من أهمّ وأقدم مراكز التعليم في العالم العربي ثلاث جامعات هي: جامعة "الأزهر" في القاهرة وجامعة " الزيتونة " في مدينة تونس عاصمة تونس وجامعة " القرويين " في مدينة فاس في المغرب.

Of course, since Levantine and other *al-ʿāmmiyya* varieties are living language varieties, variation in the pronunciation of some words among different speakers is expected, for example, ثلاث "three," مدينة "city," but such variation is predictable and can be explained by simple rules. The Arabic speaker does not need to learn two sets of words; the same set is found in both (see Younes 2015, ch. 4).

مثل *versus* زيّ *and* عمل *versus* سوّى

One question often asked in this context is, how does one choose between, on the one hand, elements shared by the two language varieties and, on the other, corresponding, nonshared elements that are as commonly or even more commonly used, such as the *al-ʿāmmiyya*-only forms يسوّي - سوّى "to do" and زيّ "like" as opposed to the shared forms عمل and مثل with the same meanings? In situations where two forms with a similar meaning are possible in conversation, the *ʿArabiyyat al-Naas* series introduces the more formal alternative first as is typically the case in foreign language instruction. For example, it is more appropriate in an English-as-a-foreign-language textbook to introduce the phrase "going to" before "gonna," although the second form might be more common.

Giving Equal Weight to Both Varieties

While it is possible in theory to treat *al-ᶜāmmiyya* and *al-fuṣḥā* equally in an Arabic program that introduces both, the general practice in programs that separate the two language varieties clearly favors *al-fuṣḥā*. There are a variety of reasons for such discrimination (see Younes 2015, ch. 3). In an integrated program that distributes language tasks in a way that truly reflects actual usage of the language, favoring one variety over the other would not be possible. A textbook that aims to equip learners to deal with the language the way it is actually used would have to focus on the four language skills equally and distribute the learning material between the two language varieties according to the function or task to be mastered. A dialogue at an airport would be presented in *al-ᶜāmmiyya* while an announcement about flight arrivals and departures would be presented in *al-fuṣḥā*.

Reflecting the Features of the IA in
Instructional Materials and Practices

In the following paragraphs I describe in some detail how the IA is actually implemented in the *ᶜArabiyyat al-Naas* textbook series designed for elementary, intermediate, and advanced classes, and in the classrooms where these texts are used. Sample units from the three textbooks are used for illustration.

ᶜArabiyyat al-Naas, part 1 (Younes, Weatherspoon, and Foster 2014) consists of twenty-one units. The first two units, which are introductory, consist of ten lessons each. Each of the remaining nineteen units, which form the body of the textbook, consists of five lessons that cover listening, reading, speaking, writing, and grammar components with accompanying exercises and activities. I use unit 10 of the book to demonstrate in some detail the principle of integration of different skills and activities in instructional materials and classroom practice.

ᶜArabiyyat al-Naas, Part 1, Unit 10 *(Younes, Weatherspoon, and Foster 2014, 175–88)*

The general theme of the unit is education. Lesson 1 consists of two video clips in which Emily, an American student studying Arabic in Jordan, talks with her Jordanian roommate, Fadwa, about studying at Jordanian and American universities. Lesson 2 consists of a reading passage about the three oldest Muslim-Arab universities, al-Azhar, al-Zaytūna, and al-Qarawiyyīn. Lesson

3 also consists of a reading passage, which includes part of Emily's diary in which she writes about the importance of the *tawjīhī* "high school exam" in Jordan. Lesson 4 focuses on the grammatical structures that appear in the preceding three lessons and includes explanations and activities to help the student learn and master these structures. Examples of the structures discussed are the difference between من ˈأهمَ and مِن أهمَ, the different uses of ما, verb-subject agreement, and relative pronouns. The lesson also includes what is called the "sociolinguistic corner," which offers explanations of the main differences in vocabulary and structures that appear in the listening and reading materials of the first three lessons. Finally, lesson 5 includes a number of activities with the goal of reviewing and recycling the vocabulary and structures presented in the unit while also adding an element of variety and fun to the unit.

Among these activities are a simple song about studying and exercises to help enrich the student's vocabulary (opposites, plurals, and a crossword puzzle). The last activity of the lesson consists of a speaking/writing exercise in which the student is asked to choose one of two topics and is given the following prompts:

1. Create a dialogue with another student in which you discuss your reasons for choosing the school you are attending. Then write it up in about 50 words.
2. Study the history of your university or college (or any other university you like), prepare a short outline and present it to the class. Then write it up in about 50 words.

True to the philosophy of the IA and in conformity with what would actually happen in comparable situations among Arabic speakers, conversation and informal speaking activities are presented and worked on in *al-ᶜāmmiyya*, while reading and writing activities are presented and performed in *al-fuṣḥā*.

ᶜArabiyyat al-Naas, part 2, Unit 8 *(Younes and al-Masri 2014, 131–47)*
The theme of the unit is the weather. Lesson 1 consists of two reading texts presented in *al-fuṣḥā*. The first is a table comparing the weather in Amman and New York and the second is a text about the weather in the Arab world. Lesson 2 includes a weather forecast, which is presented as a reading and listening text. The language used in weather forecasts in the Arab world, typically *al-fuṣḥā*, is generally the same whether it is broadcast on radio or TV or written in newspapers and on websites. That is why such a text can be

both written and spoken. Lesson 3 is built around a conversation in *al-ᶜāmmiyya* among three Arabic speakers comparing the weather in Jordan, Lebanon, and Saudi Arabia. Students listen to an audio recording of the conversation and complete accompanying activities in the textbook. Lesson 4 consists of a general review and exercises and activities to recycle the vocabulary.

Unlike *ᶜArabiyyat al-Naas*, part 1, there is no separate lesson in *ᶜArabiyyat al-Naas*, part 2 for grammar; grammar explanations are integrated into the activities of the first three lessons.

ᶜArabiyyat al-Naas, part 3, Unit 13 *(Younes and Chami 2014, 228–42)*

The theme of this unit is money and the economy. Lesson 1 includes two reading texts in *al-fuṣḥā* taken from the Al Jazeera website, both dealing with economic growth in Arab countries, the first about Jordan and the second about Bahrain. Lesson 2 includes a passage in *al-fuṣḥā* featuring the economy of the Egyptian city of Dumyāṭ, with its 0 percent unemployment, and explaining its success. Lesson 3 consists of an audio recording in *al-ᶜāmmiyya* of a woman from a Lebanese radio station interviewing three parents about the difficulties they face in making ends meet. Lesson 4, as is the case with lesson 4 in *ᶜArabiyyat al-Naas*, part 2 and lesson 5 in *ᶜArabiyyat al-Naas*, part 1, consists of exercises and activities that aim to recycle the vocabulary of the unit and culminates in a speaking/writing activity in which students are asked to "prepare at home, discuss in class and then write" on one of the following three topics:

1. Has anyone in your family or someone you know suffered from an economic crisis and lost his/her job? What happened? What did he/she do to deal with the situation?
2. Comment on the story of the success of the Dumyāṭ economy. Compare between Dumyāṭ and other cities in and outside of Egypt.
3. In your opinion, should there be governmental rules and limitations on the economic activity of the country, or do you believe that the government should not interfere in economic matters?

The key features of the IA listed above (one communication system with two complementary components, *al-ᶜāmmiyya* and *al-fuṣḥā*, building on shared elements and giving equal weight to both) are all adhered to in the material described above. The first key feature is further illustrated by the fact there is one textbook for both varieties and that each unit in each textbook contains materials representative of both and used in situations and for functions that reflect native usage.

Shared Elements

As is well known, *al-ᶜāmmiyya* and *al-fuṣḥā*, being varieties of the same language, share most of their vocabulary and grammatical structures. Many apparent differences can be easily explained and learned by a limited number of rules. Consider, for example, the correspondences between *al-fuṣḥā* and Levantine Arabic in the realization of three phonological features: the phoneme *q*, the diphthong *aw*, and the pronunciation of the vowel of the *tā° marbūṭa*:

Table 2.2 Correspondences between *al-fuṣḥā* and Levantine Arabic in the realization of three phonological features

al-fuṣḥā	Levantine	Meaning
qarīb	°arīb	near
mawza	mōzi	banana
tuffāḥa	tuffāḥa	apple

The differences between *al-fuṣḥā* and Levantine in these three examples can be explained by the following three rules:

1. *Al-fuṣḥā* <q> is realized as <ᶜ> in Levantine.
2. *Al-fuṣḥā* <aw> is realized as <ō> in Levantine.
3. The vowel of *tā' marbūṭa* is pronounced <a> after emphatic and back consonants (*ḥ, kh, ṣ, ḍ, ṭ, z,* ', and *gh*) and <i> elsewhere in Levantine. After <r>, the vowel is pronounced <a> unless it is preceded by <i> or <ī>, in which case it is pronounced <i>. In *al-fuṣḥā* this vowel is pronounced <a> throughout.

Rather than learning each set in a different class using a different textbook, the same set can be introduced once along with the rules of the distribution of the variants in the two language varieties, which can be generalized to thousands of other words.

As was pointed out earlier, in preparing and selecting materials for the textbooks, the authors made a conscious attempt to use what is common to the two varieties, rather than what separates them, in a manner that reflects real usage and without sacrificing authenticity. For example, the forms in column C in table 2.3 are chosen over those in columns A and B when such a choice is possible:

Table 2.3 Sample shared words used in the instructional materials

A (*al-fuṣḥā* only)	B (*al-ᶜāmmiyya* only)	C (Shared)	Meaning
	ballaš-yiballiš	bada-yibda	to begin
	fiyyi/fīni	mumkin, baqdar	I can
	zayy	mithl	like
nāfidha		šubbāk	window
hunālik(a)	hunīk	hunāk	there
	kthiir ḥilw	ḥilw k(a)thiir	very pretty

Finally, the thematic organization of the textbooks makes it easier to build on the shared elements of the two language varieties. A look at any of the material in the different units confirms this claim. For example, table 2.4 shows the number of shared as well as different words and expressions introduced as new vocabulary in the units discussed above:

Table 2.4 Number of shared and different words and expressions introduced in specific units

	Number of shared words and expressions	Number of different words and expressions
'Arabiyyat al-Naas, vol. 1, Unit 10	52	9
'Arabiyyat al-Naas, vol. 2, Unit 8	57	4
'Arabiyyat al-Naas, vol. 3, Unit 13	80	0

Giving Equal Weight to Al-fuṣḥā and Al-ᶜāmmiyya

Judging by current and previous attitudes and practices, presenting *al-fuṣḥā* and *al-ᶜāmmiyya* in two separate tracks will in all probability result in some form of discrimination against *al-ᶜāmmiyya*. *Al-fuṣḥā* enjoys a high level of prestige, while in the minds of many practitioners *al-ᶜāmmiyya* has negative associations. Furthermore, the ready availability of instructional materials in *al-fuṣḥā*, both written and spoken, and the relative paucity of such materials in *al-ᶜāmmiyya* will likely tip the balance in favor of using more *al-fuṣḥā* materials in an Arabic course.

In a truly integrated program, a healthy balance based on actual usage in "real life" is maintained between the two language varieties since discussions of all materials, both written and spoken and both *al-fuṣḥā* and *al-ᶜāmmiyya*, take place in *al-ᶜāmmiyya*. Such discussions, particularly at more advanced levels, typically include *al-fuṣḥā* sayings, quotes, poetry, and even verses from the Qur'ān. The simultaneous presence and opportunities for reinforcement are assured for the two varieties, just as the two varieties are found side by side in a complementary and mutually reinforcing relationship in the Arabic-speaking world.

Challenges to Integration
The major criticism that has traditionally been leveled against the IA is that it can be potentially confusing to students. This issue is addressed in detail in a previous publication (Younes 2015, ch. 5), to which the reader is referred. However, new challenges have arisen as a result of the actual implementation of the approach in integrated textbooks and in classroom practices. Among these challenges are such practical issues as the following: (1) When designing an integrated textbook or a class reading or listening activity, what variety of the language should comprehension questions be written in, considering the fact that the texts for which the questions are designed are often written in *al-fuṣḥā* while the discussion based on them is supposed to take place in *al-ᶜāmmiyya*? (2) How much spoken *al-fuṣḥā* should be used in class discussions? (3) Should we tolerate the use of *al-ᶜāmmiyya* in written compositions?

The answers to these questions are likely to vary among programs and individual teachers. In addressing these issues, the Cornell Arabic program has followed two guiding principles. First, since the main goal of the program is to graduate students who can deal successfully with the Arabic language situation, an attempt is always made to reflect native usage in the classroom as much as possible. What would native speakers do in a similar situation? Comprehension questions accompanying *al-fuṣḥā* texts are normally written in *al-fuṣḥā*. Consequently, *al-fuṣḥā* is used in the comprehension questions accompanying the written texts in the textbook series, except in the first half of *ᶜArabiyyat al-Naas*, part 1, where English and *al-ᶜāmmiyya* are used since the students' command of *al-fuṣḥā* is still quite limited. And since the writing of *al-ᶜāmmiyya* is becoming more widespread, comprehension questions on *al-ᶜāmmiyya* materials are written in *al-ᶜāmmiyya*.

The second guiding principle is to try to maintain a positive, supportive, and stress-free environment that is as conducive to learning as possible. There are undoubtedly teachers who are more comfortable speaking *al-fuṣḥā* than others, and there are teachers for whom the practice of using fully inflected *al-fuṣḥā* for conversation is quite stressful. There is no harm in using *al-fuṣḥā* as long as such use does not result in a stressful classroom situation, which may arise if or when a teacher is forced to use fully inflected *al-fuṣḥā* for functions for which it would sound artificial, such as conversing with friends or family members or discussing what one did over the weekend. When discussing politics or poetry, speaking *al-fuṣḥā* may be the more natural option both in terms of the topic and for the teacher.

These two guiding principles are also relevant when dealing with the use of *al-ᶜāmmiyya* in written compositions. For example, standards of native usage do not allow the use of *miš* "not" in written compositions. The program's policy is to be more tolerant of such errors at the elementary level and then treat them as errors of word choice at the intermediate and advanced levels. This way students would not be unduly discouraged, and the goal of graduating students who can use Arabic properly is met.

Conclusion: Integration versus Separation

There is no doubt that integration means different things to different people. For some practitioners, the mere introduction of *al-ᶜāmmiyya*—albeit in a separate course—in an Arabic program where *al-fuṣḥā* is taught is viewed as integration. For me, integration means that an elementary AFL course automatically includes both language varieties, where each variety is used in the way it is used by native speakers and where the role of *al-ᶜāmmiyya* is of equal relevance and importance to that of *al-fuṣḥā*.

There are a number of practical and pedagogical advantages to integration as opposed to separation. These advantages are discussed in some detail in Younes (2015, ch. 4). Here a list of these advantages will suffice: One course and one set of textbooks instead of two; the absence of the need to divide the indivisible; the learners prepared to deal effectively with the relationship between *al-fuṣḥā* and *al-ᶜāmmiyya* in the real world; the availability of opportunities for reinforcement of the two language varieties in a more natural manner; and, finally, a richer, more varied, and more interesting classroom environment.

References

Abdalla, Mahmoud, and Mahmoud Al-Batal. 2011–12. "College Level Teachers of Arabic in the United States: A Survey of Their Professional and Institutional Profiles and Attitudes." *Al-ᶜArabiyya* 44/45: 1–28.

Badawi, El-Said. 1973. *Mustawayāt al-ᶜArabiyya al-muᶜāSira fī miṣr* (Levels of contemporary Arabic in Egypt). Cairo: Dār al-maᶜārif.

Belnap, R. Kirk. 2006. "A Profile of Students of Arabic in US Universities." In *Handbook for Arabic Language Teaching Professionals in the 21st Century*, edited by Kassem M. Wahba, Zeinab A. Taha, and Liz England, 169–78. Mahwah, NJ: Lawrence Erlbaum.

Ferguson, Charles. 1959. "Diglossia." *Word* 15:325–40.

Husseinali, Ghassan. 2006. "Who Is Studying Arabic and Why? A Survey of Arabic Students' Orientations at a Major University." *Foreign Language Annals* 39 (3): 395–412.

Palmer, Jeremy. 2007. "Arabic Diglossia: Teaching Only the Standard Variety Is a Disservice to Students." *Arizona Working Papers in SLA & Teaching* 14:111–22.

Ryding, Karin. 2013. *Teaching and Learning Arabic as a Foreign Language: A Guide for Teachers*. Washington, DC: Georgetown University Press.

Shiri, Sonia. 2013. "Learners' Attitudes toward Regional Dialects and Destination Preferences in Study Abroad." *Foreign Language Annals* 46 (4): 565–87.

Wilmsen, David. 2006. "What is Communicative Arabic?" In *Handbook for Arabic Language Teaching Professionals in the 21st Century*, edited by Kassem M. Wahba, Zeinab A. Taha, and Liz England, 125–38. Mahwah, NJ: Lawrence Erlbaum.

Younes, Munther. 2015. *The Integrated Approach to Arabic Instruction*. London and New York: Routledge.

Younes, Munther, and Hanada al-Masri. 2014. *ᶜArabiyyat al-Naas*, part 2. London: Routledge.

Younes, Munther, and Yomna Chami. 2014. *ᶜArabiyyat al-Naas*, part 3. London: Routledge.

Younes, Munther, Makda Weatherspoon, and Maha Foster. 2014. *ᶜArabiyyat al-Naas*, part 1. London: Routledge.

3

Lessons Learned and Empirical Data from Twenty-Five Years of Using an Integrated Approach

R. KIRK BELNAP

Brigham Young University

BRIGHAM YOUNG UNIVERSITY'S (BYU) twenty-five-plus years of continuous use and tweaking of its integrated approach (IA) to the learning of Arabic is first and foremost about responding to the needs of its students, who are in many ways representative of the majority of students enrolled in Arabic courses in the United States: undergraduates with a high degree of interest in the modern Arab world and in using the language to interact with Arabs. Most put a high priority on traveling to the region, understanding Arab culture, and reading and understanding print and broadcast media. Many are also interested in its literature and cinema as well as in understanding important cultural symbols, such as the Qur'ān. In short, they fit well the national demographics described in the author's survey (2006) and in smaller surveys, such as Ghassan Husseinali's (2006). In current practice, and based on a good deal of trial and error, the BYU Arabic program seeks to strike a balance between assisting students to acquire real-world communication skills that fuel students' motivation to persist in studying Arabic and building a solid foundation on which they may build and eventually distinguish themselves as competent users of the language in both informal and formal contexts.

This chapter begins with a discussion of factors that led to the adoption and retention of an IA, followed by empirical data on student learning outcomes and qualitative and quantitative data that provide insight into the question of what happens when students begin with one dialect and later encounter another that is significantly different. The chapter also summarizes our experience with teaching different dialects and concludes by presenting evidence that indicates that an IA may actually lead to more students achieving advanced levels of proficiency in Arabic appropriate to more formal contexts. No approach is without drawbacks. This chapter illustrates one program's experience with seeking to address institutional and student priorities in an innovative manner.

Background and Rationale for Adopting an Integrated Approach

BYU's Arabic program has evolved considerably from an undergraduate program typical of the early 1980s, including limited use of Arabic for true communication in class; a sequence of six semesters of Arabic with no focus on what was then called "Colloquial Arabic"; and class time devoted largely to doing drills from the most widely used textbook series of the time. Students now speak Levantine Arabic from the first day of class and continue studying it alongside Modern Standard Arabic (MSA) throughout the first four semesters. The largest area studies major at BYU, Middle East Studies/ Arabic, and our Arabic minor require that students participate in BYU's intensive semester abroad program, which takes the place of "third year" (no longer offered on campus) and results in most students reaching Advanced-level proficiency in both speaking and reading as defined by the American Council of Teachers of Foreign Languages (ACTFL).[1] Students who reach this level are eligible to enroll in BYU's Arabic Language second major, which focuses on polishing students' abilities to use Arabic, mostly for formal contexts. Content-based instruction is a cornerstone of both the overseas and post-overseas experience.

The roots of BYU's IA go back to the 1980s and the faculty's grappling with the challenges of building an Arabic program that would assist students to effectively and efficiently acquire facility in using Arabic (Parkinson 1985b).[2] Seminal work on foreign language education, such as by Theodore Higgs and Ray Clifford (1982), and key developments in the Arabic field, such as establishing the Middlebury Summer School of Arabic (1982) and publishing the ACTFL Arabic Proficiency Guidelines (Allen 1985), played an important role in this process and were the result of language professionals who took seriously the concept of "communicative competence" (Hymes 1966). Frustration with the textbooks and practices common to the Arabic field led me to do a good deal of listening to students and teachers (Belnap 1987; 1995). Contributing local factors included the following: (1) The two faculty members responsible for BYU's Arabic program were part of campus-wide discussions that included leading national figures in foreign language teaching and curriculum development and (2) both were actively involved in doing sociolinguistic research on Arabic speech communities in the 1980s and 1990s. As a result of their research on both modern and historical lan-guage *use* (Belnap 1993, 1999; Parkinson 1985a, 1987), both were particu-larly sensitive to the fact that arguments for privileging the teaching of MSA and delaying exposure to vernacular varieties were typically the result of language ideology rather than a pragmatic assessment of the facts of Arabic speech communities and the needs of learners. Dilworth Parkinson therefore went on to investigate native ability to speak, read, and write MSA in Cairo (Parkinson 1991, 1992, 1993).

Communicative competence is about knowing *when* to say *what* to *whom* (Hymes 1966; Savignon 1983). Sociolinguistic authenticity, learning how people actually communicate, can be rather inconvenient for language learners and their teachers. For example, the complicated system of Japa-nese honorifics requires even novice learners of the language to be sensitive to how to linguistically signal respect and intimacy.[3] As a result, beginning textbooks of Japanese acquaint learners with the basics of this system. A popular textbook begins on page 4 with instructions on using "**-san** (*Mr./Ms.*) for your friends or classmates and **–sensee** (*Professor*) for your instruc-tor," as well as the following: "Notice that the question **onamae wa?** does not end in **ka**. In formal Japanese, questions end in **ka**, but in an informal, colloquial style of speech questions are often abbreviated" (Tohsaku 2004). This challenge of learning *what* to say *to whom* is universal. Charles Fergu-son, who played a pivotal role in making modern Arabic accessible to stu-dents, often quoted John Haviland: "to speak at all is to choose a register which will index the moment" (1979, 389; discussed in Belnap and Haeri 1997, 142). Failing to teach students to speak as natives do sets them up for frustration.

Like many others of my generation, I was taught to speak MSA in a manner that left me with almost no speaking ability after two years of study. As was typical, my first encounter with vernacular Arabic came in my third year of Arabic. Egyptian dialogues that were the foundation of each lesson breathed life, as did the political cartoons we read. But I did not really comprehend the problem as I should have until the first weeks of my Center for Arabic Study Abroad (CASA) experience when a classmate, who had studied at Middlebury College during the summer and could speak MSA well, expressed his anger that he had not been better prepared for the realities of Cairo. Shopkeepers and others did not speak MSA, as they were "supposed to" (students were regularly told that MSA was the language for communicating with all Arabs who are not illiterate). Students deserve to know the truth.

Interested in claims about the role of MSA for conversations between Arabs from different regions, I chose a course that focused on this skill as a CASA elective. I was convinced we needed empirical work on the topic, so, working under Elsaid Badawi's guidance, I did exploratory fieldwork and quickly learned that using MSA in Cairo rarely resulted in satisfactory communication. For example, a crowd of curious onlookers in a post office exploded in laughter when they heard me ask to buy stamps in MSA. Sonia Shiri (2013) documents similar student experiences in other countries, confirming that using MSA for everyday communication is problematic and that using the local vernacular opens doors for deeper conversations.

The experience with teaching MSA for informal conversation left the instructors in BYU's Arabic program increasingly dissatisfied. The transition to an IA accordingly began in 1989 with handouts that introduced beginning students to basic Egyptian Arabic expressions. Dr. Parkinson then returned from a year of research in Egypt with evidence from a representative sample of Egyptians that few could use MSA to communicate orally (1992), and he soon began developing supplemental material for first- and second-semester Arabic that included dialogues, vocabulary lists, grammar and culture notes, and some learning activities. This new approach meant that on the first day of Arabic 101, students were using Egyptian. During the first weeks, we focused on speaking in class while they learned the Arabic script as homework. Approximately equal attention was given to Egyptian and MSA during the first year. In second year, more time was devoted to MSA, and students read and listened to selections from an Egyptian play by Ali Salem. In 2002 we added video clips of daily life interaction that we filmed in Cairo to supplement the first four semesters of Arabic courses. BYU decided to move its Arabic program to Jordan in 2013 because of the security situation in Cairo. As a result, we switched to Levantine Arabic, given that Levantine had become widely understood in the Arab world, thanks to the popularity of Turkish TV programs dubbed into Syrian Arabic. We now use print and video materials developed in Amman, as well as some of our own audio and video, in order to supplement the Levantine materials found in the textbook series that we use.

Early results of using the IA at BYU were encouraging. Students were enthused. They spoke a lot more Arabic on campus, and they were more satisfied with their experiences in the Arab world. For example, a student returning from his summer in Cairo as a CASA fellow wryly observed that the cab drivers knew the dialogues from the BYU Egyptian materials. Another former student, who had been working in Iraq, reported that his knowledge of Egyptian was highly valuable for getting around as he worked on learning Iraqi.

Proficiency Testing and the Integrated Approach

In the mid-1990s, Ford Foundation funding that came to the American Association of Teachers of Arabic through the National Council of Organizations of Less-Commonly-Taught Languages provided an opportunity to compare the MSA reading and listening comprehension of students from two institutions that employed integration in their curricula, BYU and Cornell University, with students from five other institutions who were doing only MSA.[4] The most important finding was that students using an IA did not appear to be disadvantaged as a result of their simultaneously learning a vernacular variety of Arabic. The fact that they performed significantly better on the reading test and almost so on the listening test is likely due to the fact that both integrated programs used level-appropriate readings to help their students develop facility in reading. As for listening, it may well be that in the integrated programs students were simply getting more practice hearing Arabic in and out of the classroom.

Assessing the speaking ability of BYU students using the ACTFL Oral Proficiency Interview (OPI) has been a challenge. In his introduction to the ACTFL Arabic Proficiency Guidelines, Roger Allen (1985) discussed at some length problems associated with using MSA for informal contexts. ACTFL later abandoned language-specific guidelines, emphasizing that the proficiency guidelines are functional in nature. Testers were instructed to pose questions in MSA but allow those being tested to speak the variety they are comfortable using, especially if doing so is sociolinguistically authentic. Some testers have nevertheless pushed BYU students to speak in MSA even after publication of the Arabic Consensus Project (2012), which contains the following policy announcement: "In the ACTFL test protocol, Arabic is considered to be one language represented by a continuum from all colloquial to all MSA, and a combination of mixes along the continuum. During ACTFL OPI testing, testers accommodate to the variety of language that the test taker is producing and accept Arabic language produced anywhere along the continuum. An ACTFL OPI rating recognizes a speaker's overall functional ability in Arabic."

Testing students' oral and reading proficiency has become standard practice for the BYU Arabic program. At first this was done only at the end of its semester-long intensive study-abroad program. In recent years, students have also done an OPI at the beginning of the program. Table 3.1 gives the official

Table 3.1 Distribution of BYU semester abroad student exit OPI scores

OPI Score	Egypt 2004	Jordan 2006	Morocco 2006	Jordan 2008	Jordan 2011		Jordan 2014		Jordan 2015	
					pre	post	pre	post	pre[a]	post
AH	5	3	2	2					1	5[b]
AM	19	14	3	17		5	2	11	1	13
AL	20	6	5	19	3	14	1	12	5	16
IH	8	4	1	7	7	22	8	9	9	12
IM	1			3	22	11	9	2	16	
IL					19		11		6	
NH				1	1		2			
NM							1			

[a] Due to a miscommunication, eight of the students were interviewed by a tester in training. As a result, preprogram scores for these students were not included in this table, but the distribution of the official scores given here still gives a good sense for the range of abilities of the students at the beginning of the program.
[b] Two of the five students who reached Advanced High had previously spent over a year working with Iraqi refugees living in the United States. Another had just completed a Critical Language Scholarship program in Morocco before beginning the BYU program in Jordan.

OPI scores for these students. All interviews were conducted over the telephone, except for those in 2015, which were face-to-face interviews in Amman.

The somewhat higher scores from 2004 to 2008 reflect a time of inflated Arabic OPI ratings, which may partially account for the fact that Arabic raters at the time showed lower interrater reliability (Surface and Dierdorff 2003). We believe the greater numbers of Advanced Mid and High ratings in 2014 and 2015 primarily result from (1) more students entering the overseas program with better speaking ability and (2) program interventions in Jordan that have resulted in more opportunity for students to practice Advanced- and Superior-level functions (Bown, Dewey, and Belnap 2015). The lower scores in 2011 are also likely the result of some testers pressuring students to speak MSA, which they were not as good at as Jordanian. This type of pressure from testers has been far less common in recent years, perhaps as a result of the Arabic Consensus Project (2012).

The OPI scores reported in table 3.1 indicate that BYU students are getting the foundation they need to achieve their goal of acquiring advanced speaking ability in Arabic. Remarkably, all forty-two students in 2015 certified with at least Intermediate-High proficiency, meaning that all could function at the Advanced level most of the time. Comparable data for other Arabic programs is not available, but a comparison with Russian results shows the BYU Arabic speaking gains to be much better. For example, 38 percent of 334 Russian students who began a semester-length program with Intermediate-Mid proficiency made no measurable progress in their final OPI (Davidson 2010).

Transitioning to a Different Dialect

Until 2013, BYU students began their Arabic experience in Utah by learning to speak Egyptian, but most cohorts ended up studying overseas in BYU programs based in Jerusalem, Damascus, or Amman. The transition to Levantine took some effort but was not a major obstacle for most students. However, eleven students ended up studying in Fez, Morocco, during the fall of 2006 because the BYU administration was uncomfortable with students going to Jordan or Egypt immediately after the Israel–Hezbollah War. The considerable difference between Moroccan and Egyptian Arabic provides an excellent case study to test the proposition that studying even a dialect that is quite different from what students are accustomed to helps them to learn the new dialect. A sample of eleven students is relatively small, and nearly a decade has passed since their experience, but OPI scores and student comments in response to queries sent by email and Facebook are nevertheless revealing and provide qualitative data that could be useful in informing future research. The fact that the students' OPI scores in table 3.1 pattern closely with those programs held in other locations during the same period is also suggestive that they were not seriously impeded in developing their speaking ability because of the differences between Egyptian and Moroccan.

I sent email and Facebook messages to these former students in November 2015 asking if the Egyptian they had learned in Utah helped them learn Moroccan. Those who responded were invited to give more detail on their experience and an update on what they are now doing professionally. Seven responded. Five believe that knowing some Egyptian had been beneficial; two did not think it helped. The reasons given vary considerably. All seven expressed that they found little or no noticeable similarity between Moroccan and Egyptian. Three observed that Egyptian was a useful bridge that gave them a means of communication with their host family while they learned Moroccan.

A student who had previously lived in the Philippines and learned at least the basics of communicating in Tagalog, Ilocano, and Kapamgpangan, which are related but mutually incomprehensible, felt that learning MSA and Egyptian prepared him to expect that there are significant differences between varieties of Arabic. Another student, who had little language learning experience before starting Arabic but scored Advanced Low at the end of the program, observed: "I think that learning Egyptian, despite it being so wildly different from Moroccan, did help me as I started learning Moroccan. . . . I think it helped set up my brain for learning Moroccan, although the two dialects rarely intersected. It was good to already have a pretty clear basis for what the differences were between dialect and MSA . . . before diving into Moroccan—so in that way, I would say studying colloquial was very beneficial."

Students were actually primed with these insights in their first-semester syllabus:

All languages consist of a number of language varieties. Arabic is probably best seen as a continuum stretching between these two poles: 1. Written Arabic (often called "Modern Standard Arabic"), the officially sanctioned form of the language, is used in books and newspapers throughout the Arab World (from Iraq to Morocco), as well as for news broadcasts. 2. Spoken Arabic, sometimes called dialect or colloquial Arabic, is what Arabs speak at home and in their daily lives. Unlike Standard Arabic, the dialects differ considerably from one Arab country to another.

This class will expose you to both of these, but don't worry, they're closely related. You will learn Spoken Egyptian Arabic (Cairene, to be exact). There is good reason to start with Egyptian. It is widely understood in the Arab world because Egypt has produced most of the TV programs and movies seen in the Arab world. Approximately one third of all Arabs are Egyptians. We have found that our students are able to quickly adjust to other dialects and that Egyptian comes in very handy for communicating with speakers from all parts of the Arab world. We have also found that learning Spoken and Written Arabic together gives our students a better feel for the language. . . .

Unfortunately, the recent responses of students in email and Facebook messages suggest that this training was mostly forgotten when they arrived in Morocco. Most mentioned how difficult everyone told them Moroccan would be to learn. Some of the students spent little or no time working on learning Moroccan. Students bound for the Arab world need to be reminded before their departure and repeatedly on site of the unity of Arabic, of the parallels between the different dialects, and the dialects' close relationship with MSA.

Table 3.2 provides some detail on these former students and their responses. As noted earlier, the OPI scores are likely somewhat inflated, but it is telling that even the student with the lowest score, who was nineteen years old and

Table 3.2 Some details on BYU students from 2006 Morocco program

OPI Score	Egyptian Helped?	Some Details from Email or Facebook Responses
AM	Yes	"Knowing two forms preps you to know that there will be differences" (student who spent time in the Philippines).
AM	Yes	Lived in Arabic house at BYU where she used Egyptian a lot.
AL	No	Feels that MSA and colloquial varieties are basically two different languages; discouraged by his experience, he stopped studying Arabic after the Morocco program.
AL	No	Barely a B- student in Arabic before the abroad program but diligence in Morocco resulted in significant progress in MSA and Moroccan, the latter largely the result of his homestay experience. Now uses Arabic at work.
AL	Yes	Focused on Moroccan and used it in OPI. Went on to teach Arabic in K–12; now runs nongovernmental organization that helps Syrian refugees.
AL	Yes	Egyptian helped a lot (this is the student who commented on the structural parallels between Egyptian and Moroccan).
IH	Yes	Helped at first as common language with host family; now reviewing and studying Moroccan intensively in order to start a translation job.

began to struggle with homesickness and ended up disengaging from studying Arabic in the second half of the program, reported the following about her OPI experience: "I used both Egyptian and Moroccan. But mostly Moroccan. . . . I do remember the conversation included me pretending to be the tenant and the tester being the landlord and she is talking to me over a broken window. . . . It turned into a bargaining match as I was trying to make her pay for the window I broke. Ha! She thought that was pretty funny."

These results are supported by Emma Trentman's (2011) empirical investigation of Mahmoud Al-Batal and Kirk Belnap's statement that "experience has shown that students can move readily from learning one dialect to another. The transition from Egyptian to Levantine (or vice versa) is particularly easy and some exposure to both of these varieties is a significant plus" (2006, 396). Her study provides evidence that familiarity with one dialect helps one to understand other dialects better than knowing MSA does. Shiri (2013) found that Critical Language Scholarship students located in various parts of the Arab world widely reported that learning a second dialect is facilitated by the first, that most of her survey respondents were receptive to learning more than one, and that they value familiarity with different regional varieties.

Which Dialect?

Arabic teachers who are resistant to the idea of an integrative approach regularly counter with "There are so many dialects of Arabic. How could one choose which dialect to teach from so many?" This concern is not truly a hindrance for two reasons: First, most teachers of Arabic are native speakers of or are comfortable in Egyptian or Levantine, and these are the two varieties overwhelmingly requested by students since the mid-1980s (Belnap 1987, 2006; Shiri 2013). Second, Abdalla and Al-Batal (2011–12) found that most teachers supportive of teaching dialect are also receptive to the idea of teaching a dialect that is not their own.

The BYU Arabic program's experience indicates that measures may need to be taken to ensure positive outcomes. For example, a Moroccan graduate student at BYU had no problem teaching students to use Egyptian; later, as a teaching assistant in Jordan, she also proved adept at speaking Levantine with them. Palestinian and Jordanian graduate students, on the other hand, have typically not performed so well. In fact, many Palestinian and Jordanian students on the BYU campus have been critical of the choice to teach Egyptian; not surprisingly, they expressed this only to the students, resulting in an apparently demoralizing effect on them. BYU faculty have learned that students of Arabic need to be prepared to recognize such negative comments as culturally authentic examples of nationalistic attitudes. Likewise, they should be prepared to know how speaking Egyptian or another dialect may be received. For example, a BYU student who attended a summer program at another institution in the 1990s was subjected to what he experienced as harassment whenever he used Egyptian in class. Language professionals need to value and build on the previous efforts of students to learn Arabic, even if they do not agree with the approach at that student's home institution.

Table 3.2 hints at a related phenomenon: the widespread belief that North African dialects are so different from MSA and other dialects that they hardly qualify as Arabic. This attitude is widely held by Arabs from the East, who make up the majority of teachers in the United States, 81 percent in the survey conducted by Abdalla and Al-Batal (2011–12). One often hears derogatory comments about North African dialects being full of French (Shiri 2002), as if Eastern dialects have not borrowed a good deal from English and other languages. Teachers should help students develop an appreciation for all varieties of Arabic, which likely means that many teachers will need more training in the nature of linguistic variation as well as exposure to more of the Arab world.

Students naturally develop an emotional attachment to the dialect of a friend or favorite teacher. Part of becoming educated about Arabic should include the awareness that valorizing one dialect for some subjective reason, such as "it sounds more sophisticated," is not professional behavior. Likewise, both students and teachers need to learn to recognize as unscientific the tendency of many to claim that their own or some other dialect of Arabic is closer to MSA, a tendency that Ferguson originally discussed (1959). No study has empirically established that one dialect is more like MSA. For every feature that a dialect shares with MSA, another feature can be found that calls the closer relationship in question.

Long-Term Benefits of Using an Integrated Approach

BYU's experience with using an IA has demonstrated that assisting students to acquire solid vernacular conversational skills results in many developing a high degree of motivation for studying formal Arabic. The more proficient they become in a dialect, the more they realize that they must become proficient in a range of registers to effectively function in Arabic speech communities. This tendency is best seen in the distribution of BYU Arabic winter semester enrollments, the semester immediately after the students return from their semester of intensive in-country study of Arabic, as shown in table 3.3. All but one of these courses focus on more formal registers of Arabic.[5] The most popular of these courses by far in 2016 were the core courses of BYU's unique Arabic Language second major: (1) a debate course that includes both prepared and extemporaneous formal speaking; and (2) a research course in which students read, write about, and make a formal presentation on a professional interest.

All students and especially second majors are encouraged to simultaneously improve their spoken Arabic as they do the research for their presentations, especially in the second half of the major when some have engaged in internships in Jordan. We have witnessed impressive improvements in students' command of vernacular Arabic, whether they worked with refugees in Salt Lake City or were based in Jordan. For example, an intern in Amman conducted a series of interviews with women about sexual harassment. Applying what she had learned about sharpening to improving her speaking ability (Belnap and Abuamsha 2014; Leaver and Campbell 2014), she recorded these interviews, listened closely to them, and with the help of a tutor became better

Table 3.3 BYU undergraduate enrollments on campus after semester overseas

Course	2012	2013	2014	2015	2016
Current Events[a]	18	9	5		8
Advanced Spoken Arabic (Levantine)	14				13
Advanced Grammar (close reading of editorials, etc.)	15	11	3		
Independent Readings	2	13	4	9	3
Modern Arabic Literature[a]	5		5		8
Classical Arabic Texts	5	4			1
Business Arabic[a]	6		5	6	
Debate[a]	14	10	6	10	27
Research Tutorial[a]	14	10	3	5	21
Total	93	57	31	30	81

Note: Blank cells in this table indicate that the course was not offered. All of these students participated in BYU's study-abroad program, except perhaps one or two students in the Classical Arabic Texts course.
[a] These courses typically include significant formal presentation opportunities.

with each interview at conversing naturally. This undergraduate was certified at Advanced High in speaking at the end of her internship.

The Need for Patience and Pragmatism

While some outside observers find the dialectal interference in the written production of BYU first- and second-year students unacceptable, we consider this a small price to pay for the eventual outcomes of an IA. In fact, we would do well to reevaluate this mixing. From a traditional prescriptivist standpoint, it is negative interference, but this is shortsighted. The results reported by Michelen Chalhoub-Deville and Kirk Belnap (1995), that IA students have better reading skills, suggest that an IA facilitates students' comprehension of MSA, underscoring the unity of Arabic as one language—that is, the close relationship between MSA and vernacular varieties.

We would do well to reexamine our desires for flawless MSA production (especially in the beginning), given that few natives are capable of this and that our students are far more likely to actually need only MSA comprehension skills and informal conversational skills (the skills of the average educated native speakers).[6] This, of course, flies in the face of established Arab language ideology, which many nonnative learners buy into. It is difficult not to do so. I enjoy flawless MSA as well as the next Arabist and wince at some errors of even our best Advanced-level students. We need to continually remind ourselves, however, that error correction overdone does not end well. Rather than attempting to root out such errors as soon as possible, we have found better results through designing learning opportunities that focus on the process of learning how to sharpen one's skills, how to continue to measure one's progress and continuously improve as a life-long learner.

Acquiring proficiency in style shifting, the ability to use the resources of both informal and formal varieties of Arabic in an effective manner, takes time. We cannot expect nonnative students to quickly develop a good feel for how to use these resources, particularly given how common mixing of formal and informal elements is becoming both in the speech of educated young Tunisians (Walters 2003) and in domains such as literature (Somekh 2010). Parkinson (1993) provides convincing evidence that most Egyptians never succeed in gaining solid control of MSA, yet many are nevertheless adept at using Arabic in a variety of formal and informal contexts. Belnap and Brian Bishop (2003) document attitudes and practices of young educated Arabs that suggest that they are well aware they are mixing and feel this actually makes for better writing. Only students with a feel for the full range of Arabic are prepared to successfully negotiate the emerging linguistic landscape.

Summary

The search for the one best language-teaching method in the 1970s and 1980s proved to be misguided; to the discerning eye, local conditions will reveal advantages and disadvantages to every approach (Kumaravadivelu 2012). One method or approach might be better suited for a certain context; another for a certain type of learner. We have come to the conclusion, from over twenty-five years of sustained experimentation, assessment, and revising of BYU's IA, that the authenticity, the feel that the students acquire for how Arabic works as a complete system, the increased motivation, and the end product are well worth some initial confusion and the long process of students learning to know when to use what to whom.

We are far from where we want to be as an Arabic program. We are working both on developing quality audio and video materials and on incorporating existing materials to our first- and second-year curriculum in order to help our students become better prepared for when they land in Jordan to begin their semester of intensive study. We continue to work to both train native teaching assistants to grasp the vision of our IA and to acquire techniques that will enable them to better serve the students both in the classroom and in speaking appointments with them. Clear grading rubrics have been particularly useful for the latter, including rewarding students for "chunking" (using phrases extracted from audio or video of native models). We are especially encouraged by the results we have seen as we have shared results from Project Perseverance with first- and second-year students and as they have learned from the example of near-peer teaching assistants recently returned from Jordan (Belnap et al. 2016). Clear grading rubrics helped students to better understand themselves as learners as well as better understand the learning process; become more mindful and therefore better at self-regulating; and learn the skill of sharpening starting early in their first semester, including grasping the power of recording and rerecording themselves as they seek to close the gap between their speaking performance and level-appropriate native models that are their target.

Exclusive focus on Classical Arabic or MSA was understandable in generations past, when access to Arabic was largely restricted to print materials with little or no admixture of vernacular material. Those days are gone. Mixing has become the norm. Even the producers of satellite talk-show programs and editors of respected newspapers who once zealously suppressed the intrusion of the vernacular have come to terms with the fact that at times there is no substitute for the power of vernacular speech. In short, mixing has become so common that a student who wants to deal with the modern Arab world needs a feel for the full continuum of Arabic. Exposure to MSA or vernacular varieties alone cuts students off from appreciating the Arabic that is now everywhere, thanks to the internet. Following extensive study of the proficiency of native speakers in MSA, Parkinson found that,

> while it is true that there are many areas of the grammar that pose problems, when it comes to actual reading, listening and writing proficiency, subjects scored quite well. . . . And . . . if we accept the notion of a highly formal "mixed" form which is like *fuSHaa* but without the case endings and other 'problem' rules . . . , we find that speakers and writers express themselves very well indeed. . . . If our goal is, as it must be, preparing students to deal with the real world and the real native speakers who inhabit it, let us use this to our advantage . . . [and] focus on what real native speakers do well, instead of on what they can hardly do at all. (2004, 204–5)

The BYU student experience of constant exposure to the full range of Arabic prepares them to take the reality of the Arab world in stride as they interact with Arabs on campus and watch TV series on YouTube beginning early in their first semester of Arabic. When they find themselves immersed in a free-flowing mix of Arabic in the airport in Amman, it comes as no surprise that no-smoking signs written in a dry formal Arabic are flanked by cell phone ads that cleverly employ Jordanian Arabic. Shortly thereafter their issues class teachers are immediately able to draw on and model a natural and fuller range of Arabic resources available to them. And when these students return and enroll in courses in Utah, they continue to find opportunities to experience and use Arabic as it is actually used by educated Arabs, in formal presentations, in semiformal discussions leading up to these, and in lighter but no less critical socializing where there is no hint of formality. Their entire undergraduate experience helps them see Arabic as one seamless continuum of resources to be enjoyed and adroitly employed as they grow in true communicative competence and therefore confidence.

References

Abdalla, Mahmoud, and Mahmoud Al-Batal. 2011–12. "College-Level Teachers of Arabic in the United States: A Survey of Their Professional and Institutional Profiles and Attitudes." *Al-ᶜArabiyya* 44/45: 1–28.

Al-Batal, Mahmoud, and R. Kirk Belnap. 2006. "The Teaching and Learning of Arabic in the United States: Realities, Needs, and Future Directions." In *Handbook for Arabic Language Teaching Professionals in the 21st Century*, edited by Kassem M. Wahba, Zeinab A. Taha, and Liz England, 389–99. Mahwah, NJ: Lawrence Erlbaum.

Allen, Roger. 1985. "Arabic Proficiency Guidelines." *Al-ᶜArabiyya* 18:45–70.

Arabic Consensus Project. 2012. "Speaking." *American Council on the Teaching of Foreign Languages.* http://www.actfl.org/publications/guidelines-and-manuals /actfl-proficiency-guidelines-2012/arabic/arabic-consensus-project/speaking.

Belnap, R. Kirk. 1987. "Who's Taking Arabic and What on Earth For? A Survey of Students in Arabic Language Programs." *Al-ᶜArabiyya* 20, no. 1/2: 29–42.

———. 1993. "The Meaning of Agreement Variation in Cairene Arabic." In *Perspectives on Arabic Linguistics*, vol. 5, edited by Mushira Eid and Clive Holes, 97–117. Philadelphia: John Benjamins.

———. 1995. "The Institutional Setting of Arabic Language Teaching: A Survey of Program Coordinators and Teachers of Arabic in US Institutions of Higher Learning." In *The Teaching of Arabic as a Foreign Language: Directions and Issues*, edited by Mahmoud Al-Batal, 35–78. Provo, Utah: American Association of Teachers of Arabic.

———. 1999. "A New Perspective on the History of Arabic: Variation in Marking Agreement with Plural Heads." *Folia Linguistica* 33, no. 2: 169–85.

———. 2006. "A Profile of Students of Arabic in US Universities." In *Handbook for Arabic Language Teaching Professionals in the 21st Century*, edited by

Kassem M. Wahba, Zeinab A. Taha, and Liz England, 169–78. Mahwah, NJ: Lawrence Erlbaum.

Belnap, R. Kirk, and Khaled Abuamsha. 2014. "Taking on the 'Ceiling Effect' in Arabic." In *To Advanced Proficiency and Beyond: Theory and Methods for Developing Superior Second-Language Ability*, edited by Tony Brown and Jennifer Bown, 105–16. Washington, DC: Georgetown University Press.

Belnap, R. Kirk, and Brian Bishop. 2003. "Arabic Personal Correspondence: A Window on Change in Progress?" *International Journal of the Sociology of Language* 163: 9–25.

Belnap, Kirk, Jennifer Bown, Dan Dewey, Linnea Belnap, and Patrick Steffen. 2016. "Project Perseverance: Helping Students Become Self-Regulating Learners." In *Positive Psychology in SLA*, edited by Peter MacIntyre, Tammy Gregersen, and Sarah Mercer, 282–301. Bristol, UK: Multilingual Matters.

Belnap, Kirk, and Niloofar Haeri. 1997. *Structuralist Studies in Arabic Linguistics: Charles A. Ferguson's Papers, 1954–1994*. Leiden: Brill.

Bown, Jennifer, Dan P. Dewey, and R. Kirk Belnap. 2015. "Student Interactions during Study Abroad in Jordan." In *Social Interaction, Identity and Language Learning during Residence Abroad*, edited by R. Mitchell, N. Tracy-Ventura, and K. McManus, 199–222. EuroSLA Monographs Series 4. Colchester, UK: EuroSLA.

Buckwalter, Tim, and Dilworth B. Parkinson. 2011. *A Frequency Dictionary of Arabic Core Vocabulary for Learners*. New York: Routledge.

Chalhoub-Deville, Micheline, and R. Kirk Belnap. 1995. "Background Variables and Arabic Student's Reading and Listening Comprehension Scores on the CAL Arabic Proficiency Test." Paper presented at the Middle East Studies Association Conference, Washington, DC.

Davidson, Dan E. 2010. "Study Abroad: When, How Long, and with What Results? New Data from the Russian Front." *Foreign Language Annals* 43: 6–26.

Ferguson, Charles. 1959. "Myths about Arabic." *Georgetown University Monograph Series on Languages and Linguistics* 12: 75–82.

Haviland, John. B. 1979. "Guugu Yimidhirr Brother-In-Law Language." *Language in Society* 8: 365–93.

Higgs, Theodore V., and Ray Clifford. 1982. "The Push Toward Communication." In *Curriculum, Competence, and the Foreign Language Teacher*, edited by Theodore V. Higgs, 57–79. Lincolnwood, IL: National Textbook.

Husseinali, Ghassan. 2006. "Who Is Studying Arabic and Why? A Survey of Arabic Students' Motivations at a Major University." *Foreign Language Annals* 39: 395–412.

Hymes, Dell H. 1966. "Two Types of Linguistic Relativity." In *Sociolinguistics*, edited by William Bright, 114–58. The Hague: Mouton.

Kumaravadivelu, B. 2012. *Language Teacher Education for a Global Society: A Modular Model for Knowing*. New York: Routledge.

Leaver, Betty Lou, and Christine Campbell. 2014. "Experience with Higher Levels of Proficiency." In *To Advanced Proficiency and Beyond: Theory and Methods for Developing Superior Second-Language Ability*, edited by Tony Brown and Jennifer Bown, 5–25. Washington, DC: Georgetown University Press.

Parkinson, Dilworth B. 1985a. *Constructing the Social Context of Communication: Terms of Address in Egyptian Arabic*. Berlin: Mouton de Gruyter.

————. 1985b. "Proficiency to Do What: Developing Oral Proficiency in Students of Modern Standard Arabic." *Al-ᶜArabiyya* 18: 11–43.

————. 1987. "Constraints on the Presence/Absence of 'Optional' Subject Pronouns in Egyptian Arabic." In *Variation in Language: NWAV-XV at Stanford*, edited by Keith M. Denning, Sharon Inkelas, Faye C. McNair-Knox, and John R. Rickford, 348–60. Stanford, CA: Stanford University Department of Linguistics.

————. 1991. "Searching for Modern *Fusha*: Real-life Formal Arabic." *Al-ᶜArabiyya* 24, no. 1: 31–64.

————. 1992. "Good Arabic: Ability and Ideology in the Egyptian Arabic Speech Community." *Language Research* 28, no. 2: 225–53.

————. 1993. "Testing Native Speakers: Implications for Teaching Arabic to Non-Native Speakers." In *Investigating Arabic: Linguistic, Pedagogical and Literary Studies in Honor of Ernest N. McCarus*, edited by Raji M. Rammuny and Dilworth B. Parkinson, 191–205. Columbus, OH: Greyden Press.

————. 2005. *Using Arabic Synonyms*. New York: Cambridge University Press.

Savignon, Sandra J. 1983. *Communicative Competence: Theory and Classroom Practice*. Reading, MA: Addison-Wesley.

Shiri, Sonia. 2002. "Speak Arabic Please! Tunisian Arabic Speakers' Linguistic Accommodation to Middle Easterners." In *Language Contact and Language Conflict in Arabic: Variations on a Sociolinguistic Theme*, edited by Aleya Rouchdy, 149–74. New York: Routledge Curzon Press.

————. 2013. "Learners' Attitudes toward Regional Dialects and Destination Preferences in Study Abroad." *Foreign Language Annals* 46: 565–87.

Somekh, Sasson. 2010. "Dialogue in Literature, Modern." In *Encyclopedia of Arabic Literature*, edited by Julie Scott Meisami and Paul Starkey, 190–91. London: Routledge.

Surface, Eric A., and Erich C. Dierdorff. 2003. "Reliability and the ACTFL Oral Proficiency Interview: Reporting Indices of Interrater Consistency and Agreement for 19 Languages." *Foreign Language Annals* 36, no. 4: 507–19.

Tohsaku, Yasu-Hiko. 2004. *Yookoso! An Invitation to Contemporary Japanese*. Boston: McGraw-Hill College.

Trentman, Emma. 2011. "L2 Arabic Dialect Comprehension: Empirical Evidence for the Transfer of Familiar Dialect Knowledge to Unfamiliar Dialects." *L2 Journal* 3: 22–49.

Walters, Keith. 2003. "Fergie's Prescience: The Changing Nature of Diglossia in Tunisia." *International Journal of the Sociology of Language* 163: 77–109.

Wilmsen, David. 2006. "What is Communicative Arabic?" In *Handbook for Arabic Language Teaching Professionals in the 21st Century*, edited by Kassem M. Wahba, Zeinab A. Taha, and Liz England, 125–38. Mahwah, NJ: Lawrence Erlbaum.

Younes, Munther. 2015. *The Integrated Approach to Arabic Instruction*. London: Routledge.

Notes

Additional data and examples are freely available to view and download on this book's product page on the Georgetown University Press (GUP) website (www.press .georgetown.edu).

1. For details on this overseas program and advanced-level courses offered on the BYU campus, see Belnap and Abuamsha 2014.

2. This chapter focuses on practical aspects of BYU's experience with an IA. For a fuller treatment of the rationale for such an approach as well as for an account of the development of Cornell's model, see Younes 2015.

3. Paul Warnick, an authority on Japanese pedagogy, told me that Japanese heritage students who have never been exposed to the full honorifics system at home have a difficult time acquiring it. My experience with scores of students from many different institutions who were exposed only to MSA in the classroom is that many fail to acquire a feel for how Arabic is used naturally, even after significant in-country exposure to vernacular Arabic. They exhibit fossilized forms such as *dhahabtu* "I went" that are awkward in informal conversation. Wilmsen noted the same for "students who spend time in full-immersion environments wherein they are compelled to utilize the formal code as a vehicle of speech" (2006, 137).

4. The results of that study were never published, but the text of the Chalhoub-Deville and Belnap handout from their conference presentation of their statistical analysis of the data is included in appendix 3.1, on the GUP website.

5. Those who employ an IA are often accused of being enemies of MSA. It is noteworthy that Professor Parkinson's research for twenty years has overwhelmingly been devoted to modern print Arabic usage and to making better tools available to learners based on this research (Parkinson 2005; Buckwalter and Parkinson 2011). BYU faculty are also actively involved in producing resources for learning both Egyptian and Syrian Arabic. Michael Bush, former director of BYU's Advanced Research in Curriculum for Language Instruction and Technology in Education (ARCLITE) Lab, assisted us in the collection of video assets for the Arabic Encounters project (http://uccllt.ucdavis.edu/arabic/credits.html). We continue to fine-tune this resource for advanced-level learners.

6. David Wilmsen (2006) provides a telling illustration of the importance of such a pragmatic approach with details on the real-world needs of interpreters.

4

Preparing Arabic Teachers for Integration

The Edinburgh Model

JONATHAN FEATHERSTONE
University of Edinburgh

IN THIS CHAPTER, I demonstrate how Arabic-specific teacher-training courses, such as the five-day course developed in Edinburgh by the Centre for the Advanced Study of the Arab World (CASAW), can help to address many of the issues lying behind the ineffective nature of Arabic teaching and help prepare teachers to integrate dialect within the Arabic curriculum using the integrated approach (IA), which has been adopted in very few institutions in the United Kingdom. I also discuss the current situation regarding the teaching of Arabic in higher education in the United Kingdom. I then examine how the Edinburgh model, using the IA, led to the creation of the five-day teacher-training course in teaching Arabic using integration. I then examine the rationale behind the design of the course, while demonstrating how it succeeds in enabling teachers to teach using the IA.[1]

In 2007 CASAW at the University of Edinburgh established a new master's degree in Middle Eastern Studies, followed by the establishment of the master's degree in International Relations of the Middle East with Arabic in 2010. These are two-year master's programs, both of which include an intensive Arabic course whereby students reach a high level of proficiency (C1 in the Common European Framework or Advanced Mid-High on the American Council on the Teaching of Foreign Language [ACTFL] scale) in both Modern Standard Arabic (MSA) and a major spoken Arabic dialect.

This program is one of the few that does not use MSA as the sole medium of instruction. The method used here is the IA (Younes 1990), which involves the simultaneous teaching of a spoken Arabic alongside MSA.[2] Students are trained from the outset on how to use the appropriate language in its appropriate context. This is done by using three types of teaching material:

1. A core textbook, currently either *Al-Kitaab fii Taʿallum al-ʿArabiyya* (parts 1 and 2) (Brustad, Al-Batal, and Al-Tonsi 2013a, 2013b) or *ʿArabiyyat al-Naas* (parts 1 and 2) (Younes, Weatherspoon, and Foster 2013; Younes and al-Masri 2014).
2. A mainstream dialect textbook. Currently we use *BBC Talk Arabic* (Featherstone 2015) for Levant Arabic followed by *Breakthrough Arabic* (Auty, Holes, and Harris 1992) or *Kallimni Arabi* (Louis 2007) for Egyptian Arabic. This is not set in stone, and Arabic teachers in other institutions wishing to adopt the IA may wish to use different textbooks.
3. In-house material designed to link MSA and spoken Arabic structures together. This is crucial to ensure the smooth running of the approach, and it is here that training is key.

This intensive master's program also includes a summer in the Arab World at the end of the first academic year; by this time, students are ready to enter the Arabic "superhighway," perhaps not at seventy miles per hour, but at least at fifty or sixty miles per hour, depending on the student's own language ability. This contrasts with most undergraduate students in the United Kingdom who are taught solely MSA until their year abroad, when they are expected to "pick up" spoken Arabic on the streets with a minimal introduction to dialect in the United Kingdom.

The Edinburgh intensive master's program does not perceive integration as creating a "hybrid" language. On the contrary, integration aims at reflecting linguistic reality regarding Arabic usage. Edinburgh students are instinctively taught to choose the correct form of language when speaking and to make the necessary switches when writing. They are able to read texts in MSA but also listen to and understand popular Arabic songs, most of which are in a spoken Arabic dialect. This is in contrast to Arabic courses in the majority of academic institutions around the world that only teach MSA, thus leaving students totally cut off from a great deal of human discourse in the Arab world.

Arabic pedagogy in terms of teaching Arabic to nonnative speakers in both schools and higher education in the United Kingdom has lagged behind that of other European languages. Many universities in the United Kingdom focus on teaching students how to read MSA. When oral activities are included, they are focused on speaking in MSA, ignoring the fact that most oral exchanges in Arabic are carried in a spoken Arabic dialect. I have asked many UK colleagues why they refuse to teach a dialect alongside or even in addition to MSA, and many claim that it is too complicated, too confusing. Another argument raised is that the choice of dialect is a dilemma.

The Current Extent of the Integrated Approach in Arabic Teaching in Higher Education in the United Kingdom

If we examine the current state of Arabic teaching in higher education in the United Kingdom, for example, there exist two tiers of Arabic programs. The upper tier is universities that offer a full bachelor's degree in Arabic.[3] Most of the Arabic-language teaching is carried out by native-speaker instructors or teaching fellows of Arabic, some of whom hold PhDs from the Arab world, often specializing in fields other than Arabic-language pedagogy. Many of these teachers are often unqualified in teaching languages, let alone in the teaching of Arabic as a foreign language. The second, lower tier is where Arabic is offered as an ancillary course that contributes to a student's final degree. In the United Kingdom, some programs offer a dialect as an add-on, but this is usually kept completely separate to avoid contaminating the main task of teaching MSA. There are a few notable exceptions, such as Cambridge, where, according to their website, a dialect is introduced alongside MSA but full integration has not been implemented.[4]

Thus, in the upper tier of institutions, Edinburgh is the only university that has adopted the IA at a master's level, in which MSA and a dialect are taught side by side within the classroom, from beginning to end. In the lower tier institutions, the focus is on MSA. The favored textbook is *Mastering Arabic 1* (Wightwick and Gaafar 2014), which is in MSA, and in some institutions students are introduced to "tasters" of a wide array of dialects as if they all emanated from MSA but deviated from it. Not only is this linguistically an incorrect assumption but it will not help learners achieve fluency in Arabic. Fluency in spoken Arabic requires a large number of well-planned communicative activities as well as structural drills in one specific dialect. Although a small number of Arabic textbooks are beginning to introduce elements of spoken dialects into their modules, the IA cannot be delivered without training in its methodology. It requires a great deal of thought, creativity, and flexibility on the part of the Arabic teacher.

Often when teaching Arabic to nonnative speakers, Arabic teachers with no teaching qualifications mimic the way they were taught MSA in school as children. They forget that when they learned MSA at school, they could already speak a dialect fluently, unlike their students, who cannot. Some teachers from parts of the Arab world, for ideological reasons, feel that foreigners should study MSA and that a spoken dialect is a "private" and "intimate" language reserved solely for those who speak it as a mother tongue. There are others who incorrectly describe their dialect as "slang," claiming that it is devoid of any grammar.[5]

Convincing the Skeptics to Adopt the Integrated Approach

Despite the increase in interest in integration, there still exists in the United Kingdom a degree of skepticism among Arabic teachers (both native and non-native) toward the teaching of anything other than MSA. There are a number of reasons why I believe this to be the case:

1. Prestige. MSA is considered to be prestigious (Wahba 1996), as opposed to the dialects, which many teachers of Arabic mistakenly refer to as "slang" in English.[6]
2. Inertia. Heads of Arabic in the United Kingdom, who are often non-native speakers of Arabic themselves and who have only studied MSA, are fearful of change.[7]
3. Lack of empathy. Often those involved in teaching Arabic insist that students can "pick up" a spoken Arabic dialect through having been given a solid base of MSA. This may be possible if you are an exceptionally talented linguist or have a considerable amount of time to spend living in an Arabic-speaking country (Bacha 2014).[8]
4. "You're an Arab, therefore you can teach Arabic." This is an orientalist approach to language teaching (Said 1978).[9] There still exists in the United Kingdom the attitude that foreign languages are "subordinate" to English, and it is sufficient to be a native speaker of that language to qualify you to teach it to others.

In the light of these reasons, CASAW developed a one-week intensive training program for Arabic teachers to help them use the IA in their teaching and to enable the program to grow. This training course, which attracts Arabic teachers from all over the world, is designed for those with at least one or two years of experience in teaching nonnative speakers either MSA solely or a dialect separately.

The CASAW Training Course in Integration and the Communicative Approach

The CASAW intensive five-day course aims to achieve five goals through a series of linked workshops:

1. Breaking the barrier of fear
2. Helping teachers to deconstruct and reconstruct the Arabic language
3. Understanding the relationship between the IA and both the communicative and task-based approaches
4. Developing creativity and providing teachers with the creative tools required to use the IA in their teaching
5. Helping teachers to focus on and empathize more with their learners

The course uses the following three methods to deliver its message and to provide teachers with the skills and confidence to teach Arabic using the IA.

1. Self-discovery and reflection
2. Deconstruction and reconstruction
3. Mirroring and loop techniques

These techniques help to break down the fear of integrating dialect into the teaching of Arabic. Effective training must include both mirroring and loop activities to help the participants discover and reflect on the linguistic processes involved in moving in and out of spoken Arabic and MSA in a way that reflects linguistic reality.

Mirroring is a training activity that can be adapted by teachers in their own classes. For example, the survey used as an icebreaker on the first day of the training course to help teachers reflect on the type of language they use can later be adopted to help their students consolidate the use of the spoken Arabic verb yi'dar (to be able to) alongside the MSA version, yastaṭiᶜ.[10]

A loop activity (Woodward 2003) is one where, during the training, the teachers try out a new technique, such as mutual dictation where participants work in pairs, dictating different parts of the same text to each other; however, in this case the text discusses the effectiveness of mutual dictation as a method of integrating writing in MSA and speaking in a dialect.[11]

Breaking the Barrier of Fear

Breaking the barrier of fear is one of the major challenges of the five-day course. Many Arabic teachers tell me that they are frightened of the idea of integrating a dialect within their teaching in terms of both methodology and delivery. This fear has two sides to it: On the one hand, they fear that they do not have the expertise in teaching a dialect because they were never taught it themselves, and they do not believe that a dialect can be taught formally. On the other hand, Arabic teachers fear that learners "will not be able to cope with both a dialect and MSA simultaneously because they will get confused."

The teachers' fear that their students will be confused stems from their own sense of confusion resulting from a lack of training. They must be trained to understand that their students *can* cope with learning a dialect and MSA simultaneously without getting confused. Code-switching[12] is commonplace, particularly among bilinguals; as a result, getting students to say *shuftak imbārih* "I saw you yesterday" but to write *raᵓaytuka amsi* is not impossible or confusing, and teachers need not fear this. During the microteaching session with guinea pig beginner learners, teachers are helped to discover for themselves that adult learners can be taught on the first day to say *min wayn inta?* "where are you from?" and to write *min ayna anta?*

To further quell the fear, most students of Arabic in UK universities have studied other foreign languages at school and are able to switch from one language or dialect to another with relative ease. Moreover, students who have already successfully learned Arabic using the IA over the past eight years have consistently placed "dealing with diglossia" fairly low in the list of aspects that they found most difficult when learning Arabic, as is shown in a sample of respondents in table 4.1.

These results are based on a sample of twenty students who had studied Arabic using the IA in Edinburgh between 2013 and 2015. Ten had studied only MSA for many years in universities in Western Europe and North America and were unable to speak Arabic but only read. The other ten joined the master's program as beginners. The results demonstrate that students who had only been taught how to read MSA found "dealing with diglossia" to be the most difficult aspect. In comparison, the sample of students who were taught using the IA from the outset placed "dealing with diglossia" fairly low in terms of difficulty in comparison to other aspects of learning Arabic.

Teachers' Fear of Handling Dialect and MSA at the Same Time

Teachers' fear of teaching a dialect and MSA together stems from the fact that many teachers of Arabic have never considered teaching their own dialect, let alone integrating it into the teaching of MSA. Teachers worry about

Table 4.1

Question: Which aspects of Arabic did you find hardest to master as a student? Place the following in order of difficulty. (1 being the hardest)

	Ranking (by beginners in integrated approach)	Ranking (by students who had studied MSA exclusively)
Pronunciation	7	6
Dealing with diglossia	6	1
Broken plurals	4	4[a]
Case endings	2	8
Verb conjugations	5	9
The root system	10	2
Arabic script	8	5
Numbers	9	4[a]
Learning vocabulary	3	7
Grammar in general	1	3

[a] These were tied at 4.

which dialect to use and how to imbed it into their Arabic teaching. One workshop helps Arabic teachers understand the relationship between their own dialect and the dialects of other Arabic teachers participating in the course and helps them see that the different dialects share many aspects in common, not shared by MSA (Ferguson 1959). This realization helps teachers understand that the IA does not prescribe the use of any particular dialect over another.

The first session in the training course is an icebreaking activity that shows teachers that when they communicate with one another, even when discussing a formal topic such as teaching pedagogy, the *form* of language they use is spoken Arabic, not MSA.[13] The discussion is recorded and played back to them for reflection. They notice that they are not speaking in MSA but in their own dialects, albeit with a certain amount of "leveling" (Bassiouney 2009). They reflect on how this new awareness impacts their teaching, and they discuss in groups how they feel. The program's "reflective" nature helps the teachers' attitudes to change without being dictated to by the teacher-trainer. What inevitably occurs is that the teachers begin to understand the need to adopt strategies to teach learners to speak and function the way the teachers themselves do as native speakers.

Deconstructing and Reconstructing Arabic
and the "Diglossic Gap"

One of the aims of the Edinburgh training course is to enable teachers of Arabic to have a better understanding of "diglossia" and its impact on the delivery of communicative Arabic teaching. The course helps teachers dismantle the Arabic language and reassemble it to better understand the relationship between MSA and the dialects. This process of self-discovery through reflection not only helps the teachers understand how integration can work but also realize and accept that it is the most realistic and effective way of teaching Arabic to nonnative speakers.

The Diglossic Gap workshop is where teachers try to determine the width of the gap between spoken Arabic and MSA. The diglossic gap is the difference between spoken Arabic and MSA in any particular aspect of the language. For example, if many spoken dialects use the word *mush/mish* "not" to negate a nominal sentence, as in the phrase "I am *not* Egyptian," and MSA uses the past tense verb *laysa* to convey the same meaning, then we have a diglossic gap.

Teachers notice that the diglossic gap varies in width according to a specific structure or aspect. Because the diglossic gap is perhaps the most important variable factor affecting the learners' ability to move in between dialect and MSA, teachers' awareness of this can help them tailor their teaching material accordingly. To do this, teachers are introduced to evaluative techniques. Teachers are asked to evaluate the efficacy of different types of drills and exercises designed to help students bridge the diglossic gap, particularly in its widest areas.[14]

Two Operating Systems: Helping Arabic Teachers Understand
the True Relationship between the Dialects and MSA

To help teachers both buy into and have the confidence to teach Arabic using the IA, it is essential that they do not shy away from teaching their own dialect as part of the syllabus. There is often resistance from teachers from North Africa and Iraq, in particular, who are worried that integration cannot work with their dialects. The course is designed to help teachers realize for themselves that Arabic dialects are interrelated and operate using the same system, which differs from that used by MSA. I often equate it to MSA using the Apple Mac system, whereas the dialects use Microsoft, using different makes of computer. In my analogy, the dialects are the different brands of computer, all of which use Microsoft as opposed to Apple Mac.

To assist teachers in better understanding the diglossic gap, they are asked to choose from a selection of structures where the diglossic gap is wide and to compare how their dialect handles it.[15] For example, how is the concept of "to want" handled in various Arabic dialects? In MSA we have *urīdu an* "I want to" + subjunctive verb, as in *urīdu an arā* "I want to see." During the five-day Edinburgh course hosted at the British Council in 2009, teachers from Morocco, Syria, Egypt, and the Gulf all provided their own dialect's version of *urīdu an arā*. Teachers discovered how their dialects were closer to one another than they were to MSA in that none used *an* + the subjunctive. Each of these dialects presented the verb *shāf/yishūf* "to see," whereas MSA uses the formal version, *raʾā/yarā*. Teachers were encouraged to notice that Gulf and Moroccan Arabic use the verb *bgha/yibghi* to convey "wish" or "desire," whereas Egyptian Colloquial Arabic (ECA) uses a form 1 active participle, *ʿāwiz or ʿāyiz*, and Levantine uses the particle *biddi*, which conjugates.[16]

The aim is not only to give the Arabic teachers the opportunity to deconstruct their own language and reflect on the implications on their teaching but also to help them understand how much closer Arabic dialects are to one another than to MSA, and to accept that the dialects have their own grammar rules that sometimes differ from MSA. This gives teachers the confidence to use their own dialect in their teaching, regardless of which it is.[17]

The Relationship between the Integrated Approach and Both the Communicative and Task-Based Approaches

Foreign language teaching has gone through huge changes since the early 1960s in terms of finding the most effective way of helping both monolingual children as well as adults to acquire a new language. The IA, while being ideal for both communicative (Hymes 1972) and task-based (Ellis 2013) teaching, can also be used to make more traditional approaches such as the grammar-translation method more communicative.[18]

Developing Creativity

Teaching Arabic using the IA demands a mixture of reflection, self-evaluation, and, above all, creativity on the part of the teacher. Creativity is crucial because, although newer mainstream Arabic textbooks are trying to be compatible with the IA, they are insufficient to support teachers with the tools required to deliver effective teaching whereby MSA and a dialect are integrated. While these textbooks expose learners to either the Levant or Egyptian dialect or both, they do not have sufficient instructions or notes to help teachers to "integrate" both aspects in the classroom. Teachers must be equipped with the skills in exploiting the mainstream textbooks as well as to know how to "humanize" them (Rinvolucri 2002) so that students can get the full linguistic benefit in terms of reading in MSA and speaking in spoken Arabic.

Arabic teachers need to be creative in terms of inventing drills and activities that can integrate both aspects of Arabic effectively. For example, a teacher may be using an MSA textbook such as *Ahlan wa Sahlan* (Alosh 2000). However, this would need to be accompanied by a good dialect textbook such as *Kallimni Arabi*. Integrating this with *Ahlan wa Sahlan* may not be easy, even if the equivalent structures are covered in both books. The vocabulary and topics may be different. Teachers will have to provide supplementary material to both humanize and integrate the books they use into their teaching pedagogy so that integrated teaching can be delivered.

Creativity and Designing Supporting Material
Because teachers often need to use a good MSA textbook in parallel with a good dialect textbook to achieve integration, they need to be creative in terms of designing and delivering supporting material required to integrate MSA with spoken Arabic. Thus, a further important strand of the five-day course is aimed at allowing participants to try out, then categorize and evaluate a selection of easily created exercises for fully integrating MSA and spoken Arabic in the following areas: communicative reading, communicative writing, interactive listening, and interactive translation. In the following section, I demonstrate how the course helps teachers be creative in terms of using the IA with communicative reading.

Creativity and Communicative Reading in the Integrated Approach
More recently, textbooks have moved away from function-based formats, whereby a specific grammatical structure dominates the unit, to a more topic-based format, often revolving around one or more core texts that invariably are written in MSA. Texts might range from a short biography of a famous Arab personality, such as the poet Mahmoud Darwish, to a description of a famous city such as Cairo or Jerusalem. These texts will inevitably be written in MSA. Reading a text about Jerusalem in MSA reflects reality. Having a warm-up discussion or communicative game about Jerusalem in MSA does not. This is because native speakers of Arabic, even from a mixture of Arab countries, would not use MSA to discuss such a topic as was demonstrated in the icebreaker survey on the first day of the five-day training program.

In the communicative reading and speaking workshop, trainee-teachers are exposed to a variety of pre-reading, reading, and post-reading activities that encourage students to communicate in spoken Arabic about the text that they are reading in MSA.[19]

Pre-Reading Tasks
An example of a pre-reading task for intermediate students on a text about Jerusalem calls for dividing the class into three groups and asking one group to list five things they know about Jerusalem, the second group to list five things that they do not know about Jerusalem, and the third group to list five things that they would like to know about Jerusalem. This task can be in spoken Arabic. Each group then assigns someone to write the five points on the whiteboard in MSA and then to present to the whole class in spoken Arabic. Trainee-teachers are then provided with a number of texts of a similar level of difficulty and asked to choose from a range of different communicative activities they consider most suitable as a pre-reading task for that particular text. The essential factor is that it involves using dialect while speaking, whereas MSA is used for the reading and writing aspects of the activity. The aim is for the trainee-teachers to think creatively about how a text can be "brought to life." They are then asked to design a new pre-reading activity for a core text and then to try it out in their microteaching during the afternoons.

Reading Tasks
A reading task is an activity or exercise students do while reading a core text. There are different types of tasks or exercises, but the aim is to help the learner cope with the core text and also to help further integrate MSA and spoken Arabic. Course participants are invited to rank the efficacy of certain reading tasks but also invited to try out a communicative reading mirroring activity. This is done by using a text that discusses the teaching of Arabic. Here the jigsaw method (Aronson and Patnoe 2001) is used, whereby the trainee-teachers are divided into two groups: Alif and Ba. Group Alif is given the first half of the text and group Ba the second half. Working in two separate groups, they read through their section of the text together and try to understand it. They then practice summarizing it in their own words in spoken Arabic, trying to weave in some of the MSA vocabulary and concepts mentioned in the text. The group is divided into pairs, whereby one person from group Alif works with someone from group Ba. They then summarize orally to one another what they have read. Participants are not only mirroring what they are doing by reading an article on the teaching of Arabic but are discovering that, although they read the text in MSA, they almost invariably summarize the article in Educated Spoken Arabic (ESA) (Mitchell 1978).

Enabling nonnative speakers to communicate in ESA is the final goal of the IA because it involves using a mix of spoken Arabic sentence structures "peppered" with MSA phrases and vocabulary according to the context. Communicative reading tasks such as the jigsaw reading activity are an excellent way of helping students fully integrate MSA with spoken Arabic and developing their use of ESA.

Post-Reading Activities
In post-reading, the teachers are helped to see a correlation between the IA and the task-based approach. The aim is to ensure that students have internalized the text they have read in MSA and can discuss it or summarize it in spoken Arabic. This is done in a variety of ways. The teachers are first asked to compare a selection of communicative post-reading tasks. They are then asked to reflect on the type of language required to carry out the task in question. This is a "deconstructive" activity, helping them to instinctively match the correct type of language on the MSA/spoken scale. This could be a journalistic interview about the topic or an interpreting scenario. Teachers are then required to devise a new post-reading activity to assess to what extent it uses the IA. This again helps teachers to develop the creativity required to ensure that the spoken and MSA aspects of the lesson appear seamless to the students.

Designing Integrative Drills, Exercises, and Games
Another aspect of encouraging teachers to integrate MSA with spoken Arabic creatively is to show them how to design and then use their own drills, exercises, and games. Although some textbooks have drills, these are never enough to assist the learner in coping with the diglossic gap. First, trainee-teachers are asked to categorize different types of Arabic drills that help them understand how they function.[20] The second part of the session involves putting teachers in small syndicates and assigning them a specific structure in Arabic where there is an obvious diglossic gap, for example, future negation. In ECA, "I will not travel" is *mish hasāfir*, whereas in MSA it is *lan usāfira*. Teachers assigned to use this structure would learn how to creatively design a drill that can help learners bridge this gap.[21]

Games are an easy way of integrating MSA and spoken Arabic, a good example being the Cairo Airport Game. This game tries to imitate a conversation I overheard at the Cairo airport, between a customs officer and a Croatian student of MSA. The customs officer said loudly in ECA: *shanṭitik feen*? "Where is your suitcase?" The student, not understanding the ECA, replied with *ᶜafwan*? "Sorry?" The customs officer then retorted in MSA by saying in a patronizing tone *ayna haqibatuki*? (In very formal Arabic: "Where is your suitcase?!") The student understood him with some feeling of humiliation. This feeling of humiliation results from the fact that the student had studied Arabic in Croatia for several years but was unable to understand a simple question at the Cairo airport. The IA will help ensure that students of Arabic will no longer feel this sense of humiliation and defeat. The Cairo Airport Game is a good way of helping students practice code-switching between MSA and spoken Arabic. It is produced by preparing cards with questions written in English or in spoken Arabic. Students work in pairs. Student A takes a card and questions student B in spoken Arabic, like the officer at the airport. Student B pretends not to understand. Student A then repeats the question again, this time in MSA (even in a patronizing tone!) A similar "diglossic" game can be done the other way round, where the questions are written in MSA and are then read out by student A. Student B pretends not to understand, forcing student A to rephrase in a spoken Arabic dialect.

To help teachers develop creativity to create games to integrate MSA with spoken Arabic such as the Cairo Airport Game, they have to try out a number of preselected language games and rank their efficacy in terms of how well they help the learner deal with the diglossic nature of Arabic. It is this process of ranking that then helps the trainee-teachers reflect more deeply and become aware of what works and what does not work in terms of the IA.

The Integrated Approach and Empathizing with the Learner

Several needs-analysis studies have been carried out examining the main reasons that students in higher education in Western countries wish to learn Arabic (Alosh 1992; Martin 2006). Ultimately the most important reason is to be able to communicate in Arabic as fluently as possible with the hope of finding a job requiring Arabic.

Teachers need to match their teaching with the needs of most of their students, which is to communicate as closely as native speakers of Arabic do. Helping teachers to develop empathy means that teachers need to see the result of being only taught MSA and seeing and hearing the consequent frustration that occurs on arrival in an Arabic-speaking country. This is achieved very effectively during the session known as the diglossic playlet.

Working in pairs, the teachers are asked to write and act out a short "diglossic playlet" to demonstrate the absurdity of trying to speak in MSA in the wrong context. For example, they might pretend to be a customer in a restaurant trying to order a meal in MSA or a passenger in a Cairo taxi trying to negotiate the fare to the pyramids in MSA! Writing and performing these short playlets in front of the other participants in the course not only encourages creativity but also helps teachers reflect on the importance of the IA in an amusing way.

Another way of developing empathy is to see how students use their Arabic following graduation. At the University of Edinburgh, many of the master's students on the intensive program are studying Arabic for one purpose only: to get a job using Arabic. In all cases, whether it be working as an interpreter for the International Red Cross or working for a nongovernmental organization such as Mercy Fund or Human Rights Watch, it is essential that an applicant be able to read in MSA and speak in spoken Arabic. Many organizations do not trust UK university qualifications in Arabic as being sufficient, so they conduct their own tests, which often involve integration of MSA and spoken Arabic as determined by the particular job description. During the five-day training course, teachers watch short video clips of students who have completed the two-year intensive course using the IA and are able to see how students have managed to achieve their linguistic goals.

The Mini Lesson

The afternoons of the five-day course are devoted to mini lessons, also referred to as microteaching. These are designed using the principle of loop. As mentioned earlier in this chapter, "loop" activities help trainees internalize the aims of the course more effectively by embedding the main message (i.e., integration) in all the workshops. To achieve this in the mini lesson, the theme needs to be related to diglossia and its impact on the teaching of Arabic, which, according to the loop technique, further consolidates the aims of the course. Trainees prepare a one-hour lesson divided into four sections, each delivered by a different teacher. The others observe. It is here that teachers have the chance to experiment with the IA and get a feel for how natural it is for both their guinea pig students as well as themselves as teachers. Teachers are not only observed by their peers but are encouraged to self-evaluate and reflect on their own teaching. Teachers have two opportunities to microteach during the week so that issues or difficulties encountered in the first session can be rectified following further reflection and discussion.

Conclusion

I am convinced that the IA, in terms of teaching Arabic to nonnative speakers, fits with the linguistic needs of the majority of students who study Arabic both in schools and in higher education. There is still a considerable degree of resistance to this approach both in the United Kingdom and in many other countries where Arabic is taught to nonnative speakers. Additionally, I have found that the bulk of universities and private institutions in the Arab world who offer courses of Arabic for foreigners know little about the IA and are resistant to it. The task therefore is twofold:

1. Convincing UK universities with large Arabic departments (such as Oxford, Leeds, and Exeter, for example) to adopt the IA.
2. Ensuring that teachers are properly trained in teaching it.

In this chapter I have demonstrated how the Edinburgh CASAW five-day intensive teacher-training course works in terms of helping teachers of Arabic deliver effective Arabic teaching using the IA. At the time of writing, I have already trained over fifty teachers of Arabic in this approach. All of the participants are continuing to teach Arabic in various institutions around the world, including the United Kingdom. The questions that remain to be answered and require further research are as follows:

1. To what extent have the teachers implemented the IA in their teaching? How has this been received by their students and institutions?
2. If those teachers who attended the course still have not implemented the IA in their teaching, why not? Is this due to institutional resistance or a feeling that they are still insufficiently confident in delivering or convincing their colleagues to use it?

A possible solution to some of the above is to develop a further "follow up" training course to address issues that have arisen. Another option is to design and deliver a "training the trainer" course in the IA that could then be delivered in-house in institutions interested in adopting this methodology.

A final thought is that however effective the five-day training course is, in terms of helping teachers of Arabic develop the confidence to use the IA, it does not address the enormous gap that exists in terms of obtaining fully accredited qualifications in the teaching of Arabic to nonnative speakers as, for example, the CELTA and DELTA (Certificate in English Language Teaching to Adults and the Diploma in Language Teaching to Adults), which are prerequisites for anyone wishing to teach English to nonnative speakers. Currently in the United Kingdom there is no formal, externally accredited, internationally recognized teacher-training qualification in the teaching of Arabic either in schools or in higher education. The teaching of Arabic will continue to lag behind the teaching of English or other European languages such as French and Spanish so long as it is considered to be a profession not worthy of development, not only by the academic heads of departments where

Arabic is taught but also by the teachers themselves. In so many UK universities, Arabic is taught in the "lower tier," which is simply language centers employing part-time, hourly paid teachers with no teaching qualifications. These university language centers do encourage or fund career development or continuous professional development. Some students joining the intensive master's Arabic program in Edinburgh arrive having studied Arabic for up to three years in UK university language centers and their equivalents further afield. Their teachers, usually unqualified, have insisted on teaching them only MSA. They arrive in Edinburgh being able to read but unable to speak.

It is therefore essential to establish a number of accredited course opportunities in several countries to train Arabic teachers in the IA and to finally dispel their fears that students cannot handle studying MSA and a dialect simultaneously. Teachers also need to be convinced that the spoken dialects are an essential part of the Arabic language that learners should not be discouraged from learning. This also means that academic institutions not only in the United Kingdom but around the world must be made aware of the efficacy of the IA. The CASAW five-day intensive course is the first of its kind in the United Kingdom that attempts to achieve this.

References

Alosh, Mahdi M. 1992. "Designing a Proficiency-Oriented Syllabus for Modern Standard Arabic as a Foreign Language." In *The Arabic Language in America*, edited by Aleya Rouchdy, 284–304. Detroit: Wayne State University Press.

———. 2000. *Ahlan wa Sahlan.* New Haven, CT: Yale University Press.

Aronson, Elliot, and Shelley Patnoe. 2001. *Cooperation in the Classroom: The Jigsaw Method*, 3rd ed. New York: Pinter and Martin.

Auty, Nadira, Clive Holes, and Rachael Harris. 1992. *Breakthrough Arabic*. London: Palgrave-Macmillan.

Bacha, Meriem Bousaidi. 2014. "Mediating Cultures between and among Arabic Teachers." *Theory and Practice in Language Studies* 4, no. 7: 1319–26.

Bassiouney, Reem. 2009. *Arabic Sociolinguistics.* Edinburgh: Edinburgh University Press.

Brustad, Kristen, Mahmoud Al-Batal, and Abbas Al-Tonsi. 2013a. *Al-Kitaab fii Taᶜallum al-ᶜArabiyya*, Part One, 3rd ed. Washington, DC: Georgetown University Press.

———. 2013b. *Al-Kitaab fii Taᶜallum al-ᶜArabiyya*, Part Two, 3rd ed. Washington, DC: Georgetown University Press.

Ellis, Rod. 2013. *Task-Based Language Learning and Teaching*. Oxford Applied Linguistics. Oxford: Oxford University Press.

Featherstone, Jonathan. 2015. *BBC Talk Arabic*, 2nd ed. London: Pearson.

Ferguson, Charles. 1959. "Diglossia." *Word* 15: 325–40.

Fishman, Joshua A. 1967. "Bilingualism with and without Diglossia; Diglossia with and without Bilingualism." *Journal of Social Issues* 23, no. 2: 29–38.

Hymes, Dell H. 1972. "On Communicative Competence." In *Sociolinguistics: Selected Readings*, edited by J. B. Pride and J. Holmes, 269–93. Harmondsworth, UK: Penguin.

Louis, Samia. 2007. *Kallimni Arabi.* Cairo: American University Cairo Press.

Martin, William. 2006. "Marketing Arabic as a Second/Foreign Language Program." In *Handbook for Arabic Language Teaching Professionals in the 21st Century*, edited by Kassem Wahba, Zeinab Taha, and Liz England, 401–9. London: Routledge.

Mitchell, Terry F. 1978. "Educated Spoken Arabic in Egypt and the Levant, with Special Reference to Participle and Tense." *Journal of Linguistics* 14, no. 2: 227–58.

Rinvolucri, Mario. 2002. *Humanising Your Coursebook.* London: Delta Publishing.

Said, Edward. 1978. *Orientalism.* London: Penguin Books.

Wahba, Kassem. 1996. "Linguistic Variation in Alexandrian Arabic: The Feature of Emphasis." In *Understanding Arabic. Essays on Contemporary Arab Linguistics in Honour of Said Badawi*, edited by Alaa Elgibali, 120. Cairo: American University in Cairo Press.

Wightwick, Jane, and Mahmoud Gaafar. 2014. *Mastering Arabic 1*, 3rd ed. London: Palgrave-Macmillan.

Woodward, Tessa. 2003. "Loop Input." *ELT Journal* 57, no. 3: 301–4.

Younes, Munther. 1990. "An Integrated Approach to Teaching Arabic as a Foreign Language." *Al-ᶜArabiyya* 23, no. 1/2: 105–22.

Younes, Munther, and Hanada al-Masri. 2014. *ᶜArabiyyat al-Naas*, Part 2. London: Routledge.

Younes, Munther, and Yomna Chami. 2014. *ᶜArabiyyat al-Naas*, Part 3. London: Routledge.

Younes, Munther, Makda Weatherspoon, and Maha Foster. 2013. *ᶜArabiyyat al-Naas*, Part 1. London: Routledge.

Notes

Additional data and examples are freely available to view and download on this book's product page on the Georgetown University Press (GUP) website (www.press.georgetown.edu).

1. Examples of specific workshops covered during the course are accessible on the GUP website.

2. In this article Younes describes the situation of Arabic teaching in higher education in the United States in terms of its inability to prepare students for the linguistic complexity of the Arabic language due to diglossia. At Cornell University, Younes went on to pioneer the IA, whereby both Modern Standard Arabic (MSA) and a spoken dialect (in this case, Levantine) are taught side by side. Younes originally wrote two textbooks on his approach: *Elementary Arabic* and *Intermediate*

Arabic (1995, 1999) and, much more recently, *ᶜArabiyyat al-Naas*, parts 1, 2, and 3 (Younes, Weatherspoon, and Foster 2013; Younes and al-Masri 2014; Younes and Chami 2014). In addition to these textbooks, he has more recently (2015) written a book on the IA, which tries to not only explain more fully but also to assess to what extent this method has succeeded and has begun to be used in other institutions in the United States and elsewhere.

3. See table 4.1 on the GUP website.

4. See the University of Cambridge Language Centre website, http://www .langcen.cam.ac.uk/lc/culp/arabic/culp-arabic.html.

5. On a recent visit to a private language school in Jordan, which many UK universities use for their students' year abroad, I asked why they did not teach dialect. They said that dialect is "chaotic and devoid of any grammar."

6. A senior lecturer at a well-known university in London responded to a student, who was angry at having been laughed at in Beirut while trying to order a meal in MSA, by replying in English in an irritated tone: "We are not here to teach you how to buy chewing gum. This is a university, not Berlitz."

7. In fact, the former head of Arabic at a university in the North of England, a nonnative speaker himself, was often heard repeating the Arabic phrase: "We are here to speak the language of the educated, not the language of peasants."

8. At a recent conference held in London to discuss the future of the teaching of Arabic in UK universities, I suggested that many UK institutions should change the title of their Arabic degrees to "Arabic for Reading." This statement was met with anger from the head of Arabic at one of the UK's most prestigious universities, who dismissed the need to teach any dialect at a university, justifying his point by stating, "I only learned MSA as a student and I managed to 'pick up' Gulf Arabic after living and working in Kuwait." This demonstrates not only a total lack of empathy with the nonnative learner of Arabic but also a lack of understanding of the diglossic nature of Arabic by assuming that students of Arabic can quickly extrapolate the spoken Arabic equivalent of an MSA structure. How, for example, can an intermediate learner of Arabic who had been taught *la astaṭī' an arāka ghadan*, which is the MSA way of saying: "I cannot see you tomorrow," be expected, without help, to "pick up" the Egyptian Arabic equivalent of the same phrase which is *maᵓdarsh ashūfak bukra*? This lack of empathy pervades the profession not only among certain non-Arab teachers of Arabic but also Arab teachers of Arabic as well.

9. As a result of this orientalist attitude, many of the less prestigious UK institutions employ unqualified teachers who rely on their own experience of being taught Arabic as children. As long as the teaching of Arabic remains a subordinate profession, it will be prone to charlatanism and unprofessionalism in terms of teaching pedagogy.

10. See activity 4.1 on the GUP website.

11. An example of a mutual dictation is provided in activity 4.5 on the GUP website.

12. Code-switching is where someone moves into and out of two languages or registers of the same languages or into and out of two dialects. This is well illustrated in terms of Arabic by the renowned sociolinguist Joshua Fishman (1967).

13. The ice-breaking activity used here is a survey. See activity 4.1 on the GUP website.

14. Students do not have limitless time to learn Arabic; course designers must focus on the areas where the diglossic gap is wide and must spend less time focusing on aspects where the gap is very narrow indeed, such as noun and adjective agreement. See activity 4.2 on the GUP website.

15. See activity 4.2 examples on the GUP website.

16. The verb *bgha/yibghi* is used in the past tense in Morocco and in the present tense in the Gulf, but both convey a present tense meaning.

17. Many teachers of Arabic whom I have met, in particular from North Africa, justify their insistence on using MSA in their teaching by claiming that their students will not understand their dialect. By understanding better how all the dialects, including Maghrebi, function, they are able to overcome the fear of using it in class, which is essential when delivering the IA.

18. The communicative approach was developed in the 1980s and 1990s in both Western Europe and the United States and is well described on Scott Thornbury's blog (https://scottthornbury.wordpress.com) as having language components that reflect real-life oral exchanges, and it is from this that the concept of "communicative competence" came into being. If only MSA is taught, students will not be able to carry out the majority of oral exchanges required by this approach. The task-based approach involves setting students a task, normally in small groups or syndicates. The teacher will normally set a pretask activity whereby the necessary vocabulary and structures are provided to help learners complete the task. The task normally has a clear outcome and can result in the students presenting information in different ways. This approach does have some flexibility in terms of both the use of MSA and spoken dialect, depending on the task required of the student.

19. See activity 4.3 on the GUP website.

20. See activity 4.5 on the GUP website for examples.

21. See activity 4.2 on the GUP website.

5

Preparing Students for the Future

Integrating Dialect and Standard into the Arabic Foreign Language Classroom

ELIZABETH HUNTLEY

Michigan State University

THE STUDY OF ARABIC as a foreign language (AFL) in the United States is increasingly popular in the post-9/11 world. Between 1998 and 2013, Arabic enrollment increased over 600 percent (Welles 2004; Goldberg, Looney, and Lusin 2015).[1] Arabic is no longer studied solely for academic and religious reasons; it is increasingly seen as a lucrative skill set for future employment opportunities.[2] Consequently, students are seeking to learn the language at ever-higher levels of linguistic and cultural fluency. Arabic programs have traditionally focused on teaching Modern Standard Arabic (MSA) to facilitate academic pursuits. MSA, as the language of reading, writing, and formal interactions, is a necessary tool for traditional scholarship. With rising demand from an increasingly diverse student body, however, AFL instructors have been forced to reconsider the broader needs and goals of the booming Arabic second-language (L2) student population. This new generation of students wants to spend time abroad in order to gain the linguistic and cultural knowledge needed to pursue career options that require proficiency in spoken as well as written Arabic. Such demands necessitate the teaching of Spoken Colloquial Arabic (SCA), the language of daily interactions and informal subjects, alongside MSA.

The most recent guidelines released by the American Council on the Teaching of Foreign Languages (ACTFL) has begun to embrace this multiglossic reality.[3] In describing the attributes of a Superior-level Arabic L2 student, the guidelines state that the "mixing of both MSA and the standard dialect of the speaker is a predominant feature in Arabic speech today, and a Superior Level listener should be able to comprehend speech that displays such a mix." Even at the novice level, students are expected to engage in basic exchanges such as memorized greetings and pleasantries that would normally be carried out in SCA.

Although there is general agreement in the AFL field that both MSA and SCA must be taught, there is still widespread disagreement about when and how to introduce these two registers in the classroom.[4] One group argues they should be learned separately. They believe that students should be given a solid, multiyear foundation in MSA before they are exposed to SCA in the classroom. Another group argues that SCA can only be learned in-country and should not be taught in the foreign language classroom at all. In both cases, MSA is still the first register to which Arabic L2 students are exposed. This decision to frontload the teaching of formal, academic language and delay the teaching of everyday, communicative discourse strategies goes against general principles of foreign language pedagogy. Karin Ryding refers to this phenomenon as "reverse privileging," asserting that it is one of the main impediments that prevents the Arabic field from graduating larger numbers of students at the Superior and Distinguished proficiency levels (Ryding 2009; Younes 2015).

The most recent solution to the SCA versus MSA problem is the integrated approach (IA), wherein both the informal and formal registers are taught side by side from day one.[5] This is the approach adopted by the University of Michigan, where the third edition of *Al-Kitaab fii Ta'allum al-'Arabiyya* is taught (Brustad, Al-Batal, and Al-Tonsi 2010, 2011, 2014).[6] Mahmoud Al-Batal, one of the authors of *Al-Kitaab*, notes that this approach "does not treat these varieties of Arabic as discrete and separate entities, but as components of one integrated linguistic system" (Al-Batal 1992, 298). Those who believe in teaching only MSA for beginner students argue that the IA is detrimental to overall student learning and attitudes. It is thought that teaching MSA and SCA side by side will lead to student confusion and frustration with ultimately little linguistic gain.

This chapter evaluates the conflicting curricular claims alongside actual Arabic L2 student experiences both domestically and abroad. It analyzes how beginning-level students have engaged with the IA at the University of Michigan and compares their reactions to those reported by students studying abroad in the Arab world. In doing so, it examines students' goals in light of their successes and frustrations with pursuing Arabic competency. It argues that the IA can support students academically and psychologically at all stages of learning. Finally, it offers suggestions not only for implementation of the IA but also for general steps to move the AFL profession forward.

Methodology

This chapter uses data on Arabic L2 experiences both in study-abroad programs and in foreign language classrooms. Domestic and abroad experiences are anecdotally woven in throughout the chapter as supporting evidence as well as analyzed separately at the end.

For foreign language classroom data, this chapter draws on the National Middle East Language Resource Center's (NMELRC) 2005 survey of 641 Arabic L2 students in the United States (Palmer 2007) and Ghassan Husseinali's 2006 survey of 120 second-year Arabic L2 students. It also analyzes in depth the midterm survey responses of 68 students in the third semester of Arabic study at the University of Michigan (Midterm Survey 2013).

For study abroad, this chapter relies on five separate studies: Jeremy Palmer's 2009 cross-sectional study of 94 students across the Arab world, Hilal al-Mamari's 2011 longitudinal study of 23 students in Oman, Eva Hashem-Aramouni's 2011 cross-sectional study of 10 students in various locations, Emma Trentman's 2012 longitudinal study of 54 students in Egypt, and Sonia Shiri's 2013 cross-sectional study of 371 short-term study-abroad students across the Arab world.

Arguments against and for the Integrated Approach

There are many arguments against adopting the IA, including placing an unnecessary learning burden on the student; choosing the dialect; and meeting student needs. These are critically examined alongside reported student and instructor experience.

Unnecessary Learning Burden

The first argument against integrating MSA and SCA into one curriculum is that it places an unnecessary learning burden on the student. Many argue that students will feel they are forced to learn two languages at the same time (Al-Batal 1992, 287). Several students at the University of Michigan and in Hashem-Aramouni's study echoed this sentiment, reporting that it was often difficult to keep the two registers mentally "separated" (2011, 94). The same sentiment, albeit not necessarily negative, was found among a cohort of study-abroad students in Oman who were learning both MSA and Omani SCA side by side. Students reported that it did indeed feel like they were learning two different concepts but that this did not slow down their learning process (al-Mamari 2011). However, one University of Michigan student who had previous experience studying the language pointed out that integrating MSA and SCA together from the beginning made the overall learning process easier. This student reported that among the benefits of the IA was "not having to learn *fusha* [i.e., MSA] then immediately unlearn it in order to 'get' *masri* [i.e., Egyptian SCA]. When I took Egyptian [SCA] with Dr. [name removed], it seemed like the further along a student was in formal Arabic the more trouble they had learning colloquial. I think learning both at once is a much better strategy" (Hashem-Aramouni 2011). Thus, this student thought that learning both MSA and SCA side by side was less confusing than starting with MSA and eventually adding SCA to the Arabic L2 curriculum.

Such comments correspond with Paul Nation's suggestions for teaching vocabulary. Nation explains that "teachers can help reduce the learning burden of words by drawing attention to systematic patterns and analogies within the second language" (Nation 2001, 23). In the Arabic L2 context, this would mean that MSA and SCA should be introduced together as part of a holistic language system. Students acquire both registers side by side while learning which grammatical patterns apply to each.[7] This approach ultimately helps students to mentally comprehend them as part of a complete and mutually reinforcing language system. If students are eventually expected to learn both MSA and SCA in order to attain high levels of proficiency and for their future career goals, they would greatly benefit in seeing how both are connected from the very beginning of their studies.

Choice of Dialect

A second argument against the IA is that choosing which dialect to teach is difficult. It is natural to assume that AFL teachers would be most comfortable teaching their own spoken dialect, and yet that dialect might not have well-developed materials or match students' learning goals. Likewise, the dialects offered by an institution might not support students' academic interests and professional goals. These issues often cause teachers and program directors to simply avoid SCA instruction altogether. Yet an investigation of student and teacher attitudes and abilities reveals that a curriculum-driven dialect choice is not a deal-breaker for many. According to the NMELRC survey, 86 percent of students are interested in learning either Levantine or Egyptian SCA. These are popular dialects for which many well-developed materials are already available (Al-Batal and Belnap 2006, 396). Shiri (2013) found that students' preferences for study-abroad location and dialect focus changed after students had actually visited the Arab world. Time spent in-country led to an 18 percent increase in self-reported strong interest in that location as compared to predeparture interest levels. Among teachers of Arabic who are native speakers, Abdalla and Al-Batal found that almost 60 percent of teachers would feel comfortable teaching first- and second-year classes in a dialect other than their own if necessary (2011, 16–17).

Thus, it seems that students and teachers of Arabic are more ideologically flexible in their language preferences than what is widely purported. Likewise, it appears that students are more neurologically flexible than what had been presumed. For instance, Trentman's investigation of dialect and MSA transferability among Arabic L2 learners does not support widely held fears of forced dialect fossilization. She found that familiar dialect listening ability (i.e., for students who had some background in SCA) was a stronger predictor of foreign dialect comprehension than MSA-only listening ability (i.e., for students who had only studied MSA). For spoken texts in which native Arabic speakers were accommodating their dialects to MSA (mimicking educated spoken Arabic as a lingua franca), Trentman found that both familiar dialect listening ability and MSA listening ability were significant predictors for understanding accommodated speech, although MSA was slightly more so (Trentman 2011).

Student Needs

Many argue that dialects are not necessary because some Arabic L2 learners might not need them, particularly if their area of scholarship relies on formal written texts. Do students want to learn the dialects, and if so, what for? A primary interest seems to be in travel and communication. In the NMELRC student survey, the statement "studying Arabic is important because it will allow me to interact with people who speak it" elicited a more positive response (87.4 percent) than any other item on the survey (Belnap 2008, 55). In fact, 76.8 percent of respondents indicated that they either agree or strongly agree with the statement "I am learning Arabic in order to travel to the Arab world" (Palmer 2007, 116).

Arabic language proficiency is viewed not just as essential for travel but also as important for a potential career. Students of Arabic are increasingly seeing their language learning as a desirable job skill for employment in the post-9/11 world (Husseinali 2006, 402). The NMELRC survey reported 73.2 percent agreement with the statement, "I am determined to achieve a level of proficiency in Arabic that would allow me to function in it comfortably in my professional activities" (Belnap 2008, 57). Another survey found that study-abroad students in the Middle East, as compared to those studying in more common destinations, overwhelmingly see their study-abroad time as important for improving language skills (82 percent versus 43 percent), and for the advancement of their career goals (62 percent versus 47 percent), rather than for "having fun" (36 percent versus 72 percent). The International Institute of Education notes that students increasingly seek out language skills and regional experience for future employment, particularly in the fields of national security, foreign policy, and business (Institute of International Education 2009).

Student Experience in the Integrated Approach Classroom: Analysis of University of Michigan Arabic L2 Survey

So far, this chapter has illustrated that the majority of Arabic L2 students wish to study abroad and improve their language skills. Increasingly, these students plan to use Arabic in their future careers in fields that demand advanced linguistic and cultural proficiency across the spectrum of Arabic multiglossia. The research presented here suggests that students need exposure to both SCA and MSA as a complete and complementary system of communication, ideally before going abroad, if not earlier, in order to successfully achieve these levels of proficiency.

Despite these conclusions, most Arabic foreign language programs continue to privilege MSA at the expense of SCA. Many program administrators argue that students will not like the IA, will be overwhelmed by the workload, or will simply be confused. Despite these curricular claims made on behalf of students, no study has examined students' experiences with the IA. The University of Michigan's Arabic program aimed to shed light on this process by surveying its students. The goal of the survey was to give students an opportunity to speak for themselves about their own experiences learning Arabic through the IA. The survey was conducted three semesters after the University of Michigan had switched from an MSA-based curriculum with optional SCA classes later on to the IA with the third edition of the *Al-Kitaab fii Ta*ᶜ*allum al-*ᶜ*Arabiyya* series (Brustad, Al-Batal, and Al-Tonsi 2010, 2011, 2014).

The survey was administered to all ninety students registered for the third semester of Arabic study. Sixty-seven students responded, giving a response rate of 74.4 percent. While most of these students had only been exposed to the IA, some students had prior exposure to MSA-privileging curricula at other institutions or previously at the University of Michigan. Additionally, 28.4 percent of the respondents surveyed self-identified as heritage speakers (i.e., they had exposure to the language before starting formal study in the classroom), due to the large Arab population in southeast Michigan. Thus, the survey's results should be of broad interest to teachers and program administrators in a variety of educational settings.[8]

Do Students Like the Integrated Approach?

The first question asked students to rate their level of agreement with the statement, "I like learning a dialect and the formal Arabic in the same classroom." For this statement, less than one-quarter of students responded "strongly disagree" or "disagree," approximately one-quarter responded "neutral," and over half (52.3 percent) responded either "agree" or "strongly agree." Within the heritage student subpopulation, seven out of nineteen students (36.8 percent) said that they either strongly disagreed or disagreed with the statement (as opposed to eight out of forty-nine, or 16.3 percent of nonheritage students). Thus, the heritage student population disproportionately disliked the curriculum compared to the total population of first-year students. This may be because Michigan's program policy requires that heritage students register for a dialect other than their spoken dialect so that they will have a similar curricular load to the nonheritage students. Many heritage students anecdotally reported frustration with this policy.

For this same question, students also provided open-ended responses to clarify their Likert scale choice. These responses were analyzed thematically. Overall, two (0.03 percent) students expressed a sense of frustration, echoing the above-mentioned sentiment that they were learning two languages and were thus expected to memorize twice as much. Likewise, twelve (17.9 percent) students said they often felt confused about which register to use and when or otherwise lacked the ability to mentally differentiate between the two on the spot. Whether this confusion is a natural part of the language-learning process or an unnecessary burden created by the IA has yet to be empirically evaluated, but arguments in support of both sides are often made. In spite of these frustrations, twenty-three (34.3 percent) students seemed to grasp that the multiglossic nature of the Arabic language necessitated this learning process. One student wrote, "I believe this strategy gives the best overall ability to understand Arabic as it is used in the actual world." Another student succinctly captured the value of the IA in light of the nature of the Arabic language, explaining, "I mean, it's a question of both 'do i like it' and 'is it necessary.' I definitely think it is necessary."

What Difficulties Do Students Encounter
with the Integrated Approach?

The second question asked students to elaborate on the difficulties they have encountered in learning Arabic with the IA. Many students expressed that they had a hard time learning both registers together. Thirteen (19.4 percent) students wrote that the curriculum created an increased workload. Two (0.03 percent) students mentioned that they tend to only remember the words that are written a lot. Thus, their MSA retention is reportedly much stronger than their SCA retention. Sixteen (23.9 percent) students repeated the above-mentioned sentiments that they had difficulty keeping MSA and SCA separated in their minds, and ten (14.9 percent) students reported that they spoke in a mixture of both rather than keeping them separate.

What Are the Advantages of the Integrated Approach?

Students were also asked to share what the perceived advantages of the IA are. Forty-two (62.7 percent) students reported that the new curriculum reflected the reality of the Arabic language or that it helped them to communicate orally in a more realistic manner (i.e., knowing which register would be appropriate to use in different situations). Twelve (17.9 percent) students wrote about the added value that SCA would give them for future travel and study-abroad opportunities, demonstrating an awareness between their academic goals and the nature of the Arabic language as it is lived in the Arab world. One student wrote, "You need both [formal and colloquial registers]. This is real life. It seems like it would be a total waste of time to do anything else, although I could see how people might think it easier to work only in *fusha* [MSA]." This demonstrates an overall awareness for what pedagogical methods must be adopted in order to fully prepare students for advanced levels of Arabic study and interaction.

What Strategies Do Students Rely on to Help
Navigate the Integrated Approach?

The responses to the statement, "What strategies do you use to help you deal with the particular challenges of a mixed register curriculum?" were eye-opening regarding program implementation. Nine (13.4 percent) students reported that they had not yet figured out a good strategy for studying both registers side by side, and three (4.5 percent) more added that they would like to gain new learning strategies for the integrated curriculum beyond what they had already been doing. Regarding their actual strategies, students listed creating flashcards, extra studying, and devoting additional attention to what register they wished to use before speaking or writing, all of which are standard best practices for language learning. It is unclear whether the students who reported a lack of language strategies consider the above-mentioned techniques to be strategies. Potentially, students might be using those very same techniques but not considering them to be a "strategy" per se. Nonetheless, given students' general acknowledgment that learning MSA and SCA together is challenging, it is incumbent upon Arabic L2 teachers to explicitly instruct students in language-learning strategies alongside the language itself. This may not only boost student morale but also empower them to see that such difficulties are natural parts of the second-language acquisition process.

Overall Students' Attitudes on Curriculum Choice

Lastly, students were asked to describe their attitudes toward the mixed register curriculum. Response options are shown in figure 5.1. Students who chose "other" mainly expressed their support for the curriculum as long as they could study a different dialect of their choice. Thus, despite expressing some difficulties with the IA, it seems that University of Michigan students overall understand the rationale for and support the learning of MSA and SCA side by side. The survey in general illustrates that students are aware of the difficulties and benefits of the IA. While there is clearly room for improvement in terms of equipping students with the necessary learning strategies, overall the IA seems to successfully meet students' needs and support their learning goals.

Student Experience Abroad: Unforeseen Problems with MSA-Only Methodology

Of course, learning does not stop once students leave the classroom. As illustrated above, most Arabic students intend to study abroad and improve their language and cultural skills. Many instructors who privilege MSA in the foreign language classroom argue that students will be able to easily pick up SCA and integrate it once they get to the Arab world. Despite these claims, few have actually asked students about their experiences related to language usage and access to social experiences during study abroad. An analysis of five separate studies of student opinions regarding their linguistic and cultural skillsets before, during, and after study abroad reveals three general themes: diminished self-evaluation of acquired language skills, feeling embarrassed and isolated, and missed opportunities for cross-cultural learning.

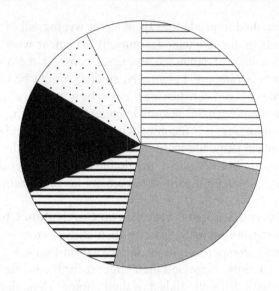

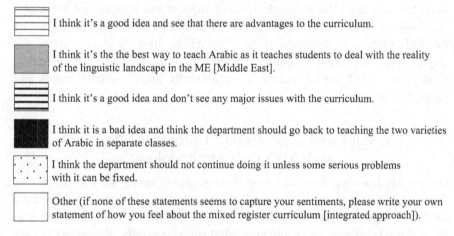

I think it's a good idea and see that there are advantages to the curriculum.

I think it's the the the best way to teach Arabic as it teaches students to deal with the reality of the linguistic landscape in the ME [Middle East].

I think it's a good idea and don't see any major issues with the curriculum.

I think it is a bad idea and think the department should go back to teaching the two varieties of Arabic in separate classes.

I think the department should not continue doing it unless some serious problems with it can be fixed.

Other (if none of these statements seems to capture your sentiments, please write your own statement of how you feel about the mixed register curriculum [integrated approach]).

Figure 5.1 Students' attitudes toward the mixed register curriculum

Diminished Self-Evaluation of Acquired Language Skills

Many of the students who had only learned MSA prior to studying abroad felt unprepared to deal with the multiglossic reality of Arabic. One student, expressing his initial experience with Egyptian SCA, explained that he felt like he "hadn't taken any Arabic at all" (Trentman 2012, 171–72). This sudden downgrade in self-perceived language abilities was often demotivating once students learned that their hard-earned MSA skills would not be required on a daily basis (al-Mamari 2011, 37). However, students who had prior experience with dialects reported feeling more comfortable operating within the multiple registers used in the Arab world (al-Mamari 2011, 34; Hashem-Aramouni 2011, 85). Many of the students who went abroad without any dialect study reported that they were able to eventually adjust, although they felt that they had lost several weeks in the process (Trentman 2012, 172; Hashem-Aramouni 2011, 79).

Feeling Embarrassed and Isolated

In addition to the sense of frustration, students also reported feeling embarrassed due to their lack of SCA skills (al-Mamari 2011, 45; Hashem-Aramouni 2011, 82–83). Many reported feeling left out of important cultural interactions because they could not operate within the colloquial framework. Palmer explains that "it is also not uncommon for native Arabs to snicker at foreigners who only speak the formal language, thus potentially causing a sense of humiliation" (Palmer 2007, 112). This frustration may discourage students from practicing their language skills in the study-abroad setting and may negatively affect their ability to integrate into the host culture or feel they have a sense of place there. In fact, many students reported that their lack of SCA ability caused people to speak to them in English while studying abroad, further limiting their chances to practice their Arabic and restricting their exposure to Arab culture across the social and educational spectrum (Trentman 2012, 174; al-Mamari 2011, 1).

Conversely, students who communicated with SCA reported feeling more welcomed to participate in local culture. This is likely because SCA is used for daily activities and informal interactions. One learner reported that using SCA seemed to put interlocutors at ease and dissolve suspicions. He shared his belief that "people trust you more as a foreigner speaking in a local dialect because it shows an immediate and specific interest in that local culture" (Hashem-Aramouni 2011, 79–80). Another learner, however, believed that the key to establishing interpersonal relationships was not by speaking in SCA but by demonstrating cultural awareness (Hashem-Aramouni 2011, 80). It is unclear what the student meant by "cultural awareness" in this context, but it seems to be an act which exists outside of the social grammar of language register choice.

Missed Opportunities for Cross-Cultural Learning

In the post-9/11 job market, employers are looking not simply for machine-grade translators but for Arabic speakers equipped with the necessary cross-cultural knowledge to navigate any range of professional situations. Many students travel to the Arab world hoping to improve both their language proficiency and their cultural awareness as marketable skillsets after graduation. Unfortunately, study-abroad students with MSA-only backgrounds may lose not only opportunities to improve their language skills but also opportunities to broaden their understanding of cultural norms in the Arab world through social interactions (Trentman 2012, 174–78; al-Mamari 2011, 39–42; Hashem-Aramouni 2011, 78–79).

This connected loss has not only been reported anecdotally but has also been supported through empirical research. Palmer found a direct correlation between language study background, language usage while abroad, and rates of acculturation among study-abroad students. Study-abroad students who had prior SCA experience reported significantly higher initial levels of acculturation than students who had only studied MSA (Palmer 2009, 103). For overall acculturation levels, a striking correlation between modes of communication and acculturation gain was also found. Although all students reported acculturation gains, those who communicated the *least* in MSA showed the *highest* increase in level of acculturation (Palmer 2009, 214). Furthermore, no parallel significant correlation was found between communicating in MSA and increased interactions (Palmer 2009, 215). In fact, most students reported that they did not need to use MSA beyond the classroom setting during their time studying abroad.

Thus, these multiple studies demonstrate that equipping students to operate comfortably in SCA bolsters their sense of confidence when studying abroad. Furthermore, it helps them to experience more positive and frequent interactions with native speakers across a broader range of social and educational backgrounds. Such interactions are key to developing the necessary cultural knowledge and awareness students will use in their desired professional paths. If foreign language teachers are truly dedicated to supporting this generation of learners' academic and intellectual goals, they must start preparing students appropriately in the classroom.

Conclusion

Although the IA is a relatively new phenomenon in the AFL classroom, this methodology is clearly satisfying a growing demand for overall language proficiency. It has been demonstrated that SCA and MSA can be taught side by side and effectively synthesized into students' mental representations of the language as a whole. Doing so will not only give them early exposure at the novice levels of measured language proficiency but will also pave the way for students to access new dialects alongside their first Arabic dialect of study. The research reviewed here has shown that a workable knowledge of SCA alongside MSA broadens students' opportunities to interact within the larger Arab world. Given that the overwhelming majority of Arabic L2 learners plan to study abroad, the IA best prepares students to practice their language and expand their cross-cultural expertise. These are mutually reinforcing skillsets that not only improve students' employment opportunities but also give them a healthier and happier sense of themselves as they relate to Arabic and the Arab world. If teachers of Arabic wish for their students to succeed in their academic and professional goals, they must give them adequate tools to do so.

Further Directions

While the research reviewed in this chapter suggests great promise for the IA, many issues remain to be addressed. First, AFL teachers need to provide better support for their students in the integrated foreign language classroom. As noted in the University of Michigan survey, many students felt that they lacked the skills necessary to successfully navigate the IA. Instructors and program administrators alike must identify L2 strategies and incorporate methods to teach them alongside the language. This is an area in which teachers who also learned Arabic as a foreign language can make a significant contribution by sharing lessons from their own learning.

Furthermore, the AFL profession needs to seriously reflect on how proficiency levels should be defined and measured. This, in large part, means defining what types of students the profession wants to graduate and on what timeline. At the end of four years of undergraduate study, do AFL teachers want students whose communication patterns match those of educated native Arabic speakers in their daily lives? Do they want students who can easily read historical and religious texts with academic competency? To answer those questions, AFL professionals must continue to ask students about their own needs, preferences, and goals, rather than making assumptions on their behalf.

Finally, the AFL profession needs to reevaluate how it measures Arabic L2 proficiency. While the ACTFL guidelines have begun to incorporate the social grammar of register, generally accepted oral proficiency exams like the Oral Proficiency Interview continue to privilege MSA. Thus, it rewards students who produce socially inappropriate language choices by calling it "proficiency." This is a false proficiency that only exists in foreign language classrooms, and propagating it may harm students once they go abroad. It constricts their chances to practice the language and feel positive about their efforts as L2 learners. It hinders their ability to establish meaningful relationships and gain cross-cultural knowledge as they navigate new social geographies. It stunts the development of desired skills for future employment opportunities.

The AFL field should not squander this unprecedented period of growth in student interest and program expansion. AFL professionals need to seriously consider the issues discussed here as they make curricular decisions and as they continue to advance the field forward.

References

Abboud, Peter F. 1971. "State of the Art IX: Arabic Language Instruction." *Middle East Studies Association Bulletin* 5, no. 2: 1–23.

Abdalla, Mahmoud, and Mahmoud Al-Batal. 2011–12. "College-Level Teachers of Arabic and Attitudes." *Al-ᶜArabiyya* 44/45:1–28.

Al-Batal, Mahmoud. 1992. "Diglossia Proficiency: The Need for an Alternative Approach to Teaching." In *The Arabic Language in America*, edited by Aleya Rouchdy, 284–304. Detroit: Wayne State University Press.

Al-Batal, Mahmoud, and Kirk R. Belnap. 2006. "The Teaching and Learning of Arabic in the United States: Realities, Needs, and Future Directions." In *Handbook for Arabic Language Teaching Professionals in the 21st Century*, edited by Kassem M. Wahba, Zeinab A. Taha, and Liz England, 389–99. Mahwah, NJ: Lawrence Erlbaum.

al-Mamari, Hilal. 2011. "Arabic Diglossia and Arabic as a Foreign Language: The Perception of Students in World Learning Oman Center." Capstone Project Paper 2437. School for International Training Graduate Institute.

Badawi, El-Said. 1973. *Mustawayāt al-ᶜArabiyya al-muᶜāṣira fī miṣr* (Levels of contemporary Arabic in Egypt). Cairo: Dār al-maᶜārif.

Belnap, Kirk R. 2008. "If You Build It, They Will Come." In *Linguistics in an Age of Globalization: Perspectives on Arabic Language and Teaching*, edited by Zeinab Ibrahim and Sanaa Makhlouf, 53–65. Cairo: American University in Cairo Press.

Brustad, Kristen, Mahmoud Al-Batal, and Abbas Al-Tonsi. 2010. *Alif Baa: Introduction to Arabic Letters and Sounds*, 3rd ed. Washington, DC: Georgetown University Press.

———. 2011. *Al-Kitaab fii Taᶜallum al-ᶜArabiyya*, Part One, 3rd ed. Washington, DC: Georgetown University Press.

———. 2014. *Al-Kitaab fii Taᶜallum al-ᶜArabiyya*, Part Two, 3rd ed. Washington, DC: Georgetown University Press.

Central Intelligence Agency. 2015. "Career Opportunities: Open Source Officer." https://www.cia.gov/careers/opportunities/analytical/open-source-officer -foreign-media-analyst.html.

Ferguson, Charles. 1996. "Epilogue: Diglossia Revisited." In *Understanding Arabic: Essays in Contemporary Arabic Linguistics in Honor of El-Said Badawi*, edited by Ala Elgibali, 49–68. Cairo: American University in Cairo Press.

Goldberg, David, Dennis Looney, and Natalia Lusin. 2015. "Enrollments in Languages Other Than English in United States Institutions of Higher Education, Fall 2013." New York: Modern Language Association of America.

Hashem-Aramouni, Eva. 2011. "The Impact of Diglossia on Arabic Language Instruction in Higher Education: Attitudes and Experiences of Students and Instructors in the US." PhD dissertation, California State University of Sacramento.

Husseinali, Ghassan. 2006. "Who Is Studying Arabic and Why? A Survey of Arabic Students' Orientations at a Major University." *Foreign Language Annals* 39: 395–412.

Institute of International Education. 2009. "Expanding US Study Abroad in the Arab World: Challenges and Opportunities." IIE Study Abroad White Paper Series. http://www.iie.org/en/Research-and-Publications/Publications-and-Reports/IIE-Bookstore/Expanding-US-Study-Abroad-in-the-Arab-World#.V_w8Y7W1xXA.

Midterm Survey for Arabic 201 Students. 2013. Unpublished survey. Ann Arbor: University of Michigan.

Nation, Paul. 2001. *Learning Vocabulary in Another Language*. Cambridge: Cambridge University Press.

National Association of Colleges and Employers. 2015. "Overall Average Starting Salary Climbs 5.2 Percent for Class of 2015 Grads." *Targeted News Service*.

Palmer, Jeremy. 2007. "Arabic Diglossia: Teaching Only the Standard Variety Is a Disservice to Students." *Arizona Working Papers in SLA & Teaching* 14: 111–22.

———. 2009. "Student Acculturation, Language Preference, and L2 Competence in Study Abroad Programs in the Arabic-Speaking World." PhD dissertation, University of Arizona.

Ryding, Karen. 2009. "Educated Spoken Arabic: A Flexible Spoken Standard." *NECTL Review* 64: 49–52.

Shiri, Sonia. 2013. *Teaching and Learning Arabic as a Foreign Language: A Guide for Teachers*. Washington, DC: Georgetown University Press.

Trentman, Emma. 2011. "L2 Arabic Dialect Comprehension: Empirical Evidence for the Transfer of Familiar Dialect Knowledge to Unfamiliar Dialects." *L2 Journal* 3: 22–49.

———. 2012. "Study Abroad in Egypt: Identity, Access, and Arabic Language Learning." PhD dissertation, Michigan State University.

Welles, Elizabeth B. 2004. "Foreign Language Enrollments in the United States Institutions of Higher Education, Fall 2002." *ADFL Bulletin* 35: 7–26.

Younes, Munther. 1990. "An Integrated Approach to Teaching Arabic as a Foreign Language." *Al-ᶜArabiyya* 23, no. 1/2: 105–22.

———. 2015. *The Integrated Approach to Arabic Instruction*. London: Routledge.

Younes, Munther, Makda Weatherspoon, and Maha Foster. 2013. ᶜ*Arabiyyat al-Naa*s, part I. London: Routledge.

Notes

Additional data and examples are freely available to view and download on this book's product page on the Georgetown University Press (GUP) website (www.press .georgetown.edu).

1. The total enrollment for students of some variety of Arabic (including MSA, SCA, classical, and Qur'ānic) appears to have peaked at 34,908 students in 2009, then decreased to 33,520 students in 2013. Interestingly, according to the Modern Language Association, Arabic is *not* considered a less commonly taught language (LCTL) because it ranks among the top fifteen foreign languages taught in the United States and has done so since at least 1998 (Welles 2004; Goldberg, Looney, and Lusin 2015).

2. In 2015 the overall average salary for graduates holding a bachelor's degree was $50,651. For bachelor's degrees in the social sciences, the average drops to $39,931 (National Association of Colleges and Employers 2015). In comparison, the starting salary for an open source officer with the CIA ranges between $50,864 and $118,069 (Central Intelligence Agency 2015).

3. Al-Batal (1992) describes Arabic as a multiglossic, rather than diglossic, language, "with more than two varieties and a continuum along which native speakers shift according to a number of different variables." For further discussion of di- and multiglossia in Arabic, see Badawi (1973) and Ferguson (1996).

4. Of course, there are still many traditionalists who believe that SCA has no place in academia whatsoever because, according to them, it is not the language of literature and scholarship (Hashem-Aramouni 2011, 86–91). Others argue that no other foreign language expects its L2 learners to master all varieties of its dialects and sociolects (such as asking English language learners to master rural white New Zealander English dialects alongside African American Vernacular English dialects alongside Shakespearean English). I find the latter a poorly structured straw man argument, for no other foreign language and its registers have a complementarity that is as historically rich and unique as Arabic. Furthermore, integrated approach Arabic curricula do not teach highly regionalized dialects or sociolects but rather focus on Educated Spoken Arabic as a lingua franca between native speakers. For an outline of Educated Spoken Arabic, see Ryding (2009).

5. The integrated approach as a concept was already being discussed as early as the 1970s but not widely implemented outside of the Defense Language Institute (Abboud 1971, 4). By 1990 Cornell University was already integrating MSA and SCA as a part of its regular curriculum, but the integrated approach did not catch on in other institutions until much later (Younes 1990).

6. The integrated approach is also effectively demonstrated in the *ᶜArabiyyat al-Naas* textbook series (Younes, Weatherspoon, and Foster 2013), which focuses on the complementary nature of MSA and SCA. Rather than giving side-by-side equivalents of both registers, *ᶜArabiyyat al-Naas* organizes word lists functionally according to the task. See Younes (2015) for an in-depth explanation of the *ᶜArabiyyat al-Naas* curriculum.

7. For example, students learn that the active participle in Egyptian and Levantine SCA is the approximate semantic equivalent to the conjugated imperfect verb found in MSA. Both patterns are derived and applied regularly within the tri-radical root system, allowing students to learn both sets of vocabulary within these grammatical parameters.

8. A list of the survey questions and answers is also provided in appendix 5.1 on the GUP website. The questions relevant to this chapter have been reordered for the purposes of analysis. The questions are presented one at a time, with student responses analyzed after each question.

PART 2

Curricular Models and Approaches to Integration

6

A Digitally Assisted Model of Integration of Standard and Colloquial Arabic Based on the Common European Framework

MANUELA E. B. GIOLFO AND FEDERICO SALVAGGIO

The University of Genoa

THE COMMON EUROPEAN FRAMEWORK of Reference for Languages (CEF) is based on the concept of "language proficiency" conceived of as the ability to use language to cope with several sociocommunicative tasks referring to various real-life situations.[1]

At first, learners are confronted with situations involving basic tasks aiming at the fulfillment of needs of concrete types. At later stages, they will have to cope with situations involving more advanced tasks such as understanding complex texts for social, academic, and professional purposes (Council of Europe 2001, 24). The progression of the learning process is described by CEF through a set of different levels, each of which represents a different degree of competence.

CEF, which has become the common reference method for assessment and evaluation throughout Europe, should not be conceived of as a reference framework for the teaching of European languages alone but rather as a reference framework for the teaching of foreign languages in Europe. Its theoretical background, which is grounded in approaches to communicative language teaching, is shared by other international teaching and assessment guidelines such as the American Council on the Teaching of Foreign Languages (ACTFL) Proficiency Guidelines.

No wonder that, due to the increased interest in the teaching of non-European languages (Arabic, Chinese, etc.), one witnesses in Europe a growing need for the standardization through CEF guidelines of the teaching and assessment of non-European languages (Bellassen 2012).

When we apply the task-based approach proposed by CEF to the teaching of Arabic, we are immediately confronted with the fact that, unlike what we see in most European languages, Arabic native speakers would not resort to just a single variety of the language to carry out the linguistic acts related to CEF tasks. When dealing with some communicative acts (e.g., asking for the price of an item) native speakers of Arabic would normally use a local Colloquial Arabic (CA) variety, whereas when dealing with other communicative acts (e.g., writing an essay) they would use a Standard Arabic (SA) variety. To conform to CEF pedagogical principles, we should therefore look for a teaching approach that integrates the teaching of SA with that of CA. The integration of the latter in the teaching of Arabic poses a series of delicate methodological and even practical problems.

One of the main questions we deal with in this chapter is how to manage the simultaneous teaching of both varieties while also keeping CA and SA separated during the teaching process. To tackle this question, we show the existence of a correlation between the resort to CA or SA on one side and the use of "listening and speaking" (L/S) or "reading and writing" (R/W) skills, respectively, on the other.

We then introduce a more explicit distinction between these two sets of skills for each CEF level as well as a clearer identification of language varieties associated with each of them. This way CA and SA, although mostly concurrent throughout the learning process, are separated based on the nature of the skills involved. Keeping spoken and written domains separated and associating to each of them the specific variety involved, in our opinion, serves at best the purposes of integration. In the classroom, the linguistic choices of teachers who follow the proposed model will need to be made accordingly.

The teachers' role is also essential in providing the students with the linguistic and metalinguistic information they need to successfully manage linguistic variation in ways that emulate native speakers' linguistic behavior in real-life situations without, at the same time, losing a unified perception of the Arabic language as a whole. To reproduce the complexity of such a linguistic reality, the role played by information and communications technology (ICT) cannot be overestimated. ICT in our model is not just an important source of aid and support; rather, it should be regarded as a founding and constitutive element of the model itself—that is, "the condition of possibility" of our model. In fact, ICT allows the reproduction of CA samples in the form of audio outputs, which is the form colloquial varieties are mostly associated with in real-life situations.[2]

The role played by ICT, particularly computer technologies, in our model is not confined to that. Unlike other technologies that allow sound reproduction such as tape recorders, computer technologies enable listening activities to be easily and effectively integrated into more complex activities involving multiple skills. More importantly, by managing different sets of data through distinct input/output channels (aural versus visual), ICT allows the contemporary separation and integration of spoken and written domains throughout the learning process. This is of utmost importance because, by doing so, ICT produces a virtual learning environment (VLE) in which learners are confronted with linguistic inputs that reproduce as faithfully as possible the linguistic environment in which native speakers learn, teach, and use Arabic.

In this chapter we aim, therefore, to present a model of integration based on both CEF and ICT. Although we do not enter into the details of the application of our model to the development of specific syllabi and curricula, in the last part of our chapter we show how the basic principles and general guidelines of our model can be applied to the designing of some illustrative computer-assisted teaching activities.

Language Proficiency and Communicative Competence in Light of CEF

The concept of language proficiency as defined by the CEF refers to the ability to use language to cope with several sociocommunicative tasks (SCT).[3] All SCTs are related to real-life situations occurring in various contexts called domains. Different language users can develop different degrees of competence in each of these domains. To describe these various degrees of competence, the CEF provides a set of six common reference levels, A1, A2, B1, B2, C1, and C2, and provides a description of what language learners should be able to do at each level.[4]

In the CEFs perspective, the ability to carry out specific linguistic acts and tasks is related to the use and development of several competences. Among these competences, communicative competence is particularly emphasized. Communicative competence is divided into linguistic, sociolinguistic, and pragmatic competence. Linguistic competence includes "lexical, phonological, syntactical knowledge and skills and other dimensions of language as system" (Council of Europe 2001, 13). Sociolinguistic and pragmatic competences are respectively concerned with "the sociocultural conditions of language use" and "the functional use of language resources" (ibid).

Therefore, in the CEF's perspective, to reach authentic communicative competence, linguistic competence must be integrated with sociopragmatic competence. This, as we discuss later, is particularly relevant to the case of teaching Arabic.

CEF and the Teaching of Arabic

When applying the six-level system to the teaching of Arabic, we are compelled to take into account several factors. First, the CEF's emphasis on using the language in real-life situations implies that the language varieties used by language learners should be the ones to which native speakers would normally resort in such situations. This has extremely important implications for Arabic.

To carry out the various linguistic acts required by the six CEF levels, Arabic native speakers do not normally resort to only one variety. Such a complex linguistic situation is described by Charles Ferguson in terms of diglossia, which he defines as "a relatively stable language situation in which, in addition to the primary dialects [Low] of the language . . . , there is a very divergent, highly codified . . . superposed variety [High], . . . which . . . is used for most written and formal spoken purposes but is not used by any sector of the community for ordinary conversation" (1959, 435). As Ferguson points out, in a diglossic linguistic situation, "ordinary conversation" and "written and formal spoken purposes" are not covered by the same language variety.

When considering the six CEF levels, which include both "ordinary conversation" and "written and formal spoken purposes," we should then be able to differentiate for each of the SCT the language variety normally associated with it in that particular context. If we go back to the description of the six levels, we notice that basic levels mainly refer to daily situations in which learners have to cope with different basic tasks (fulfillment of needs of concrete types, etc.).

In Arabic, these domains are not normally covered by SA but are instead predominantly associated with CA. However, more advanced levels involve, alongside more complex listening and speaking skills (which involve both CA and SA), the comprehension and production of increasingly challenging written texts. These texts, despite being normally associated with SA, can well consist of a mix of CA and SA or even of CA only. Interestingly, if the separation between tasks performed in CA and those performed in SA becomes more and more fluid as the level progresses (A1>A2>B1>B2>C1>C2), it appears as a more static separation as the level decreases (C2>C1> B2>B1>A2>A1).

The Six-Level System and Language Variation

As seen, CA and SA are differently represented throughout CEF's six levels. Lower levels show a predominance of CA, which tends to be associated with oral communication and with listening and speaking skills. This is a consequence of the particular nature of the SCT considered by CEF at lower levels, which mostly require communicative acts based on oral communication and the use of CA. On the other hand, at lower levels SA is predominantly associated with written communication and consequently with reading and writing skills. This does not imply that the linguistic reality behind the resort to CA or SA is that of a sort of bimodalism in which CA often reflects "the speech modality" while "SA often reflects the writing modality" (Hamam 2014, 165). Rather, it means that, at lower stages, learners are confronted with the predominant association of CA with tasks requiring listening and speaking skills and the predominant association of SA with tasks requiring reading and writing skills. At the higher levels of CEF, this association of CA with listening and speaking tasks and SA with reading and writing tasks is progressively weakened. At the middle and upper levels, learners are confronted with oral texts that exhibit CA alone, SA alone, or a mix of both as well as with written texts that exhibit SA alone, CA alone, or a mix of both. This is due to the particular nature of the SCTs considered by the CEF at middle and upper levels that can require the use of SA in oral communication as well as the use of CA in written communication or the use of both varieties in both oral and written communication. We describe this distribution of CA and SA by associating the various communicative competences required by each CEF level to the language variety native speakers would normally resort to for the carrying out of the specific tasks implied by those competences.[5] Different levels show not only a different distribution of CA and SA but also a weakening of the initial association of CA with listening and speaking on one side and SA with reading and writing on the other. Despite the increasing presence of SA in comparison to CA, as the levels progress many of the middle-upper levels show that a speaker can use both CA and SA together in fulfilling the requirement of the tasks. Thus, the respective proportions of the two varieties vary based on the level considered. We can roughly represent the distribution of CA and SA by means of the following chart.

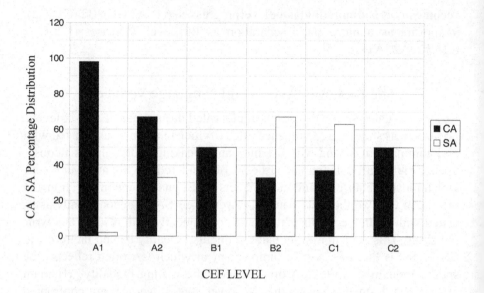

Figure 6.1 Percentage distribution of CA and SA within CEF's six levels

Figure 6.1 shows an unequal distribution of the two varieties throughout CEF levels. Level A1 appears as almost exclusively associated with CA. Level A2 is mostly associated with CA, although several tasks require SA (e.g., tasks dealing with local geography, employment). Level B1 entails SCTs such as dealing with matters regularly encountered in work, school, and leisure and the production of simple texts describing experiences, hopes, and so on. Therefore, level B1 implies the use of both CA and SA, where CA and SA at level B1 are shown in equal proportions. Level B2 is mostly associated with SA (e.g., understanding texts on concrete, abstract, and specialized topics) and to a minor extent to CA (e.g., interacting without strain with native speakers). At this level, some tasks may also include the use of a mix of CA and SA as well as the awareness of sociolinguistic values embedded in the choice of varieties. Level C1 is still predominantly associated with SA, but CA starts increasing again. This is because, while written skills at this level are still predominant and primarily associated with SA (e.g., understanding demanding and complex texts), many of the SCTs involved at this level (e.g., expressing oneself fluently for social, academic, and professional purposes) are mostly related to the resort to CA (but might as well imply the resort to a mix of CA and SA or even SA alone). Level C2 has an equal distribution of CA and SA because at this level there is an equal proportion of tasks requiring CA and tasks requiring SA. As we can observe, very significantly, both B1, the threshold level, and C2, the proficiency level, require a perfectly balanced competence in both varieties.

Language Variation and the Four Basic Language Skills

To shed light on the constraints that determine the particular distribution shown in figure 6.1, we can try to associate the tasks required by each CEF level to the four basic language skills: listening (L), speaking (S), reading (R), and writing (W).[6] We can further analyze the levels by dividing the four skills into oral and written skills. This way we will have two sets of skills: L/S and R/W.

Figure 6.2 represents the distribution of these two sets of skills and shows unequal distribution of the two sets throughout CEF levels. Level A1 appears in the CEF level description as almost exclusively associated with L/S in that the SCTs considered at this level are mostly associated with L/S skills (e.g., communicating on familiar and routine matters). At this level, there is also a very low percentage of R/W, which derives from the presence at this level of some tasks such as filling simple forms. Level A2 is mostly associated with L/S, although several tasks require R/W. Level B1 shows L/S and R/W in

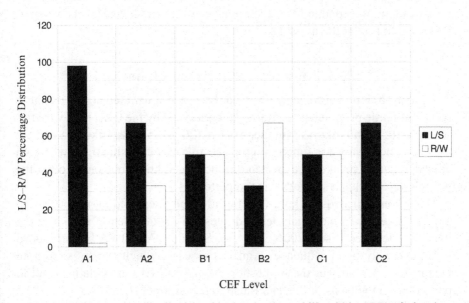

Figure 6.2 Percentage distribution of oral and written skills within CEF's six levels

equal proportions. Level B2 is mostly associated with R/W and to a minor extent to L/S. Level C1, like level B1, shows L/S and R/W in equal proportions. Level C2, like level A2, is mostly associated with L/S, with several tasks requiring R/W.

The concordance between figure 6.1 and figure 6.2 at levels A1, A2, B1 and B2 is extremely significant and allows us to identify a strong correlation (at these specific levels) between the resort to CA or SA on one side and the tasks based on the use of L/S or R/W skills, respectively, on the other. At more advanced levels there is a progression toward a mixed use of CA and SA, which can be more freely associated with both sets of skills (L/S and R/W). The lack of concordance between figure 6.1 and figure 6.2 at levels C1 and C2 is particularly significant as it proves that, at the more advanced levels, CA does not necessarily imply the resort to L/S skills and SA does not necessarily imply the resort to R/W skills.

In the next section, the relevance of this correlation to the teaching process will be dealt with in detail as well as the significance of the divergence in levels C1 and C2.

The analysis of the description of the six-level system has shown that both varieties are required to reach the goals envisaged by CEF for each level. At the same time, it has shown that, based on the tasks and the skills required by each level and the linguistic behavior adopted by native speakers, the two varieties tend to separate from each other only for the lower levels, whereas they tend to mix at the upper levels.

A Model of Integration Based on the CEF

The most obvious consequence of what has been illustrated so far is that to reach authentic proficiency in Arabic, as conceived by the CEF, both varieties will have to be taught.[7] As Munther Younes (2006, 159) remarks, CA and SA are both "necessary for functioning in the full range of situations where an educated native speaker is expected to function. Without one or the other the proficiency of such a speaker is incomplete."

Having established that both varieties must be integrated into the teaching process takes us to the much-debated question about when to introduce the two varieties (see Eisele 2006, 218–19). Should CA and SA be introduced simultaneously or in sequence? And in this case, which variety should be taught first? We answer these questions in light of CEF's guidelines and in particular on the basis of the data illustrated in figure 6.1.[8]

Figure 6.1 clarifies that the two varieties are not equally distributed in the various CEF levels. As we can see, the tasks required by the first level (A1, beginner) can be carried out by almost exclusively resorting to CA and only marginally to SA. This is because the vast majority of the tasks required at this level appear as almost exclusively associated with CA, whereas only a few tasks are normally associated with SA.[9] The CEF in itself does not deny the possibility of resorting to a mix of CA and SA to carry out these tasks but clearly suggests that at this level, due to the nature of the SCTs involved, the exposure to SA is minimal.

With the second level (A2, elementary) the contemporary presence of both varieties becomes more significant, although at this level most of the tasks still require CA. The third level (B1, intermediate) requires CA and SA in equal proportions. The following level (B2, vantage) shows a mirror symmetry with A2 and presents inverted proportions of CA and SA. This means that at this level most of the tasks will need SA. In the penultimate level (C1, advanced) SA is still predominant, but CA starts rising again due to the nature of the tasks involved at this level, which include activities such as listening to TV programs in which people speak a mix of CA and SA or reading novels written in CA or in a mix of CA and SA. In the last level (C2, mastery), for the same reasons, CA keeps rising to the extent that, as in the case of level B1, it reaches an equal distribution with SA.

Consequently, during the teaching process, when dealing with level A1, the focus will be almost exclusively on CA and only incidentally on SA. At level A2, although the focus will still be on CA, SA will be progressively introduced. At levels B2 and C1, the emphasis will be on SA, while also keeping on developing skills in CA. At level C2, equal attention will have to be drawn to both varieties, thus implying that proficiency can only be attained by a very high and perfectly balanced competence in both CA and SA. Equal attention to CA and SA will have to be reserved also in the case of B1, a fact that is particularly noteworthy as this level holds a special position within the six CEF levels and is considered the threshold level (Van Ek 1975)—that is, the take-off point for the independent use of the language.[10]

Therefore, after an initial exclusion of SA to the benefit of CA (from the first classes until the introduction of the alphabet), for most of the teaching process, CA and SA will have to be approached simultaneously.[11]

This leads us to the second main question, namely, how to manage the concurrent teaching of both varieties. We answer this question by drawing on the analysis illustrated in two preceding sections. As we have seen, the comparison between figure 6.1 and figure 6.2 shows, at least for levels A1, A2, B1, and B2, the existence of a strong correlation between the resort to CA or SA, on one side, and the use of, respectively, L/S or R/W skills, on the other.

As far as the lower (A1, A2) and intermediate (B1, B2) levels are concerned, the alternation of CA and SA in covering the different tasks is more strictly related to the nature (oral versus written) of the basic language skills required by the levels' tasks. In levels A1, A2, B1, and B2, CA tends to be more strictly associated with oral skills and SA with written skills.

In addition to that, at these levels tasks tend to show a strong polarization in terms of "purely CA" tasks versus "purely SA" tasks (e.g., asking the price versus consulting a timetable). Therefore, at this stage of the teaching process, the separation between CA and SA is realized through the division between oral and written skills and we mainly have CA oral activities on one side and SA written activities on the other.

At the advanced levels (C1, C2), while written skills are still predominantly associated with SA, some SCTs (e.g., giving a public speech) require the association of SA to oral skills. This accounts for the divergences between figure 6.1 and figure 6.2 at these levels.

At level C1, as illustrated in figure 6.1, the focus on SA is predominant. However, due to the resort to SA to perform oral tasks (such as delivering a lecture) the distribution of oral and written skills is equally balanced. For the same reason, in C2, although CA and SA are equally balanced, oral skills prevail on written skills (typical SCTs at this level include using SA to perform oral and written acts in a series of professional, academic, and highly formal situational contexts in which, of course, a mix of CA and SA may as well easily occur). Also, advanced levels tasks tend to show a less polarized situation. In fact, alongside "purely CA" and "purely SA" tasks, we have "mixed CA and SA" tasks (such as listening to a TV program in which a mix of CA and SA is used). Learners at this stage will be confronted with oral and written tasks that present a more nuanced linguistic situation, including communicative contexts in which native speakers would normally adopt different linguistic strategies: code-switching, code-mixing strategies, mixed varieties, and so on.

CEF and ICT

Both at lower levels (where we have a stricter separation of CA and SA) and at higher levels (where we gradually move toward mixed and integrated forms), the role of ICT is essential in allowing the reproduction of this peculiar linguistic situation. As stated in the first section of this chapter, ICT first allows the reproduction of CA samples in the form of audio outputs, which is the form colloquial varieties are normally associated with in real-life situations. This avoids presenting the learners with written transcriptions of oral conversations, which by their very nature cannot fully convey all the socio-pragmatic implications of the original spoken texts. Technologies that allow sound reproduction are essential when working on listening skills since this cannot be done by means of written texts. Furthermore, through ICT, particularly through computer technologies, listening activities can be integrated into more complex activities involving tasks that encompass both L/S and R/W skills, on one side, and CA and SA, on the other. This is essential at the lower levels, where CA and SA tend to be separated based on the skills involved. For instance, as illustrated in the digital learning activities provided on the website accompanying this volume, in order to verify the comprehension of the conversation in CA at level A1, we can ask students to listen to a conversation in CA (reproduced by the audio channel via speakers or headphones) and then to answer a set of written questions in SA (reproduced by the video channel via monitor or touch screen). This activity, when done by ICT (instead of book and tape), has the big advantage of keeping the learners within a unified learning environment, which positively impacts attention and motivation. Furthermore, through ICT, this same activity can be more accurately regulated in terms of timing of the different stages of the exercise, number of repetitions of the single elements, and immediate feedback with comments on the answers produced. Last, but not least, ICT uniquely allows the contemporary managing of different colloquial varieties so that learners can choose within the same learning activity which colloquial variety they want to focus on.

At the higher levels where learners are confronted with language inputs related to complex real-life situational contexts—where, as seen, CA and SA tend to mix and integrate each other—the resort to ICT is as essential as at lower levels. This is because ICT, by means of audio and video devices, allows the faithful reproduction of real-life language materials that are fundamental at higher levels.

As already mentioned, this is of utmost importance because, by doing so, ICT enables the establishment of a virtual learning environment in which learners are confronted with linguistic inputs that reproduce as faithfully as possible the linguistic environment in which native speakers learn, teach, and use Arabic. Furthermore, ICT can manage different sets of data through distinct input/output channels (aural versus visual), thus enabling the simultaneous separation and integration of spoken and written domains throughout the learning process within a unified learning environment.

As we can see in the following table, L/S activities are processed via the audio output devices (e.g., speakers, headphones) whereas R/W activities are processed via electronic visual displays (e.g., computer monitors, tablet screens). In the next section, we show how this can be applied to the realization of some illustrative teaching activities.

Table 6.1 Computer devices and channels involved in processing oral and written activities

Activities	Computer devices		Computer channel
Skills involved	Input	Output	
oral	microphone	speakers/ headphones	aural (audio)
written	keyboard/mouse/ touch screen	screen	visual (video)

The Role of ICT in Designing Digital Learning Activities

As stated in the first section of this chapter, our intention here is not to enter into the details of the construction of specific curricula and syllabi aiming at building up particular morphosyntactic or sociopragmatic notions. Our intention is to present a general theoretical framework from which specific teaching approaches, methods, and strategies can be derived. Nevertheless, we present a possible application of our model for the realization of some illustrative teaching activities in a computer-assisted language-learning environment.

We have so far divided the four skills into oral and written skills. As we are now considering designing teaching activities based on the interaction of human beings (i.e., the learners) with ICT (namely, computers), it is necessary to introduce a further division of the four skills into productive skills (speaking and writing) and perceptive skills (listening and reading).

Humans' oral and written productions (which are based on productive skills, speaking and writing) reach computers in the form of input data and are received through input devices (microphone, keyboard, touch screen, and mouse). Conversely, computers' productions (generated by output devices: speakers, headphones, screen) are received by humans in the form of aural and visual information interpreted by means of their perceptive skills (listening and reading). For practical and technical reasons in designing our digital activities, here we only deal with the perceptive skills.[12]

In order to tailor our activities to the tasks required for a specific level, we need to identify the language varieties we need to employ in our activities. We can do that by going back to the CEF's description of the six levels and adapting that by selecting what refers to perceptive skills.[13] In this way we are able to clearly identify the constraints (i.e., the different SCT tasks and related situational contexts) that determine at each level the association between perceptive activities and the corresponding language variety involved (see table 6.2). The results obtained are consistent with those already illustrated in the previous sections. Lower and intermediate levels exhibit a strict correlation between, respectively, oral and written skills, on one side, and the resort to CA and SA, on the other. At the more advanced levels, both varieties can be associated with both sets of skills.

Consequently, at the lower and intermediate levels we have spoken and written texts that mostly present one language variety at a time. Listening activities at A1, A2, B1, and B2 mostly include CA spoken texts (but also oral texts in SA, particularly texts that were originally conceived as written texts and then read out loud, such as public announcements at railway stations, airports, etc.). Reading activities at A1, A2, B1, and B2 are mostly based on SA texts (but also include texts that were originally written in CA, such as advertisements, commercials, etc.).[14] At the advanced levels, spoken and written texts present various combinations of language varieties. Listening activities at C1 and C2 are based on oral texts that may include pure CA or pure SA as well as a simultaneous resort to CA and SA. Reading activities at C1 and C2 are based on written texts that may include pure SA or pure CA as well as a simultaneous presence of SA and CA. We summarize this in table 6.2.

If we want to realize, for instance, three different digital activities focused on perceptive skills and tailored to three different CEF levels, A1, B1, and C1, we would mostly have the situation shown in table 6.4.

As we can see, for each level, perceptive skills imply the use of both varieties. Therefore, in designing our activities we would have to select appropriate contexts in which the two varieties can be exercised simultaneously while being kept separated through different digital channels.

To set the two varieties within the same situational and communicative context is of paramount importance because this provides a general framework that incorporates what is taught in CA and SA into the same acquisition process. As Paolo Balboni (2010, 44) points out, "acquisition occurs through a global perception at first, followed by a phase of analysis, and it ends with a synthesis, where the mind fixes what it has observed and analysed."

Based on the above, for each level considered we can select specific situational contexts and SCTs and individuate the language varieties involved and the computer channels activated. Then, for each situational context, we can design digital activities that integrate oral and written skills on one side and CA and SA on the other.[15]

Table 6.2 Distribution of CA and SA in association with perceptive skills within the CEF's six levels

Level	Activities	Description	Language variety involved
A1	Listening	Can understand familiar, everyday expressions and very basic phrases aimed at the satisfaction of needs of a concrete type and questions about personal details such as where he lives, people he knows and things he has (provided the other person talks slowly and clearly and is prepared to help).	CA
A2	Listening	Can understand sentences and frequently used expressions related to areas of most immediate relevance (e.g., very basic personal and family information, shopping, local geography, employment).	CA
	Reading	Can read texts related to areas of most immediate relevance (e.g., very basic personal and family information, shopping, local geography, employment).	SA
B1	Listening	Can understand the main points of clear oral input on familiar matters regularly encountered in work, school, leisure, etc.	CA
	Reading	Can understand the main points of clear written text on familiar matters regularly encountered in work, school, leisure, etc.	SA
B2	Listening	Can understand native speakers' in spontaneous regular spoken interactions without strain for either party.	CA
	Reading	Can understand the main ideas of complex text on both concrete and abstract topics, including technical discussions in her field of specialization.	SA
C1	Listening	Can understand oral inputs where language is used flexibly and effectively for social, academic, and professional purposes.	CA/SA
	Reading	Can understand a wide range of demanding, longer texts, and recognize implicit meaning.	CA/SA
C2	Listening	Can understand with ease virtually everything heard from different spoken sources and can differentiate finer shades of meaning even in the most complex situations.	CA/SA
	Reading	Can understand with ease virtually everything read from different written sources and can differentiate finer shades of meaning even in the most complex situations.	CA/SA

Table 6.3 Association of CA and SA with listening and reading skills within the CEF's six levels

Skill	Level	Language variety
Listening	A1, A2, B1, B2	CA (with some SA)
	C1, C2	CA or SA or CA and SA
Reading	A1, A2, B1, B2	SA (with some CA)
	C1, C2	SA or CA or SA and CA

Table 6.4 Association of CA and SA with listening and reading skills at levels A1, B1, and C1

Level	Skill	Language variety
A1	listening	CA
	reading	SA
B1	listening	CA
	reading	SA
C1	listening	CA or SA or CA and SA
	reading	SA or CA or SA and CA

The Role of the Teacher

As seen in the previous section, we can effectively work on the development of students' perceptive skills through ICT. This can be done both inside the classroom, where the teacher can coordinate the use of ICT, and in distance learning, where students are autonomously exposed to learning activities designed for that purpose. As for the productive skills, these can also be enhanced via ICT. In the classroom, teachers can select digital listening and reading activities aimed at the consolidation of speaking and writing abilities. Through distance learning, those same activities can be incorporated into digital exercises and activities. Nevertheless, as already seen, ICT cannot substitute for teachers in the accurate assessment of productive skills, so the role of the teacher in the classroom is essential in ensuring that all the skills are harmoniously developed. This is not the only field in which the role of the teacher is indispensable. We have so far suggested that in order to reach authentic proficiency in Arabic, more than one variety has to be mastered by the learners. This is of course a necessary condition, but it is not a sufficient condition by itself.

As seen in the second section of this chapter, proficiency in the CEF's perspective is based on the concept of communicative competence, which the CEF further divides into three components: linguistic, sociolinguistic, and pragmatic competence. The mere linguistic knowledge of both CA and SA, even if advanced, would only fall into the definition of linguistic competence, which is but one of the components of communicative competence. The other fundamental components are sociolinguistic competence and pragmatic competence. Therefore, linguistic competence in itself would not be enough to reach authentic proficiency, as conceived by the CEF, and needs to be supplemented by pragmatic and sociolinguistic competence.

This means that a model aimed at developing authentic proficiency cannot confine itself to focusing on linguistic competence in CA and SA but must integrate the necessary sociolinguistic and pragmatic competence that will guide the learners in choosing the variety appropriate to each given context or task.[16] This sociopragmatic competence must be developed through the whole learning process by providing the learners with the metalinguistic competence they need to successfully manage linguistic variation in ways that emulate native speakers' linguistic behavior in real-life situations. Metalinguistic competence should therefore include the ability to recognize and interiorize rhetorical, ideological, and sociological values associated with CA and with SA (Giolfo and Sinatora 2011, 120). In other words, learners must learn to evaluate the appropriateness of their choice of the language variety used to carry out each particular SCT on the basis of rhetorical, ideological, and sociological implications associated with each variety within each particular situational context. Learners must be aware, for instance, of the sociopragmatic implications of ordering kebab in SA (which could mean being taken for a foreigner) or writing an official report in a mix of CA and SA (which could mean being taken for someone who has not received proper education).

In this respect, the role of the teachers is of utmost importance because, while transmitting a unified perception of the Arabic language as an organic whole, they help students to develop that awareness of variation that will guide them in the choice of the language variety appropriate to each particular context.[17] The role of the teachers is essential in illustrating how, in everyday life within the Arabic-speaking community, CA and SA complement each other, and native speakers resort to both varieties to convey and acquire the information needed to successfully carry out complex SCTs in wider situational contexts.

Concluding Remarks

Managing integration in the classroom is a challenging task that confronts researchers and practitioners with extremely difficult theoretical and methodological problems. Nevertheless, in our opinion, any serious attempt to apply the CEF to the teaching of Arabic cannot leave out integration. Adopting a "fictional" approach in which SA is used to indifferently cover all the socio-communicative situations described by CEF does not represent, in our perspective, a valid alternative to integration. Although this seems to be the case for a large number of Arabic teaching programs throughout the world, including Europe, such a choice would not only be in clear discordance with CEF guidelines but, more importantly, would be in discordance with the Arabic sociolinguistic reality itself. As David Wilmsen states: "Telephone conversations, bargaining in the marketplace, or booking hotels are conducted in the local vernacular or nothing else. Teaching programs based in written Arabic are faced with the choice of either constructing artificial conversations . . . or to ignore such situations entirely" (2006, 127).[18]

If CEF puts extreme emphasis on real-life language, this is because, within a communicative language teaching approach, presenting learners with linguistic inputs as faithful as possible to real-life linguistic inputs is believed to have an extremely positive impact on the learning process.

It is precisely for this reason that, in our view, any attempt to apply CEF to the teaching of Arabic cannot leave out ICT too. By producing a VLE, ICT represents a powerful means to reproduce the complexity of the Arabic sociolinguistic reality. Through VLE, learners can be confronted with complex teaching activities that require the simultaneous use of CA and SA, and this leads to the feasibility of authentic assessment of learning within an integrated approach. The adoption of the approach presented in this chapter will face many challenges and forms of resistance. In Europe, and elsewhere, CA and SA have for a long time been confined into separate fields of Arabic studies. University courses of Arabic are still traditionally intended as courses in SA, whereas CA is confined within the field of dialectology. Even when recently compelled or invited to adapt their courses to the CEF standards, many institutions opted for an exclusively nominal adoption limited to a general reference to the CEF level the course is meant to achieve. This has so far been done without considering the implications that the reference to a particular CEF level (and to its specific SCT) would imply in terms of language varieties needed to achieve full competence within that particular level.[19]

We believe that rethinking the teaching of Arabic in light of CEF represents a pressing need because of the growing demand for standardization of teaching and assessment of non-European languages. Besides that, for the specialists in the field of teaching Arabic as a foreign language (TAFL), it constitutes a great opportunity to reflect on the characteristics of Arabic and its sociolinguistic dimensions and to develop more efficient strategies to enhance authentic proficiency in Arabic. Adopting the pedagogical principles of CEF impacts TAFL-based research because it compels us to elaborate a theoretical approach that can be justified in communicative and sociolinguistic terms and integrates CA and SA in the same teaching process. Thus, on one hand, the need for integration of CA and SA arises as a consequence of the application of CEF guidelines to the teaching of Arabic. On the other hand, the principles that inspire the CEF clearly attest to the fundamentality of integration. Moreover, a deeper analysis of CEF levels on the basis of the tasks involved, such as the one we have conducted, demonstrates that the CEF does not simply indicate the necessity of integration of SA and CA but that it also indicates (more explicitly than implicitly) the modality by which such integration can be achieved within the teaching process.

References

Al-Batal, Mahmoud. 1992. "Diglossia Proficiency: The Need for an Alternative Approach to Teaching." In *The Arabic Language in America*, edited by Aleya Rouchdy, 284–304. Detroit: Wayne State University Press.

Balboni, Paolo E. 2010. *Language Teaching Research Based on the Theory of Models.* Perugia, Italy: Guerra Edizioni.

Bellassen, Joël. 2012. "Is Chinese Eurocompatible? Is the Common Framework Common? The Common European Framework of Reference for Languages Facing Distant Languages." In *International Symposium Report 2011: New Prospects for Foreign Language Teaching in Higher Education—Exploring the Possibilities of Application of CERF*, edited by Nobuo Tomimori, Masashi Furihata, Kiyoshi Haida, Naotoshi Kurosawa, and Masahi Negishi, 23–31. Tokyo: World Language and Society Education Centre, Tokyo University of Foreign Studies.

Benchina, Hocine, and Nadia Rocchetti. 2015a. *ILA. Test preparatori per la certificazione della lingua araba.* Livello A1. Milano: Jouvence.

———. 2015b. *ILA. Test preparatori per la certificazione della lingua araba.* Livello A2. Milano: Jouvence.

Canale, Michael, and Merrill Swain. 1980. "Theoretical Bases of Communicative Approaches to Second Language Teaching and Testing." *Applied Linguistics* 1: 1-47.

Council of Europe. 2001. *Common European Framework of Reference for Languages: Learning, Teaching, Assessment.* Cambridge: Cambridge University Press.

Durand, Olivier, Angela D. Langone, and Giuliano Mion. 2010. *Corso di arabo contemporaneo*. Milano: Hoepli.

Eisele, John. 2006. "Developing Frames of Reference for Assessment and Curricular Design in a Diglossic L2: From Skills to Tasks (and Back Again)." In *Handbook for Arabic Language Teaching Professionals in the 21st Century*, edited by Kassem M. Wahba, Zeinab A. Taha, and Liz England, 197–220. Mahwah, NJ: Lawrence Erlbaum.

Ferguson, Charles. 1959. "Diglossia." In *Word* 15: 325–40.

Giolfo, Manuela E. B., and Francesco L. Sinatora. 2011. "Rethinking Arabic Diglossia. Language Representations and Ideological Intents." In *Multilingualism: Language, Power and Knowledge*, edited by Paolo Valore, 103–28. Pisa: Edistudio.

Hamam, Marco. 2014. "Bimodalism: Arabic Diglossia as a Double Modality of Communication." In *Romano-Arabica* 14:165–92.

Ladikoff Guasto, Lucy. 2002. *Ahlan. Grammatica araba didattico-comunicativa*. Roma: Carocci.

Kallas, Elie. 1995. *Yatabi lebaaniyyi: Un "livello soglia" per l'apprendimento del neo-arabo libanese*. Venezia: Cafoscarina.

Taha, Zeinab A. 2006. "Toward Pragmatic Competency in Arabic." In *Handbook for Arabic Language Teaching Professionals in the 21st Century*, edited by Kassem M. Wahba, Zeinab A. Taha, and Liz England, 353–62. Mahwah, NJ: Lawrence Erlbaum.

———. 2008. "Educated Spoken Arabic: How Could It Help in Redefining ACTFL Guidelines?" *Al-ᶜArabiyya* 40/41: 104–14.

Van Ek, Jan A. 1975. *The Threshold Level in a European Unit/Credit System for Modern Language Learning by Adults*. Strasbourg: Council of Europe Publishing.

Wilmsen, David. 2006. "What Is Communicative Arabic?" In *Handbook for Arabic Language Teaching Professionals in the 21st Century*, edited by Kassem M. Wahba, Zeinab A. Taha, and Liz England, 125–38. Mahwah, NJ: Lawrence Erlbaum.

Younes, Munther. 2006. "Integrating the Colloquial with Fusha in the Arabic-as-a-Foreign-Language Classroom." In *Handbook for Arabic Language Teaching Professionals in the 21st Century*, edited by Kassem M. Wahba, Zeinab A. Taha, and Liz England, 157–68. Mahwah, NJ: Lawrence Erlbaum.

Notes

Although the ideas expressed in this chapter come from a joint research project of both authors, Manuela E.B. Giolfo is responsible for the following sections: "The Six-Level System and Language Variation," "Language Variation and the Four Basic Language Skills," "A Model of Integration Based on the CEF," "The Role of the Teacher," and "Concluding Remarks". Federico Salvaggio is responsible for the introduction, "Language Proficiency and Communicative Competence in Light of CEF,"

"CEF and the Teaching of Arabic," "CEF and ICT," and "The Role of ICT in Designing Digital Learning Activities."

Additional data and examples are freely available to view and download on this book's product page on the Georgetown University Press (GUP) website (www .press.georgetown.edu).

1. A copy of the Common European Framework of Reference for Languages is included in a website we created for teachers, A Digitally Assisted Model of Integration of Standard and Colloquial Arabic—Sample, http://arabicintegrationsamples .blogspot.it/.

2. This does not exclude the fact that, in real-life situations, CA might also occur in connection with the written form or that SA might be associated with spoken productions.

3. Based on the notion of communicative competence; see Canale and Swain 1980.

4. Table W6.1 (on the GUP website) presents a global description of the six levels provided by the CEF (Council of Europe 2001, 24).

5. See table W6.2 on the GUP website.

6. See table W6.3 on the GUP website.

7. We will not address the question of which regional CA to teach alongside SA (see Al-Batal 1992, 288). We would just like to remark that our digitally assisted model permits the realization of interchangeable modules based on different regional CA that can be freely combined with the SA module (see the volume companion website for a sample of such digital activities).

8. For an approach to the same problem in ACTFL guidelines' perspective, see Al-Batal 1992, 299; Eisele 2006; and Taha 2008.

9. Although the CEF global overview of A1 does not include SA-based tasks, more detailed overviews (Council of Europe 2001, 26) do list at level A1 SA-based tasks (e.g., understanding familiar names and words on posters and filling out simple forms).

10. For the notion of "threshold level" referred to the teaching of Arabic, see Kallas 1995.

11. This is the method applied in designing the learning activities provided within this volume's companion website and the curriculum for an experimental integrated course launched at the University of Genoa by Manuela E. B. Giolfo and Abdeljalil Bentajar (see appendix 6.1 on the GUP website).

12. Most commonly available ICT resources for analysis of human written and spoken productions, at the present stage of development, do not allow a complete recognition of all the necessary linguistic features needed for a full and thorough assessment of written and spoken productions. As we see in the next section, for an exhaustive evaluation of productive skills the role of the teacher is essential. For this reason and for the reasons exposed in the next section, the role of teachers within our model is essential and the model itself would not be conceivable without the active action of teachers. This also accounts for the fact that we have decided to call our

model "a digitally assisted model of integration" and not "a digital model of integration" *tout court.*

13. See, again, table W6.1 on the GUP website.

14. See note 7.

15. See table W6.4 for situational contexts at levels A1, B1, and C1 with tasks, skills, language varieties, and channels involved, and table W6.5 for digital activities targeting levels A1, B1, and C1, both on the GUP website.

16. For pragmatic competence related to Arabic, see Taha 2006.

17. As Younes (2006, 164) points out, presenting Arabic as one system of communication "is not only an accurate reflection of the sociolinguistic realities of the language but is also pedagogically more effective."

18. Similar "artificial" conversations can be found in some recent European manuals claiming to adopt the CEF (Durand, Langone, and Mion 2010) or a communicative approach (Ladikoff Guasto 2002).

19. This is also the case of the Italian ILA project for the certification of Arabic. This recently launched certification project aims at establishing a system of assessment and certification for Arabic based on CEF levels. While claiming to adhere to CEF guidelines and to specifically focus on oral competences, ILA confines itself to the sole evaluation of SA communicative skills. In our opinion, such a claim constitutes, due to the ideolinguistic choices that it represents, an evident disregard of CEF principles and guidelines (Benchina and Rocchetti 2015a, 2015b).

7

Developing a Genre-Based Curriculum to Teach Arabic Diglossia

EMMA TRENTMAN
University of New Mexico

TO BECOME PROFICIENT in a language, learners must develop socio-linguistic competence, or "acquire native-speaker (NS) patterns of variation" (Bayley and Regan 2004, 325). All languages contain sociolinguistic variables, such as the *–ing/in'* variation in English or the *ne* deletion in the *ne pas* construct in French. Native speakers choose different realizations of these variables according to social context, and nonnative speakers must also learn this skill. While the majority of research on the acquisition of sociolinguistic competence has focused on learners of French (e.g., Dewaele 2004; Howard, Lemée, and Regan 2006; Regan, Howard, and Lemée 2009), sociolinguistic variation exists in all languages. As a diglossic language, Arabic presents interesting opportunities for the study of sociolinguistic variation (Bassiouney 2009; Holes 2004). However, the question of how to teach sociolinguistic variation in the context of Arabic diglossia has remained a persistent debate in the field of teaching Arabic as a foreign language. In this chapter, I describe the potential of a genre-based curriculum to integrate the teaching of Modern Standard Arabic (MSA) and a dialect and an initial attempt to develop this type of curriculum in first-year Arabic. Finally, I analyze student oral and written data to evaluate the development of sociolinguistic competence in this curriculum.

Genre-Based Curricula

Genre-based approaches to curriculum and instruction in the foreign language classroom advocate for a multiyear curriculum sequenced according to textual genres (Arens 2008; Byrnes 2002; Byrnes et al. 2006). The concepts of text and genre are defined based on systemic functional linguistics (SFL). SFL views language as a context-based system with agentive users rather than a collection of structural elements (Halliday and Matthiessen 2013). This system includes both immediate communicative contexts and larger socio-cultural-historical ones, and language users display agency, identity, and social positioning (Kern and Schultz 2005).

Using SFL leads to an expanded definition of both text and genre. Texts can be written, oral, or multimodal: "The term 'text' refers to any instance of language, in any medium, that makes sense to someone who knows the language; we can characterize text as language functioning in context. . . . Language is, in the first instance, a resource for making meaning; so text is a process of making meaning in context" (Halliday and Matthiessen 2013, 3). Furthermore, the production and interpretation of texts is always context-dependent. This has important implications for foreign language learners, who must understand the context-based nature of language in order to choose culturally appropriate modes of expression while also expressing their own social identities, as Heidi Byrnes (2006, 49) explains: "When oral and written language is explicitly located within its cultural contexts, learners begin to appreciate how language is constitutive for cultural functions and begin to explore what flexibilities exist between relatively fixed expectations associated with different contexts of situation and choices that can validly be made within them."

Genres are collections of these texts that form a particular level of context. James Martin (1997, 13) defines genre as "the system of staged goal-oriented social processes through which social subjects in a given culture live their lives." By defining genres as social processes, this definition draws attention to the fact that texts belonging to these genres are supposed to follow certain expected steps and are produced with an audience in mind, whether or not this audience is physically present (Martin 1997). Language learners must learn to mimic these steps to produce culturally acceptable models of these genres. At the same time, an emphasis on learner agency means that learners can also critique and resist these models to some degree (Martin 2000). Examples of genres typically included in an introductory language curriculum are giving directions, introducing a colleague, answering the telephone, and many other basic language functions. Texts are specific examples of these functions, and the context is the social context in which these texts are meaningful.

Developing Genre-Based Curricula for the
Foreign Language Classroom

Using the definitions of text and genre from SFL to develop a foreign language curriculum involves three main steps: sequencing the genres, finding example texts for students to analyze, developing materials to structure students' analysis and production of the genres, and assessing students' abilities regarding their comprehension and production of these genres (Byrnes 2006). The most prominent example of a genre-based curriculum in US foreign language higher education is that of Georgetown University's German Department, which pursued a multiyear project to transform their curriculum into a genre-based one.[1]

There are numerous ways to sequence textual genres. Byrnes (2006, 2008) recommends sequencing texts "from personal to public narrativity" (2006, 49), as this follows James Paul Gee's (2002) distinction between the primary discourses of everyday life and the secondary discourses of public life and society, and it reflects fundamental developmental concepts in SFL. Thus, this type of sequencing provides a clear progression from basic to more advanced language learning (Byrnes 2008; Byrnes et al. 2006).

After sequencing the genres, the next step is to find examples of these genres for students to analyze (Byrnes 2006; Byrnes et al. 2006). With the help of their instructor and peers, students analyze the unfolding stages of the genre using tasks and organizers that scaffold their comprehension and analysis (Byrnes 2006; Byrnes et al. 2006). Using this method, even beginning language students are able to read the cultural messages contained in authentic materials and analyze them as representative of specific genres (Maxim 2002, 2006). Following their analysis, students move on to creating their own examples of these genres using the textual moves they have analyzed. These assignments become assessments that can help clarify instructional goals and learning outcomes (Byrnes 2002).

Research on genre-based curricula demonstrates that this approach has a number of favorable outcomes. These include bridging a gap between a focus on oral abilities in the lower divisions and critical textual analysis in the upper divisions (Byrnes et al. 2006; Swaffar 2006), helping foster the translingual and transcultural competence called for by the 2007 report of the Modern Language Association (Barrette, Paesani, and Vinall 2010; Modern Language Association 2007), and helping students reach advanced level proficiencies within the limited time of an undergraduate language program (Byrnes et al. 2006)

Genre-Based Curricula to Address Diglossia

To date, applications of genre-based curricula have focused on more commonly taught languages, particularly German, French, and Spanish (Byrnes 2006; Byrnes et al. 2006; Maxim 2006; Allen 2009; Barrette, Paesani, and Vinall 2010; Kern 2008). However, developing a curriculum based on theories of language use in context is particularly appealing for addressing one of the most persistent challenges in the teaching of Arabic, that of Arabic diglossia. Speakers of Arabic vary their language between two idealized poles of dialect and MSA (or Classical Arabic) based on a variety of contextual and speaker elements, including the immediate situation, interlocutor, educational level, language ideology, and social identities (Bassiouney 2009; Holes 2004; Versteegh 1997). As such, using the framework of SFL provides useful insights into the choices Arabic speakers make in different contexts. Providing students the opportunity to analyze the use of MSA and dialect as part of genre-based conventions rather than two separate systems is a productive way of integrating these varieties in the classroom. In the next section, I describe an initial attempt to build a genre-based curriculum in Arabic, starting at the introductory level.

Developing a Genre-Based Curriculum for Elementary Arabic

Based on the beneficial outcomes of genre-based curricula and their potential for helping students gain sociolinguistic competence in Arabic, I decided to try this approach in the Arabic program at the University of New Mexico starting in the fall of 2014. The initial implementation coincided with the introduction of six-credit Elementary Arabic classes that met five days a week and the hiring of a new faculty member, Heather Sweetser, who participated in the genre-based curriculum development. In the remainder of this section, I describe the choice of the National Council of State Supervisors for Languages–American Council on the Teaching of Foreign Languages (NCSSFL–ACTFL) can-do statements as genres, the sequencing of these can-do statements, materials development for the classroom, and assessment of student work.

Choosing the Genres / Can-Do Statements

Although the genre-based curriculum was theoretically appealing, there was little guidance for implementing it at the elementary levels and particularly in a less-commonly taught language where students need to learn a different script. Although Hiram Maxim (2002, 2006) used a romance novel in a first-year German class, this seemed difficult in a first-year Arabic class, as these materials are difficult to find in Arabic and reading is typically slower due to the challenges of the Arabic script.

However, the expanded definitions of texts and genres used in SFL and incorporated into genre-based pedagogies mean that language functions at an introductory level, such as everyday conversations or the text of basic announcements, can also be viewed as a type of genre (Arens 2008). Thus, we decided to use the NCSSFL–ACTFL can-do statements as the target genres for this project. The NCSSFL–ACTFL can-do statements are a list of language functions organized by ACTFL proficiency level and language skill. They include items such as "I can introduce myself and others" (inter-personal communication, Novice Mid) and "I can write a postcard message" (presentational writing, Novice High). The complete list of these can-do statements can be found on the ACTFL website.[2]

For Elementary Arabic, can-do statements at the Novice and Intermediate levels were targeted to lead to the overall goal of having students reach Inter-mediate Low in all five modes of communication by the end of the year (two semesters of six-credit Arabic classes). Can-do statements at the Intermediate Mid and High levels were included to push students to higher levels on spe-cific tasks, helping them develop the overall proficiency levels necessary to perform consistently at Intermediate Low.

Sequencing and Textbook Analysis

Following the decision to use the NCSSFL–ACTFL can-do statements, the next step was to sequence them. The first step in this process was to analyze the two textbooks used in the first year of Arabic, *Alif Baa*, 3rd edition (Brus-tad, Al-Batal, and Al-Tonsi 2010) and *Al-Kitaab fi Taᶜallum al-ᶜArabiyya*, Part One, 3rd edition (Brustad, Al-Batal, and Al-Tonsi 2011) for the presence of the can-do statements at the Novice and Intermediate levels. Since the can-do statements are language functions, they were primarily found in the story of Maha and Khaled, the dialogues (*al-ḥiwārāt*), and other authentic or semiauthentic audiovisual and written material in the textbooks. For exam-ple, the can-do statement "I can write simple statements about where I live" was listed as corresponding to the first chapter of *Al-Kitaab*, Part One, where Maha explains that she lives in Brooklyn, New York.

After analyzing the textbooks in light of the can-do statements, there were two categories of can-do statements that needed to be addressed: those included in the NCSSFL–ACTFL can-do statements but not present in the textbooks and those that were present in the textbooks but not in the NCSSFL–ACTFL list (which is not meant to be exhaustive). For each can-do statement missing from *Al-Kitaab*, the decision was made to either add it to the curriculum using supplemental materials or to reject it as inappropriate for a college-level class. An example of a can-do added to the textbook was "I can ask for directions to a place," which was added in *Alif Baa* chapter 6. An example of a can-do rejected was "I can follow along with simple arithmetic problems when I can see the figures," as this seemed irrelevant to an introductory university class. Can-do statements present in *Al-Kitaab*, such as "I can respond to bad news," based on the dialogue in chapter 7, were added to the list of can-do statements that formed the curriculum. These can-do statements were then sequenced into the lessons for each day in the first-year Arabic curriculum.[3]

Materials Development

Once the can-dos were sequenced, the next step was to develop materials using these can-do statements and the theories informing genre-based curricula. Specifically, students needed examples of these can-do statements to analyze activities to scaffold their analysis of these texts, and activities encouraging them to create their own versions of the texts. Finding example texts proved to be the most challenging step, as locating authentic examples of the can-do statements accessible to first-year students was at times impossible, given the time constraints of the semester. As a result, we frequently relied on the authentic and semiauthentic materials in *Al-Kitaab* as examples of the can-dos or developed our own semiauthentic materials. Authentic materials we did find included items such as Coca-Cola and Fanta advertisements and a website that advertises vacation packages. Materials from *Al-Kitaab* included the story of Maha and Khaled, reading passages pulled from websites and newspapers, additional listening drills from Arab TV or recorded by members of Maha's family, and the dialogue (*al-ḥiwār*) videos in the textbook.

Lesson Plans

Daily lesson plans were developed around one or more can-do statements with a framework of guided, at-home textual analysis followed by a presentation, practice, evaluation format in class. This section describes the framework for developing the lesson plans, and specific examples using this framework are included in the section "Sample Lesson Plans," below. For the at-home analysis, students watched or read an example of the targeted can-do statement (itself listed on the homework schedule) and completed an activity asking basic comprehension questions (in addition to other homework). In class, the can-do statement was addressed through a presentation, practice, evaluation scheme. The presentation portion typically lasted two to ten minutes and involved reviewing the can-do statement, the text students had worked with at home, and any related grammar or vocabulary they had studied at home. During the practice part of the lesson, students completed an activity that allowed them to create their own versions of the can-do statement. For example, they might interview other students using a chart organizer or perform a skit or write a postcard. Finally, the evaluation portion of the lesson allowed students to demonstrate their ability to "do" the can-do statement and also provided an opportunity for the instructors to evaluate students' abilities. For the evaluation, students might write about the classmate they interviewed, answer questions about a skit, or read each other's postcards and respond. Students were not formally graded on this activity, but the instructor's assessment of their abilities (yes, no, sort of) was recorded in a spreadsheet. The sample lesson plans discussed below provide further information on the implementation of this framework.

Dialect Integration

Focusing on the can-do statements provided a context that allowed for the natural incorporation of sociolinguistic information relevant to particular language functions. While this frequently focused on the imperfect distinction of spoken versus written genres, having a specific context made it easier to draw students' attention to the language sociolinguistically appropriate in that context. Although the dialect focus of the class was Egyptian, all dialects were welcomed, and students who preferred to use other dialects were permitted to do so for their homework or in class. For example, one heritage student often used his own Gulf dialect in assignments, and another student frequently chose to watch the Levantine videos and use this dialect. Furthermore, since the focus of the elementary class was encouraging students to use Arabic of any variety, students were allowed to write in Colloquial Arabic and speak in MSA, although the instructors would indicate which variety might be more appropriate for the situation. However, students were not penalized on formal assessments such as tests or presentations for using a variety of Arabic inappropriate to the situation.

Sample Lesson Plans

To give a more concrete idea of how these lessons organized around the NCSSFL–ACTFL can-do statements worked in practice, I discuss several examples below. These examples include a lesson using the *Al-Kitaab* story as an example of a can-do statement, a lesson using the *Al-Kitaab* dialogue as an example of a can-do statement, a lesson using instructor produced semiau-thentic materials, and a lesson using authentic materials.

Example 1: I can talk about jobs and career plans

The can-do statement "I can talk about jobs and career plans" was matched to the lesson 12 *Al-Kitaab* story, where Muhammad Abu al-ᶜila talks about his career and his decision to stay in the United States after finishing his PhD. Prior to class, the students watched this video in Egyptian Arabic and com-pleted the corresponding drill for homework, which asked basic comprehen-sion questions about the video. In class, the presentation phase consisted of watching the video and then arranging the scrambled sentences of the story in order in small groups. The practice phase involved discussing in small groups a difficult decision supplied by the teacher, such as "the decision between a job that has a lot of vacations and a job that has a high salary." The evaluation phase consisted of a written summary of the decision the group had made and their reasons. This setup also allowed students to discuss the same information (a difficult career decision) in both speaking (their initial discussion) and writing (the summary). By repeating the same task in both spoken and written genres in the same class period, it was possible to remind students of the suitability of using dialect to discuss their decision and then MSA to write about it. For further practice, students read and commented on their peers' writing.[4]

Example 2: I can respond to bad news

The can-do statement "I can respond to bad news" was not in the original NCSSFL–ACTFL list but was added based on material in the textbook. This can-do statement occurs in the dialogue in chapter 7 of *Al-Kitaab*, where two women discuss the news of a car accident. Students watched the dialogue at home in Egyptian Arabic and completed the corresponding drill as part of their homework before class. The presentation portion of the lesson consisted of reviewing and discussing the video. A review of the standard phrases used to respond to bad news (which the students had also studied at home in prepa-ration) was also included. Each phrase was displayed on the screen, and stu-dents were asked for scenarios in which they would use this phrase. The practice section of the lesson involved students calling each other on Skype (mimicking the telephone call in the video) to give each other various pieces of bad news and practice responding using these key phrases. Students could create their own bad news or use phrases supplied by the teacher such as "my cousin is very sick and went to the hospital." To emphasize that bad news would most likely be related in dialect, the phrases supplied by the teacher were written in Egyptian dialect. This practice activity doubled as the evaluation—as the instructor moved around the classroom listening to and assisting students on their calls, it provided an opportunity to assess whether they could respond to bad news appropriately. Immediately after the class, the teacher recorded her opinion of whether students were able to do this can-do statement in the spreadsheet.[5]

Example 3: I can buy a ticket

The can-do statement "I can buy a ticket" is an example of a can-do statement that was included in the NCSSFL–ACTFL can-do statements but was not in the textbook. It was added to chapter 7 of *Al-Kitaab*. Within the time constraints of the semester, it was not possible to find an authentic and accessible video, so we recorded our own example of this genre in Egyptian dialect because buying a ticket is a language function that would typically be performed in dialect.[6] Notably, while this video does contain a ticket exchange, it is also clearly geared toward our students, as demonstrated by the finger gestures to help explain the number of tickets and the price, and the inclusion of a joke about one of the teachers' favorite actors. The presentation part of this lesson involved presenting the can-do statement, the word for ticket, and a review of negation in MSA and Egyptian dialect. In the practice part of the lesson, students were asked to prepare a skit that involved buying a ticket based on the video. The evaluation portion was the performance of the skit, and the instructor recorded her evaluation in the spreadsheet following the class.[7]

Example 4: I can write a postcard message

The can-do statement "I can write a postcard message" was included in the NCSSFL–ACTFL can-do statements but not in *Al-Kitaab*. It was added in chapter 12, which contains information in the *Al-Kitaab* story on the Abu al-ᶜila family's upcoming vacation to Egypt and is an example of how we used genre-based pedagogy to incorporate authentic materials into the classroom. In the presentation part of class, students were introduced to the can-do statement and vocabulary related to trips (e.g., ticket, reservation, five-star). Students were then directed to a travel website to read about package vacations to various places.[8] To scaffold their understanding of the site and help them plan their trip, they were given an organizer that asked them to find specific information such as the price, hotel, and daily program. In the evaluation portion of this lesson, they used this organizer to help write a postcard about this trip to their classmates. Because postcards are a highly variable genre in terms of MSA and dialect use, students were encouraged to write these postcards as they liked. Although following the theories of genre-based pedagogy exactly would have had the students analyze actual postcards rather than websites about packaged trips, it was not possible to find these sources, and this lesson did allow them to incorporate authentic information into their postcards.[9]

Assessments

As noted earlier, students were not formally evaluated on the evaluation portion of each lesson plan. However, the formal assessments were also based on the can-do statements, including tests, blogs, presentations, and the final exam. Students completed five blog assignments throughout the semester that asked them to demonstrate their ability to do a particular can-do statement, such as describing their daily routine or the schedule of an event. The can-do statements were also incorporated into a section of each test. For example, one test included a section on filling out information related to an identification card (I can understand what is asked for on an ID card) and another required them to read short biographies to justify their choice of a potential suitor for Khaled (I can give basic biographical information about others).

At the end of the semester, students completed an oral presentation and a final exam with speaking, reading, listening, and writing sections. All of the can-do statements covered in the semester were included in at least one part of these evaluations.[10]

Challenges and Developments

As this description of the initial development shows, there were numerous challenges in implementing a genre-based curriculum in the Elementary Arabic classroom, especially in terms of finding authentic examples of the genres for students to analyze. Nevertheless, it was successful for teaching Arabic generally and also for integrating the teaching of MSA and dialect. We are continuing to refine the curriculum and develop it at higher levels.

In the next section, I analyze student data to evaluate the genre-based curriculum in terms of teaching sociolinguistic awareness and integrating the teaching of dialect and MSA.

The Development of Sociolinguistic Competence

This section analyzes first-year Arabic students' development of sociolinguistic competence in the first year of this curriculum.

Participants

The participants in this study were enrolled in the second semester of first-year Arabic (Arabic 112). They attended class five days a week and were invited to participate in the research project by giving permission for their classwork to be analyzed for research purposes. Fourteen of the nineteen students enrolled in Arabic 112 consented to participate. One of the participating students was a heritage learner from the Arab Gulf region and another was a nontraditional student who had lived for several years in a North African country.

Data

The data analyzed for this project were students' final oral presentations, the writing section of the final exam, and their final grades on the entire exam. Since this data was collected at the end of the first year, it represents the culmination of the first year curriculum. It also represents both written and oral production, an important—albeit imperfect—distinction in the use of MSA and dialect. The oral presentation asked students to prepare a short recorded presentation for their classmates on one of five topics drawn from the can-do statements covered throughout the semester. The final writing consisted of two prompts (one of at least one hundred words, and one of at least seventy-five words). For each prompt, students could choose between one of two options. All four options were based on the can-do statements covered in the semester. The final exam score was used as a measure of their overall language abilities, since the exam included reading, listening, writing, and speaking sections and covered all of the can-do statements targeted in the semester. Any variety of Arabic was accepted on the exam, and students were not marked higher or lower based on the instructor's assessment of their ability to use MSA and dialect appropriately.

Analysis

To analyze the data, the writing prompts and the presentations were transcribed into searchable texts (from scans for the writing and recordings for the presentations). Word frequency lists were generated for each text using the MAXDictio program.[11] Using this frequency list, all lexical, morphosyntactical, and phonological elements that could vary between Egyptian Arabic (EA) and MSA were selected. An example of a lexical element that could vary is the word for "also, too" realized as *kamān* in EA and *ayḍan* in MSA. An example of a lexical element that could not vary is the word for "book" (*kitāb*). An example of a morphosyntactical element that could vary is the future tense, which is marked by *ḥ/h-* in Egyptian dialect and *s-/sawfa* in MSA. An example of a morphosyntactical element that could not vary is the use of the definite article *al-*. An example of a phonological element that could vary is the Arabic letter *jīm*, realized as [g] in EA and [ʒ] in MSA. An example of a phonological element that could not vary is the Arabic letter *bā'*, realized as [b] in both Egyptian and MSA. On average, about 25 percent to 30 percent of the words in the student texts could vary.

For each word that could vary, it was documented whether students used the EA or MSA variant, and this resulted in a total number of MSA elements and EA elements in the text. The number of EA elements in the text was divided by the number of elements that could possibly vary to give a percentage of EA in the document. For example, one student's oral presentation contained a total of 237 words, 79 of which could vary between MSA and EA. He used the MSA variant in 63 of these instances and the EA variant in 16. This resulted in an EA percentage of 20 percent for the oral presentation.[12] Although MSA and dialect are sometimes portrayed as completely separate systems, only about 25 percent to 30 percent of the words on average had the possibility of varying between MSA and EA in these students' texts.

Results

Table 7.1 contains individual results, means, and standard deviations for the percentages of EA in the presentations and writing prompts; the difference in EA use between these two texts; and the final exam grades. These results show that, overall, students used similar amounts of EA on the writing (27 percent) and the presentations (21 percent). However, the standard deviations are quite large, indicating that there is considerable variation among students, as the individual student scores also demonstrate. While students such as Mike and Dan used considerably more EA on the presentations, others such as Ken and Ella used much more EA on the writing prompt.[13] While the former choice demonstrates developing sociolinguistic competence through the use of EA and MSA to distinguish between spoken and written genres, the reverse seems to directly contradict sociolinguistic expectations. However, the students' final exam scores also varied considerably, indicating variation in their overall language abilities. For this reason, further analyses were conducted to examine the relationship between sociolinguistic competence and overall Arabic proficiency.

Correlational Analysis

The first analysis was a correlation conducted between students' final exam scores and the difference between their use of EA in the presentation and final exam. If sociolinguistic competence develops along with general linguistic competence, it might be expected that more EA use on the presentation than

Table 7.1 Comparison of writing, presentations, and final grades

Student[a]	EA Writing (%)	EA Presentation (%)	Difference	Final Grade[b]
Aaron	48	20	-27	67
Alice	13	22	9	103
Carrie	61	0	-61	84
Dan	25	64	39	101
Ella	63	33	-29	79
Jalal	4	12	8	101
Ken	50	26	-24	57
Mark	22	21	-1	89
Mary	8	3	-5	96
Mike	4	45	41	106
Rachel	4	5	1	105
Rob[c]	15			85
Sandy[c]	28			75
Tammy	6	0	-6	56
Mean	26	21	-5	87
SD	23	19	27	18

[a] All names are pseudonyms.
[b] Students received extra credit for turning in a practice exam, which explains why some scores are over 100.
[c] Students' presentations were not recorded due to technology failure.

on the writing prompts would correlate with higher exam scores. This turned out to be a strong and statistically significant correlation, $r = .584$, p (one-tailed) $= .023$.[14]

Individual Analysis

Given the small sample size as well as the existence of students who scored well on the exam but used more dialect in the writing prompts, it was necessary to look more closely at the individual results. In terms of their use of EA on the presentation compared to the exam, students fell into three groups: students who used more EA in the presentation ($n = 4$), students who used roughly equal amounts of EA and MSA in the presentation and writing section ($n = 4$), and students who used more EA in the writing prompts ($n = 4$).

In terms of sociolinguistic competence, it was expected that students would use more EA on the presentation (a spoken genre) than the writing prompts. Thus, it is not surprising that all four of the students who used more EA in the presentation (Mike, Dan, Alice, and Jalal) scored highly on the final exam. These students' results support the fact that students are developing sociolinguistic competence through the genre-based curriculum and that this competence parallels overall linguistic competence.

Of the four students who used roughly equal amounts of EA and MSA, three simply used very little EA in either the presentation or the written exam (less than 8 percent). Two of these students, Rachel and Mary, scored highly on the exam, indicating that their overall language proficiency was nevertheless high. While it is impossible to know exactly what guided their choices, one explanation of these results is that they viewed both the writing prompts and the presentation as formal assessments, and this guided their choice to use predominantly MSA on both. The other student, Tammy, scored poorly on the final exam (partially due to her decision to answer the listening section entirely in English). While it is possible that Tammy was guided by the same decisions as Rachel and Mary, it is worth noting that she was extremely resistant to learning EA throughout the semester. This is an instance where the need to consider learner agency and social identity is clear: even in classroom situations where Tammy was guided to use EA due to its sociolinguistic appropriateness, she resisted, drawing upon her experience living in a North African Arabic-speaking country (during which time she did not speak Arabic) to state that all Arabs spoke MSA and she did not like EA. Finally, there is the case of Mark, who used 21 percent to 22 percent EA on both his writing prompts and his presentation. While this is more EA than Rachel and Mary, he too may have felt that these situations called for similar language levels since they were both final assessments.

The fact that three of the students who used more EA in the writing prompts than the presentation also scored poorly on the final exam supports the idea that sociolinguistic competence develops along with overall linguistic competence. Examples 1 and 2, below, demonstrate the contrast in writing skills between Ken, a low-scoring student who used considerably more EA in his writing, and Mike, a high-scoring student who used considerably more EA in his presentation. Both students were writing about their daily routine, and while both passages contain linguistic errors, Ken's passage contains several incomprehensible runs in comparison to Mike's passage.

Example 1. Ken's routine

في السيمستر الدبح رانا عني الفصل خلمسن إأنا لازم أروح ألنع كثيراً .أنا صبحأ في اساء ٧ في صبح .بعدّ دنلك ، أنا أروح في الفصل للتريخ في اساء ٩ في صبح.

Example 2. Mike's routine

في هذا الفصل الدراسي برنامج اليومي كان غريب قليلا لانني لا عندي نفس البرنامج كل اليوم فعادة أصحو من النوم حوالي الساعة السابعة والنصف ثم أفطر مع نفسي وأشرب قهوة كثيرا لانني لا أحبّ النوم.

However, there was also a student who used more EA on the writing but scored relatively high on the final exam, Carrie. While at first this seems to contradict the pattern of sociolinguistic competence paralleling linguistic competence, a closer look at Carrie's writing prompts reveals that this may not be the case. She chose to write about her daily routine and a postcard. The postcard prompt contained 71 percent EA, and since a postcard is a fairly informal writing event, this could actually be a sign of sociolinguistic awareness compared to the 0 percent EA used in her presentation. In contrast, the prompt describing her routine contained only 57 percent EA. While this is still high, seven out of twelve of the EA elements in the prompt were the result of her choice to write times and dates in EA (*as-sā^ca sitta* "six o'clock") rather than MSA (*as-sā^ca as-sādisa*). Whether this choice was guided by sociolinguistics or ease of use, it is clear that despite her unusual results, Carrie was also developing sociolinguistic competence, and this is one reason why the speaking/writing distinction is imperfect as a measure of sociolinguistic awareness.

Discussion

The data analyzed in this chapter provides compelling evidence that when exposed to opportunities to approach Arabic diglossia via genre-based pedagogies, students' sociolinguistic competence develops along with their overall linguistic competence. Although this result is not particularly surprising, it demonstrates that following an integrated approach of teaching both MSA and dialect in the classroom can support students' understanding of Arabic diglossia and guide them to make sociolinguistically appropriate choices. Although the genre-based curriculum described here remains under development, the initial iteration demonstrates that this is a promising method for addressing these issues. The remainder of this chapter outlines the implications of this research for the ongoing development of genre-based Arabic curricula as well as recommendations for future research.

Curriculum Development

As noted earlier, further development of this Arabic curriculum will require finding more authentic or even semiauthentic examples of the can-do statements for students to analyze. Despite the fact that an integrated approach was used in the classroom rather than a more traditional MSA-only approach, students' overall use of dialect remained quite low. Even in cases when students were actively trying to use dialect, they rarely exceeded an EA percentage of 50 percent to 60 percent. Although data of native speakers performing these can-do statements in authentic contexts is needed to confirm this statement, this seems quite low for many of the everyday interactional situations covered by the can-do statements at the Novice and Intermediate levels. Thus, while finding authentic materials that provide examples of these can-do statements is challenging and time consuming, students' low levels of dialect use overall indicate the importance of pursuing this goal.

However, this also addresses a common reservation about using integrated approaches to teach Arabic—the impact of this approach on students' MSA abilities. The results of this study indicate that this should not be a concern because the majority of students, and especially those with higher level language abilities, were able to express themselves using predominantly MSA. In fact, it is their abilities in dialect that need to be further developed if they are to be proficient in both varieties and gain the sociolinguistic competence to switch between them.

Future Research

The limitations of this study also raise a number of issues that should be addressed in subsequent research on this topic. While this study delivers promising results for the impact of a genre-based curriculum in developing sociolinguistic awareness in Arabic, it focuses solely on a small group of learners in their first year of Arabic. Since two of the main arguments for using a genre-based curriculum are the ability to link upper- and lower-division classes and to develop students with advanced levels of proficiency during an undergraduate degree, it is important to continue this research at higher levels of Arabic. This will allow for insights into students' future development of sociolinguistic competence and the proficiency levels they can reach.

Furthermore, it is clear that the distinction between spoken and written genres is imperfect for both curricular development and research analysis, and it is important to look more closely at the actual context, particularly in terms of perceived or actual interlocutors and learner agency. Future research should address these issues in two main ways. First, it would be useful to examine the authentic and semiauthentic materials that students are exposed to using the same technique used to analyze EA and MSA percentages in this chapter. The percentages found in these materials can then become instructional targets. Even if they vary wildly, examining the potential reasons for these discrepancies can lead students to a greater understanding of the diglossic situation in Arabic and the complicated relationships between context and speaker agency. Second, it would be useful to collect student production data throughout the semester to track ongoing developments in sociolinguistic awareness. Although in the current study the instructors recorded their impressions of students' abilities to complete the can-do statements throughout the semester, this rarely included production data and did not include data specifically relating to sociolinguistic competence. Adding analysis of both the input that students received as well as their ongoing development across multiple levels of the curriculum would paint a clearer and more complete picture of their language acquisition.

However, in including and analyzing authentic materials as instructional goals in terms of increasing sociolinguistic awareness, the agency of individual speakers must also be taken into account, both for native speakers and for learners. Although there are conventions for the use of MSA and dialect by native speakers, it is also the case that speakers sometimes choose to deliberately flout these conventions for particular interactional goals or to establish specific social identities. For example, news broadcasts are typically considered the domain of MSA. However, in an episode of Al-Jazeera I watched that included an interview with a poet who wrote in Colloquial Arabic, he insisted upon speaking in his dialect despite the interviewer's urging him to speak in MSA. In an episode of BBC Arabic, I once heard the newscaster, who typically speaks only MSA even when interviewees use Colloquial Arabic, switch to Colloquial Arabic when interviewing a woman who had been imprisoned for prostitution and had given birth in jail. This choice seemed to indicate the newscaster's desire to make an interviewee in a delicate situation feel at ease. Similarly, it cannot be assumed that learners merely want to mimic the language of native speakers; they, too, exert agency and may resist conventional sociolinguistic practices to better display their own identities or language learning goals (e.g., van Compernolle and Williams 2012; Kinginger and Farrell 2004). While it is crucial to develop students' sociolinguistic awareness so they will recognize when their language is unconventional, there must also be a place in the classroom for them to exert their individual agency even if it is through unconventional sociolinguistics.

Overall, it is clear that using genre-based pedagogies to integrate the teaching of MSA and dialect in the classroom is a promising method that helps develop students' sociolinguistic awareness. Continued curricular development and future research will add to our knowledge about this type of pedagogy and its impact on the development of sociolinguistic competence. In turn, this will allow Arabic programs to produce students with sociolinguistic competencies that match their overall language abilities, a goal that many programs have historically struggled to accomplish.

References

Allen, Heather Willis. 2009. "A Literacy-Based Approach to the Advanced French Writing Course." *French Review* 83: 368–85.

Arens, Katherine. 2008. "Genres and the Standards: Teaching the 5 C's through Texts." *The German Quarterly* 8: 35–48.

Barrette, Catherine M., Kate Paesani, and Kimberly Vinall. 2010. "Toward an Integrated Curriculum: Maximizing the Use of Target Language Literature." *Foreign Language Annals* 43: 216–30.

Bassiouney, Reem. 2009. *Arabic Sociolinguistics*. Washington, DC: Georgetown University Press.

Bayley, Robert, and Vera Regan. 2004. "Introduction: The Acquisition of Sociolinguistic Competence." *Journal of Sociolinguistics* 8: 323–38.

Brustad, Kristen, Mahmoud Al-Batal, and Abbas Al-Tonsi. 2010. *Alif Baa: Introduction to Arabic Letters and Sounds*, 3rd ed. Washington, DC: Georgetown University Press.

———. 2011. *Al-Kitaab fii Taᶜallum al-ᶜArabiyya: A Textbook for Beginning Arabic*, Part One, 3rd ed. Washington, DC: Georgetown University Press.

Byrnes, Heidi. 2002. "The Role of Task and Task-Based Assessment in a Content-Oriented Collegiate Foreign Language Curriculum." *Language Testing* 19: 419–37.

———. 2006. "A Semiotic Perspective on Culture and Foreign Language Teaching: Implications for Collegiate Materials Development." In *Language and Culture out of Bounds: Discipline-Blurred Perspectives on the Foreign Language Classroom*, edited by Vicki Galloway and Bettina Cothran, 37–66. Boston, MA: Heinle Thomson.

———. 2008. "Articulating a Foreign Language Sequence through Content: A Look at the Culture Standards." *Language Teaching* 41: 103–18.

Byrnes, Heidi, Cori Crane, Hiram H. Maxim, and Katherine A. Sprang. 2006. "Taking Text to Task: Issues and Choices in Curriculum Construction." *International Journal of Applied Linguistics* 152: 85–109.

Dewaele, Jean-Marc. 2004. "The Acquisition of Sociolinguistic Competence in French as a Foreign Language: An Overview." *French Language Studies* 14: 301–19.

Gee, James Paul. 2002. "Literacies, Identities, and Discourses." In *Developing Advanced Literacy in First and Second Languages: Meaning with Power*, edited by Mary J. Schleppegrell and M. Cecilia Colombi, 159–75. Mahwah, NJ: Lawrence Erlbaum.

Halliday, Michael A. K., and Christian M. I. M. Matthiessen. 2013. *Halliday's Introduction to Functional Grammar*. New York: Routledge.

Holes, Clive. 2004. *Modern Arabic: Structures, Functions, and Varieties*. Washington, DC: Georgetown University Press.

Howard, Martin, Isabelle Lemée, and Vera Regan. 2006. "The L2 Acquisition of a Phonological Variable: The Case of /l/ deletion in French." *Journal of French Language Studies* 16: 1–24.

Kern, Richard. 2008. "Making Connections through Texts in Language Teaching." *Language Teaching* 41: 367–87.

Kern, Richard, and Jean Marie Schultz. 2005. "Beyond Orality: Investigating Literacy and the Literary in Second and Foreign Language Instruction." *Modern Language Journal* 89: 381–92.

Kinginger, Celeste, and Kathleen Farrell. 2004. "Assessing Development of Meta-Pragmatic Awareness in Study Abroad." *Frontiers: The Interdisciplinary Journal of Study Abroad* 10: 19–42.

Martin, James R. 1997. "Analysing Genre: Functional Parameters," In *Genre and Institutions: Social Processes in the Workplace and School*, edited by Francis Christie and James R. Martin, 3–39. New York: Continuum.

———. 2000. "Design and Practice: Enacting Functional Linguistics." *Annual Review of Applied Linguistics* 20: 116–26.

Maxim, Hiram H. 2002. "A Study into the Feasibility and Effects of Reading Extended Authentic Discourse in the Beginning German Language Classroom." *Modern Language Journal* 86: 20–35.

———. 2006. "Integrating Textual Thinking into the Introductory College-Level Foreign Language Classroom." *Modern Language Journal* 90: 19–32.

Modern Language Association. 2007. "Foreign Languages and Higher Education: New Structures for a Changed World." *Modern Language Association. MLA.* Accessed March 19, 2013. http://www.mla.org/flreport.

Regan, Vera, Martin Howard, and Isabelle Lemée. 2009. *The Acquisition of Sociolinguistic Competence in a Study Abroad Context*. Tonawanda, NY: Multilingual Matters.

Swaffar, Janet. 2006. "Terminology and Its Discontents: Some Caveats about Communicative Competence." *Modern Language Journal* 90: 246–49.

van Compernolle, Rémi A., and Lawrence Williams. 2012. "Reconceptualizing Sociolinguistic Competence as Mediated Action: Identity, Meaning-Making, Agency." *Modern Language Journal* 96: 234–50.

Versteegh, Kees. 1997. *The Arabic Language*. Edinburgh: Edinburgh University Press.

Notes

Additional data and examples are freely available to view and download on this book's product page on the Georgetown University Press (GUP) website (www.press .georgetown.edu).

I would like to thank Heather Sweetser for her assistance with the curriculum development described in this chapter and the student participants for allowing me to analyze their classwork.

1. For more details, see the Department of German at Georgetown University web page, https://german.georgetown.edu/page/1242716500101.html.

2. "NCSSFL-ACTFL Can-Do Statements: Performance Indicators for Language Learners," American Council on the Teaching of Foreign Languages, second printing 2015, http://www.actfl.org/sites/default/files/pdfs/Can-Do_Statements_2015.pdf.

3. For a color-coded draft of these can-do statements, see Item 7.1 on the GUP website.

4. For lesson materials, see folder 7.2 on the GUP website.

5. For lesson materials, see folder 7.3 on the GUP website.

6. For the video, see the link in the lesson plan, in folder 7.4, available on the GUP website.

7. For lesson materials, see folder 7.4 on the GUP website.

8. Travel in Jordan website, http://www.travelinjordan.com/travel-tours.html.

9. For lesson materials, see folder 7.5 on the GUP website.

10. These assessments are included in folder 7.6 on the GUP website.

11. For more details, see the MAXQDA website, http://www.maxqda.com.

12. Table W7.1, on the GUP website, lists these calculations for each student.

13. All names are pseudonyms.

14. The Kolmogorov-Smirnov test indicated that the data were normally distributed. One-tailed correlation was used because the directionality was predicted.

8

An Integrated Moroccan and Modern Standard Arabic Curriculum for First-Year Learners

MIKE TURNER

The University of Texas at Austin

IN THIS CHAPTER I introduce a program for integrating the teaching of Moroccan Arabic dialect materials into a first-year Arabic course that uses the *Al-Kitaab*, 3rd ed., textbook series (Brustad, Al-Batal, and Al-Tonsi 2010; 2011). The need for an integrated curriculum for Moroccan Arabic and Modern Standard Arabic (herein MA and MSA) is a direct outcome of changes that have occurred in the teaching of Arabic as a foreign language landscape in recent years. On one hand, growing acceptance of the "integrated approach" (Al-Batal 1992; Al-Batal and Belnap 2006; Younes 2006), in which colloquial Arabic varieties are taught in tandem with the formal language, has increased demand for such curricula on the whole, regardless of the particular variety that is to be taught. On the other hand, ongoing political instability in Egypt and the Levant, which formerly served as key destinations for study abroad, has led to the emergence of Morocco as one of the premiere sites for language study in the Arab world and, in turn, a focal point on students' radars.

Because communicative proficiency in Arabic should assume knowledge of a colloquial variety, and because Moroccan is increasingly likely to be the variety in which students will have immersive language-learning experiences, it is paramount that effective resources for teaching MA be developed and implemented in as short a time as possible and that this effort should begin now. It is no longer sufficient for Moroccan to be reserved for study-abroad programs or relegated to supplemental courses for advanced students, as has traditionally been the case; it should, rather, assume a proper role as part and parcel of established Arabic programs in the United States. A key task in achieving this goal is making Moroccan pedagogically accessible at the most fundamental of levels—namely, the first year of Arabic language instruction.

Although not without challenges, this task is easily feasible on the whole. The third editions of the *Al-Kitaab* series have already laid much of the theoretical groundwork required to successfully integrate colloquial varieties into the first-year classroom. The series provides all vocabulary in both Egyptian and Levantine Arabic, a complete series of scripted videos for each variety, and various activities for activating and reinforcing the colloquial language both at home and in the classroom. Where this approach has succeeded, there is no need to invent a new method; instead, the most effective use of resources is to model Moroccan materials on those that already exist for other varieties, with effort put toward ensuring contiguity in format and presentation. The program outlined here represents a practical attempt to do precisely that by providing a set of Moroccan colloquial materials that plugs directly into the *Al-Kitaab* curriculum and allows for simultaneous engagement of MA and MSA.

Needs in Teaching Diglossia

The integrated approach, described by Mahmoud Al-Batal (1992) as one in which the various varieties and levels of Arabic are treated as "components of one integrated linguistic system" and explored in depth in this volume, serves as the pedagogical underpinning of the third editions of the *Alif Baa* and *Al-Kitaab* textbooks (2010; 2011). In keeping with the integrated approach, all vocabulary in *Alif Baa* and *Al-Kitaab* is introduced in three varieties: MSA, Levantine, and Egyptian; the expectation is that students in any given course will simultaneously engage both MSA and one of the two colloquial varieties. The colloquial plays a central role in the course as the language of instruction and the primary vehicle for nearly all speaking and most listening activities. Courses that employ *Al-Kitaab* in the way that the authors recommend, then, are heavily dependent on the use of a dialect; in turn, one of the most significant achievements of the textbook is that it provides a substantial set of materials for teaching one within a unified Arabic second-language acquisition framework.

For instructors who wish to use the integrated approach in their Arabic courses, there is a clear solution available today in *Al-Kitaab*. This solution, however, comes with a caveat: it is available only insofar as the instructor chooses to use Egyptian or Levantine as the colloquial variety within the course. Although a trained and competent instructor should be able to instruct first-year students in either variety, to do so is not always optimal. First, instructors' backgrounds should be seen as a resource in its own right; in the case that suitable resources are available, instructors should ideally instruct in the dialect—or one similar to it—with which they are most familiar, to best use their cultural and linguistic knowledge. For instructors whose primary backgrounds are in Moroccan, Algerian, or Tunisian Arabic, being able to instruct in a variety that makes their minimally leveled speech accessible—rather than a more geographically removed dialect—reaffirms to students the value of the instructors' linguistic and cultural experience within the larger Arab cultural context.

It is likewise important to consider practical factors such as the likelihood that students will be able to use the colloquial variety they are learning in real-life situations, particularly in the Arab world itself. Egypt has been a central destination for Arabic study for decades, but the political uncertainty that has troubled the country in the wake of its 2011 revolution means the future of such programs is indeterminate; meanwhile, the possibility of study in Syria will clearly be off the table for many years. Already high-profile programs, such as the Arabic Language Flagship's "capstone" year abroad, have relocated. In the wake of these changes, Morocco is now increasingly likely to be the Arab country that foreign learners of Arabic will visit and MA the variety they will encounter in day-to-day communicative situations. Because the ability to navigate tasks of a practical and personal nature is one of the key skills we hope to impart at the Novice and Intermediate levels, and because many of our students will put these skills to the test with Moroccan native speakers, we are in dire need of materials to teach MA in the first-year integrated classroom.

It is this gap in resources that the curriculum and materials outlined herein seek to fill. Taking the established framework within which the Levantine and Egyptian colloquial varieties are already presented in *Alif Baa* and *Al-Kitaab* and taught in courses that use them, I briefly outline a curriculum for an integrated classroom within which MA is taught in tandem with MSA. I then specifically discuss the design of the Moroccan materials that are currently in development, touching on various theoretical issues that they raise and the solutions that best answer these issues. The goal of this curriculum is to set first-year students on a path toward real Arabic proficiency, where they are able to use their command of both MA and MSA in sociolinguistically appropriate contexts and to develop a skill set that will also allow them to access other varieties with relative ease.

Curriculum Design

The integrated MA and MSA curriculum proposed here assumes a first-year Arabic program that meets for five hours per week, as is common at a number of universities in the United States. It provides materials sufficient for two semesters of instruction at this pace, by the end of which students can be expected to have mastered the material in *Alif Baa* and most of *Al-Kitaab* Part One. The curriculum is informed by a number of policies and philosophies regarding the course objectives, materials, assignments, classroom dynamics, and language use. The guiding principles for each of these aspects are summarized here.

Course Objectives

The primary goal of the course is to establish student's proficiency. Proficiency in Arabic, as first described in the framework put forth by the American Council on the Teaching of Foreign Languages (ACTFL 1989) and more recently updated with Arabic-specific annotations (ACTFL 2012), covers four primary skills: speaking, writing, listening, and reading. Although not codified in the ACTFL guidelines, Thomas Garza (2010) also makes a convincing case that culture should be considered a "fifth skill"; for this reason, the course also seeks to provide cultural learning opportunities commensurate with the other skills. The course seeks to push students toward a balanced mastery of each of these skills at a predictable pace, with the expectation that they will reach the Novice High level by the end of the first semester and Intermediate Low to Intermediate Mid level by the end of the second.

   In the context of this course, where a key component of proficiency is being able to use diglossic varieties in a way that corresponds with sociolinguistic expectations, development of some skills favors the colloquial MA, and development of others favors MSA. Speaking tasks are almost entirely in MA. Listening tasks favor the colloquial but also include exposure to the formal language; similarly, writing tasks favor the formal language but do not discourage students from using the colloquial. Reading tasks are almost entirely in the formal language. At this level, acquisition of cultural knowledge primarily occurs in MA although exposure to some topics (such as religious terms) may call for MSA.

Course Materials

The primary materials for this integrated course are *Alif Baa: Introduction to Letters and Sounds*, 3rd ed. (2010) and *Al-Kitaab fii Taᶜallum al-ᶜArabiyya*, Part One, 3rd ed. (2011), accompanied by the online *Al-Kitaab Moroccan Arabic Supplement*, currently in development and described in greater detail below. Each unit in *Alif Baa* is engaged for two to four contact hours, and each in *Al-Kitaab* Part One is engaged for between seven to twelve contract hours, during which students work inside and outside the classroom to activate and solidify their new vocabulary and their grammatical and cultural knowledge. Additional supplemental resources, particularly listening activities in the forms of songs and videos as well as games and props, are used at the instructor's discretion.

The role of the proposed *Moroccan Arabic Supplement* is significant. On one hand, it simply serves as an alternative to the currently extant online companion website for *Alif Baa* and *Al-Kitaab* Part One, providing all of the same MSA materials and drills. On the other, it significantly expands the content of the companion website by providing a Moroccan counterpart for all audiovisual content types that are, to date, offered in Egyptian and Levantine Arabic, and for extended vocabulary usage notes, grammatical sketches, and cultural addendums that cannot be retroactively added to the printed textbook. The goal of combining the former *Al-Kitaab* Part One companion website with the new materials in a single website is to decrease redundancy and make it easier for students to access homework and assignments.[1]

Assignments

This intensive first-year Arabic course relies heavily on assignments completed outside of class. The five hours of in-class instructional time per week allowed by the course are only sufficient for advancement in the language if they are used effectively as a chance to activate and reinforce learning that has primarily taken place at home. For this reason, most initial exposure to vocabulary and grammatical structures occurs outside of class and with the aid of computer-based audiovisual aids that permit students to hear the material both in isolation and in context. As Dilworth Parkinson (1992) notes, one of the primary advantages of such aids is that they allow students to engage the language at their own pace and at a time of their choosing. This gives each student an opportunity to adequately prepare the language for use in class prior to arriving, regardless of individual differences in learning style.

Assignments meant to be completed outside of class include daily homework, corrections to previous homework, cultural response papers, and preparation for in-class skits and presentations. Daily homework is completed in two formats: either (1) handwritten drills corresponding to material in *Alif Baa*, *Al-Kitaab* Part One or the corresponding *Moroccan Arabic Supplement* or (2) drills directly within the online *Moroccan Arabic Supplement*. Both homework types are graded manually; automated online submissions are checked for appropriate attempts at completion and evaluated holistically.

Classroom Dynamics

Because out-of-class assignments are the primary avenue for introduction of new concepts, the role of actual in-class time is to provide students an opportunity to activate and reinforce vocabulary and structures to which they already have some exposure. For this reason, the curriculum embraces the notion of "the communicative classroom" (Hedge 2011, 57) to push students toward a command of the language that is based first and foremost on its use in accomplishing communicative tasks. Classroom activities are targeted at developing particular skills: a listening activity, for example, may see students approach a video in MA that includes a number of new vocabulary items in multiple stages, with the goal of each stage being to extract a subsequently greater amount of information and to more accurately identify key words and phrases.

Maintaining a communicative environment requires both an appropriate physical setup and instructional philosophy. The classroom should have movable seating that allows the instructor to freely rearrange the classroom on demand, thus enabling various group configurations. Within the communication-based curriculum that this course entails, work with a variety of partners and different groups constitutes a majority of the time spent in class; although the instructor may, as needed, direct activities or clarify linguistic points from the front of the classroom, lecturing for any extended period is to be avoided. This is in keeping with the notion that first encounters with material should take place at home and that the class should allow students to practice their language through situationally appropriate use.

Language Use in the Classroom

The language of classroom instruction itself is MA to as much of a degree as is possible. At the beginning of the first semester, the instructor models this philosophy by presenting common instructions in Moroccan and using them consistently.[2] This instructional language is subsequently expanded, and students are encouraged to adopt Arabic as their default speaking language and to progressively avoid English. By the second semester, a strict rule should be implemented by which neither the students nor the instructor speak any language other than Arabic without asking and obtaining the other party's permission. This policy ensures that students are not only exposed to as much Arabic as possible while in the classroom but also that they develop strategies to communicate even when they do not have a full range of vocabulary at their disposal.

A particularly salient issue regarding language use in this course concerns the place of linguistic diversity, particularly regarding the use of Arabic varieties. In the context of the communicative classroom, particularly where speaking and listening activities are conducted, this choice often defaults to MA, which is the variety the instructor most often models for the students. This does not, however, mean that Moroccan is the only acceptable variety for interaction in the classroom. Instead, a key tenet of the course philosophy is that students are free to produce language in any Arabic variety, and that they are in turn responsible for negotiating communicative situations with other students regardless of the variety those others choose. In short, Moroccan remains the default colloquial variety—a sort of localized lingua franca that all students can be expected to know and fall back on for clarity—but all varieties of Arabic are seen as equally viable vessels for accomplishing communicative tasks.[3]

The Moroccan Supplement

The Moroccan Arabic Supplement for *Alif Baa* and *Al-Kitaab* Part One is a proposed electronic resource that has already been fully prototyped and implemented in a first-year course at the University of Texas at Austin; its primary goal is to enable simultaneous instruction in MA and MSA. The materials envisioned here represent a refined version of the *Moroccan Arabic Supplement*, which functions as a standalone alternative to the currently extant companion websites for *Alif Baa* and *Al-Kitaab* Part One. The proposed Moroccan site combines the functionality of the companion website, specifically its MSA material and automated drills, with the newly developed Moroccan materials. The latter set of materials and the rationale under which they are constructed are the focus of the next section.

Supplement Design

The *Moroccan Arabic Supplement* is ultimately a website, a series of web pages organized into thematic units that correspond with those present in the *Alif Baa* and *Al-Kitaab* Part One textbooks. Robert Blake (2013, 41) lists a number of advantages in using such a format, arguing that "web pages can include sound files that harness a sensorial channel lacking in books" and that "sound files increase the prospects of building lasting mental images for words and phrases in a phonological, semantic, and even aesthetic context." Regarding the new Moroccan materials, one of the main uses of this advantage is to present vocabulary accompanied by a recording of each new term. The same principle of embedded media also allows students to use the supplement to watch videos, including a themed story that follows the lives of two young Moroccans while incorporating acquired vocabulary and grammatical structures.

One of the most important design factors for the *Moroccan Arabic Supplement* is a need for contiguity with the printed textbook it is designed to accompany. Several steps are taken to ensure that students can easily move between the two sources. One of the most basic of these involves the system of color coding each variety, in which the scheme presented in *Al-Kitaab* Part One—where blue is used for MSA, purple for Levantine, green for Egyptian, and black for items shared between all varieties—is replicated and expanded to accommodate the new Moroccan materials. The color chosen for Moroccan is orange, which is easily contrastive and not used for other varieties or for styling of headings of subheadings. This scheme allows students to easily recognize the variety in use. Students viewing the website, for example, see two distinctly Moroccan vocabulary items that are presented in orange, contrasting with their MSA counterparts in blue. Meanwhile, two other items, for which no colloquial variants exist, are given in black.[4]

Beyond the color scheme, other steps are taken to approximate the look and feel of *Al-Kitaab* and interface the online Moroccan components with the printed textbook. A system of headings and subheadings is maintained, along with recognizable icons that indicate the availability of audiovisual media within a given section. A familiar layout of rows and columns is also used to present vocabulary, with MSA terms given on the right, colloquial items in the center, and an English gloss on the left. In addition, because much of the material in the Moroccan supplement corresponds with particular sections of the textbook, a page reference number (visible in the top left corner) is provided for each section, allowing students to move between the two resources with ease and compare material in other colloquial varieties if they desire.

Content Development

Although a well-considered design is paramount to the efficacy of the *Moroccan Arabic Supplement*, its content is what propels day-to-day instruction. Here the same principle of contiguity applies: specifically, where *Alif Baa* or *Al-Kitaab* Part One provide a particular set of materials for Egyptian or Levantine colloquial, the supplement should provide an equivalent set in Moroccan. There are several different categories of content types in this regard, each of which demands its own considerations. For the purposes of this chapter, they are (1) **vocabulary**, or the most basic presentation of words and meanings; (2) **grammatical sketches**, or explanations of how given linguistic categories behave; (3) **standalone audiovisual aids**, meaning audio or video recordings meant to activate particular structures but not thematically related to each other; (4) a **themed story**, or series of interconnected audiovisual aids that feature the same characters; and (5) **cultural addendums**, meaning sections and notes that expand explicitly on facets of Moroccan culture beyond what is contained in the other sections. At least one instance of each content type generally occurs in each unit.

Vocabulary

Effective acquisition of vocabulary represents the most basic building block of a communicative curriculum. Al-Batal (2006, 332) calls it "the most important challenge that learners of Arabic face" and advocates that it should play a central role in all aspects of teaching the language, including in materials design. Recognizing vocabulary's key role in developing competency in in Arabic, every unit of *Alif Baa* and *Al-Kitaab* Part One is headed by a new vocabulary chart; the Moroccan supplement in turn does the same. Because learning to perceive and produce spoken words is a fundamental part of knowing vocabulary, every item in every vocabulary chart in the supplement has a corresponding sound file that allows the student to hear and mimic its pronunciation. This allows a learner to approach vocabulary at a self-directed pace, listening to each item as many times as needed, and to draw connections between etymologically related items in MSA and Moroccan, which are presented side by side. In any column headed by an audio icon, clicking on a vocabulary item results in immediate playback of the associated recording.[5]

The choice of Moroccan vocabulary and how to present it raises two main theoretical issues, both of which are addressed consistently throughout the supplement. The first of these is how to represent the phonology of Moroccan items in the Arabic script consistently; the second is how to select representative Moroccan vocabulary items while balancing between transparency with MSA and accurate representation of the dialect, which has a good deal of intradialectical variation and several ubiquitous foreign loanwords.

As a starting point, it is critical that materials designed for an integrated approach to Arabic teaching represent the colloquial variety—here, Moroccan—in Arabic script. Not only is this in keeping with the strategy adopted in *Al-Kitaab* Part One, 3rd ed., upon which the Moroccan supplement is modeled, but it allows students to practice reading and writing the script in more contexts, and highlights the similarities between the colloquial and standard language. There are two main challenges in representing Moroccan in Arabic script. The simpler of these involves the question of how to represent consonants while maintaining transparency with MSA, an issue that affects Egyptian and Levantine materials as well. A more complex and distinct issue is the representation of the Moroccan vowel system, for which length—unlike in other varieties—is not distinctive and short vowels can be seen not as phonemic but rather epenthetic (Boudlal 2009).[6] While seeking to mirror the *Al-Kitaab* strategy as much as possible, the guiding principle for Arabic script representations of Moroccan is that they are partially logographic, prioritizing transparency with MSA over a fully accurate representation of the phonology, which is more precisely given in the accompanying recordings.

In representing consonants, the *Moroccan Arabic Supplement* follows the lead of *Al-Kitaab* in most regards. Where Moroccan has lost the distinction between two letters that are present in the standard language—as is the case with *tāʾ/thāʾ, dāl/dhāl*, and *ḍāḍ/ẓāʾ*—the form that most closely approximates the standard pronunciation is used; thus, MSA ثانوي (secondary) is given as ثانوي in Moroccan. Where Moroccan has split a sound represented by a single letter in MSA into two different sounds, on the other hand, the orthography represents the sound etymologically. This means that both قهوة and قال are written with a letter *qāf*, although the former is pronounced /qhwa/ and the latter /gal/; the same is true of the *jīm* in جدة and جلس, respectively /jdda/ and /gls/. The advantage of this approach is that it makes historical etymological links between both varieties readily apparent; at the same time, it requires that students rely on the audio recordings for exact pronunciations.

In representing vowels, the supplement likewise seeks first and foremost to maintain transparency with the consonantal skeleton of MSA. Although Moroccan does not have the same long/short vowel system that MSA does, all of the etymologically long vowels in Moroccan are pronounced as "full" vowels, thus they are written in the Arabic transcriptions. Since the /a/ in /daṛ/, for example, is etymologically long, the word is written as دار. The short vowels present in MSA cognates can undergo one of two fates in Moroccan. In most cases, they lose phonemic status entirely; in these cases, they are simply not represented (e.g., /ktb/ is written كتب, with no attempt to give the epenthetic [ə] of the surface form [ktəb]). The other possible case, usually seen with recent borrowings from MSA, is that the short vowels will be realized as full vowels, equal in length to etymologically long vowels. In such cases the short vowel is written so that a word like /ḥadita/ is transcribed حادِتة, even with the understanding that the /a/ vowel and /i/ vowel are functionally equal in length. Once again, with the help of recordings, this compromise allows students to develop a tentative understanding of the differences in sound systems between varieties while drawing connections between shared vocabulary items.

The second theoretical issue in determining the presentation of vocabulary involves the selection of individual items, particularly when multiple options may be suitable. Here the supplement seeks to strike a balance, highlighting the similarities between MSA and Moroccan while remaining truthful to the language as it is actually used. As with other dialect groups, there is a good deal of intradialectical variation within Moroccan (see Heath 2002). At the same time, an argument can be made for the existence of an increasingly prominent Moroccan "koine" (see Maas 2000), modeled largely on the speech of Casablanca and used throughout the country; it is this subvariety from which vocabulary is drawn unless there is a specific pedagogical justi-fication in using a different term. Admittedly, there are some items for which variation is so ubiquitous that it is hard to identify a "standard" form (e.g., /faš/, /mlli/, /mnin/, all [when]). In these cases, one item is simply chosen and used consistently (/faš/). Finally, regarding loanwords, particularly from French, the supplement treats ubiquitous loans as normal colloquial vocabu-lary items and renders them accordingly in Arabic script.

Figure 8.1, which gives Moroccan equivalents of the first five vocabulary items in lesson 7 of *Al-Kitaab* Part One, highlights these various solutions in action.[7] The first row gives an example of a Moroccan item, لۆّلة, for which the consonant skeleton is distinct from that of the MSA أولى and is represented accordingly. The second row gives two items that are essentially the same except the dental letter *thāʾ*, which is instead pronounced as *tāʾ* in Moroccan. The third row shows an item for which the standard colloquial item is etymo-logically unrelated to the MSA term and is simply given as is. In the fourth row, two colloquial items are presented: one, حادِثة, closely approximates the

الْمُفْرَدات Vocabulary 🎧

المعنى	◀ المغربية	◀ الفصحى
first (adj.)	لۆّلة / لّوّل	أُولى (مؤنث) (مذكر: أُوّل)
secondary (also referring to high school)	تانوي/ة	ثانَوِيّ/ة
crazy	حمق / حمّاق	مَجنون ج. مَجانين
accident	حادْثة ج. حَوادْث / كسيدة ج. كْسايد	حادِث ج. حَوادِث
saddening, distressing *	تايقْلّق	مُحزِن

Figure 8.1 Presentation of vocabulary items

MSA term but with some pronunciation differences; the other, كسيدة, is the more common term, originally from French but now characterized by fully Arabic morphology. Finally, the fifth row reveals a Moroccan expression that is neither etymologically related nor of the same word class (the MSA item is presented as an adjective, whereas the Moroccan item functions as a verb). In cases where the grammatical rules that govern a given vocabulary item are in need of explanation, the item is marked with an asterisk, and the rules are given in more detail in a "Notes on Vocabulary Usage" underneath the vocabulary chart.

Grammatical Sketches

In the *Moroccan Arabic Supplement*, grammar is presented primarily as a functional tool that allows students to better communicate with the vocabulary that they already know: a means rather than an end in itself. This approach relies heavily on the concept of "noticing" (Hedge 2011, 146), where students' first exposure to a given structure should come not from a grammatical blurb in the textbook or online supplement but rather in a real-life-use context that prompts them to notice, and thus begin to question, the structure on their own. Only after the opportunity for initial exposure has been given is further, more detailed information provided. The presentation of grammar is tempered; like with vocabulary, not all possible structures and variants are given but rather the ones that most effectively allow students to engage in communicative tasks.

The process of interfacing the Moroccan supplement with *Al-Kitaab* calls for different types of grammatical sketches, the depth of detail of which varies according to the immediate pedagogical goal. The first of these types is usage notes, which accompany vocabulary items and provide extended grammatical information on their use. Figure 8.2 gives an example of such notes for the Moroccan future marker غادي or غـ, presented in lesson 7. For most of these items, the other colloquial varieties present parallel information at the same time; on occasion the information is unique to the Moroccan item.

2. The future tense is indicated by a prefix on المضارع:

غادي، غـ	سـ
غادي نمشي معاك للسبيطار.	سأذهب معك إلى المستشفى.
واش غادي تتخرجوا هاد العام؟	هل سَتَتَخرّجون هذه السنة؟
غناكل مع صحابي هاد المسا.	سآكُل مع أصدقائي هذا المساء.

Figure 8.2 Extended grammatical information in usage notes

For grammatical topics that require more complex treatment, the supplement follows the lead of *Al-Kitaab* by introducing them in independent subsections. The primary goal of such sections is to take a grammatical structure with which students already have some basic familiarity and further clarify its role. They thus mark the point at which students begin to transition into conscious recognition of structures and, later, the ability to control them. The subsection "Main Verbs and Dependent Verbs," for example, gives the first explicit grammatical discussion of the Moroccan indicative marker تا, which students are assumed to have previously "noticed." This parallels the conditions under which a similar Egyptian/Levantine marker بـ is profiled on pages 74–75 of the printed textbook.[8]

Occasional challenges arise when providing grammatical information on Moroccan. Although most structures that students engage have direct parallels in either MSA or one of the other colloquial varieties, there are a limited number of cases in which achieving the same communicative task in Moroccan may require a greater degree of grammatical complexity.[9] I suggest that there are three possible solutions in such cases: (1) an alternative (although perhaps less frequent or semantically ideal) construction can be used, (2) supplemental grammar notes beyond those contained within *Al-Kitaab* can be provided, or (3) students can simply be asked to memorize a paradigm without delving into the grammar at the time. Each of the solutions has advantages, but the choice of which one to use must be balanced against the task at hand. The first solution, for example, is employed when students learn the basic semantic concept "need" in *Alif Baa* unit 7, expressed in other varieties with the term لازم. The most common Moroccan equivalent here would be the verb خصّ plus an attached personal pronoun, but at this stage students do not yet know the attached pronouns; thus, an alternative structure is given in the word ضروري. Although such decisions are made on a case-by-case basis, the guiding principle is that grammatical idiosyncrasies should not introduce undue difficulty into otherwise level-appropriate communicative tasks.

Standalone Audiovisual Aids

Alif Baa and *Al-Kitaab* Part One contain a number of audiovisual aids that are used to activate and reinforce grammatical structures but are not thematically linked to each other. These include the "Listen and Interact" videos and all of the videos for *Alif Baa*, as well as a number of videos for *Al-Kitaab* Part One in which the characters or storylines do not reoccur. All of these audiovisual aids make use of colloquial Arabic, so they are among the most essential components of the *Moroccan Arabic Supplement* to be recast in MA. The scripts for these audiovisual recordings are highly controlled for vocabulary and structure, and they parallel the other colloquial scripts as closely as possible. One of the greatest advantages of the online supplement is that it allows for direct embedding of the appropriate media files so students can, as with vocabulary, access them at their own pace at home and come to class prepared to use the same language in a communicative environment.

The "Listen and Interact" drills in *Alif Baa*, for example, consist of a speaker who poses simple greetings and questions, with a pause between utterances to allow the student to practice appropriate responses.[10] One of the advantages of embedded media is that it allows for a degree of interaction not possible with traditional resources. The dialogue on the *Alif Baa* companion website, for example, asks students to identify their gender; doing so not only makes the appropriate recording available but also implicitly transfers knowledge of gender as a grammatical category in Arabic that can affect linguistic output.

Video scenes typically feature two or more speakers interacting in real-life settings and give students an opportunity to understand simple, everyday speech in clear contexts, as the ACTFL guidelines (1989) stipulate that students at the Novice and Intermediate levels should be able to do. The scenes feature native speakers of MA in various settings in Morocco and highlight cultural practices associated with greetings, leave-taking, and respectfully addressing others. In the video scene that corresponds with unit 7 of *Alif Baa*, a young teacher enters the room and greets a colleague with a customary handshake. After returning greetings, the colleague offers the teacher a customary drink of tea or coffee, an offer that she ultimately accepts.[11]

In a classroom context, such videos allow the instructor to encourage students to provide information about the exchange, both linguistic and cultural. Over the course of multiple viewings, the instructor may ask students to identify the general context, repeat familiar phrases, and extract more difficult ones by listening closely; the instructor may also ask for students' observations on cultural practices and body language. These practices set the stage for more involved listening activities, where students' first engagement with the material primarily takes place at home. As students move toward a higher level of proficiency, videos become longer and more linguistically complex; they are likewise increasingly accompanied by comprehension questions that are first answered at home and then brought to the classroom for discussion.

Themed Story
One of the most salient offerings of the *Al-Kitaab* series is a "themed story" that is told over the course of the series, primarily in monologues. It alternates between two main characters, both young Arabic-speaking college students

who discuss their personal background and emotions in accessible, level-appropriate language. The themed story, which the third edition of *Al-Kitaab* provides in MSA, Egyptian, and Levantine Arabic, is one of the primary venues through which new vocabulary is encountered in context, and serves as a base for classroom activities in which the characters and their lives serve as the object of discussion. As one of the most central components of the curriculum, it is imperative that the Moroccan materials replicate the story to as great a degree as possible with believable Moroccan characters.

To this effect, the *Moroccan Arabic Supplement* provides its own rendition of the themed story based on the lives of two Moroccan youth named Karima and Yassine. Karima, like her counterparts in the other colloquial varieties, is a student at New York University whose Moroccan father works at the United Nations and whose Palestinian mother works at the university's admissions office. Yassine, like his counterparts, lives in a major city in the Arab world—here, Marrakech—and studies business administration in the city's largest public university (Cadi Ayyad University). In each unit, Karima and Yassine provide subsequently more information about their personal lives, hobbies, and opinions; this information serves as a target for assignments inside and outside of class, as figure 8.3 demonstrates.

In producing videos for the themed story, special care is taken to maintain consistency with the curricular goals, with an emphasis on creating materials that are both of sufficient difficulty to be challenging but still within students' grasp. As is to be expected for learners who have attained, at a maximum, intermediate proficiency, the topics in these videos are limited to personal affairs, hobbies, and interests. Vocabulary is strictly controlled so that most of the new items in each video are in the same unit's vocabulary chart; similarly, care is taken to ensure that vocabulary and grammar from previous lessons is recycled, thus reinforcing student's ability to recognize them in context. The rate of speech is fast enough not to seem unnatural but at the same time tailored for nonnative speakers, as should be expected at this level,

---

Listen to ياسين using the strategies you have learned. Write a **paragraph** for each question. You may use الفصحى and/or المغربية words and expressions.

1. واش ياسين طالب مزيان؟ علاش/علاش لا؟

2. أش كان بغى يقرى ياسين؟ وعلاش ما قراهش؟

3. شنو رأي الوالد في مستقبل ياسين؟

4. في رأيكم، واش ياسين مقلّق حيت هو ما دخلش لقسم الأدب؟ علاش/علاش لا؟

Figure 8.3 Discussion questions for themed story

and extended pauses between speech segments are included in order to signal transitions between topics and give students additional time to parse the speech. Because students' comprehension at the Novice and Intermediate levels is often dependent on context, visual cues also play an important role in the video production. For this reason, when Karima discusses New York University, for example, a picture of the university briefly flashes onto the screen; likewise, when Yassine mentions smoking, he simultaneously holds up a cigarette.

On a cultural level, the themed story also exposes students to several practices and traditions common to Morocco, many of which are shared with other Arabic-speaking countries. Familial relationships are emphasized as particularly important, and frequent references to various family members give students an opportunity to improve their command of a key set of culturally significant vocabulary. Other topics, such as leisure time and the educational system, also feature prominently. Yassine speaks at length about the time he spends at the coffee shop with his friends, for example, and his many references to his educational and career goals serve as a launching point for comparing and contrasting the experiences of students in the United States with those in Morocco. Finally, on an extralinguistic level, the scenes filmed in Morocco, which feature traditional architecture and are accompanied by music, are designed to give students as aesthetic feel for the country and to cast it in a positive light, further encouraging students to take interest in Moroccan culture and explore it on their own.

Cultural Addendums

Culture, which is seen in this curriculum as a "fifth skill" regarding proficiency (Garza 2010), is difficult to disentangle from language use. Most of the cultural learning that takes place in the *Moroccan Arabic Supplement* is, as described earlier, engaged implicitly alongside other tasks, as in listening activities or classroom discussion of them. At the same time, again following the lead of *Alif Baa* and *Al-Kitaab*, there is room for content that explicitly informs students of cultural practices. Like with vocabulary and grammar, this cultural exposure is best obtained in a functional context, giving students not abstract encyclopedic knowledge but rather information that is immediately useful in comprehension or communication. The short blurb featured in figure 8.4, for example, allows student to understand a cultural reference that they will shortly thereafter hear in drill 15 of *Al-Kitaab* Part One, lesson 10.

In other cases, a cultural addendum expands upon information that is presented in the printed textbook and is generally applicable to all Arabic varieties by giving additional common phrases that are used in Moroccan. A

اللغة والثقافة: بنت النّاس

The phrase بنت النّاس is literally "the people's daughter," and refers to someone of good upbringing who is respected in the community. When Moroccans speak of finding بنت النّاس or ولد النّاس, the implication is that this is the person they will marry.

Figure 8.4 Example of a cultural reference

number of Moroccan forms of address given in addition to the Syrian terms on page 89 of *Alif Baa*, 3rd ed., for example, feature prominently in a number of standalone videos and are used daily in classroom interactions between students and instructors.[12]

Meanwhile, there are some cases in which the *Moroccan Arabic Supplement* must part ways with *Al-Kitaab* Part One, particularly where cultural elements and associated linguistic terms in the eastern Arab world depart from those of North Africa. This dilemma is particularly relevant in lesson 7, where the educational system plays a prominent role in the themed story. Because the educational system in Morocco is somewhat different from that of Egypt and Syria and because many common terms are unrelated, a decision is made here to present both realities in their own standalone cultural addendum.[13] This is in keeping with a philosophy, relevant to the teaching of both language and culture, that although similarities should be highlighted wherever possible, differences should likewise not be artificially glossed over.

Future Directions

In this chapter I have laid out the predominant themes and methodologies that should inform a first-year course in which Moroccan colloquial and MSA are taught side by side in the same classroom, and I have sought to contextualize them within larger trends within the field of teaching Arabic as a foreign language. In doing so, I hope to have shown that using MA as the language of instruction in a communication-based course that uses the integrated approach to diglossia instruction is not only possible but is a project in which serious Arabic programs should take interest. Particularly given the changing reality of study abroad in the Arab world, which means students are more likely than ever to encounter Moroccan as the colloquial variety of real-life interactions, these programs must recognize that effective Arabic instruction cannot remain centered in only the language and culture of the eastern Arab world. In considering this change, we should not see it as a challenge to overcome but rather an opportunity to push our students toward cultural and linguistic proficiency in a previously unexplored way.

Beyond the practical implications of allowing us to teach Moroccan, the materials proposed here in the form of an online *Moroccan Arabic Supplement* to the *Alif Baa* and *Al-Kitaab* textbook series also serve a theoretical purpose. Specifically, they speak to the benefit of using preexisting curricula as "scaffolding" upon which modular supplemental materials can be built, allowing methods that have already been established as effective to serve as the models for innovation. In theory, a Gulf Arabic or Iraqi supplement to *Al-Kitaab* Part One is just as attainable as a Moroccan one precisely because the current edition of the textbook has already put forth a model for teaching a choice of colloquial variety and clearly marked those materials as such. Future Arabic pedagogical materials should adopt this principle and expand upon it, taking modular and variety-neutral content design as their foundation and ensuring a legal and technological framework that encourages outside contributors to build directly upon them.

References

American Council on the Teaching of Foreign Languages (ACTFL). 1989. "ACTFL Arabic Proficiency Guidelines." *Foreign Language Annals* 22, no. 4: 45–71.
———. 2012. "Arabic Consensus Project." American Council on the Teaching of Foreign Languages. May 19, 2016. http://www.actfl.org/publications/guidelines-and-manuals/actfl-proficiency-guidelines-2012/arabic/arabic-consensus-project.
Al-Batal, Mahmoud. 1992. "Diglossia Proficiency: The Need for an Alternative Approach to Teaching." In *The Arabic Language in America*, edited by Aleya Rouchdy, 284–304. Detroit: Wayne State University Press.
———. 2006. "Playing with Words: Teaching Vocabulary in the Arabic Curriculum." In *Handbook for Arabic Language Teaching Professionals in the 21st Century*, Kassem M. Wahba, Zeinab A. Taha, and Liz England, 331–40. Mahwah, NJ: Lawrence Erlbaum.
Al-Batal, Mahmoud, and Kirk Belnap. 2006. "The Teaching and Learning of Arabic in the United States: Realities, Needs, and Future Directions." In *Handbook for Arabic Language Teaching Professionals in the 21st Century*, edited by Kassem M. Wahba, Zeinab A. Taha, and Liz England, 389–400. Mahwah, NJ: Lawrence Erlbaum.
Blake, Robert J. 2013. *Brave New Digital Classroom: Technology and Foreign Language Learning*, 2nd ed. Washington, DC: Georgetown University Press.
Boudlal, Abdelaziz. 2009. *The Prosody and Morphology of a Moroccan Arabic Dialect: An Optimality-Theoretic Account*. Saarbrücken: VDM-Verl. Müller.
Brustad, Kristen, Mahmoud Al-Batal, and Abbas Al-Tonsi. 2010. *Alif Baa: Introduction to Arabic Letters and Sounds*, 3rd ed. Washington, DC: Georgetown University Press.

————. 2011. *Al-Kitaab fii Taᶜallum al-ᶜArabiyya: A Textbook for Beginning Arabic*, Part One, 3rd ed. Washington, DC: Georgetown University Press.

Garza, Thomas. 2010. "Culture." Foreign Language Teaching Methods. May 18, 2016. https://coerll.utexas.edu/methods/modules/culture/.

Heath, Jeffrey. 2002. *Jewish and Muslim Dialects of Moroccan Arabic*. New York: Routledge.

Hedge, Tricia. 2011. *Teaching and Learning in the Language Classroom*. Oxford: Oxford University Press.

Maas, Utz. 2000. "Moroccan: A Language in Emergence." In *Arabic as a Minority Language*, edited by Jonathan Owens, 385–404. Berlin: Mouton de Gruyter.

Parkinson, Dilworth B. 1992. "Computers for Arabic Teaching: The Promise and the Reality." In *The Arabic Language in America*, edited by Aleya Rouchdy, 305–26. Detroit: Wayne State University Press.

Younes, Munther. 2006. "Integrating the Colloquial with Fuṣḥā in the Arabic as a Foreign Language Classroom." In *Handbook for Arabic Language Teaching Professionals in the 21st Century*, edited by Kassem M. Wahba, Zeinab A. Taha, and Liz England, 157–66. Mahwah, NJ: Lawrence Erlbaum.

Notes

Additional data and examples are freely available to view and download on this book's product page on the Georgetown University Press (GUP) website (www .press.georgetown.edu).

1. While the current *Al-Kitaab* companion website has been used as is in a prototype course, with the Moroccan materials provided as a standalone supplement, this situation is not preferable in the long term; the proposed combined site is the ideal solution.

2. For example, an instructor may initiate group work for a listening activity by saying:

دابا، بالجوج، بغيتكم تتكلموا على الفيديو من الواجبات. "Now, in [groups of] two, I'd like you to talk about the video from the homework."

3. Nevertheless, in the case of homework, all students should engage materials in the same colloquial variety; this is a necessary part of maintaining a shared language base.

4. For a screenshot of this example, see figure W8.1 on the GUP website.

5. See video 8.1 on the GUP website for an example showing how the website functions.

6. For example, native Moroccan phonology does not distinguish between الأَدَب and الآداب, both of which are pronounced *l-adab*.

7. All figures that appear in the book in black and white also appear on the GUP website in color.

8. See figure W8.2 on the GUP website.

9. This is not to say that Moroccan is more grammatically complex than any other variety, or vice versa; rather, the grammatical complexity of performing the same communicative task in one variety or the other may vary.

10. A video demonstration of one such drill can be seen in video 8.2 on the GUP website.

11. See video 8.3 on the GUP website.

12. See figure W8.3 on the GUP website.

13. See, in full, in figure W8.4 on the GUP website.

9

Arabic Diglossic Speaking without Mixing

Practices and Outcomes from a Beginning Level

SONIA SHIRI AND CHARLES JOUKHADAR
The University of Arizona

A VARIETY OF language program models were developed over the past half century or so in order to tackle the issues of diglossic proficiency development among learners of Arabic as a foreign language and the importance of learning how to speak a dialect in particular. Among the most successful but most difficult to implement has been the model adopted by certain universities, including several in the United Kingdom, that requires combining three years of Modern Standard Arabic (MSA) learning on the home campus with compulsory study abroad in an Arabic-speaking university, typically during the second or third year. Offering a dialect class, typically Egyptian or Levantine, on the home campus for third-year students with a prerequisite of two years of MSA has constituted another option that has privileged this kind of sequencing while attending to this issue in the home program.

A prominent argument in favor of this approach purports that knowledge of MSA leads to the learning of dialects, particularly when combined with overseas study. Opportunities for short-term study abroad have become more common although study abroad is rarely compulsory and few institutions offer the option of completing a full year abroad. In the United States, the number of students completing summer study abroad remains modest compared to the number of students taking Arabic on their home campuses. Only 2 percent of the over 304,000 American students who conducted study abroad during 2013–14 traveled to the Middle East and North Africa region while around 8 percent majored in foreign languages and international relations (Institute of International Education 2015). According to the Modern Language Association (MLA), close to 32,000 studied Arabic throughout US institutions of higher education in 2013 (MLA Language Enrollment Database 2013). The number of students of Arabic traveling abroad during the last few years has been higher than ever before and constitutes an opportunity for a sizable number of them to experience life in Arabic-speaking countries along with the Arabic dialect(s) spoken there.

Yet, without knowledge of a dialect that allows them to engage and connect with their host society, these students seem to be linguistically unprepared for their time abroad, regardless of the level of Arabic they achieved at home, as a recent study indicated (Shiri 2013). Students also report difficulty accessing Arabic native speakers while abroad and challenges in speaking Arabic with them when they do (Palmer 2012; Trentman 2013a, 2013b). Moreover, learners from universities throughout the United States (Shiri 2013, 2015a) who participate in summer abroad programs in five Arabic-speaking countries overwhelmingly report gaining an appreciation for the importance of learning an Arabic dialect, any dialect, as part of any Arabic education. This is because of the opportunities it affords students for connecting with Arabic speakers and understanding their cultures. A study of the role of dialect and MSA in developing intercultural competence in short-term study abroad further confirms the complementary relationship between these two varieties and emphasizes the key role dialect plays in learners' cultural literacy (Shiri 2015b). This study indicates that dialect mediates many cultural interactions, including higher-level interactions. The study also points out that, while MSA plays an important role in higher-level interactions, it plays a secondary role in lower-level interactions. Such findings make the purposeful instruction of dialect at the home campus a necessity to prepare students for sociolinguistically appropriate and meaningful connection with Arabic speakers and as a medium for learning important aspects of Arab culture.

Calls for the teaching of Arabic dialects along with MSA have been made since the 1990s (Al-Batal 1992; Al-Batal and Belnap 2006; Ryding 2006; Younes 2006, 2015), and a variety of applications of the "integrated approach" emerged over time. However, one of the longstanding objections to simultaneously teaching MSA and an Arabic dialect has been the fear that students would be "confused" by the two varieties; this, in turn, would jeopardize their overall language development the argument goes—a second important objection to this approach (Younes 2015). The question of which dialect to teach in the absence of an agreed upon "standard" vernacular variety of the language adds to the complexity of the issue. As Mahmoud Abdalla puts it, "the teaching of colloquial Arabic and the place of the dialects in the Arabic curriculum is still debatable. As a result, some coordinators and planners seek refuge in study abroad programs as an alternative solution. Students will immerse in the culture while learning the target language, but, here again, the questions of which culture they should be immersed in and which type of Arabic medium should be used are important points to be considered" (2006, 328). This issue seems to be less important to students, however, as most are open to learning *any* dialect and even multiple dialects, while some believe Egyptian and Levantine are the most popular so far, as Sonia Shiri (2013) reports. Studies on Arabic student and teacher beliefs about language learning indicate that some important discrepancies in perspective exist between the two groups (Kuntz 2000; Kuntz and Belnap 2001), signaling a potential mismatch between language program design and student needs and beliefs (see chapter 13 in this book). Moreover, data-driven studies investigating student outcomes in the various applications of the integrated approach remain thus far limited and are mostly incorporated in this volume.

The current study investigates the effectiveness of an implementation of this approach that teaches both MSA and dialect simultaneously within the same course but following two parallel curricula that are implemented during the first two semesters of college-level Arabic learning at the University of Arizona. The aim of the investigated approach is to develop student proficiency in *both* varieties and to minimize if not avoid the mixing between them by purposefully heightening students' "noticing" (Schmidt 1990) of the two varieties at the curricular and instructional levels. The current study investigates the strategies used by first-year-level instructors to keep the two varieties separate and explores the level of success achieved in students' speaking of MSA and dialect varieties both in classroom activities and in skits and oral presentations. More specifically, this study focuses on the degree of success of this approach as measured by the proficiency levels achieved in these beginning-level students' speaking, the amount of mixing they exhibit between MSA and dialect, the level of noticing revealed by students when mixing is evident, and strategies used by instructors to minimize mixing.

Arabic Varieties and the Teaching of Arabic as a Foreign Language

While classical diglossia (Ferguson 1959) still characterizes the linguistic situation of Arabic and while the High (H) variety still sustains its prestige and overall function compared to the Low (L) variety, the situation is further complicated by a number of other practices. On the one hand, the differences between the L and H varieties widely exhibited in phonology, morphology, syntax, and semantics persist alongside differences that can be drastic among the L varieties themselves. On the other hand, code-switching between the H language and the spoken regional vernaculars that constitute the L variety is common among educated speakers (Mitchell 1986; Ryding 2006), although its rules may vary from country to country. Conventions for when the H and the L varieties are expected to be used also can vary by region and by time period, although knowledge of the H variety remains tightly connected to literacy and the status that it bestows on its speakers. Moreover, speakers of Arabic from different regions or backgrounds tend to use several strategies when in a contact situation. In fact, across dialects, communication is negotiated mostly through a strategy termed "accommodation," whereby speakers change to varying degrees the way they speak when in contact with speakers of other dialects (Abu Melhim 1991; S'hiri 2002). The amount of accommodation and whether it is unidirectional or mutual tends to be governed by factors such as language ideologies, power relations, and hierarchies ascribed to the regional vernacular varieties (Chakrani 2015; Hachimi 2013; S'hiri 2002). Moreover, while code-switching is common among the spoken varieties of Arabic themselves (Albirini 2014; Schulthies 2014), code-switching is also practiced between Arabic and the foreign languages that are used in the region (Sayahi 2014). Furthermore, with the advent of new media, rules governing which Arabic variety may be written and in what contexts have become more complex. For instance, it has become common to see dialects transcribed on blogs and social media as they are used to tackle from the most informal to the most formal topics. While these factors inevitably make the teaching of Arabic as a foreign language a challenging endeavor for language programs and students, they also underscore the importance of teaching dialect, and not merely at the introductory level, alongside the established standard language of literacy, government, and media.

The Arizona Arabic Program

When revamping the Arabic curriculum after the University of Arizona program became a Language Flagship in the fall of 2013, the language program director, also the first author of this chapter, undertook to implement an approach that teaches MSA and dialect simultaneously that she had adopted with success in other settings. The goal of the Language Flagship is to help undergraduate students from all areas of specialization become global professionals with a high level of proficiency in their language of choice. The

Arabic Flagship Program trains students stateside to reach the American Council on the Teaching of Foreign Languages (ACTFL) Advanced level in preparation for a year of study in an Arabic-speaking country, with the goal of reaching professional proficiency (ACTFL Superior Level) by the time of graduation.

Benefiting from lessons learned from the attempts of other institutions to tackle the diglossia issue using different integrated approach models, the Arizona Arabic Flagship Program includes dialect instruction in the curriculum from the first day of class through the advanced levels. However, it seeks to develop a relatively equal level of speaking proficiency in both MSA and the dialect in the program while being particularly intent on minimizing, if not avoiding, the amount of confusion and mixing reported by other applications of this approach. The curriculum is designed on the premise that MSA and vernacular Arabic are distinct but complementary varieties within the larger category of Arabic language and that professional-level proficiency in Arabic means an ability to operate in both with accuracy and confidence. As such, and in order to reach higher levels of proficiency in each, it is recognized that there may be overlap and even redundancy in the learning process akin to learning two close languages in one program. Naturally, this is more demanding than is generally attempted in a single language course. This approach entails that students of these varieties will have to learn, in most cases, double sets of vocabulary items, syntactic and morphological rules, and sounds as well as a whole set of skills involved in the selection of the appropriate variety needed for a given context. However, because the dialect is mostly spoken, the effort needed to develop literacy (reading and writing) will only be tackled in MSA instruction, although students are also exposed to written examples of dialect, especially on social media.

The Arizona approach differs from Munther Younes's (2015) approach, which suggests that because MSA is used in reading, writing, and scripted speech and since dialect is used for daily communication, the two do not need to overlap during instruction of speaking. He explains that in the integrated approach as implemented in Cornell's Arabic program, confusion between the two varieties is minimized because MSA "materials are presented in the form of passages to be read and understood but not to be actively spoken," while dialect materials "are introduced and regularly used as a foundation for speaking activities" (2015, 55–56). Furthermore, Younes questions the value of introducing an activity in MSA along with its "translation" in the dialect, as is the case in the *Al-Kitaab* lesson that he uses to illustrate this practice, and suggests that this may be "more confusing to Arabic students than integration" (2015, 55). This, as with other models that attempt to tackle the diglossia challenge, might serve the needs of its specific language program. The argument on which the Arizona approach is based, however, purports that, while there might be a few domains where it is safe to divide and "specialize" instruction in one Arabic variety or the other, these domains are limited. MSA is not merely a written language but rather an Arabic variety that indexes education when spoken in the contexts where it is expected, whether entirely by itself or mixed in with a dialect. Developing higher-level proficiency in Arabic involves instruction in both varieties and not privileging one over the other, regardless of the sequence or order in which the two varieties are introduced. To develop advanced proficiency in Arabic, it is necessary to begin with the lower-level proficiency for both varieties, then build on it and integrate it into higher-level discourse as the context dictates. There is therefore no shortcut for reaching higher-level proficiency in Arabic (MSA and dialect) without building the basics, even though it might be tempting from a language program administration perspective to focus on providing this level merely in dialect or merely in MSA. In other words, there may be no way to avoid what looks like redundancy when teaching the same content in MSA and dialect if the goal is to develop ACTFL Intermediate-level proficiency and beyond in both. The pedagogical challenge resides, therefore, in how to efficiently develop proficiency in both varieties while keeping the boundaries between the two systems clear in the minds of the learners to minimize unnatural or random mixing, allowing each variety to develop without interfering with the development of the other, and preparing students for mixing the two according to recognized conventions.

Noticing

The approach adopted in the Arizona Arabic Flagship Program relies on Richard Schmidt's (1990) Noticing Hypothesis, which stresses the importance of conscious noticing in second-language learning. Schmidt formally proposed the Noticing Hypothesis in 1990 when he suggested that noticing is a necessary and sufficient condition for converting input into intake. In other words, intake is the part of input that the learner notices. Hence, learning can only take place in situations when the learner can consciously register or notice the differences between the remembered form (or the interlanguage form) and the form in the input—that is, the process is not an implicit or a nonconscious one. Understanding a form is not a sufficient condition for learning it; the learner needs to focus his or her conscious attention in order to learn it. In Jeff Siegel's book on second dialect acquisition (SDA), in which he introduces his vision for this new subfield of second-language acquisition that focuses on learning a second dialect of the same language, Siegel (2010) proposes noticing as an important predictor of ultimate attainment in SDA. Siegel suggests that conscious perception of unique second-dialect features is a necessary means to reducing negative or unsuccessful transfer from the first dialect. Although research on the subject of noticing in SDA remains limited, Siegel cites ample evidence regarding persistent intrusions from the first dialect into the second dialect that slow down or thwart successful acquisition. He also reports how some scholars believe that the similarities that connect two varieties of the same language can facilitate acquisition whereas other scholars believe those same similarities make learning a second dialect more difficult than learning a second language. Noticing becomes, therefore, an important prerequisite for aiding SDA.

Although the current study investigates the learning of two varieties (MSA and dialect) of the same second language (Arabic) that are learned simultaneously rather than in succession, it still posits that noticing is an important tool in supporting proficiency in both varieties, and one that is essential in avoiding mixing between them. The approach thus suggests that the explicit drawing of students' attention to the existence of diglossia or multiglossia in Arabic as well as to the linguistic and sociolinguistic differences between the varieties is crucial in helping students deal with potential confusion and random mixing, especially in the lower level, and therefore in promoting higher levels of proficiency in each.

The Study

As applied on the Arizona Arabic Flagship Program 2013 and 2014–15 first-year student cohorts, heightening students' noticing of the existence of the two varieties and their distinct structures and sociolinguistic functions was attempted first at the program level (through the separation of the two segments during instruction), and then metalinguistically and pedagogically through the teaching techniques, the course syllabus, and the curriculum. The goal of this study is to evaluate the effectiveness of this hypothesis by looking at first-year students' production of the two varieties, both during classroom activities and unmediated end-of-year skits, and in examining students' proficiency levels during those interactions. More specifically, the study tackles the following three main research questions:

1. How much and what kind of MSA and dialect mixing did Arabic students exhibit in their speech, and did they show any signs of awareness of the difference between the two varieties?

2. What was the learners' level of proficiency as exemplified by the topics discussed, the degree of accuracy of their speech, and the degree to which they were able to maintain speaking in one or the other variety during classroom interactions and skits/oral presentations?
3. What were the strategies (if any) that instructors used in order to support learning of the two varieties without random mixing?

Methods

The following section provides a description of (1) the setting under which our research project was carried out, (2) the participants who took part in our study, and (3) the process through which our data were collected and analyzed.

Research Setting

This study examines students' speaking in MSA and in Arabic dialect during classroom interactions and in skits of a first-year Arabic class at the University of Arizona. The five-days-a-week, fifteen-week-per-semester program curriculum is divided into two parallel components, one for MSA and one for dialect, both taught from the first day of class. The MSA component uses the MSA materials in the *Al-Kitaab* book series (*Alif Baa* and *Al-Kitaab* Part One) (Brustad, Al-Batal, and Al-Tonsi 2010, 2011, 2014). The dialect component does not use the *Al-Kitaab* materials but is designed to teach Egyptian, Levantine, or Moroccan Arabic with the goal of developing student proficiency in that specific dialect through the ACTFL Intermediate level. The dialect materials are thematically organized and include a variety of Novice to Intermediate topics such as greetings, family, ordering food and using appropriate eating manners, money, shopping and bargaining, and visiting the doctor. The topics involve technology-assisted content that accelerates learning as well as authentic cultural materials such as songs and film clips. Although the dialects offered are selected depending on the proficiency of the instructors, at least two dialects are offered each year. The curriculum for all three dialect courses is identical, and classes follow the same instructional and testing pace throughout both semesters. During the first four weeks of the first semester, students spend half of the daily fifty-minute class learning how to speak in the designated dialect and the other half of the session developing their reading and writing skills using the materials from the sounds and letters textbook, *Alif Baa*. As students move on to *Al-Kitaab* Part One, the curriculum switches to one day a week of dialect and four days of MSA for the rest of the year. This ratio was decided because, while the dialect class focuses mostly on speaking with a minimal exposure to writing in social media, the

MSA class teaches literacy (reading, writing, and grammar) in addition to speaking. Each dialect class, thus, covers a new theme per week on average and includes around fifteen to twenty new words or expressions. Conversation tables are offered twice a week for each of the three dialects and for MSA throughout the year, and students may earn extra credit if they attend these sessions. Because attendance is not compulsory, only a few students attend regularly.

It is worth noting that, although both courses cover content appropriate for the beginning level and do overlap in many places, such as when introducing oneself or speaking about school or family members and their occupations, the dialect class introduces a variety of themes that are not handled by the MSA component of the program and its textbooks. Such topics include giving directions, going to the doctor, and interacting politely and appropriately in a variety of situations such as those involving eating, shopping, or travel, none of which are addressed in the MSA class.

During classroom activities, the teacher acts as a model for students in terms of using only MSA during the MSA sessions and only the dialect during the dialect sessions. The only exception is at the start of MSA class, when the teacher may use the dialect for warm-up before switching to MSA. The teacher does not accept random mixing of the two varieties from students, and the students are explicitly corrected when they use a form from the other variety. Students are asked to prepare two major skits for the end of the semester: one in MSA and one in the dialect. The skit guidelines sent to students emphasize the fact that the variety in question should be used.

Participants

Participants in the study are the instructors and students from two first-year sections. Both sections are taught by professional male instructors holding higher degrees in second-language acquisition and teaching. One is a native speaker of Levantine Arabic while the second is a native speaker of Egyptian Arabic. A total of thirty-six students are included in this study, seventeen of whom are male and nineteen are female. Students who had prior knowledge of Arabic dialects, such as heritage learners, are not considered in this study. Only students who started off as total beginners in both MSA and the dialect are included. Data from very low-performing students are also not included.

Data Collection and Analysis

Data were obtained from video recordings of classroom interactions and end-of-semester students' skits filmed at the end of the first year of Arabic at the University of Arizona during the spring 2014 and spring 2015 semesters. The classroom recordings were part of an overall set of recordings gathered from all levels for program evaluation purposes. Two sections of the first-year course were chosen: one that taught MSA and Levantine and the other MSA and Egyptian. A total of four 50-minute classroom periods were recorded, two for MSA and two for dialect. Student-to-student and student-to-instructor classroom interactions were analyzed in search of MSA-dialect mixing instance frequency and patterns, accuracy levels in each variety, and instructor strategies vis-à-vis mixing. Students' skits were also used to examine the degree of mixing along with the level of proficiency achieved in the two varieties at the end of the first year. A total of two hours and fifteen minutes of MSA, Levantine, and Egyptian skits were collected. In the data analysis, the following criteria were adopted. Self-corrected segments were counted correct. All prepositions (including *bi* and *li*), particles, and personal pronouns were counted as individual words. For lexical items that shared the same consonants in MSA and dialect, the way they were uttered, that is, whether they carried a particular vowel from one variety or the other, determined their category classification. Words that were close in both varieties but did not share all the consonants were counted as different. The word "mixing" is used to describe the use, by students, of a dialectal feature or lexical item in a class or activity where MSA is the designated variety and vice versa. "Random mixing" is used to describe switching between MSA and dialect that is not intentional and is merely considered as interlanguage.

Results

The following section provides a detailed description of the observations and results drawn from our study.

Students' Level of Mixing of the Two Varieties

The first research question examines end-of-first-year classroom oral interactions and skits / oral presentations in order to investigate the degree and nature of MSA-dialect mixing that Arabic students exhibited as well as identify any signs of awareness, from the student's perspective, of the difference between the two varieties. Table 9.1 summarizes the degree of mixing observed in students' production in the MSA classes and the dialect classes as well as the signs of students' awareness of the existence of the two varieties, particularly self-correction or clarification about which variety to use. Overall, 6 percent of the words spoken in all of the classes were from the other variety. This percentage encompasses words that were uttered more than once within the same segment. The rest of the interactions were conducted without mixing with the other variety.

Table 9.1 Student level of mixing and diglossic awareness in classroom activities

Student Language	MSA	Dialect	Total for Both Varieties	Average for Both Varieties
Number of words in incorrect variety, including repeated words	46	89	135	67.5
Number of words	1232.0	1025.0	2257.0	1128.5
Percentage of MSA-dialect mixing	3.5	8.5	12	6
Student self-correction to the variety at hand	2	13	15	N/A
Students seeking clarification as to which variety to use in class activity	0	2	2	N/A

According to the results, the dialect classes seem to contain slightly more mixing than the MSA classes did (8.5 percent and 3.5 percent, respectively).

In terms of signs of learner awareness of Arabic variety in the classroom, students corrected themselves fifteen times overall in class when they realized that they were using the other variety. Most of the self-corrections (thirteen out of fifteen instances) took place from MSA to dialect during the dialect classes. Only two self-corrections were observed from dialect to MSA in one of the MSA classes. Moreover, students only asked twice for clarifications about which variety to use in the class activity. Both occasions occurred during dialect classes. The rest of the time they engaged in the classroom activity using the designated variety (either MSA or dialect) without need for clarification.

Table 9.2 summarizes the degree of MSA-dialect mixing observed in students' production in their MSA and dialect skits or oral presentations. Results indicate that mixing in this pre-prepared student language was very limited.

Table 9.2 Degree of variety mixing in student skits and oral presentations

Arabic Variety	Percentage of Variety Mixing
MSA	2
Dialect	4 (Egyptian 5; Levantine 3)

A close look at the type of mixing that was taking place in the students' speaking in these different environments indicates that it primarily fell into four main categories. The most frequent type of mixing (34 percent of the instances) occurred at the lexical level and in both environments. However, lexical mixing was most noticeable in the skits. For example, a student said *jamīl* "beautiful" in the Levantine class where *ḥilw* would have been expected. The second most-frequent mixing occurs at the phonological level. In this category, students would use a word that was essentially the same in both MSA and dialect but would pronounce it using sounds from the other variety. Examples of this type of mixing include, for instance, saying *qiṭṭa* ("cat" in MSA) in an Egyptian class instead of *ʿuṭṭa* ("cat" in Egyptian Arabic). This type of mixing constitutes 17 percent overall of all the instances of mixing and seems to be less frequent in the environments dedicated to MSA. The third and fourth categories are morphological and grammatical in nature and the least frequent overall (14 percent and 8 percent, respectively) and even less frequent when MSA was produced, both in class and during skits or oral presentations. The morphological mixing took place a dozen times in the data, mostly during verb conjugation in both dialects as in *ʾadrus* ("I study" in MSA) instead of *b-adrus* ("I study" in Levantine). No mixing was observed during the conjugation of verbs in MSA; that is, all verbs that were produced where MSA was expected contained the correct MSA morphological forms. The type of mixing that is classified as grammatical mostly affected negation, specifically verb negation in the imperfect, and only occurred three times in the data. When producing dialect verb negation in these instances, learners used the MSA equivalent.

Students' Proficiency Levels

The second research question investigates the learners' level of MSA and dialect proficiency. This is determined by examining the topics discussed as well as the degree to which students were able to maintain speaking in a given variety during classroom interactions and skits/oral presentations and the level of accuracy of the speech produced in that variety. The data indicates that the topics addressed during classroom activities as well as in students' skits and oral presentations are at the Intermediate level according to the ACTFL speaking proficiency scale. In both venues students focused on topics pertaining to their personal and daily lives. In the classroom interactions, the instructors asked students to perform role plays or engage in interactions where they had to greet each other; introduce themselves to classmates; talk about their families, studies, hobbies, daily schedules; describe their apartment and city; and talk about what they did during the spring break and what they will do during the summer.

The dialect skits address, overall, the same topics practiced in the classroom interactions captured in the data but naturally add a more personalized twist mixed in with some creativity or imagination. For instance, while in one Levantine skit students spoke about their studies, families, and schedules; what they did over the weekend; and what they were planning for the following weekend, in another skit students played a "Guess Who?" game in which one of them described a personality and the others had to guess, or ask questions for more information on the personality. Another group spoke about the weather, what countries they liked to visit and why, and what they did the previous summer, while another group acted out visiting the doctor, reserving an airplane ticket, talking about the weather, ordering food in a restaurant, and bargaining. In the Egyptian skits students addressed similar topics in addition to speaking about hobbies and renting an apartment.

It is noticeable, however, that the students' speaking production in MSA contains similar topics but differs from their dialect production in two ways. First, in addition to the skit format, some students opted for a different format. They did individual oral presentations, typically using PowerPoint and speaking from written prompts or commenting on images. Second, some students introduced new topics in addition to the ones tackled in the dialect skits. The new topics pertain to schooling and literacy-related matters. For example, one group spoke about their majors, whether they liked them or not, and about their final exams. Another group referred to classified advertisements in a newspaper. A number of the students who opted for individual oral presentations seem to prefer recounting stories about trips that they had undertaken to Arab and other countries.

When it comes to the degree to which students were able to maintain speaking in one or the other variety, the results show that they spoke at the level of the sentence (ACTFL Intermediate level), staying focused on the variety at hand and mixing only during the relatively infrequent instances noted in the response to the first research question, above. There is a difference between the length of their production during classroom interactions and during skits and oral presentations, however. Classroom production that consisted of student pair and group interactions or interactions with the instructor tended to contain one question followed by a response, typically spanning between one to six sentences. The skits, on the other hand, included turns that consisted of strings of sentences, typically one to four sentences per student. Consisting mainly of monologues, the oral presentations included the longest amount of uninterrupted speech in MSA, averaging around three and a half minutes and consisting mostly of strings of sentences.

The level of accuracy of the speech produced in both varieties is also consistent with expectations for the Intermediate level on the ACTFL scale (comprehensible to sympathetic speakers of the language). Actual errors within each variety are overall limited, averaging 9 percent in class interactions and around 5 percent in the scripted speech of skits and oral presentations. Although errors span several categories, including phonology, lexicon, and grammar, the most frequent errors are of the expected type for this level: 27 percent of all errors pertain to verb conjugation, followed by errors pertaining to noun–adjective agreement and the 'iḍāfa construct (18 percent and 16 percent, respectively). Pronunciation and lexical errors affect around 9 percent of all the errors each.

Strategies Used by Instructors

The third research question examines the strategies implemented by the two instructors during class time to enhance their students' awareness of the difference between MSA and the dialect and to encourage maintenance of production of the variety at hand. Three strategies are observed in the data although they were used to different degrees. The strategies are corrective feedback, recast, and modeling. Corrective feedback includes direct and indirect types whereby the instructor either helped the student find the correct form or gave them the correct form. Recast involves rephrasing what a student said in the desirable variety of the language without drawing explicit attention to it while modeling involved speaking in the desirable variety to encourage students to emulate it. It is noticeable that the explicit corrective feedback strategy was used significantly more frequently than the recast strategy. Only two instances of recast are noted in all four sessions whereas sixteen instances of explicit correction are witnessed overall. Interestingly, none of this corrective feedback was implemented during the MSA classes when students used dialect forty-six times. Conversely, students were corrected by the instructor during the dialect classes once out of every three times that they used MSA.

Another observable pedagogical strategy that is noted in classes is modeling. Both instructors adhered to speaking the variety at hand in a consistent manner during interactions with students throughout the classes. Only six dialect words are observed in the instructors' speech during MSA classes. In addition to greetings that were pronounced with dialectal vocalization, lexical items from the dialect were used to signal transition such as *ṭayyib* "good/ok" or to urge students to start a new activity such as *yalla!* "let's go!"

Discussion and Implications

One of the most important findings of this study is the indication that it is possible to attain Intermediate-level proficiency both in MSA *and* in an Arabic dialect in first-year classes that teach them simultaneously while avoiding random mixing between the two varieties. Arabic learners in this study are shown to be overwhelmingly able to understand and sustain speech in MSA as well as in the dialect, equally, over prolonged interactions both in class and during pre-prepared, student-led speech produced in skits and oral presentations. Students show awareness of and the ability to differentiate between the two varieties in their speech and limit mixing between them to no more than 6 percent of their overall speech in this data set. The topics they addressed in both varieties span different daily activities and personal interests typically addressed in first-year language courses at the college level. Their relatively high level of grammatical accuracy in both varieties, their rare use of hybrid constructs, and ability to self-correct indicate a grasp of the lexicon and structures of both varieties and ability to control spoken production in one or the other variety.

These findings run counter to expectations and concerns within the Arabic learning field regarding achievable proficiency levels and the ability to keep the two varieties distinct while teaching them simultaneously. The findings also run counter to observations in the field about students' unnatural, MSA-dialect "hybrid" speech as a result of learning Arabic following the "integrated approach." The results of this study are possible in this Arabic program because of the curricular choices and pedagogical strategies that were designed to increase student noticing of the distinctions between the two varieties while encouraging using each in a sustained manner throughout the year. Both varieties were taught in a parallel manner, with each advancing through its own curriculum and therefore restricting the need to "borrow" from the other variety in order to communicate adequately. The instructors' implementation of a curriculum that helped students advance in each variety and their consistent modeling of the desired variety during classroom interactions supported students' noticing and distinct acquisition of the two varieties. Although a remote second, underscoring its secondary importance for this beginning-level class compared to modeling, explicit corrective feedback is the other pedagogical strategy instructors implemented in this data set, contrary to recasting, which was barely used at all. Using corrective feedback primarily in the dialect class and hardly at all in the MSA class might be an indication of the instructors' concern for the importance of supporting a naturally sounding dialectal speech in that one class period dedicated to dialect compared to the more frequent opportunities for working on MSA in the other four classes dedicated to building literacy. An accurate understanding of the instructors' motivation behind this behavior, however, requires the incorporation of polling of the instructors in future research. Assessing each variety separately also further clarifies the importance of keeping them separate in order to promote proficiency in each and not rely on code-switching to compensate for the forms that have not been acquired yet.

These results indicate that it is possible to build a strong foundation in the language of daily life as well as in the language of literacy—that is, to lay the basis for a diglossic language development that will foster a higher language proficiency that is sociolinguistically appropriate. In other words, as students continue to advance in their proficiency in these two varieties, they will be well equipped to switch back and forth between the two according to the situation, as needed. As they become more advanced, they will further diversify their Arabic linguistic repertoire by learning how to mix the two varieties appropriately according to the complex rules of MSA-dialect code-switching. As demonstrated by this study, no additional time is needed to achieve this goal. Nor is it necessary to conflate the two linguistically distinct varieties and allow students to use them in free variation. Pedagogical strategies that enlist students' awareness or noticing, combined with a curriculum that promotes autonomy and self-paced learning through language technology similar to the ones described in this study, might bring the field closer to addressing the diglossia issue in a manner that enhances students' language proficiency and sociolinguistic readiness. Students could avoid feeling confused and, by producing hybridized language from the start, then could proceed to rapidly build their proficiency with confidence.

Although primarily applicable to a diglossic language such as Arabic, these findings may bear implications for the learning of standard and vernacular varieties within the same language where the linguistic differences may not be as stark. They may also be relevant to the simultaneous teaching of languages from the same family or cluster as in the case of romance languages or Scandinavian languages.

A secondary finding of this study that might bear pedagogical implications on the instruction of MSA alongside the dialect is the primarily lexical and phonological nature of the mixing that took place in the participants' speaking, both in class and in skits and oral presentations. Some of the phonological mixing occurred in an intentional rather than random manner because students were missing a vocabulary item within the variety at hand. They therefore used or "borrowed" that item from the other variety and did so wholesale. Perhaps because they are still in their first year of study, they have not yet developed coherent and comprehensive strategies for applying the phonological rules of a dialect, for instance, to words they know from MSA. They therefore take the word wholesale and do not attempt to modify its phonology and make it fit into the rules of the particular dialect the way more advanced learners would. Thus, it might be beneficial to provide some explicit guidance to lower-level learners on how to make such phonological shifts. This way they are able to capitalize on the vocabulary that they know in MSA, for example, and try to use it in the dialect when they try to be creative, as observed in the data. In the example earlier from Egyptian speech, where the word for "cat" was "borrowed" from the MSA repertoire, the student pronounced the "q" instead of converting it to the expected glottal stop of Cairene Arabic. Although this would not have helped with the necessary, but hard to guess, change in vowel after the "q," such a phonological change would have brought the student closer to producing speech that sounds more Egyptian.

It is important to note that some of the mixing that took place, however, was not the result of a strategic borrowing from the other variety but merely resulted from expected confusion around similar lexical items. This happened, for instance, several times when students were producing numbers in all three varieties represented in the data. Where lexical proximity between MSA and a dialect is obvious, it might be helpful for instructors to highlight the differences in a systematic manner, especially when they are minor or merely phonological, as in the case of numbers, for instance. Although the jury is still out on whether proximity between varieties (and specifically dialects) promotes faster learning or whether it hampers it (Siegel 2010), it might be worth harnessing Arabic students' noticing ability and language awareness to help them navigate lexical proximity by addressing phonological rules governing the different varieties in a way that is appropriate to their level.

Future research is needed to determine how the proficiency of students using the approach that relies on noticing and differentiation between the two varieties outlined in this study will develop at higher levels. Also, what happens to these students' proficiency and comprehension when they encounter code-switching, whether between MSA and a dialect or among dialects? What will happen to students' dialect proficiency when their literacy becomes stronger, and what pedagogical interventions would be needed in order to foster continued parallel development of both varieties?

References

Abdalla, Mahmoud. 2006. "Arabic Immersion and Summer Programs in the United States." In *Handbook for Arabic Language Teaching Professionals in the 21st Century*, edited by Kassem M. Wahba, Zeinab A. Taha, and Liz England, 317–30. Mahwah, NJ: Lawrence Erlbaum.

Abu Melhim, Abdel-Rahman. 1991. "Code-Switching and Linguistic Accommodation in Arabic." In *Perspectives on Arabic Linguistics*, edited by Bernard Comrie and Mushira Eid, 231–50. Amsterdam: John Benjamins.

Al-Batal, Mahmoud. 1992. "Diglossia Proficiency: The Need for an Alternative Approach to Teaching." In *The Arabic Language in America*, edited by Aleya Rouchdy, 284–304. Detroit: Wayne State University Press.

Al-Batal, Mahmoud, and R. Kirk Belnap. 2006. "The Teaching and Learning of Arabic in the United States: Realities, Needs and Future Directions." In *Handbook for Arabic Language Teaching Professionals in the 21st Century*, edited by Kassem M. Wahba, Zeinab A. Taha, and Liz England, 389–99. Mahwah, NJ: Lawrence Erlbaum.

Albirini, Abdulkafi. 2014. "The Socio-Pragmatics of Dialectal Codeswitching by Al-Keidaat Bedouin Speakers." *Intercultural Pragmatics* 11: 121–47.

Brustad, Kristen, Mahmoud Al-Batal, and Abbas Al-Tonsi. 2010. *Alif Baa: Introduction to Arabic Letters and Sounds*, 3rd ed. Washington, DC: Georgetown University Press.

———. 2011. *Al-Kitaab fii Taᶜallum al-ᶜArabiyya*, Part One, 3rd ed. Washington, DC: Georgetown University Press.

———. 2014. *Al-Kitaab fii Taᶜallum al-ᶜArabiyya*, Part Two, 3rd ed. Washington, DC: Georgetown University Press.

Chakrani, Brahim. 2015. "Arabic Interdialectal Encounters: Investigating the Influence of Attitudes on Language Accommodation." *Language & Communication* 41: 17–27.

Ferguson, Charles A. 1959. "Diglossia." *Word* 15: 325–40.

Hachimi, Atiqa. 2013. "The Maghreb-Mashreq Language Ideology and the Politics of Identity in a Globalized Arab World." *Journal of Sociolinguistics* 17: 269–96.

Institute of International Education. 2015. "Host Regions of US Study Abroad Students, 2001/02–2013/14." Open Doors Report on International Educational Exchange. January 2016. http://www.iie.org/opendoors.

Kuntz, Patricia. 2000. "Beliefs about Language Learning: Students and Their Teachers at Arabic Programs Abroad." *African Issues* 28: 69–76.

Kuntz, Patricia, and R. Kirk Belnap. 2001. "Beliefs About Language Learning Held by Teachers and Their Students at Two Arabic Programs Abroad." *Al-ᶜArabiyya* 34: 91–113.

Mitchell, Terence F. 1986. "What Is Educated Spoken Arabic?" *International Journal of the Sociology of Language* 61: 7–32.

MLA Language Enrollment Database. 2013. Modern Language Association. January 2016. https://apps.mla.org/cgi-shl/docstudio/docs.pl?flsurvey.

Palmer, Jeremy. 2012. "Intercultural Competence and Language Variety on Study Abroad Programs: L2 Learners of Arabic." *Frontiers: The Interdisciplinary Journal of Study Abroad* 22: 58–83.

Ryding, Karin C. 2006. "Teaching Arabic in the United States." In *Handbook for Arabic Language Teaching Professionals in the 21st Century*, edited by Kassem M. Wahba, Zeinab A. Taha, and Liz England, 13–20. Mahwah, NJ: Lawrence Erlbaum.

Sayahi, Lotfi. 2014. *Diglossia and Language Contact: Language Variation and Change in North Africa.* Cambridge: Cambridge University Press.

Schmidt, Richard W. 1990. "The Role of Consciousness in Second Language Learning." *Applied Linguistics* 11: 129–57.

Schulthies, Becky. 2014. "Do You Speak Arabic? Managing Axes of Adequation and Difference in Pan-Arab Talent Programs." *Language & Communication* 41: 1–13.

S'hiri, Sonia. 2002. "Speak Arabic Please! Tunisian Arabic Speakers' Linguistic Accommodation to Middle Easterners." In *Language Contact and Language Conflict in Arabic*, edited by Aleya Rouchdy, 149–74. London: Routledge Curzon.

Shiri, Sonia. 2013. "Learners' Attitudes Toward Regional Dialects and Destination Preferences in Study Abroad." *Foreign Language Annals* 46: 565–87.

———. 2015a. "The Homestay in Intensive Language Study Abroad: Social Networks, Language Socialization and Developing Intercultural Competence." *Foreign Language Annals* 48: 5–25.

———. 2015b. "Intercultural Communicative Competence Development during and after Language Study Abroad: Insights from Arabic." *Foreign Language Annals* 48: 541–69.

Siegel, Jeff. 2010. *Second Dialect Acquisition.* New York: Cambridge University Press.

Trentman, Emma. 2013a. "Arabic and English during Study Abroad in Cairo, Egypt: Issues of Access and Use." *Modern Language Journal* 97: 457–73.

———. 2013b. "Imagined Communities and Language Learning During Study Abroad: Arabic Learners in Egypt." *Foreign Language Annals* 46: 545–64.

Younes, Munther. 2006. "Integrating the Colloquial with *Fusha* in the Arabic-as-a-Foreign-Language Classroom." In *Handbook for Arabic Language Teaching Professionals in the 21st Century*, edited by Kassem M. Wahba, Zeinab A. Taha, and Liz England, 157–66. Mahwah, NJ: Lawrence Erlbaum.

———. 2015. *The Integrated Approach to Arabic Instruction.* London: Routledge.

PART 3

Integration and Skill Development

10

Integrating Colloquial Arabic into the Arabic L2 Curriculum

An Analysis of Learner Speech

LAMA NASSIF

Williams College

We came here and started out speaking *fusha* [Modern Standard Arabic] to taxi drivers, restaurant owners, etc. Some knew *fusha* and were able to speak to us but many didn't. We were laughed at, not understood, and stood out as foreigners. Then, when I began to pick up and use the dialect, reactions immediately changed. I was taken more seriously; I was complimented on my Arabic, I was asked if I was Jordanian, and I was able to hold lengthy conversations with people. The doors that can open for you if you know the dialect (or at least attempt to use it) are unlimited. (Quoted in Shiri 2013, 14)

THE REMARK that opens this chapter, by a student following a study-abroad experience in Jordan, represents a reality that learners of Arabic as a second language (L2) who have only studied Modern Standard Arabic (MSA) face as they interact with Arabic speakers. While knowledge of spoken varieties of Arabic affords learners opportunities for naturalistic communication and enhances the quality of their interactions with Arabic speakers, introducing Colloquial Arabic (CA) in the Arabic L2 curricula in the United States has thus far been the exception rather than the norm (Al-Batal and Belnap 2006; Palmer 2007; Ryding 2013; Shiri 2013, 2015). The MSA that most learners acquire today is not spoken in day-to-day interactions, creating a "fake model of oral proficiency," as Mahmoud Al-Batal notes (1995, 123).

Karin Ryding (2006, 2009, 2013) uses the term "reverse privileging" to describe the situation in which the secondary, more formal discourse (i.e., MSA) is introduced prior to the primary, day-to-day discourse (i.e., spoken varieties). While seemingly counterintuitive, privileging MSA in the Arabic L2 curricula is intertwined with several philosophical, sociolinguistic, pedagogical, and programmatic issues. In many contexts, CA is stigmatized as being a less prestigious variety of Arabic, or even a corruption of MSA (Bassiouney 2009; Holes 2004; Palmer 2007; Versteegh 2001, 2004). In addition, questions such as how to approach the marked differences between MSA and CA, what spoken variety to teach, and what kind of Arabic to teach continue to raise interest and stimulate debates.

These challenges notwithstanding, many L2 Arabic practitioners have long called for the simultaneous integration of MSA and spoken varieties early on in Arabic L2 instruction (Al-Batal 1992, 1995; Al-Batal and Belnap 2006; Younes 1995, 2015). Al-Batal and Belnap argue that "the Arabic classroom can and should be a place in which multiple registers co-exist, as they do in real life" (2006, 397). Munther Younes argues, "If the goal of an Arabic-as-a-foreign-language program is to prepare students to function successfully in Arabic, then they should be introduced to both a spoken Arabic dialect and [formal Arabic] from the beginning of an Arabic course" (1995, 233).

Changing Arabic as an L2 Field

In response to an increasing interest in interacting with Arabic speakers (Belnap 2006; Husseinali 2006; Kuntz and Belnap 2001), some programs have adopted an integrated approach in which MSA and a variety of CA are introduced in the Arabic L2 classroom from the early stages of Arabic instruction. While pedagogical experiences abound, no research exists on the simultaneous development of MSA and CA in L2 Arabic learning, a gap that the current study seeks to address. The study explores the development of MSA and CA as reflected in the speech of learners who have undergone integrated MSA-CA training. In so doing, it aims to evaluate MSA-CA integration into the Arabic L2 curriculum as measured by the learners' development of speaking competence in both varieties. It also studies the learners' ability to attain an understanding of the sociolinguistic reality of MSA and CA use as reflected in their speech productions in a variety of contexts.

The Study

The current study explores the speech productions of learners of L2 Arabic enrolled in a program that offers integrated MSA-CA instruction. Its goals are to study features that might clarify the process of simultaneous development in the two Arabic varieties (CA and MSA), and to determine whether learners show marked similarities (i.e., systematic patterns) in their use of these features. It also seeks to assess learners' success in developing the ability to use these varieties appropriately (i.e., "sociolinguistic competence"; Canale 1983), and to show awareness of "register" (e.g., formality and informality). The following research questions guided the study:

1. What features of speech do learners in integrated MSA-CA instruction display?
2. Do learners display systematic patterns in their speech productions?
3. Do learners show awareness of appropriate register in their use of MSA and CA?

Method

This section provides information on the research participants and the design and data analysis of the study.

Participants

The participants (N = seventy; thirty-six males and thirty-four females) were L2 learners of Arabic as a foreign language at the University of Texas at Austin. The participants were enrolled in first-, second-, and third-year Arabic courses, as shown in figure 10.1. They were of typical university age and studied a variety of majors.

The participants were enrolled in six sections of intensive Arabic; first- and second-year participants came from multiple sections, outlined in table 10.1. Sections at the same level were guided by the same syllabus and course objectives. The participants were involved in training in MSA and Levantine Arabic or in MSA and Egyptian Arabic. The sections also shared the same daily schedule of activities and assignments and took the same exams. Third-year participants came from one section that involved training in MSA and Levantine Arabic. All of the sections used the *Al-Kitaab fii Taʿallum al-ʿArabiyya* series (Brustad, Al-Batal, and al-Tonsi 2006, 2011, 2013). Table 10.1 provides an overview of the sections, the variety of Arabic training, and hours of instruction.

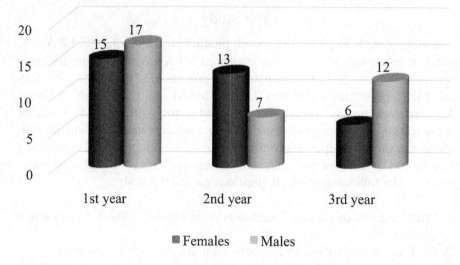

Figure 10.1 Profile of the participants

The participants were exposed to input in both MSA and a spoken variety (Levantine or Egyptian), as determined by the variety assigned to the class (See Al-Batal's chapter in the current volume for information on the integration model at the University of Texas at Austin). Input was provided through teacher speech and learner speech and through authentic and semiauthentic written and spoken texts.

Table 10.1 Overview of the sections, Arabic variety training, and hours of instruction

Group	No. of sections	Training	Semester	Hours of Instruction
1st-year Arabic I: Novice Mid to Novice High	3	MSA & Levantine (2) MSA & Egyptian (1)	Fall 2013	6 hours a week, 15 weeks: 90 hours
2nd-year Arabic II: Intermediate Mid to Intermediate High	2	MSA & Levantine (1) MSA & Egyptian (1)	Spring 2014	6 hours a week, 15 weeks: 90 hours
3rd-year Arabic I: Intermediate High to Advanced Low	1	MSA & Levantine	Summer 2011	15 hours a week, 5 weeks: 75 hours

Study Design and Tasks

Given the research questions above, this study adopted an exploratory approach. The study did not seek to assess the participants' levels of accuracy or fluency; rather, it aimed to detect and explore emerging speech patterns. The study relied on tasks that had already been designed as part of the course work in order to provide an ecologically valid and meaningful representation of the participants' learning. All of the students' "productions" were made during the final two weeks of the academic semesters of focus; they included student presentations, class skits, recordings, and end-of-course interviews. Table 10.2 provides an overview of the study tasks.

Table 10.2 Overview of the study tasks

Group	No. of tasks	Type of task
1st-year Arabic I	1	End-of-course interviews
2nd-year Arabic II	1	End-of-course presentations
3rd-year Arabic I	2	End-of-course presentations
		End-of-course skits

First-Year Tasks

The productions from the first-year participants (Novice Mid), administered during the last week of the semester, involved spontaneous student–interviewer interactions. It included recordings of a "Your Upcoming Weekend" task in the second part of the interviews. The participants were guided with specific prompts; six questions were used, which required details on upcoming weekend activities at different times of the day (e.g., "What are you going to do in the morning?" "What time?"). The participants were not directed to use a particular variety of Arabic or to employ specific structure; instead, they were merely instructed to "speak in Arabic."

Second-Year Tasks

The productions from the second-year participants (Intermediate Mid to High) were drawn from end-of-course presentations. The task involved a four- to five-minute class presentation on a topic of interest. The participants were instructed to "present a report in Arabic." When the participants inquired about CA use in the presentations, the course instructor commented that they should use the form that they felt to be most appropriate.

Third-Year Tasks

The productions from the third-year participants (Advanced Low to Mid) were drawn from end-of-course presentations and end-of-course skits. The presentation task involved a ten- to twelve-minute formal class presentation on a topic of interest; a more predominant use of MSA was thus expected of them. The students were also required to include a follow-up questions-and-answers component after each presentation, but they were not given specific instructions about which variety to use in that component. The skit task involved a seven- to ten-minute dialogue in Levantine Arabic.

Data Analysis

Given the study's focus on the patterns that emerge in learner speech, we conducted a qualitative, multistep analysis of the data. First I performed a data-driven analysis using a grounded theory approach (Strauss and Corbin 1998). I identified emerging themes (MSA features, CA features, and common MSA-CA features) during the initial data analysis, which served as a "preliminary thematic framework" (Lynch 1996). Next I coded the data according to the major themes that I had identified, and I created subcategories (e.g., MSA conjunctions). In conducting the analysis, I carried out a process of categorical aggregation (Creswell 2007) and grouped instances of the data according to their relevant categories and subcategories; I uncovered different patterns in the process. I did not conduct a statistical analysis, given the exploratory nature of the study, but I calculated descriptive statistics.

This chapter reports on the use of specific features in learners' production—verbs, negation markers, and conjunctions—and provides an overview of the lexis used in the productions (see table 10.3). These features were chosen because they display some of the most marked differences between CA and MSA, and they provide insights into the learners' developing grammatical, discourse, and sociolinguistic abilities (Canale 1983).[1]

In analyzing the verbs, verb voweling, and the presence or lack of CA prefixes that denote a time frame (i.e., the present-tense aspectual marker /b-/ [ـبـ] or the future-tense marker *ḥa-* [ـﺣ]) determined verb categorization since these features reflect the grammar associated with verb usage.[2] In analyzing other aspects of lexis, however, word voweling was not a factor in word categorization as long as the word stem (i.e., consonantal and long-vowel structure) remained intact and was a form that is commonly used in both MSA and CA. For example, the word بيت "home" was categorized as a common MSA-CA word, regardless of whether the speaker used the Levantine pronunciation *bēt* or the MSA pronunciation *bayt*. This method of analysis was

Table 10.3 Examples of categories and subcategories in data analysis

Feature categorization	Verbs		Negation markers		Conjunctions		Lexis	
MSA	He watches	يُشاهد	not	لا\ليس	but	ولكن	tomorrow	غداً
	She studies	تَدرس			also	أيضاً	only	فقط
					because of	بسبب		
CA	She works	بتشتغل1		مو\ما\مش	but	بس	a lot	قوي
	I did	سَوّيت			also	كمان	at all	خالص
	They say	بيؤولوا			because of	منشان	will	حـارح
Common CA-MSA	They were.	كانوا	I didn't have	ما كان عندي	and so	فـ	week	أسبوع
			He didn't study	ما درس	or	أو	wonderful	رائع
							first	أول

The aspectual marker *baa* [ـ] attached to the verb بيشتغل ("works") marks present tense actions and states in CA. It is used in Egyptian and Levantine CA.

done to acknowledge the richness of expression in both MSA and CA and the difficulty of separating many words into distinct MSA or CA features.

Findings and Discussion

The current study investigates (1) the features of the speech that learners in integrated instruction display, (2) the existence of systematic patterns in the participants' speech productions, and (3) the participants' awareness of the appropriate register in their MSA-CA use. The study findings reflect the coexistence of features of both MSA and CA in the learners' speech. The learners "code-switched" between the varieties in their use of words, phrases, and sentences in instances of intrasentential and intersentential mixing. The data also shows examples of word-level hybridization. As the learners advanced in their Arabic studies, their code-switches and language choices seemed to be determined by the suitability of each language variety to the target context—that is, "diglossic" code-switching (Mejdell 2006). Some aspects of *lughat al-muthaqqafin* ("the language of the educated"; Mejdell 2000) are also seen in the data. The following sections discuss the findings and present examples related to the three research questions, organized by the year of Arabic instruction and emerging language patterns.

First-Year Learners' Productions

Figure 10.2 shows a visual display of features of the first-year productions. The first-year participants display variation in their use of features in the data sample while also showing an overall preference for CA (see also the stage 1 findings from Thomas Leddy-Cecere's chapter in the present volume). Apart from verbs, CA features predominate, while MSA and common MSA-CA features are also visible in the data (e.g., conjunctions). CA negation markers and conjunctions are more frequently used than MSA negation markers and conjunctions. These findings are expected, given the training provided in first-year Arabic I, which emphasizes immediate needs and day-to-day interactions that are usually used in CA (e.g., basic self-introductions and talking about hobbies, interests, and daily routines). The participants also show personal preferences for MSA or CA (as shown by the predominance of features from one variety over the other). The participants, however, used features from both. One student sample production includes MSA, CA, and common MSA-CA features but shows preference for the use of verbs in MSA, a common observation in the data (as demonstrated in figure 10.2).[3] This pattern is also visible in sample productions with CA prefixes attached to verbs that are pronounced in an MSA fashion; in one such sample, the student used the CA-specific future-tense marker ha- (ـه, "going to"[4]) and pronounced verbs

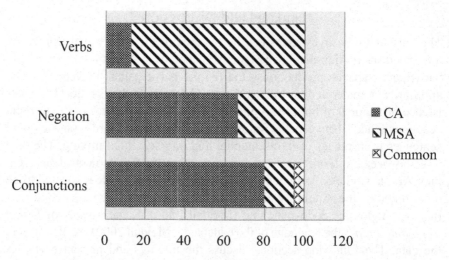

Figure 10.2 A visual display of features in first-year productions

in an MSA fashion although he showed an overall preference for Levantine Arabic in his production.[5]

While the MSA-CA word-level hybridization shown in this sample production may seem incorrect by prescriptive standards, it is not uncommon in the speech of educated Arabic speakers. In an analysis of six speeches of the late Egyptian president Gamal Abdel Nasser—well known as a powerful public speaker—Clive Holes reports instances in which Nasser attached the marker *ḥa-* to verbs pronounced in an MSA fashion (e.g., حِنُحارب, حِنُقاتَل "We will fight"). In describing this linguistic practice, Holes (1993, 19) comments that it is "not just the interweaving of dialect and standard features which occurs, but word-level hybridization." Bassiouney reports on the frequency of the use of the aspectual marker *baa* (بـ).[6] This distinctive feature of present-tense verbs in spoken varieties expresses the habitual nature of actions "even with 'pure' MSA verbs" (2009, 58). Bassiouney cites examples such as بِيَقَّع "is located" and بِتُناقَش "is being discussed."

Similarly, in Nasser's speeches, Holes reported instances such as بِيُقبَل "is being accepted," in which the speaker used /b-/ with a passive-tense verb that is used in MSA (as shown in Bassiouney 2009), and بِيَستَطيعوا "are able to," in which /b-/ was used with an MSA verb; Holes described this practice as "undoubtedly a rule-governed process, even if no one has yet demonstrated for any dialect where its permissible limits lie." He continued:

> Hybridization is the evidence of the co-existence and mutual accommodation of rival language systems, and hybrid forms of the *byuqbal* ["is being accepted"] and *byastaṭiiʕu* ["are able to"] type can and do occur to varying degrees in the speech of almost all speakers. Educated speakers may use them a lot, and less educated speakers little . . . but that is simply to do with speakers' relative familiarity with the contributing linguistic systems. The as-yet undiscovered rules that generate such hybrids must be substantially if not entirely shared by all speakers. (1993, 19)

Accordingly, one could argue that these participants are performing a similar hybridization as in the instances shown in Holes (1993) and Reem Bassiouney (2009) by affixing CA tense markers to MSA verbs. This linguistic practice signals the coexistence and accommodation of two language systems in a way that is similar to that shown in the speech of Arabic speakers (Holes 1993).

Verbs in First-Year Productions
Verbs are some of the most distinctive features of learner productions across the entire data sample. Unlike other features in the data, verbs are more pre-

dominantly used in an MSA fashion. One could argue that verbs are carriers of action, and thus a more formal way of expressing them may be expected, especially in a formal end-of-course conversation with an interviewer. These productions may thus indicate an emerging sense of register that would necessitate the use of certain formal features (verbs, in this case). The learners' verb use may also indicate an emerging grammatical competence in MSA. As Ryding remarks, "Verbs to a great extent determine the syntactic structures of sentences" (2013, 200).

One distinctive feature in the analysis of verb usage in the data is the use of the aspectual marker /b-/ (ـِ). Overall, the percentage of verbs with /b-/ usage compared to total verb usage is 25.5 percent. Over a quarter (27 percent) of the participants at this level consistently used /b-/ in their verbs, while 16 percent affixed this prefix to certain verbs (but not others) within the same utterance. One student, for example, integrated /b-/ in the first occurrence of the verb arūḥ (أروح, "I go") but consistently dropped this prefix in the rest of the utterance.[7] Another time, however, the student showed an overall preference for CA verb usage.[8]

Negation in First-Year Productions

Another distinctive feature of the learner productions is the use of negation markers. CA negation markers predominate (65 percent of the participants used CA markers only); when they did use MSA negation markers, instances of CA markers were also usually found within the same utterance.[9] Only 10 percent of the participants exclusively used MSA markers. This finding could be explained by the training that usually occurs in the first semester of Arabic, where the focus is on expressing negation in CA.

Conjunctions in First-Year Productions

Similarly to negation markers, CA conjunctions predominate in the first-year participants' productions (as shown in figure 10.2). Nearly two-thirds (65.22 percent) of the participants only used CA conjunctions in their speech, while 4.35 percent only used MSA conjunctions. Again, when MSA conjunctions were used, there were usually instances of CA conjunctions within the same utterance.[10] As noted earlier, this finding could reflect course training.

Second-Year Learners' Productions

Figure 10.3 shows a visual display of the features in the second-year productions. The second-year participants show an increased usage of MSA and common MSA-CA features compared to the first-year participants. This pattern may indicate an increasing awareness of register given the formality of the presentations from which second-year data were collected. Linguistically,

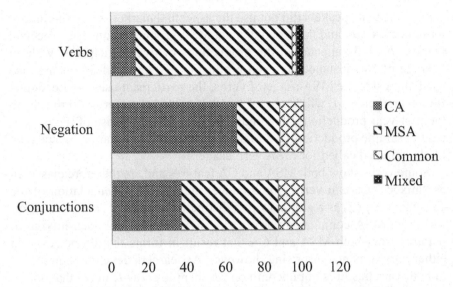

Figure 10.3 Visual display of features in second-year presentations

this pattern reflects an evolving language-development process with increased mixing of MSA and CA features (see stage 2 findings in Leddy-Cecere's chapter in this volume). It also mirrors course training; in second-year Arabic courses, students are more widely introduced to MSA and common MSA-CA features, and higher-level topics (e.g., abstract concepts such as Arab history, traditions, and journalism) are integrated into the course. Accordingly, some sort of formality and a wider range of usage of MSA and common MSA-CA features are expected. The scope of writing, usually conducted in MSA, also increases in second-year Arabic. Nevertheless, the data sample also shows the use of CA features, and that the percentages of usage varies by feature type.

In the student samples, we can hear a predominance of MSA and common MSA-CA features along with the simultaneous use of features from Levantine Arabic. For example, one participant (who had had training in both Egyptian and Levantine Arabic in different semesters) used Levantine to express desire: كان بدّي "I wanted." This habit may have stemmed from the speaker being more comfortable with a spoken variety while expressing emotions, thus reflecting an evolving sense of appropriate language use, as is discussed further below.[11]

Verbs in Second-Year Productions
As was the case with the first-year participants' productions, the verbs used by the second-year participants are more predominantly MSA in nature;

this means that speakers did not use the aspectual marker /b-/ or the future-tense marker ḥa-, and they used distinct MSA pronunciation. The aspectual marker /b-/ only appears in the productions of five participants, with an average of two instances in each production. Other CA features are also used alongside the MSA usage of verbs; the participant uses the Levantine future marker رح ("will"; see table 10.3) with MSA verbs. Similarly to the first-year productions, this finding may reflect the sense of the participant in sample production 10.8 to the formality of the situation, which they likely believed called for MSA verb usage.[12]

Some verbs show both MSA and CA features and are therefore classified as "mixed." Certain verbs, for instance, include the pronunciation of the consonant qāf (ق) as a glottal stop (a distinctive feature of some CA varieties) in an MSA-conjugated verb (e.g., يؤولون "they say"). Such mixing of features from both MSA and CA that result in forms that do not exist in either variety is not surprising, however. As learners develop competence in both varieties, it is not uncommon for them to show features that do not exist in their first or target language as they advance toward consistent target-like production (Gass and Selinker 2008). Still, the percentage of mixed MSA-CA verbs compared to total verb usage is minimal in the data (3.62 percent).

Negation in Second-Year Productions

The second-year students' use of negation markers showed a different pattern than that of verb usage. While there was still variation, CA markers were more frequent in the data (65 percent of negation marker use). This finding could be interpreted by the participants' comfort in using CA negation markers (or as necessitated by the specific content that they were negating) as well as by their use of MSA or CA in that specific utterance. For example, one student used the MSA negation marker ليس "not" in an utterance that represents historical information.[13] On the other hand, the student used MSA and CA markers within the same discourse; he shifted from MSA negation (لا تدخنها "you don't smoke it") to CA negation يعني مش . . . ما بتشوف "that is not . . . you don't see" when he changed the whole discourse to CA as he was explaining an idea.[14] This shift reflects a developing sense of appropriate language use, which is discussed further below.

Conjunctions in Second-Year Productions

The use of conjunctions show variation in the second-year productions; MSA conjunctions are more frequently used than CA conjunctions (50.4 percent and 36 percent, respectively). Most of the participants (85 percent) used CA and MSA conjunctions in the same presentation. Interestingly, while 65 percent of the first-year participants only used CA conjunctions, none of the participants in the second year did this, which reflects their language training and evolving sense of register. Expectations of MSA use increase in formal presentations, and teachers could have emphasized cohesive features as the type of forms that will provide an organized structure to the presentation.

We find a range of uses of conjunctions: (1) the use of CA and MSA features within the same presentation, (2) the use of one feature in Levantine (كمان) and in MSA (أيضاً) (both meaning "also") within the same presentation, and (3) the use of MSA features only. One could argue that some conjunctions (e.g., كمان) persist in the productions of second-year students given these words' predominance in first-year Arabic.[15]

Additional Patterns in Second-Year Learners' Productions

Two additional (and interesting) patterns are observed in the second-year participants' productions. First, all of the participants consistently pronounced key words in an MSA fashion.[16] This finding displays an increasing sense of register, with an expectation of MSA use in formal presentations. It is also reminiscent of the aforementioned *lughat al-muthaqqafīn* (Mejdell 2000), with frequent usage of MSA and common MSA-CA lexis.

The second pattern involves shifting to CA when expressing opinions or providing clarifications. One student used the Levantine words كتير "a lot" and حلوة "beautiful," placing the intensifier "a lot" before the adjective "beautiful" and elongating the long vowel ي in كتير (all of which are CA features) to express her opinion.[17] A second student shifted to a spoken variety when attempting to clarify an idea.[18] Such a practice indicates an evolving sense of appropriate and real-life use of Arabic.

The participants' shift to CA lexis and grammatical structures to express opinions and to clarify ideas is not uncommon in Arabic speech. Holes observes that Nasser employed MSA to express more abstract and impersonal concepts but shifted to Egyptian Arabic to express concrete ideas that were "strongly associated with the personalization of issues" (1993, 35). This observation is also documented in the speech of former Egyptian president Hosni Mubarak, who used MSA when assuming the role of the president (i.e., a more formal role) while shifting to Egyptian Arabic when attempting to indicate closeness to the audience (see Bassiouney 2009). It would thus seem that the participants' experiences in integrated instruction advance their sociolinguistic competence by providing them with the ability to make linguistic choices that reflect appropriate language use.

Third-Year Learners' Productions

Figures 10.4 and 10.5 show a visual display of the features in the third-year presentations and skits. The third-year participants were the most systematic in their use of language features compared to the first- and second-year participants. The participants used a wide range of features of MSA in their presentations and a similarly wide range of features of Levantine Arabic in their skits, which reflects their course training and their evolving native-like "diglossic competence" in both varieties (see stage 3 findings in Leddy-Cecere's chapter in this volume). In third-year Arabic courses, students are more widely introduced to MSA than in any other previous year of Arabic study, and speaking and writing are largely conducted in MSA. The participants also demonstrated consciousness of expected register, which is reflected in the linguistic choices they made vis-à-vis the continuum of Arabic varieties in each of their assigned tasks.

MSA Use in Third-Year Presentations

The third-year course instructor described the presentation task as a formal one, with expectations of MSA use. The participants, however, showed predominant use of MSA and common MSA-CA features not only in their formal presentations but also in the spontaneous question-and-answer component that followed each presentation. Nearly one-third (29 percent) of the participants did not use any CA features, and 43 percent used minimal CA features; this could be interpreted as an indication of overconsciousness of register manifested as attempts to strictly adhere to MSA and common MSA-CA features.[19]

Verbs in Third-Year Presentations

The verbs used in the third-year participants' productions are predominantly MSA; the aspectual marker /b-/ only appears twice in the entire data sample. In one of these instances, a participant used the verb بعرف "I know" but immediately used the MSA version أعرف without the /b-/. Somewhat less than 1 percent of the verbs were used in a spoken variety. As noted above, speakers could view verbs as being carriers of actions in an utterance; thus, we may expect that speakers would use more formal vocabulary to express such verbs.

Negation in Third-Year Presentations

The data sample shows frequent use of MSA negation markers; over half (57 percent) of the participants did not use any CA markers. The use of CA negation, however, is more prevalent in the third-year presentations than other

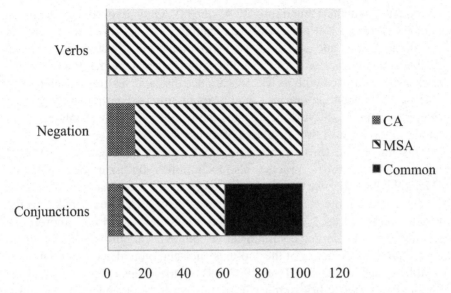

Figure 10.4 Visual display of features in third-year presentations

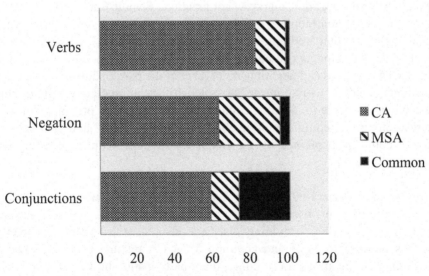

Figure 10.5 Visual display of features in third-year skits

colloquial elements (see figure 10.4, above). Only two spoken negation markers were used in the entire data sample: ما "not," used with verbs in Levantine Arabic, and مش "not," used with nouns and adjectives in Egyptian Arabic and some varieties of Levantine Arabic. It may be that the use of the spoken ما is confused with its MSA uses since the same feature is used in both varieties. The negation marker مش appears in only one participant's production; interestingly, the student adjusted the word to an MSA counterpart (ليس "not") in three out of four instances of its use.[20]

This immediate shift from CA to MSA indicates overconsciousness of register. This linguistic practice also exemplifies diglossic code-switching (Mejdell 2006) because the speaker switched to one form that was deemed to be more appropriate for the topic that was being discussed (or due to the formal context of use). This shift reflects an increasing sense of appropriate register and a developing communicative competence. Further, this linguistic choice presents evidence of the "co-existence and mutual accommodation of rival language systems" (Holes 1993, 19). While Holes originally used this notion to describe hybridization, this notion could be extended to accommodate instances in which the use of a feature from one variety is immediately supplemented by its counterpart in another variety, as deemed appropriate by the context of use.

Conjunctions in Third-Year Presentations
Like verbs and negation markers, conjunctions demonstrate frequent MSA use. The use of common MSA-CA conjunctions increases among third-year students when compared to first- and second-year students' productions, and half of the participants (50 percent) did not use any CA conjunctions. Like the data from verbs and negation, 43 percent of the participants who used CA conjunctions demonstrate instances in which they immediately shifted their use of a CA feature to its MSA counterpart. The two most predominant features among CA conjunctions in this study are بس "but" and كمان "also," which could be explained by the frequency of these features in everyday speech.[21]

Additional Patterns in Third-Year Learners' Presentations
Unlike the pattern observed in second-year productions—where speakers shifted to CA when providing clarifications—the third-year participants strictly adhered to MSA and common MSA-CA features when they were providing clarifications. In so doing, these participants show overconsciousness of register; they might have overestimated the predominance of MSA in Arabic speakers' presentations to the exclusion of CA features.[22] This habit contrasts with the actual formal speech of Arabic speakers such as that of

Nasser, as analyzed by Holes (1993; see above). The third-year participants' overconsciousness of register is also evident in their immediate self-corrections, as noted earlier.

Third-Year Skits: Overall Features
Unlike the formal presentation task, the third-year skit task represents a day-to-day dialogue in which CA use is expected of the learners. Figure 10.5 shows a visual display of the features in the skits.

The participants show marked similarities in their colloquial productions. While MSA and common MSA-CA features predominate in the presentations, CA and common MSA-CA features predominate in the skits; this represents the participants' evolving knowledge of CA and adherence to the expectations of CA and common MSA-CA usage in day-to-day dialogue.[23] The percentages of CA feature use are lower than those of MSA and common MSA-CA features in the formal presentations, however, which could be interpreted by the larger scope of focus on MSA and common MSA-CA features in third-year instruction.

It could well be that these findings reflect the language choices the participants make. In describing Arabic speakers' speech, Kees Versteegh (2001, 195) notes that "since the colloquial and the standard language are not discreet varieties, but only abstract constructs at the extremes of a continuum, linguistic choice does not involve a two-way selection, but rather a mixture of variants." One could argue that the same would apply to the description of learner productions in the current study. The productions show developing and simultaneous knowledge in MSA and CA, and they involve a mixture of variants. The following discussion provides evidence of these remarks.

Verbs in Third-Year Skits
Verbs used in a CA-specific fashion are prevalent in the data sample. MSA verbs are also observed, for example, لا أعرف "I don't know."[24] Instances of MSA verbs with CA features (e.g., the future marker رح [25]) are also used, although there is minimal evidence of this mixing in the data.[26] As with the presentations, the participants' skits include examples of immediate shifting of verb forms from one variety to the other, which signals the participants' consciousness of register, the conscious language choices they made, and the accommodation of two linguistic systems.[27]

Negation in Third-Year Skits
Nearly two-thirds (62.6 percent) of the negation instances in the skits are in CA, and roughly one-third (32.3 percent) is in MSA. The present-tense negation marker لا "not," used with verbs or for negating an entire clause, is the

only MSA negation marker used in the entire data sample.[28] Interestingly, ﻻ is only used to express disagreement or in imperative structures, as is typically used in the Levantine variety of Arabic.[29] It could be argued that the participants' use of MSA negation is a signal of disagreement rather than an MSA feature that is used to negate present-tense verbs in an informal conversation.

Conjunctions in Third-Year Skits
Within the skits, 58.25 percent of the conjunctions are in CA, while 15.05 percent are in MSA; common MSA-CA use of this feature (26.7 percent) exceeds that of verbs and negation markers. In fact, of all the features across the entire data sample in this study, conjunctions show more common MSA-CA usage than any other features. This finding could be explained by the frequency of common MSA-CA lexis in real-life Arabic use and the increasing frequency of this feature in learners' speech as they advance toward target-like Arabic production, as is discussed below. Similarly to all of the features above, one instance of immediate shifting of form is also observed.[30]

Additional Patterns: Lexis
One-quarter (25 percent) of the productions in each task and across each year of Arabic study were analyzed for the use of lexis. In so doing, the study aims to attain an idea of the participants' overall use of lexis as a reflection of their real-life use of Arabic. Figure 10.6 presents an overview of lexical use across

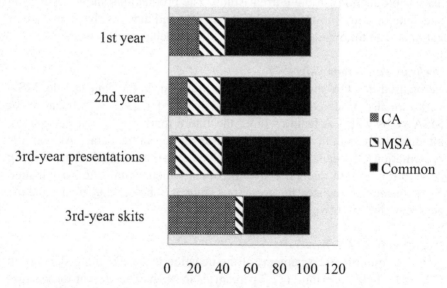

Figure 10.6 Overview of lexical use across the years of Arabic study

the years of Arabic study. Similar to the findings presented thus far, the participants' productions show the coexistence of MSA, CA, and common MSA-CA lexis. The participants were speaking in Arabic—in MSA, CA, and in common MSA-CA features of speech—just as Arabic speakers do.[31]

An interesting pattern also appears in the participants' lexical use; some participants used words from more than one CA variety within the same presentation. This finding indicates that they had had previous training in a variety other than the one introduced in the semester of focus; this represents a unique variety of Arabic and the accommodation of multiple language systems in developing Arabic competence.[32]

In third-year participants' presentations, the use of CA lexis is limited to 4.68 percent of overall lexical usage. These CA words mostly served a certain function such as naming items (e.g., food and sports equipment). This finding likely indicates that the participants were aware of the presentational nature of their task and were, therefore, selective about which items should be presented in a CA format within a formal presentation (namely, items that relate to day-to-day living).

Concluding Remarks

The current study aims to evaluate the integration of MSA and CA in the Arabic L2 curriculum, as measured by the learners' ability to develop competence in both varieties and to gain a better understanding of the sociolinguistic reality of Arabic use. To accomplish these goals, the study investigated the following: (1) learners' features of speech in integrated instruction display, (2) the existence of systematic patterns in the learners' speech productions, and (3) the learners' awareness of appropriate register in their use of MSA and CA. Overall, the findings show evidence of the learners' developing MSA-CA competence across years of Arabic study. The learners expressed meaning in Arabic along the MSA-CA continuum and displayed an evolving sense of register and appropriate language usage.

The participants' productions show marked similarities that reflect their evolving competence in both MSA and CA and their accommodation of multiple linguistic systems. As they advanced in their Arabic studies, their code-switches and linguistic choices seem to be determined by the suitability of each variety to the target context (i.e., diglossic code-switching). The learners code-switched between the varieties in their use of words, phrases, and sentences; as they advanced in their Arabic study, their choices seem to reflect their awareness of the appropriate language forms depending on the context of use. The data also show examples of word-level hybridization along the same lines of the linguistic choices that Arabic speakers make. The data also show aspects of *lughat al-muthaqqafīn* (Mejdell 2000); this is seen by the participants' increasing use of MSA and common MSA-CA features in formal contexts while still maintaining the ability of self-expression in CA in day-to-day dialogue.

Other patterns that reflect awareness of register are also observed in the data. Immediate shifts from one form in one variety to its counterpart in another variety (determined by the context of use) reoccur in third-year student productions. These shifts signal an evolving knowledge of appropriate forms in different contexts with the advance of Arabic study, the conscious language choices that learners make, and the "co-existence and mutual accommodation of rival language systems" (Holes 1993, 19). The data also includes instances in which learners shift to CA to express opinions or present clarifications, as is done in the real-life use of Arabic.

Taken together, these findings support the integration of MSA and CA in the Arabic L2 curricula. The simultaneous presentation of MSA and CA varieties in the Arabic curriculum seems to have advanced learners' sociolinguistic competence, enhanced their linguistic repertoire, and enriched their command of Arabic in ways that afforded them opportunities for linguistic choices that reflect the real-life use of Arabic. The participants not only made decisions that pertained to the syntactic accuracy of their speech; they also made linguistic choices in which they drew on a uniquely varied linguistic repertoire across the MSA-CA continuum.

It could also be argued that the participants' evolving knowledge and the coexisting features of MSA and CA in their speech reflect a process of language development with stages of evolving knowledge of a language variety, as expected in a learner's developing "interlanguage" (Selinker 1972). This refers to the internalized language system of the learner: a system with its own structure that uses elements from one's target language, one's mother language, and one's developing language (Gass and Selinker 2008). In developing their interlanguage, the learners in this study not only seem to be accommodating multiple language systems but they also display evidence of the structure that they themselves "impose" on their "available linguistic data" (Gass and Selinker 2008; see the "Verbs in Second-Year Productions" section of this chapter, for instance). This structure evolves into a more target-like system as they advance in their Arabic learning experiences. This unique interlanguage of the Arabic learner represents in itself a continuum of varieties that mirror the rich and powerfully complex nature of Arabic.

Further, the current study also provides insights that address a major question of many Arabic L2 practitioners: Will the learners' ability to speak in MSA be negatively impacted by the exposure to CA? The data show that exposure to CA as early as the beginning of Arabic instruction does not hinder the development of the learners' linguistic competence in MSA; rather, it augments their understanding of its appropriate contexts of use and provides them with a richer repertoire of linguistic competence that feeds into their knowledge of Arabic speech.

As a beginning step in the process of exploring MSA-CA training in Arabic L2 curricula, this study calls for future research that will inform curricular decisions in Arabic L2 instruction. Future research should expand the data sample to include larger student populations at different programs and should involve more varieties of task types and contexts. The field also requires longitudinal research in which the progress of learners in integrated and nonintegrated programs is studied and compared across different years of Arabic study.

The notes above notwithstanding, the findings of the current study present evidence of the learners' ability to attain a high command of Arabic varieties and develop an understanding of the sociolinguistic reality of Arabic use. The study thus offers implications for L2 Arabic practitioners. It encourages all those who are involved in Arabic learning and instruction to embrace the task of introducing Arabic as spoken by Arabic speakers rather than privileging one variety; the latter is a curricular decision that does not reflect the complexities and nuances of real-life Arabic use. The study also calls for certain attitudinal shifts. First, we should acknowledge the richness of introducing different varieties of Arabic and the opportunities such an approach would grant to the experiences of Arabic learners; spoken varieties are an integral part of Arabic, without which the Arabic learning experience is incomplete. Second, the coexistence of varieties in the Arabic learners' speech should not be viewed as a reflection of deficiency but as an indication of the richness of Arabic learners' linguistic systems. Finally, inspiring Arabic learners with confidence in their ability to master different varieties is essential to their success as they engage in the challenging yet exhilarating experience of Arabic learning.

References

Al-Batal, Mahmoud. 1992. "Diglossia Proficiency: The Need for an Alternative Approach to Teaching." In *The Arabic Language in America*, edited by Aleya Rouchdy, 284–304. Detroit: Wayne State University Press.

———. 1995. "Issues in the Teaching of the Productive Skills in Arabic." In *The Teaching of Arabic as a Foreign Language: Issues and Directions*, edited by Mahmoud Al-Batal, 115–33. Provo, UT: American Association of Teachers of Arabic.

Al-Batal, Mahmoud, and R. Kirk Belnap. 2006. "The Teaching and Learning of Arabic in the United States: Realities, Needs, and Future Directions." In *Handbook for Arabic Language Teaching Professionals in the 21st Century*, edited by Kassem M. Wahba, Zeinab A. Taha, and Liz England, 389–99. Mahwah, NJ: Lawrence Erlbaum.

Bassiouney, Reem. 2009. *Arabic Sociolinguistics: Topics in Diglossia, Gender, Identity, and Politics*. Washington, DC: Georgetown University Press.

Belnap, R. Kirk. 2006. "A Profile of Students of Arabic in US Universities." In the *Handbook for Arabic Language Teaching Professionals in the 21st Century*, edited by Kassem M. Wahba, Zeinab A. Taha, and Liz England, 169–78. Mahwah, NJ: Lawrence Erlbaum.

Brustad, Kristen, Mahmoud Al-Batal, and Abbas al-Tonsi. 2006. *Al-Kitaab fii Ta͒allum al-͒Arabiyya: A Textbook for Intermediate Arabic*, 2nd ed. Washington, DC: Georgetown University Press.

———. 2011. *Al-Kitaab fii Ta͒allum al-͒Arabiyya: A Textbook for Beginning Arabic*, Part One, 3rd ed. Washington, DC: Georgetown University Press.

———. 2013. *Al-Kitaab fii Ta͒allum al-͒Arabiyya: A Textbook for Intermediate Arabic*, Part Two, 3rd ed. Washington, DC: Georgetown University Press.

Canale, Michael. 1983. "From Communicative Competence to Communicative Language Pedagogy." In *Language and Communication*, edited by Jack C. Richards and Richard W. Schmidt, 2–27. New York: Longman Group.

Creswell, John W. 2007. *Qualitative Inquiry and Research Design: Choosing among Five Approaches*. Thousand Oaks, CA: Sage.

Gass, Susan, and Larry Selinker. 2008. *Second Language Acquisition: An Introductory Course*. New York: Taylor and Francis.

Holes, Clive. 1993. "The Uses of Variation: A Study of the Political Speeches of Gamal Abd Al-Nasir." *Amsterdam Studies in the Theory and History of Linguistic Science Series* 4: 13–45.

———. 2004. *Modern Arabic: Structures, Functions, and Varieties*. Washington, DC: Georgetown University Press.

Husseinali, Ghassan. 2006. "Who is Studying Arabic and Why? A Survey of Arabic Students' Orientations at a Major University." *Foreign Language Annals* 39, no. 3: 395–412.

Kuntz, Patricia, and R. Kirk Belnap. 2001. "Beliefs about Language Learning Held by Teachers and Their Students at Two Arabic Programs Abroad." *Al-͒Arabiyya* 34: 91–113.

Lynch, Brian. 1996. *Language Program Evaluation: Theory and Practice*. New York: Cambridge University Press.

Mejdell, Gunvor. 2000. "Aspects of Formal Spoken Arabic in Egypt—Lugha wusta or Lughat al-muthaqqafiin. A View from the North." *Al-Logha* 2:7–25.

———. 2006. *Mixed Styles in Spoken Arabic in Egypt*. Leiden: Brill.

Palmer, Jeremy. 2007. "Arabic Diglossia: Teaching Only the Standard Variety Is a Disservice to Students." *Arizona Working Papers in SLA & Teaching* 14: 111–22.

Ryding, Karin C. 2006. "Teaching Arabic in the United States." In *Handbook for Arabic Language and Teaching Professionals in the 21st Century*, edited by Kassem M. Wahba, Zeinab A. Taha, and Liz England, 13–20. Mahwah, NJ: Lawrence Erlbaum.

———. 2009. "Educated Spoken Arabic: A Flexible Spoken Standard." *NECTFL Review* 64: 49–52.

———. 2013. *Teaching and Learning Arabic as a Foreign Language: A Guide for Teachers*. Washington, DC: Georgetown University Press.

Selinker, Larry. 1972. "Interlanguage." *International Review of Applied Linguistics* 10: 209–31. Reprinted from 1983. *Second Language Learning: Contrastive Analysis, Error Analysis, and Related Aspects*, edited by B. W. Robinett and J. Schachter, 173–96. Ann Arbor: University of Michigan Press.

Shiri, Sonia. 2013. "Learners' Attitudes toward Regional Dialects and Destination Preferences in Study Abroad." *Foreign Language Annals* 46, no. 4: 565–87.

———. 2015. "Intercultural Communicative Competence Development During and After Language Study Abroad: Insights from Arabic." *Foreign Language Annals* 48, no. 4: 541–569.

Strauss, Anselm, and Juliet Corbin. 1998. *Basics of Qualitative Research: Procedures and Techniques for Developing Grounded Theory*, 3rd ed. Thousand Oaks, CA: Sage.

Younes, Munther. 1995. "An Integrated Curriculum for Elementary Arabic." In *The Teaching of Arabic as a Foreign Language: Issues and Directions*, edited by Mahmoud Al-Batal, 233–55. Provo, UT: American Association of Teachers of Arabic.

———. 2015. *The Integrated Approach to Arabic Instruction*. London: Routledge.

Versteegh, Kees. 2001. "Linguistic Contacts between Arabic and Other Languages." *Arabica* 48, no. 4: 470–508.

———. 2004. "Pidginization and Creolization Revisited: The Case of Arabic." In *A Festschrift for Manfred Woidich*, edited by Martine Haak, Rudolf de Jong, and Kees Versteegh, 343–58. Leiden: Brill.

Notes

Additional data and examples are freely available to view and download on this book's product page on the Georgetown University Press (GUP) website (www.press.georgetown.edu).

1. Table W10.1 on the GUP website provides examples of categories and subcategories from the data analysis. The data analysis and reporting use a variety of colors: common MSA-CA features are presented in black font, MSA features in blue, Levantine features in purple, and Egyptian features in green.

2. Again, see table W10.1.

3. See sample production 10.1 on the GUP website. All of the sample productions are presented on the GUP website with their English translations.

4. See table W10.1.

5. See sample production 10.2 on the GUP website.

6. Also in table W10.1.

7. See sample production 10.3 on the GUP website.

8. See sample production 10.4, also on the GUP website.

9. This is shown in sample production 10.5 on the GUP website.

10. See sample production 10.6 on the GUP website.

11. See sample production 10.7 on the GUP website along with an audio recording of the student.

12. See sample production 10.8 on the GUP website.

13. See sample production 10.9 on the GUP website.

14. See sample production 10.10 on the GUP website.

15. See sample production 10.11 on the GUP website.

16. See sample production 10.12 on the GUP website.

17. As shown in sample production 10.13 on the GUP website.

18. This shift also was shown in sample production 10.10.

19. Sample production 10.14 on the GUP website, along with an audio recording, presents examples from a student presentation that shows the predominance of MSA and common MSA-CA features.

20. Two examples are shown in sample production 10.15 on the GUP website.

21. Sample production 10.16 on the GUP website presents examples.

22. See sample production 10.17 on the GUP website.

23. See sample production 10.18 on the GUP website.

24. In sample production 10.18 on the GUP website.

25. As in table W10.1 on the GUP website.

26. See sample production 10.19 on the GUP website.

27. Sample production 10.20 on the GUP website presents two examples.

28. See table W10.1 on GUP website.

29. See sample production 10.21 on the GUP website.

30. See sample production 10.22 on the GUP website.

31. See sample production 10.23 on the GUP website from a first-year student.

32. At the participants' university, students might not necessarily study the same colloquial varieties throughout their Arabic studies. See sample production 10.24, from a second-year student, on the GUP website.

11

Diverse Speaker Output in the Integrated Arabic Classroom

Trends and Interpretation

THOMAS LEDDY-CECERE

The University of Texas, Austin

THIS STUDY EXAMINES and describes dialectal and register-based variation observed in the production of undergraduate students of Arabic as a foreign language at the University of Texas, Austin (UT). As a point of curricular design, these students receive explicit instruction in multiple, discretely identifiable varieties of their target language, including Modern Standard Arabic (MSA), Egyptian Colloquial Arabic (ECA), Levantine Colloquial Arabic (LCA), and (for those beginning their education during or after the fall of 2014) Moroccan Colloquial Arabic (MCA). This research investigates the ways in which this diversity of input is reflected and reshaped as an element of student output.

As such, the work represents a convergence between analyses and goals traditionally attributed to either "theoretical" or "applied" linguistic research. It is theoretical in that its focus rests on the interaction of linguistic systems as observable in students' usage, with an attempt to link such systemic interactions to those more broadly hypothesized to exist in speech communities worldwide. It is applied in that an informed understanding of the results of these interactions is of clear advantage in the engineering and realization of desired pedagogical outcomes. Regarding approach and execution, the study also bridges both camps: although the subjects are students and a large portion of the data is gathered from a classroom setting, I have relied heavily and fruitfully on the conventional "field" techniques of participant observation and the sociolinguistic interview. My investigation of diverse output among students of Arabic is thus an attempt to supersede the often artificial applied/ theoretical divide to provide findings of use and interest to both Arabic language educators and to students of linguistic variation and contact more broadly.

Study Purpose and Rationale

This study is poised to help fill a gap in the general literature surrounding the study of dialectal variation, acquisition, and contact in world language education settings. There are studies that examine L2+ learners' production of dialectal variants in "naturalistic," largely untutored scenarios of acquisition, such as those authored by H. Douglas Adamson and Vera Regan (1991) and Michael Friesner and Aaron Dinkin (2006), both of which document the English usage of non-Anglophone immigrant groups to the United States. A small number of additional works have tackled the acquisition of L2+ dialectal variation in classroom contexts, such as Lauren Schmidt's (2011) investigation of Spanish learners, that of Raymond Mougeon, Katherine Rehner, and Terry Nadasdi (2004) concerning learners of French, and the more general, cross-linguistic summary provided by Robert Bayley (2005). Generally, these studies find that language learners' perception and production of dialectal variation in the target language is limited, and what little is found is usually triggered by above-average degrees of experience and native-speaker exposure on the part of individual students. Crucially, these findings arise from scenarios in which the dialectal usages are not explicitly taught or perhaps even tacitly licensed as part of language education; this fact sets them dramatically apart from the circumstances generated by the Arabic curriculum at UT, which forms the backdrop for the present inquiry. What little discussion is available on explicit instruction in dialectal variation is centered on the education of native speakers of nonstandard varieties in more prestigious forms of their own language (see Siegel 2010), again a situation qualitatively different from the present case.

The present study thereby addresses a serious lacuna in existing research: the nature and products of explicit instruction in dialectal variation in foreign language education. It provides descriptive, observational insight to complement the pedagogical assertions convincingly argued for in the preceding and following chapters of the present volume. Additionally, it extends the scope of inquiry beyond desiderata in Arabic instructional input to include the form of resultant student output as well. Finally, as described above, I strive to fruitfully connect the primarily applied linguistic focus of the volume with findings and techniques drawn from theoretical research into contact between related language varieties.

Arabic Instruction at UT

Before proceeding, I will offer a brief description of the Arabic curriculum under which my research participants study. UT uses the third edition of the *Al-Kitaab* textbook series (Brustad, Al-Batal, and Al-Tonsi 2011, 2013), completed by the fifth semester of study before transitioning to *Al-Kitaab* Part Three, 2nd ed. (Brustad, Al-Batal, and Al-Tonsi 2007). As the fifth and sixth semesters progress, increasing amounts of authentic materials from nontextbook sources are introduced into the classroom. Once the fourth year of instruction is reached, students join content-based courses, which draw entirely on authentic materials and do not use a particular textbook. Some students in the sample (particularly those in their fourth year of study) have studied Arabic abroad in various locations and with various entities—these details were collected on an individual basis from interview participants and will be reported when relevant in conscientiously interpreting the data.

Regarding philosophies and policies surrounding the place of dialect in the Arabic classroom, the position of UT's program is that the use of any dialect is sanctioned at any time, save in the context of a form-focused drill encouraging mastery of a specific variety's forms. Students are encouraged to use what they know to effectively communicate and accomplish task-based objectives and are free to bring their full Arabic repertoire to bear. As instruction continues and students' awareness of diglossic and dialectal variation grows, they are offered guidance as to the effectiveness of different forms in different situations, but care is taken to frame this in terms of the positive value of employing a certain variety in a given scenario and not as the "outlawing" of any alternatives. UT's courses use three dialects of instruction: ECA, based on the dialect of Cairo; LCA, based on that of Damascus; and MCA, following the speech of Casablanca. For the first four semesters of study, each course section adopts one of these three as its designated variety, which is then taught alongside MSA throughout the course. It is not uncommon for students to transition multiple times between Egyptian, Levantine, and Moroccan sections as they progress through the curriculum—enrollment is left open to their choice. An important outcome of this fact is that, even should a student opt to persist with a single dialect of instruction, the same need not be true of all students, and thus a high potential for passive exposure to other varieties exists by way of peer interaction (as well as students' shared access to course materials of the target dialect and otherwise). Beyond the second year of instruction, no specific dialect is designated, and classroom language use is determined organically by the body of students and the instructor. Clearly, instructors' usage presents an additional source of diverse input; interestingly, however, its effect on variation in student production is largely indirect, with evidence pointing to peer practices as the primary external influence—this point is demonstrated and elaborated below.

Research Questions and Project Description

This chapter addresses the following two-part research question:

1. Is the interaction of Arabic varieties in student production within an integrated Arabic program guided by generally theorized, naturally occurring processes of language/dialect contact?
2. If so, do these processes occur in a predictable manner with the subsequent potential for pedagogical application?

The methods used to evaluate answers to these inquiries are described immediately below.

Methods

My study's data is drawn from two sources. The first consists of field notes taken during 24.5 hours of classroom observation among the students of UT's undergraduate Arabic program, approximately evenly distributed between first- through fourth-year courses. All observations were conducted during the spring of 2015, during which I joined as a licensed (and often repeat) participant in classroom activities. The second source of data is a series of sixteen individual interviews carried out with undergraduate Arabic students of the same program during the same time period. These were based on standard practices of the sociolinguistic interview and consisted of an initial phase of general conversation prompts in Arabic followed by an opportunity for metalinguistic commentary in English; interviews averaged approximately twenty minutes apiece. The Arabic prompts both encouraged conversation on concrete, descriptive topics (e.g., "What's your favorite hobby?") and pushed students to engage with more abstract use of language (e.g., "Is the study of foreign language an important part of education?"), with the intent to evaluate possible changes in mixing patterns across usage contexts. All students interviewed began their primary education in Arabic at UT, progressing through the standard course sequence to arrive at their current level of attainment. Four interviewees each represented the four levels described above. All interviews were audio recorded and transcribed for further review.

These two sources of data were consulted in concert to generate a qualitative description of the interactions of linguistic systems observable in student output, as realized in the form of mixed utterances containing elements of more than one discretely identifiable Arabic variety (of MSA, ECA, LCA, and MCA) as well as the evolution of those interactions across student experience levels. This description is composed of analyses along four essential lines of inquiry. The first is a structural one and concerns the types of mixing behavior encountered in the data. Toward this end, I use Pieter Muysken's (1997) tripartite theorization of code-mixing typology—which classifies mixed utterances (intrasentential mixing) as representing examples of alternation, insertion, or congruent lexicalization—with additional reference to Peter Trudgill's (1986) notion of fudged forms. The second analysis addresses global patterns of switching behavior and systemic interaction within emergent subsets of the observed population. In this case, I have drawn heavily on Trudgill's seminal (1986) formulation of the principles of dialect contact and new dialect formation, also referred to as koineization; my conclusions are informed by additional work on the topic by Jeff Siegel (1985), Donald Winford (2003), and Paul Kerswill (2012). It is here that evidence most strongly indicates continuity between general theories/principles of dialect contact and the phenomena encountered in the polylectal Arabic classroom. Third, I consider the potential motivating factors, both cognitive and social, behind the emergence of the above-mentioned patterns. These also are framed in reference to general theory, relying on the sources listed above with the critical addition of Robert LePage and Andrée Tabouret-Keller (1985). Finally, I employ field notes and interview commentary to identify "on-the-ground" factors that facilitate the actuation of these motivations in the manners observed.

Results

On the basis of the classroom observations and individual interviews, I have identified four general classes of mixing behavior in the output of the study's participating students; these correlate strongly with the presence of generally theorized outcomes of dialect contact in "natural" contexts. Moreover, these four classes appear to occur in a more or less sequential manner across differing experience levels of Arabic students involved in the research and thus give the impression of representing successive stages in the evolution of systemic interactions in these students' speech. Therefore, in short, the answers to both components of the study's research question would appear to be "yes": general processes of dialect contact are active in the speech of the Arabic students, and these processes seem to occur in a predictable manner, in accordance with the characteristics of the stages discussed below.

Stages of Dialect System Interaction Observed among Learners in UT's Integrated Arabic Classes

In the following subsections, I describe each of four stages in detail with discussion of the types of mixing behavior evidenced, the overall pattern of such behavior, the motivations for its occurrence, and the factors leading to its actuation. In all cases, examples of actual student output are presented to both illustrate and support these characterizations.[1]

Stage 1. The first stage is most typically attested by the productions of first-year Arabic students observed in the study, although the correlation is not a perfect one—among the interviewees, I classify three of the four first-year students and one of their second-year colleagues as displaying its characteristic features. Overall, at this stage interaction between Arabic varieties gives the impression of being somewhat restricted, at least in comparison to other stages of mixing behavior to be examined shortly. Critically, MSA appears to exist in a horizontal (i.e., nondiglossic) relationship alongside ECA, LCA, and MCA, with mixtures representing all possible relevant combinations attested in the data—thus, at this stage, MSA interacts with other varieties as "just another dialect," albeit one in which students are generally quite proficient (and often dominant) given its relative prominence in the curriculum.

Regarding type, most switches belong to Muysken's (1997) classes of alternation or insertion. An alternation, in brief, consists of a "clean" break from one variety to another, either between sentences or within a sentence along the boundary of a major syntactic unit; an insertion consists of a single word or constituent of one variety incorporated into a larger utterance of another. The first sentence below is an example of an alternation between *LCA* and **MSA**, the second from **MSA** to *LCA*. The third and fourth examples display <u>ECA</u> and <u>MCA</u> insertions into otherwise **MSA** sentences.

1. *minshān huwwe* **lā yurīd ʾan yaʾkul.**[2]
   (Because he doesn't want to eat.)
   First-year class observations

2. **ʿindamā kuntu fī al-jaysh,** **ʾabdaʾ ʾajrī kathīran** *li-ʾannu biddī* . . .
   (When I was in the army, I started running because I wanted . . .)
   "Aaron," a first-year interviewee*

3. **ar-rajul** <u>it-tānī</u> **lā yuṣallī fī ṣ-ṣabāḥ.**
   (The other man doesn't pray in the morning.)
   First-year class observations

4. **yatakallam al-ᶜarabiyy maᶜa ᶜāʾilathu** <u>bzzāf</u>.
   (He speaks Arabic with his family a lot.)
   "Samuel," a first-year interviewee*

Only rarely is mixing observable below the level of the word, involving a combination of morphemes or phonemes from distinct varieties. Such instances may be classed as representing Muysken's third type of intrasentential mixing, that of congruent lexicalization. This phenomenon is more prominent in the second stage of mixing behavior and is discussed below. Here a single example will suffice, consisting of the combination of the <u>ECA</u> verb stem *-rūḥ* with the **MSA** inflectional prefix *ya-* (plain text indicates common elements not assignable to a sole, specific Arabic variety found in the sample):

5. huwa **ya**<u>rūḥ</u> fī ᶜirāq
   (He goes to Iraq.)
   "Rita," a first-year interviewee*

To these three types defined by Muysken, I add a fourth typical of this stage: the repair. Similar in many respects to an alternation, the repair consists of an utterance begun in one variety and subsequently aborted and recast in another with an "overlapping" portion of the utterance repeated in both varieties. The following demonstrate repairs from <u>ECA</u> to **MSA** and from **MSA** to *LCA*, the moment of the repair itself (prosodically marked in speech) noted by the symbol //:

6. ᶜalshān [sic] // **li-ʾanna al-wālida mātat.**
   (Because // because the mother died.)
   First-year class observations

7. **lā ʾurīd** // *mā biddī ʾadrus.*
   (I don't want // I don't want to study.)
   First-year class observations

As an example of these traits embodied in a stage 1 speaker, let us take "Rita," a first-year student who studied in ECA sections for her first and second semesters. Her speech during her interview was predominantly MSA with an admixture of ECA and contained a total of 10 intrasentential switches—an average of 2.5 switches per 100 words. These switches comprised 3 alternations, 4 insertions, 2 congruent lexicalizations (both consisting of the same morpheme-stem combination), and 1 repair. Thus, her overall rate of mixing is fairly low (as is seen in comparison to students of other stages), and insertions and alternations dominate. Additionally, the single repair is infrequent yet salient insofar as it explicitly demonstrates control of multiple linguistic alternatives for the expression of particular words and grammatical functions. She does not appear to situate MSA and ECA in a vertical (diglossic) relationship, as variation between the two does not obviously correlate with changes in topic, stance, or other relevant factors (see Holes 1993; Albirini 2011) over the course of her interview.

As represented by Rita, the overall patterns of systemic interaction in this stage present a fairly limited degree of mixing behavior: students generally tend toward dialectally homogenous utterances, although which dialect is used may differ from student to student and from task to task (such a tendency is corroborated by findings reported in Lama Nassif's chapter in the present volume for a distinct sample of first-year students from the same Arabic program). Intriguingly, this generally mimics the state of affairs described by Trudgill (1986) and others as pertaining to the earliest stages of dialect contact among the first generation of interacting speakers.

Though the outcomes present similarly I believe the motivations underlying the observable mixing behavior to differ in each case. In general cases of dialect contact, early generations of interacting speakers are thought to avoid mixing behavior for the primary reason that they are "set" in their linguistic ways and lack a clear target to induce them away from their established patterns (Trudgill 1986). This is not the case for first-year Arabic students, who do not command preexisting linguistic habits upon which to fall back. Rather, I believe their motivation for limited mixing behavior to be a cognitive one, favoring principles of isomorphy (one form, one meaning) in early stages of language acquisition (see Winford 2003). Such a position is supported by information supplied by several students during the individual interviews, who stated that they preferred—at least in the initial phases of their studies—to acquire a single form of a given item that "works" and then move on to acquire a second item, rather than investing the time to learn two variants of the same word. Such a preference particularly well explains the prevalence of insertion-type mixes in the data, although the presence of repair-type mixes reveals that students do sometimes control multiple variants to express a single meaning (e.g., *ᶜalshān* vs. *li-ᵓanna* from example 6, above).

The actuation of these primarily cognitive motivators seems to be largely self-generated, as evidenced by the metalinguistic commentary mentioned above regarding preferences and study habits. Peer interaction plays a role as well, as classmates are the most common arbiters of which forms "work" on a day-to-day basis in the communicative classroom: in the student-to-student interactions that form the bulk of in-class activities, what defines the effective use of Arabic is not teacher approval but peer comprehension. It thus seems that in such cases the instructor—generally observed to be more permissive and encouraging of variability than students are regarding their own speech or that of others—takes somewhat of a backseat in shaping mixing behavior. Not surprisingly, however, the eventual transmission of that same permissiveness to the class body strongly foreshadows the second stage of dialect interaction observed in the study, to which I now turn.

Stage 2. This stage is generally associated with the speech of second-year students and a few third-year students observed during class visits; of the interviewees, two second-year and one first-year student present output typical of the classification. Overall, this second stage of systemic interaction represents a dramatic increase in mixing behavior over the first stage, with qualitative differences also observable. Similarly to stage 1, MSA exists in a horizontal relationship to ECA, LCA, and MCA.

As compared to the three types of mixing described for stage 1, stage 2 attests a notable rise in the prominence of one strategy in particular—that of congruent lexicalization. As defined by Muysken, the latter "refers to a situation where the two [or more] languages share a grammatical structure which can be filled lexically with elements from either language" (1997, 362). This process of interaction between linguistic systems produces far more heterogeneous and intermingled utterances than those of insertion, alternation, or repair, and the emergence of such typifies stage 2 in contrast to stage 1. The following are examples involving items from **MSA**, <u>ECA</u>, *LCA*, and <u>MCA</u>; those attributable to more than one variety are indicated in the text by means of combined styles (e.g., <u>*ECA/LCA*</u>, **<u>MSA/ECA</u>**), while items common to all varieties are left in plain text.

8. huwa **yajlis** fī ṣ-ṣālōn wa-<u>yiᶜmal</u> *shī* gharīb ᶜashān *hēk*.
    (He sits in the salon and does something weird because of that.)
    Third-year class observations

9. [ʾanā] lā na^crif, mumkin maknās aw fās aw . . . mā ba^crif.
   (I don't know, maybe Meknes or Fez or . . . I don't know.)
   "Hillary," a first-year interviewee*

10. hinā ʾanā ikhtartu maṣrī bass ba^cdēn fī s-sana ath-thānī ʾanā
    badaʾ ət ʾan ʾadrus bi-sh-shāmī kamān, li- li-l-itneen, fa-nuṣṣ wa-
    nuṣṣ.
    (Here I chose Egyptian, but afterward in the second year I started
    to study in Levantine, also, for—for the two [semesters], so half
    and half.)
    "Heidi," a second-year interviewee*

11. bi-l-ḥaqīqa ʾanā ʾuḥibb al-lughāt. ʾanā darastu al-ʾisbānī wa
    l-faransī wa ^candamā ruḥt ʾilā l-jāmi^cat Texas ʾanā simi^ct ʾinnu
    al-barnāmaj al-^carabī ʾaḥsan barnāmaj fa ʾanā qarrartu ʾan bədrus
    al-^carabiyy.
    (Honestly, I love languages. I studied Spanish and French and when
    I went to the University of Texas I heard that the Arabic program
    was the best program, so I decided to study Arabic.)
    "Sally," a second-year interviewee*

The same process of congruent lexicalization may be observed even below
the level of the word. Such mixing behavior extends to involve individual
bound morphemes, as in example 12, below, or phonological features, as in
example 13. In the first example, an **MSA** inflectional prefix combines with
an _ECA/LCA_ verb stem, followed by an _ECA/LCA_ pronoun cliticizing to an
MSA complementizer. The second example contains a mixed production of
the word meaning "the region," in which we find applied to the **MSA** lexeme
al-ʾminṭaqa (identifiable via its vocalism) both the glottal realization of /q/
and the penultimate stress of the ECA equivalent il-man'ṭiʾa. Mixing of both
types is common in the stage 2 data, and parallel practices among second-
year Arabic students are also identified by Nassif in the present volume.

12. yaʾūl ʾann-u . . .
    (He says that . . .)
    Second-year class observations

13. al-min•ṬA•ʾa (penultimate stress)
    (the region)
    "Heidi," a second-year interviewee*

It is also notable that repair mixes, though still present, are of lower frequency than attested in stage 1. This is likely due in part to the increased flexibility in mixing represented by the congruent lexicalizations and in part to general increases in fluency, which result in lower numbers of repairs and recasts overall.

Illustrative of general stage 2 patterns is "Hannah," a second-year interviewee. Hannah spent her first semester of Arabic in an ECA section and the following three semesters in LCA sections. During her interview, she speaks primarily in LCA and MSA, roughly evenly split between the two, in addition to a much smaller but still detectable presence of ECA. Her speech contains a total of 64 intrasentential switches, for an average rate of 6.9 switches per 100 words (nearly three times as frequent as the 2.5 observed for Rita of stage 1). Of these, 27 are alternations, 26 are insertions, 10 are congruent lexicalizations, and one is a repair. Similarly to stage 1, the relationship between MSA and LCA/ECA does not show evidence of being a diglossic one.

As Hannah demonstrates, global patterns of mixing at this stage are highly variable, both between speakers and across the productions of a single speaker: multiple forms are paired together in often ephemeral combinations without clear evidence of convention or rationale. While such a statement may seem unsatisfactory or even dismissive of potential patterns as yet uncovered, it is important to note that (1) both dialect contact and second-language acquisition are inherently variable phenomena (see Bayley and Preston 2008) and (2) such lack of readily apparent order is not without value in the search for cross-linguistic correlates, indicative as it is of what LePage and Tabouret-Keller (1985) term a "diffuse linguistic system." In fact, just such a diffuse nature is ascribed by Trudgill (1986) to the second generation active in koineization scenarios. These speakers move beyond the relatively static mixing behaviors of their predecessors to embrace a highly expanded repertoire of forms although the precise assemblage of variants employed in any given utterance is difficult to predict. Thus, the pattern of systemic interactions in stage 2, like that in stage 1, continues to parallel the gradual and evolving contact of dialects theorized to occur in cases of koineization.

I believe the motivations for this mixing behavior, similarly to those in stage 1, to be primarily cognitive. Moving beyond the isomorphic tendencies identified previously, students producing stage 2 output begin to draw equivalencies between synonymous or cognate items of differing dialectal origins and to consider them equally viable alternatives for use in a given utterance. This development is consistent both with the appearance on the scene of congruent lexicalization as an important mixing type and with the largely unpredictable combinations of variables attested in the output. Under such a framework, the word *yiᶜmal* 'he does' in example 8, above, could as easily have been rendered as *yafᶜal*, *yisāwī* or *ydīr*, *shī* 'thing' as *shayᵓ*, *ḥāja* or *ḥāga*, *ḥēk* 'thus' as *ḥākkā*, *kidā* or *ḥākadhā*, and so on, depending on the individual choices and knowledge of the student at the time of speaking. Such freedom is evidenced in example 9, when Hillary employs both MCA and LCA forms of 'I know' and MSA and LCA verbal negators as part of the same utterance. The drawing of these cognitive equivalencies between linguistic items is almost certainly actuated by the express efforts of instructors and instructional materials to encourage just that: both orally and in print, corresponding dialectal variants are posed as reflecting a single, shared meaning or grammatical function. This is a consistently observed feature of "teacher talk" in UT's Arabic classrooms, where utterances such as example 14, which stress the equivalence of **MSA**, MCA, and *LCA* items, are de rigueur among instructors:

> 14. ṣāḥḥ yā shabāb, lākin **limādhā**? ᶜalāsh? *lēsh*?
> (Correct, guys, but why? Why? Why?)
> First-year class observations–instructor

The resultant perception of unqualified equivalency between contrasting dialect forms is what leads to the largely unrestrained combination of distinct linguistic systems in the output of stage 2 students. As we will see, this sets the stage for the continued evolution of mixing behavior defined as stage 3.

Stage 3. The third stage of systemic interaction is most often attested in the speech of third-year and some fourth-year students. Of the individual interviewees, the mixing behaviors of one second-year student, three third-year students, and one fourth-year student are identified with this category. As described for stage 2, intra-utterance combinations of discrete Arabic varieties are extremely common in the data, and MSA continues to exist in a primarily horizontal relationship to ECA, LCA, and MCA (although some individual learners begin to show a predictable distribution of MSA versus other varieties on the basis of topic and stance, which hints at an increased level of native-like diglossic competence). However, important differences are found between stage 3 and stage 2, primarily regarding global mixing patterns and the respective motivations for their occurrence.

Concerning mixing type, stage 3 is largely similar to stage 2, attesting congruent lexicalizations, alternations, and insertions; repairs continue to decrease in frequency. What sets stage 3 apart, then, is a dramatic increase in the stability of patterns of dialect mixing—in the terminology of LePage and Tabouret-

Keller (1985), an increase in focus. This does not imply that mixing behavior is in any way less common in stage 3 than previously but rather that the precise form it takes is demonstrably more predictable as specific combinatory possibilities rise in prominence and are conventionalized at the expense of competing alternatives. Strikingly, the result of this increased focus appears to be a form of dialect leveling, the third and most theoretically central phase of koineization/new dialect genesis as described by Trudgill (1986), Kerswill (2012), and others. In this way, the already evident parallels linking stage 1 and stage 2 to steps in general processes of new dialect formation are continued in stage 3, in a specific manner unlikely to represent coincidence.

The phenomenon of leveling to which I refer defines the production of Trudgill's (1986) third and culminating generation in processes of koineization. Leveling consists of the disfavoring of language forms which are marked, or uniquely indicative of a particular dialect origin. Thus, when three or more dialects interact, individual variables that represent the "odd man out" in comparison to other available alternatives are likely to be avoided and substituted with a more generic form. Put in formulaic terms, imagine a scenario involving interaction between dialects A, B, and C. Assuming that dialect A expresses a given value by means of feature X, while both dialects B and C express the same value by means of feature Y, speakers of dialect A may level their speech by adopting the unmarked, majority form Y in place of the marked, minority form X, despite the fact that X is native to their dialect and Y is not.

The same process is evident in the stage 3 output of UT's Arabic students, where unmarked forms common to two or more dialects are often substituted for forms specific to one dialect, even if the latter is otherwise the individual student's dominant variety. This leveling is observable at virtually all levels of systemic interaction, including phonology (MSA/LCA [ʤ ~ ʒ] preferred over ECA [g]; MSA/ECA word-final [a] over LCA [e], distinctively ECA penultimate stress lost in favor of shared MSA/LCA patterns), morphology (ECA/LCA imperfective plural -*ū* over MSA -*ūn*; MSA/ECA third plural object clitic -*hum* over LCA -*hon*), and lexicon (ECA/MSA *kull* 'all' over LCA *kill*; LCA/MSA *ʾadrus* 'study' over ECA *ʾadris*; ECA/LCA *rāḥ* 'go' over MSA *dhahaba*).[3] With regard to syntax, similar patterning of interactions is present in negation strategies, interrogative sentences, and demonstrative placement. MCA is not generally included in these determinations because it was not a dialect of instruction at UT until 2014 and thus had not been a significant source of input for third-year students at the time of study.

To ground these phenomena in an example, let us consider an excerpt from an interview with "Lily," a third-year student who studied her first two semesters in LCA classes, her second two in ECA classes, and one third-year semester each with ECA- and LCA-speaking instructors. As will be shown in the quotation, Lily's speech throughout the interview may be pre-dominately identified as ECA but exhibits a number of important departures—the majority of which may be interpreted as instances of leveling (marked in **bold**):

> 15. fa baḥibb **hādhā** l-lugha bass ya⁼nī mā darast-**hā-Ø**, wa mish mum-kin **ʾaktub** bi-fārsī ʾabadan fa-ya⁼nī kunt ⁼āyza ʾaʾrā wa **ʾaktub**, bass kunt ⁼āyza ya⁼nī **shē** jidīd wa mukhtalif. ʾakhī daras fārsī fī jām⁼it Texas . . .
> (So I like this language but I haven't studied it, and I can't write in Farsi at all so I mean I wanted to read and write, but I wanted, like, something new and different. My brother studied Farsi at UT . . .)
> "Lily," a third-year interviewee*

With the exception of MSA ʾakhī 'my brother,' all departures from ECA rep-resent cases of leveling behavior, diverting as they do to a form shared by both MSA and LCA (albeit occasionally with slight variation). Thus, we observe the preposed MSA demonstrative hādhā (≈ LCA hādā) in place of postposed ECA dā, MSA/LCA pronominal clitic -hā instead of ECA -ahā (with accompanying stress shift), and MSA/LCA ʾaktub rather than ECA ʾaktib 'I write.' On the level of phonology, both jidīd and jām⁼it are pro-nounced with LCA [ʒ] instead of ECA [g], and syntactically we may note the absence of the uniquely ECA post-clitic -sh with the negated verb. Finally, the item shē 'thing' is of particular interest in that it represents an analog to Trudgill's (1986) notion of the "fudged form," meaning a realization interme-diate between (but not precisely matching either of) two similar variants attested among interacting dialects—in this case, MSA shayʾ and LCA shī (as opposed to ECA ḥāga).

Leveling such as this account for 20 of 30 intrasentential switches in Lily's (shorter than average) interview. Her overall rate of switching is 7.4 per 100 words; 8 of the switches are alternations, 18 insertions, and 4 congruent lex-icalizations, with no repairs. While the distribution of MSA versus dialectal forms is not overtly patterned, it is perhaps notable that all of her switches are between ECA and either MSA or a shared MSA/LCA form (despite her strong LCA background); this indicates a differentiation from stage 1 and stage 2 behaviors in which MSA is treated on equal footing with other interacting varieties. This development perhaps presages a transition to more a native-like diglossic model in which the relationship of MSA to ECA is orthogonal to that of ECA and other dialects in her speech.

It is also important to note that the results of leveling are at times subtle, manifesting as one- or two-word insertions like those seen below in examples 16 and 17, in which first marked MSA *ayḍan and then ECA *faṣl, ma*ʿāhā* are replaced by leveled *kamān, ṣaff* and *ma*ʿahā*, respectively. Despite their less prominent nature, these are nonetheless attributable to the same overarching process described just above.

16. kāna ʿindī ṣaff al-fuṣḥā wa **kamān** ṣaff al-ʿāmmiyya, al-ithnayn.
    (I had MSA class and also colloquial Arabic class, both.)
    "Hope," a third-year interviewee*

17. bass ʿandī **ṣaff** tānī **ma**ʿ**ahā** fī yōm al-ʾarbaʿ.
    (But I have another class with her on Wednesday.)
    "Nicholas," a third-year interviewee*

As a final point regarding patterns of mixing in stage 3, it is notable that even in cases of differentiation between interacting dialects in which no clear unmarked form emerges, such as MSA *jayyid* versus LCA *mnīḥ* versus ECA *kwayyis* 'good,' the general increase in focus (i.e., decrease in variability) still obtains: for example, with regard to the above-listed items specifically, I have noted a strong tendency toward the use of ECA *kwayyis* by speakers of all dialects. Although the factors that have led to the preferencing of these specific items over their counterparts are not immediately clear, what is important is the regularity and consistency of usage across speakers; these instances of stability are thus set apart from the individualized patterns of invariance described for stage 1 and point to a process of community-wide conventionalization.

This last point is an important one in considering the motivations behind the leveled, focused patterns of linguistic interaction in stage 3. In the koineization context, it is clear that the factors behind the emergence of these patterns are social, corresponding to the formation and promulgation of a novel, unified group identity (see Trudgill 1986; Kerswill 2012). I contend that a similar drive underlies the evolution of mixing behavior observed in the Arabic classroom. As students increase in competency and their experience with Arabic and with one another grows, learners of similar attainment levels begin to form a recognizable, functioning speech community in which numerous varieties of the language are actively employed. This development

allows for the entry onto the scene of social influences over language variation, in addition to the primarily cognitive factors operating in stages 1 and 2.
This way the interactive processes observed in a classroom setting come to
resemble even more strongly those present in "natural" dialect contact where
marked minority forms are disfavored, shed, and replaced by unmarked
majority variants.

I therefore argue that the principal mode of actuation for the leveled, sta-
bilized mixing described for stage 3 lies in the increased and more complex
sociolinguistic interactions within the speech community formed by Arabic
students and their classmates. The systemic interactions attested in student
output of this stage are attributable to the emergence of micro-community
sociolinguistic norms among the group of peers with whom individual student communicate and to whom they relate.

Stage 4. Stage 4 describes the interaction of Arabic varieties in the production
of advanced students of Arabic at UT, most participating in their fourth year
of study. Of the interviewees, one third-year student and three fourth-year
students produce output typical of this stage. In contrast to the previous three
stages, stage 4 entails a small global decrease in mixing behavior in addition
to a fundamental rearrangement of the relations between interacting dialects,
thus veering from the essentially unidimensional trajectory observed to this
point. Regarding mixing type, stage 4 continues the congruent lexicalization,
alternation, and insertion strategies active in stages 2 and 3. It departs from
the earlier two, however, in the return to prominence of repair mixes, as
noted for stage 1. Representative of these trends is "Adam," a fourth-year
interviewee who studied his first four semesters in ECA sections but has
since studied for two years under only LCA-speaking instructors. Adam's
interview contains 39 intrasentential switches, or 5.2 per 100 words, of which
14 are alternations, 17 insertions, 6 congruent lexicalizations, and 2 repairs.
The vast majority of switches are between ECA and MSA (only one involves
a uniquely LCA item) and are largely executed in a diglossically competent
manner. In contrast to stage 3 behavior, only 12 of Adam's 39 switches are
attributable to leveling.

What these counts do not immediately show is that the primary differentiation between stage 4 and stage 3 is not one of mixing type but of overall
mixing patterns. The tripartite, horizontal relationship between MSA, ECA,
and LCA evidenced in stage 3 is overturned in favor of a bipartite, vertical
(i.e., diglossic) relationship between MSA, on the one hand, and either ECA
or LCA on the other. This state of affairs thus comes to more closely resemble
the systemic interactions active in the production of most native Arabic
speakers, which generally consist of a single colloquial dialect (or closely

related complex of dialects, such as a local and a national form) positioned in a diglossic relationship with MSA, which will have been acquired to varying levels of proficiency. From the stage 4 data, the following example is provided from a fourth-year student who successfully uses a register alternation from *LCA* to **MSA** to "wax philosophic" in challenge to another student's point regarding popular art in Egypt:

18. *bass kīf nistakhdam* **hādhā al-fann kayy nafham ar-rabīᶜ al-ᶜarabiyy?**
   (But how do we use this art to understand the Arab Spring?)
   Fourth-year class observations

Conversely, "Bruce," a fourth-year interviewee, incorporates ECA elements into otherwise **MSA** discourse to serve a similarly native-like explanatory function (see Holes 1993):

19. **al-fikra al-ᶜāmma fī hādhihi al-qaṣīda hiya** ᵓ**innu kull shay**ᵓ**, kull** hāga **fī ḥayātnā hiya muṣādafa, ṣudfa bi-shakl** ᶜ**āmm. mā ikhtarnā** ᶜ**ayiltnā, mā ikhtarnā jinsiyyātnā, mā ikhtarnā** ᵓ**ayy** hāga **fī ḥayātnā.**
   (The general idea in this poem is that everything, everything in our lives is coincidence, chance in general. We didn't choose our families, we didn't choose our nationalities, we didn't choose anything in our lives.)
   "Bruce," a fourth-year interviewee*

This is not to say that other patterns of mixing are categorically absent in student productions at this stage but rather that such patterns appear to be limited in both frequency and function: some examples represent holdovers from former leveled norms (such as the high incidence of MSA/LCA/MCA *hādhā/hādā*-type demonstratives among speakers of ECA) while others appear to be idiosyncratic preferences for specific words/phrases from other varieties (such as the consistent use by "Diana"—a fourth-year interviewee who had studied abroad in Morocco—of MCA *bzzāf* 'very' and *bḥāl ḥākkā* 'like so' in otherwise LCA speech). However, although replication of native-like patterns is not total, it is clear that a single, specific colloquial dialect has assumed precedence in the output of stage 4 and that its interaction with MSA takes place based on a range of situational (Ferguson 1959), relational (Holes 1993), and sociopragmatic factors (Albirini 2011), not simply the deterministic ones operative in stages 1–3. Thus, the pattern of systemic interaction evidenced in this stage diverges from the classically hypothesized progression of dialect contact and koineization to approach theories of diglossia and register variation. Continuity, however, may be observed with reference to the Trudgillian principle of reallocation, whereby former dialectal variants are reanalyzed to reflect other sociolinguistic considerations, and to the notion of a progressive focusing process setting the second two stages identified by this study apart from the first two. This combined presence of dialectal and diglossic interaction processes is by no means contradictory and is in fact to be expected in cases of language variation, as noted by Kerswill (2012).

Similarly to the motivations discussed for stage 3, I believe those behind the developments associated with stage 4 to be primarily sociolinguistic. In stage 3, the establishment of a peer-based speech community results in focusing and leveling phenomena; in stage 4, that initially restricted speech community expands beyond the original core of fellow learners to include instructors, nonacademic native-speaker contacts, and learners of Arabic from different backgrounds. The protected, ex nihilo microcosm, which fostered the above-mentioned processes paralleling phases of koineization/new dialect formation, now functions only as one component of a much larger whole. Correspondingly, community norms and speaker profiles active in Arabic-speaking society at large begin to take center stage and come to represent targets of reorientation and reorganization in variable and combinatory linguistic behavior.

These motivating forces are likely actuated via increased day-to-day and cumulative exposure to users of Arabic beyond the classmate-based peer group, both directly (in interpersonal communication) and indirectly (through media and other authentic materials, instructional and otherwise). The study-abroad experience seems to play a powerful role in initiating the split between stage 3 and stage 4 patterns, although it does not appear to be a necessary nor a sufficient condition in every case. Study abroad dramatically expands the arabophone sociolinguistic networks of which the student is a part and critically exposes the student to large numbers of Arabic speakers unaccustomed to interacting with foreign learners. From student reports gathered during the study interviews, it seems that this fact triggers a sharp rise in the amount of negative reinforcement students receive in response to relatively non-native-like (stage 3) mixing behavior, whether that takes the form of explicit correction, ridicule, or simple surprise on the part of a native interlocutor. The considerable potential of such experience to encourage focusing of variable linguistic production is noted by authors from LePage and Tabouret-Keller (1985) to Penelope Eckert (2008) and likely explains the return to prominence of repair-type switches as students attempt conscious manipulation of variant forms (also observed by Nassif in the present volume among the highest-level students in her sample). These may involve moves away from leveled to "pure" (i.e., dialectally homogeneous) elements, as in the self-enforced use of an ECA demonstrative in example 20, or from "school" forms derived from instructional materials to alternates acquired from outside sources, as seen in the student's attempt in example 21, to mimic the usage of his instructor's regional Levantine ⁼ishī at the expense of UT's *classroom LCA shī*:

20. **hāzihi** l-ḥāgāt // il-ḥāgāt dī . . .
    (These hobbies // these hobbies . . .)
    "Bruce," a fourth-year interviewee*

21. mumkin hādhā *sh-shī* // hādhā l-ʾishī ʾahamm *shī* // ʾahamm ʾishī.
    (Maybe this thing // this thing is the most important thing // the most important thing.)
    Fourth-year class observations

Finally, the agency of individual students should not be ignored as they more specifically delineate their future goals for Arabic language use and begin to selectively seek out new, relevant targets for acquisition on that basis.

In the preceding sections, I have described the major findings of the present study regarding stages of systemic interaction between Arabic varieties in student output, which are summarized in table 11.1:

Table 11.1 Summary of stages of systemic interaction

Stage	Type	Distribution	Motivation	Actuation
1	Alternation, insertion, repair	Restricted	Cognitive (isomorphism)	Study habits
2	Alternation, insertion, congruent lexicalization	Frequent, diffuse	Cognitive (equivalence)	Instructional patterns
3	Alternation, insertion, congruent lexicalization	Frequent, focused (leveled)	Sociolinguistic (micro-community norms)	Peer interaction, establishment of group practices
4	Alternation, insertion, congruent lexicalization, repair	Reduced, focused (native-like target)	Sociolinguistic (macro-community norms)	Non-peer interaction, negative reinforcement

Conclusions and Contributions

This study demonstrates the presence of cross-linguistically hypothesized processes of dialect interaction among foreign learners of Arabic. Moreover, it establishes a predictable trajectory for the development of these processes with potential ramifications for pedagogical best practice. On the theoretical front, these conclusions speak to at least a partial continuity of forces shaping dialect contact outcomes across both L1 and L2+ contexts, the existence of which continues to represent an open line of inquiry (see Howard, Mougeon, and Dewaele 2013). Regarding classroom application, the study's results are perhaps more immediately interpretable, sketching a progressive trajectory of evolution in the diverse output of Arabic learners. This finding argues against fears of fossilization of the non-native-like mixing patterns that may come to temporarily dominate any of the initial stages of learning. The striking parallels with dialect contact phenomena in nonclassroom contexts show these developmental patterns to be anything but unnatural: rather, they represent predictable and explicable phases in the acquisition of linguistic variability, which—allowed proper opportunity for acculturation (Schumann 1978) and explicit exposure to form (Swain 1995; Johnson 2008)—will eventually lead to target-like diversity in production. Knowledge of this progression has clear ramifications ranging from assessment to classroom management to curricular design.

This study's results are thus of interest and relevance both to teachers of Arabic as a foreign language and to researchers in the theoretical study of socio- and contact linguistics—and, consequently, to those individuals who are fortunate to count themselves as members of both professions. It is my hope that findings like these will encourage theoretical and applied linguists to focus on the continuities between their domains of research rather than the often artificial distinctions between them, and to move forward with an eye toward future collaboration, cooperation, and mutual enrichment.

References

Adamson, H. Douglas, and Vera Regan. 1991. "The Acquisition of Community Speech Norms by Asian Immigrants Learning English as a Second Language." *Studies in Second Language Acquisition* 13: 1–22.
Albirini, Abdulkafi. 2011. "The Sociolinguistic Functions of Codeswitching between Standard Arabic and Dialectal Arabic." *Language in Society* 40: 537–62.
Bayley, Robert. 2005. "Second Language Acquisition and Sociolinguistic Variation." *Intercultural Communication Studies* 14: 1–13.

Bayley, Robert, and Dennis Preston. 2008. "Variation and Second Language Grammars." *Studies in Hispanic & Lusophone Linguistics* 1: 385–97.

Brustad, Kristen, Mahmoud Al-Batal, and Abbas Al-Tonsi. 2007. *Al-Kitaab fii Taʿallum al-ʿArabiyya: A Textbook for Arabic*, Part Three, 2nd ed. Washington, DC: Georgetown University Press.

———. 2011. *Al-Kitaab fii Taʿallum al-ʿArabiyya: A Textbook for Beginning Arabic*, Part One, 3rd ed. Washington, DC: Georgetown University Press.

———. 2013. *Al-Kitaab fii Taʿallum al-ʿArabiyya: A Textbook for Intermediate Arabic*, Part Two, 3rd ed. Washington, DC: Georgetown University Press.

Eckert, Penelope. 2008. "Where Do Ethnolects Stop?" *International Journal of Bilingualism* 12: 25–42.

Ferguson, Charles. 1959. "Diglossia." *Word* 15: 325–40.

Friesner, Michael L., and Aaron J. Dinkin. 2006. "The Acquisition of Native and Local Phonology by Russian Immigrants in Philadelphia." *University of Pennsylvania Working Papers in Linguistics* 12: 91–104.

Holes, Clive. 1993. "The Uses of Variation: A Study of the Political Speeches of Gamal Abd al-Nasir." In *Perspectives on Arabic Linguistics V: Papers from the Fifth Annual Symposium on Arabic Linguistics*, edited by Mushira Eid, and Clive Holes, 13–46. Amsterdam: John Benjamins.

Howard, Martin, Raymond Mougeon, and Jean-Marc Dewaele. 2013. "Sociolinguistics and Second Language Acquisition." In *The Oxford Handbook of Sociolinguistics*, edited by Robert Bayley, Richard Cameron, and Ceil Lucas. Oxford: Oxford University Press.

Johnson, Keith. 2008. *An Introduction to Foreign Language Learning and Teaching.* Harlow: Pearson Longman.

Kerswill, Paul. 2012. "Contact and New Varieties." In *The Handbook of Language Contact*, edited by Raymond Hickey, 230–51. Hoboken, NJ: Wiley.

LePage, Robert B., and Andrée Tabouret-Keller. 1985. *Acts of Identity: Creole-Based Approaches to Language and Ethnicity.* Cambridge: Cambridge University Press.

Mougeon, Raymond, Katherine Rehner, and Terry Nadasdi. 2004. "The Learning of Spoken French Variation by Immersion Students from Toronto, Canada." *Journal of Sociolinguistics* 8: 408–32.

Muysken, Pieter. 1997. "Code-Switching Processes: Alternation, Insertion, and Congruent Lexicalization." In *Language Choices: Conditions, Constraints, and Consequences*, edited by Martin Pütz, 361–80. Amsterdam: John Benjamins.

Schmidt, Lauren B. 2011. "Acquisition of Dialectal Variation in a Second Language: L2 Perception of Aspiration of Spanish /s/." PhD diss., Indiana University.

Schumann, John. 1978. *The Pidginization Process: A Model for Second Language Acquisition.* Rowley, MA: Newbury House.

Siegel, Jeff. 1985. "Koines and Koineization." *Language in Society* 14: 357–78.

———. 2010. *Second Dialect Acquisition.* Cambridge: Cambridge University Press.

Swain, Merrill. 1995. "Three Functions of Output in Second Language Learning." In *Principle and Practice in Applied Linguistics*, edited by Guy Cook and Barbara Seidlhofer, 125–44. Oxford: Oxford University Press.

Trudgill, Peter. 1986. *Dialects in Contact*. Oxford: Basil Blackwell.

Winford, Donald. 2003. *An Introduction to Contact Linguistics*. Malden, MA: Blackwell.

Notes

Additional data and examples are freely available to view and download on this book's product page on the Georgetown University Press (GUP) website (www.press .georgetown.edu).

1. Examples drawn from recorded interview content may be heard as audio on the GUP website; these are marked with an asterisk. The student names used in this chapter are pseudonyms that were assigned to the participants, not their real names.

2. For this and all subsequent examples, English glosses reflect the intended communicative content of the utterance, regardless of errors in execution.

3. For further discussion of the dominant role of multivalent ("common") lexis in the production of students at this stage, see Lama Nassif's chapter in the present volume.

12

Effects of Integrated Arabic on Written Language Skills at West Point

A Longitudinal Study

GREGORY R. EBNER AND JEFF R. WATSON

The United States Military Academy at West Point

WHILE THE DISCUSSION of teaching spoken Arabic in the university classroom in the United States reaches back to the 1970s (see, for example, Rammuny 1978), the conversation began, in earnest, in the mid-1990s (see, Al-Batal 1992a, 1992b; Younes 1995; Ryding 1995). In that period, professionals in the teaching Arabic as a foreign language (TAFL) field began to question the decades-long focus on Classical Arabic or Modern Standard Arabic (MSA) within the American university. A recognition that the population of students who wanted to study Arabic was growing and diversifying was a driving consideration supporting the change. While previous generations of scholars learned Arabic as a tool toward enabling future research, the current cohort began to learn the language so that they could communicate with native speakers and more fully immerse themselves in the cultures of the Arabic-speaking world (Palmer 2007). In order to satisfy student demand, it became clear that Colloquial Arabic needed space in the general Arabic curriculum at the university level.

Throughout that period, an increasing number of university Arabic programs have transitioned from *al-fuṣḥā*-dominated curricula that relied upon focus on the formal register of the language for all modalities to programs that attempt to teach a more natural method of communicating that aims to replicate how Arabic is used among native Arabic-speaking populations. In an effort to teach students to communicate in a manner that more closely resembles the language one hears when interacting with native speakers, these newer programs place a stronger emphasis on the use of *al-ᶜāmmiyya* or colloquial forms of Arabic when speaking them in the past.

In these programs, *al-fuṣḥā* remains critical to learner success. When reading and writing, *al-fuṣḥā* still dominates, and to abandon it risks creating a generation of illiterate practitioners of the language. Recognizing the diglossic dilemma presented by Arabic, educators developed programs that allowed, in various forms, the two registers of the language to exist simultaneously in the classroom. Some programs strive to teach the two forms of the language in sequence, such as at the Defense Language Institute, and some universities traditionally save colloquial studies for later in the course sequence. Alternatively, the two forms of the language appear side by side, as presented in the *al-Kitaab fii Taᶜallum al-ᶜArabiyya* series of textbooks (Brustad, Al-Batal, and al-Tonsi 2011, 2013). Others, such as those using *ᶜArabiyyat al-Naas* (Younes, Weatherspoon, and Foster 2014), attempt to blend the two registers by elevating the spoken form to that of an educated speaker of the language and, in essence, teaching one composite language. Regardless of the method, integrated programs seek to find ways to essentially teach two Arabic varieties in the space previously allotted for one. Students are taught to read and write (and listen to specified texts) in *al-fuṣḥā* but to speak using one of the various forms of *al-ᶜāmmiyya*. The end goal is that graduates of these programs will be able to function similarly to native speakers, developing the nuances of understanding that will allow them to effectively and efficiently move between the various registers of the language as the culturally contextual situation dictates appropriate.

A common question when examining the effectiveness of the blended approach focuses on the resources required to teach languages. It expects that, if *al-ᶜāmmiyya* is added to the materials taught in a particular course, then those items already present must suffer some reduction of attention within the syllabus. Given limited classroom time and student resources available to outside work, the logic of this argument implies that, if *al-ᶜāmmiyya* is added to the curriculum, then something that was previously taught in the program would have to be put aside. Students focused on speaking would, of necessity, decrease the attention that they give to the written language. The logic of the argument is pleasingly rational—ambitious Arabic programs do not leave empty space in their curriculum, and anything added to the syllabi must result in something else coming out. In the blended program, the expectation is that *al-fuṣḥā*, the previously dominant form of the language, exclusively taught as the language of the classroom, must suffer a decline in emphasis and, therefore, a reduction in course resources devoted to its mastery. Continuing the logic, if *al-fuṣḥā* is no longer emphasized, then the rational expectation is that student proficiency in the written form of Arabic will decline even as their abilities to speak in a more natural manner improve.

A slow degradation of student abilities in *al-fuṣḥā* would threaten the measured effectiveness of any Arabic program. Just as many faculty in Arabic programs worried over the results of sending our students into the Arabic-speaking world armed only with *al-fuṣḥā*-driven skills, having our students lose a significant part of those skills would trouble faculty today. If we purport to teach Arabic at a university level, then we must be able to produce graduates who can function among the educated native-speaker population, read texts in the language, and effectively follow discourse in the formal form.

To determine if the field's movement toward a blended program is helping or hurting our students, we need to take measure of our efforts. To this point, no systemic assessment of the effects of *al-ᶜāmmiyya* instruction upon *al-fuṣḥā* proficiency has been published. Without such an assessment, we are left to base our curricular developments upon pedagogical hunches and to defend our decision to provide *al-ᶜāmmiyya* content on often-emotional arguments, anecdotal evidence, or purely personal experiences with the language.

This chapter attempts to provide the systematic assessment that can calm the fears of those cautious of an integrated approach. It helps to show that, while there may be some loss of *al-fuṣḥā* proficiencies when *al-ᶜāmmiyya* is added to the curriculum, that degradation need not be severe or even statistically significant. It helps to open the door to development of students who are comfortable with the diglossia present in Arabic and able to navigate the linguistic cues that mark transition from one form of the language to another. Evidence demonstrating limited decrease in *al-fuṣḥā* capabilities of students should help to reassure the field that integrated programs do not sacrifice proficiency in the written language in order to produce gains in the oral proficiencies.

West Point's Arabic Program

The United States Military Academy at West Point is a fully accredited, four-year undergraduate institution.[1] The Academy offers a broad liberal arts program based on a thirty-course core curriculum paired with a variety of majors that lead to a bachelor of science degree upon graduation.[2] In addition to dozens of other fields of study, cadets can major in one of seven foreign languages, including Arabic.

The first two semesters of Arabic (LA203/204) are taught five times per week in fifty-five-minute sessions and provide 3.5 credit hours toward graduation. In the 2013–14 academic year, West Point also converted its two-semester Intermediate Arabic sequence into an intensive one-semester course (LA371) for 4.0 credit hours. All courses beyond the three-course Beginner/Intermediate sequence are taught every other day for 3.0 credit hours. Arabic majors must take ten Arabic courses beyond the first two semesters of language study for a total of 37 credit hours in Arabic.[3]

Prior to the 2012–13 academic year, the Department of Foreign Languages taught Arabic with an *al-fuṣḥā*-only approach. Over the course of four semesters, except in the most anecdotal of cases, students were not exposed to *al-ᶜāmmiyya*, in any form, in the classroom. After completion of a fourth semester of *al-fuṣḥā*-driven instruction, only cadets majoring in Arabic were able to take a semester of Levantine Arabic as part of the major.

During that period, most Arabic instructors in the department were graduates of the Defense Language Institute, which, until the second decade of this century, did not routinely teach *al-ᶜāmmiyya* to its students. Most of those instructors had served multiple tours with the Army in the Middle East and had been exposed to the spoken forms of Arabic. These experiences both broadened their linguistic abilities and demonstrated to them some of the deficiencies in their own language education. Operational military assignments in the region had especially demonstrated the need to provide tools that would allow students to communicate in a more natural form than allowed by an *al-fuṣḥā*-only approach.[4]

Integrating Dialect Studies into the Curriculum

Spurred by exposure to other university-level Arabic programs and a growing commitment to a communicative approach to language learning, the faculty of the Arabic section at West Point began discussing the merits of adding *al-ᶜāmmiyya* to the *al-fuṣḥā*-based curriculum. The faculty decided to move from its then-current curriculum to one based upon the *al-Kitaab* series of textbooks, which allow for the mixing of the colloquial and formal forms of the language. They also resolved to use the Levantine form of the spoken language as the language of the curriculum, based upon the career experiences of the faculty and applicability of that form of the language to future careers of the programs' graduates.

In fall of 2012, the department moved to an integrated Arabic approach in the first two semesters of the language (LA203/204). Those students who continued beyond the beginning level continued to study *al-fuṣḥā* and Levantine Arabic side by side. Since the transition, conversations and many of the listening exercises in the classroom are conducted in *al-ᶜāmmiyya*. Written exercises, to include short essays and reading exercises, continue to be completed in *al-fuṣḥā*.

Those cadets who had already matriculated into the Intermediate-level course (LA361) had completed the first two semesters using an *al-fuṣḥā*-only approach to the language, so they continued with that emphasis. Those who stayed with Arabic beyond the first two years and majored had the opportunity to experience Levantine Arabic in the colloquial course offered in subsequent years.

The transition to an integrated curriculum presented some challenges. Many of the initial challenges were typical of those any language program faces when deciding to modify the approach or the focus of the classroom. A new curriculum potentially requires attention to a vocabulary different from the current set, and the textbook selected to support the new curriculum will nearly always present that vocabulary and the supporting grammar in a different manner. In the entry-level language courses that support large numbers of students, syllabi and lesson lists, perhaps developed and refined over the course of several years, must be rewritten. Supporting materials such as audio-visual presentations may no longer be valid, and course administrators must recreate or repurpose them for different parts of the courses. Making the jump to a new curriculum requires far more planning than simply ordering new textbooks for a course.

At West Point, the movement toward an Arabic curriculum that introduces the spoken forms of the language in the beginning courses provided an additional challenge, primarily in the areas of teaching approach and the training of instructors, some of whom were educated in *al-fuṣḥā*-only environments. At the time, the Arabic faculty consisted of two civilian native speakers, both from countries within the Levantine region, and one nonnative-speaking civilian who possessed advanced speaking skills but mainly focused in Iraqi dialect. In addition to the civilian faculty, the Arabic section included two nonnative speakers who had completed doctorates in Arabic. One nominally focused on Egyptian but was comfortable in Levantine and the other had focused his dialect studies primarily on Levantine. Finally, the group included two military instructors who had completed the Basic Arabic Course at the Defense Language Institute. Those members had studied only MSA and had no formal exposure to the spoken form of the language.

In the summer prior to the implementation of the integrated curriculum, the section provided instruction to the faculty members without experience in Levantine Arabic in order to make them comfortable with the spoken form.

Having taught MSA for a year at the Academy, they were familiar with class-room activities and lesson planning but needed to understand the differences in the spoken form that they would be using in the classroom. Since they were predominately teaching the beginning course, they were able to continue this professional development through the first several weeks of the course as the students focused on *Alif Baa* (Brustad, Al-Batal, and al-Tonsi 2010), learning the letters and sounds of the language. This gradual introduction allowed the instructors to be ready to teach the spoken form as well as the differences between it and MSA before the course reached that point in the text.

Many university-level Arabic programs rely on graduate students or instructors without terminal degrees for teaching at the lower levels of their programs. These instructors, often nonnative speakers of the language, may not have significant experience in the spoken forms of the language if they arrived from programs that focused on *al-fuṣḥā*. Other instructors and more experienced professors may have focused predominately on a dialect other than that considered for instruction in their current program. The experience at West Point demonstrates that, as long a supportive core of professors exists at a university, the transition to an integrated approach should not be rejected simply because some faculty members do not possess extensive experience in the dialect selected for instruction.

While West Point faced challenges in the transition to an *al-ᶜāmmiyya*-supported curriculum, the shift also presented a unique opportunity to measure the longitudinal effectiveness of each approach, *al-fuṣḥā*-only or integrated, especially in terms of reading proficiency in Arabic. Since the 2009–10 academic year, the department has assessed the reading proficiency of students completing both the basic (LA203/204) and Intermediate courses (LA361/362) for every language taught at West Point. Each year, near the end of the Beginning and Intermediate course sequences, the department's Prochievement Test (ProC) is administered to all language students. Commissioned by the department from ACTFL, the ProC is a forty-item multiple-choice test of grammar/vocabulary control and reading proficiency in MSA, which produces a rating on the ACTFL proficiency scale. As a means to assess year-to-year programmatic changes in student language ability, the ProC assesses a blend of students' reading proficiency and their achievement of course objectives specifically in terms of the discrete vocabulary and grammar presented in the first two years of language study. Because the ProC has been administered to almost all Arabic students both before and after the transition to the integrated approach, these test scores can be used to study the longitudinal effect of the transition on student performance. Decreases in reading proficiency, as measured by the ProC, could implicate the integrated approach as a possible cause of the decline.

Furthermore, since West Point cadets are also active-duty military personnel, the department also has access to the Defense Language Proficiency Test (DLPT), a standardized computer-based test of listening and reading proficiency in MSA, which rates test-takers on the Foreign Service Institute's Interagency Language Roundtable (ILR) proficiency scale (n.d.). As the Army's official measurement of listening and reading proficiency, the DLPT is designed to determine a respondent's operational language proficiency (i.e., proficiency at a level 2 or above on the ILR scale, which equates to the Advanced level or above on the ACTFL scale). Because the DLPT does not test as well at the lower levels of proficiency, where students would be expected to perform during the first two years of language study, the ProC is better suited for beginning and intermediate students. Nonetheless, as is discussed later, the DLPT does work well for more advanced students such as the department's Arabic-language majors. For this reason, the DLPT is used as an official culminating assessment to assess the overall language program by testing Arabic majors during the spring semester of their final year at the Academy just before graduation.

Research Questions

To assess the effect of integrating spoken Arabic into a historically *al-fuṣḥā*-only curriculum, this study asked the following research questions:

1. Is there a statistically significant difference in test scores between students who studied only MSA and those who studied MSA plus the Levantine dialect in Beginning and Intermediate Arabic courses at West Point?
2. Is there a statistically significant difference in test scores between Arabic majors who studied only MSA and those who studied MSA plus the Levantine dialect throughout their Arabic studies, including Advanced courses?

Population

For this study, language proficiency test scores from 910 college students of Arabic at West Point were analyzed: 514 in Beginning Arabic, 261 in Intermediate Arabic, and 135 Arabic majors upon graduation; 86 percent (N = 781) were male, and 14 percent (N = 129) were female. Additionally, most students in this population began language studies during their sophomore year at West Point and took Intermediate language during their junior year. The Arabic-language majors continued studying Arabic during their senior year.

Method

As mentioned earlier, the Department of Foreign Languages uses two standardized tests to assess progress and proficiency at several points during a student's foreign language studies at West Point. After completion of Beginning Arabic (two semesters; 160 hours of instruction) and Intermediate Arabic (one or two semesters; 80 hours of instruction), all cadets are tested using the Department of Foreign Languages ProC. Just before graduation, all Arabic majors take the DLPT. To assess whether the integration of dialect studies into the *al-fuṣḥā*-based curriculum affected student scores on the ProC or DLPT assessments, four years of test scores were compared: two years for the control group (preintegration: 2010–12) and two for the experimental group (postintegration: 2012–14).

Findings

Using the Statistical Package for Social Science (version 20), the test scores for both groups were compared. After 160 hours of instruction in Beginning Arabic, ACTFL ratings for both the control group (MSA only) and the experimental group (integrated MSA plus dialect) were identical (Novice-Mid). When converted to numeric rankings (0 = Novice-Low, 1 = Novice-Mid, 2 = Novice-High, etc.), the average postintegration scores were slightly higher (M = 1.31; SD = 0.621) than the preintegration scores (M = 1.29; SD = 0.519). Statistical testing confirmed that this difference was not statistically significant (See table 12.1).[5]

After eighty additional hours of instruction in Intermediate Arabic, ACTFL ratings again showed an average rating of Novice-Mid for both groups. Converted numeric scores, however, showed a larger difference between the preintegration and postintegration groups with the control group (1.87) scoring higher than the experimental group (1.65). A statistical comparison confirmed that the difference between these groups was statistically significant ($p = 0.048$; see table 12.2). A follow-up effect size statistic, however, showed that this difference had only a small-to-medium magnitude (ES = 0.4[6]),

Table 12.1 Wilcoxon Rank-Sum and Mann–Whitney U comparison for Beginning Arabic

Beginning Arabic		N	Mean Rank		Mann–Whitney U	31341.00
ProC	Pre	289	253.45		Wilcoxon W	73246.00
	Post	225	262.71		Z	–0.86
	Total	514			Sig.	0.392

Table 12.2 Wilcoxon Rank-Sum and Mann–Whitney U comparison for Intermediate Arabic

Intermediate Arabic		N	Mean Rank		Mann–Whitney U	3009.00
ProC	Pre	118	95.00		Wilcoxon W	4900.00
	Post	61	80.33		Z	−1.98
	Total	179			Sig.	0.048

meaning that only 27.4 percent of scores within these two groups were non-overlapping.

As mentioned earlier, in addition to the students in Beginning and Intermediate Arabic, 135 Arabic-language majors were also tested using the DLPT (listening and reading proficiency) during their final semester at West Point: 108 prior to al-ʿāmmiyya integration and 27 after.[7] In contrast to the ProC, the DLPT rates test-takers using the ILR proficiency scale, which provides ratings on a scale of 0–4 with sublevels at 0, 0+, 1, 1+, 2, 2+, and so on. See table 12.3 for how these sublevels align with ACTFL sublevels.

For both the listening and reading portions of the DLPT, student ILR ratings were within the 0 level (Novice-Mid equivalent on the ACTFL scale).

Table 12.3 ILR and ACTFL rating scale alignment

ILR scale	ACTFL scale
4	Distinguished
3+	Superior
3	
2+	Advanced-High
2	Advanced-Mid
	Advanced-Low
1+	Intermediate-High
1	Intermediate-Mid
	Intermediate-Low
0+	Novice-High
0	Novice-Mid
	Novice-Low

Table 12.4 Wilcoxon Rank-Sum and Mann–Whitney U comparison for Arabic-language majors

Arabic Majors (Seniors)		N	Mean Rank		Listening	Reading
ProC	Pre	108	67.33	Mann–Whitney U	1385.5	1300.5
	Post	27	70.69	Wilcoxon W	7271.5	7186.5
Reading	Pre	108	66.54	Z	−0.43	−0.91
	Post	27	73.83	Sig.	0.667	0.362

When converted to numeric rankings in an equivalent fashion to the ProC scores (0 = 0, 0+ = 2, 1 = 3, 1+ = 5, etc.), postintegration scores in both listening and reading were slightly higher (L = 1.07; SD = 1.27/R = 1.44; SD = 1.28) than preintegration scores (L = 0.96; SD = 1.22/R = 1.24; SD = 1.39). Once again, however, statistical testing showed that these differences were not statistically significant (see table 12.4).

Discussion

Based on these findings, several conclusions can be drawn. First, for the population of Beginning Arabic students at West Point, integrating a dialect into the previously MSA-only curriculum did not have a negative effect on proficiency ratings. Scores on the ProC were statistically similar for both groups both before and after the integration. Second, for the population of Intermediate Arabic students, there was a slight educationally significant difference in performance on the ProC test prior to al-ᶜāmmiyya integration. While this finding was unexpected, it can be explained. In addition to integrating new dialect studies into the MSA-only curriculum after the 2011–12 academic year, West Point also consolidated its two-semester Intermediate language sequence into one intensive semester. While the number of contact hours remained the same (eighty hours), the length of time taken to cover the material was reduced. This curricular change affected proficiency ratings across all of West Point's foreign language classes. Although the effect was statistically insignificant, it could explain why the postintegration scores were slightly lower than before integration for the Intermediate students. In conjunction with the small-to-medium effect size demonstrated in the data, this additional variable further lowers the importance of the difference between the two Intermediate groups.

Finally, for the selected Arabic-language majors, no statistically significant difference was observed between the two groups. Although the sample
size of the postintegration group is limited at the moment (N = 27), this trend
is expected to continue. Furthermore, while the difference between the two
groups of majors is not statistically significant at the moment, there has been
some statistical movement in the data leading us to believe that the postintegration group will continue to outperform their preintegration counterparts—
perhaps even to a statistically significant degree in the future. Hypothetically,
the integration of dialect studies into the curriculum may provide an additional linguistic reference point that supports and enhances the MSA portion
of the courses. We will continue to observe and study this trend. For this
initial study, however, the lack of difference between these two groups further supports our conclusion that integration of dialect studies into the MSA-
only curriculum did not negatively affect student performance on language
proficiency tests.

Conclusions and Implications

These data provide strong support for the claim that integrating dialect studies into an *al-fuṣḥā*-based Arabic curriculum does not negatively affect student
performance on *al-fuṣḥā*-based language proficiency tests. While integration
does present certain challenges that must be addressed, students at West Point
have proven that they are capable of maintaining skills in MSA and learning
new skills in a colloquial dialect. Despite the different L2 learning experiences of the faculty and their varying teaching styles based on these experiences, instructors have been able to integrate the Levantine dialect without
sacrificing student proficiency in MSA.

These results should serve two purposes for directors of university-level
Arabic programs. First, they demonstrate the importance of continuous
assessment of student progress and program effectiveness. Assessment of our
programs is critical to sustaining and, as appropriate, growing opportunities
for students to study Arabic at our colleges and universities. Assessment
allows program directors to definitively measure and demonstrate whether
our programs are having a positive effect on our students. Without assessment, we are left with only general impressions of our students' progress or
limited and personal anecdotal measures of individual student progress.
Those measures may help us to identify the exceptional students in our program but cannot give us a sense of the program's overall health. In the case
of this study, such assessment will allow the directors of the program at West

Point to confidently measure the effect of moving from one method of teaching to another.

Of immediate concern, the results show that introducing spoken Arabic, in an integrated manner, into an *al-fuṣḥā*-driven program, while it necessarily takes resources from *al-fuṣḥā*, does not have to result in a degradation of student proficiency in the more formal register. Program directors considering a similar transition can eliminate at least one concern from consideration. Certainly, there are many other issues to resolve before executing the transition. Directors will have to determine how to introduce the spoken form (sequentially with *al-fuṣḥā*, integrated, or as a mixed, comprehensive form of the language) and which dialect of the spoken form will be the language of instruction.[8] The basic question of the effect of colloquial instruction on *al-fuṣḥā* proficiency, however, should not be a concern.

This study only measured student abilities using the written language. While this limitation allowed a comparison that may give the field some reassurance regarding the integrated approach, it lacks a measure of the speaking proficiency of the students. Since the main purpose of moving to an integrated approach was to allow enhancement of students' oral communication abilities in Arabic and development of more natural speech patterns, it would have been beneficial to measure speaking proficiencies discretely. Unfortunately, the instruments available for such an assessment simply do not allow effective measure of students at the lower levels of proficiency. The ACTFL Oral Proficiency Interview (OPI), with its focus on MSA as the expected language of dialogue, leaves the students who focuses their early speaking skills in a dialect without a reliable measure of progress. In the future, it will be important to develop new oral proficiency assessment tools (or expand old ones) to assess learners with lower-level proficiency in both MSA and a colloquial dialect. Whereas the ability to speak Colloquial Arabic may have been a characteristic of advanced learners in the past, beginning and intermediate learners are now being educated in Colloquial Arabic earlier on. These new assessment tools will provide insight into a learner's proficiency that is more complete and more representative of the language's diglossic nature. The assessment procedures for commercial tests such as Language Testing International's OPI will need to be modified and customized to test both MSA and a chosen colloquial dialect at the lower levels of proficiency. While the OPI in its current form allows for testing in the dialect, preference is still given to MSA. As the TAFL field continues to move toward more comprehensive presentation of spoken forms of the language, it will be increasingly important to maintain standardized tools that allow both educators and learners to accurately assess progress within a program. In order to regularly assess the progress of our students in both the written and spoken forms, the field needs reliable instruments that can effectively measure those proficiencies at the lower levels in order to better support the assessment of programmatic changes.

As demonstrated in this study, individual institutions are capable of developing such instruments for self-evaluation of programs. Universally recognized measures such as the OPI and the government's DLPT, when calibrated to measure proficiency and progress at the lower levels, may also indicate if a program is improving or in decline. The standardized tests, however, give an added benefit of allowing educators to assess their programs in comparison to the field at large. Evaluation against a broader standard can allow educators to identify, across the field, which programs are achieving higher levels of success with their students. Emulation of those programs, adjusted appropriately for local realities, may serve to improve the entire field of Arabic education.

References

Al-Batal, Mahmoud. 1992a. "Diglossia Proficiency: The Need for an Alternative Approach." In *The Arabic Language in America*, edited by Aleya Rouchdy, 284–304. Detroit: Wayne State University Press.

———. 1992b. "Issues in the Teaching of the Productive Skills in Arabic." In *The Teaching of Arabic as a Foreign Language: Issues and Directions*, edited by Mahmoud Al-Batal, 115–33. Provo, UT: American Association of Teachers of Arabic.

Brustad, Kristen, Mahmoud Al-Batal, and Abbas al-Tonsi. 2010. *Alif Baa: Introduction to Arabic Letters and Sounds*, 3rd ed. Washington, DC: Georgetown University Press.

———. 2011. *Al-Kitaab fii Taᶜallum al-ᶜArabiyya*, Part One, 3rd ed. Washington, DC: Georgetown University Press.

———. 2013. *Al-Kitaab fii Taᶜallum al-ᶜArabiyya*, Part Two, 3rd ed. Washington, DC: Georgetown University Press.

Grissom, Robert, and John Kim. 2012. *Effect Sizes for Research: Univariate and Multivariate Applications*, 2nd ed. New York: Taylor and Francis.

Interagency Language Roundtable. (n.d.). "Descriptions of Proficiency Levels." Interagency Language Roundtable. http://www.govtilr.org/Skills/ILRscale1.htm.

Palmer, Jeremy. 2007. "Arabic Diglossia: Teaching Only the Standard Variety Is a Disservice to Students." *Arizona Working Papers in SLA and Teaching* 14 (August): 111–22. http://slat.arizona.edu/sites/default/files/page/awp14palmer.pdf.

Rammuny, Raji. 1978. "Tadrīs al-lugha al-ᶜarabiyya fi al-jāmiᶜāt al-ᵓamrīkiyya." In *Seminar on the Present and Future of Arabic and Islamic Studies: Final Report*, edited by A. Baghdadi and Raji Rammuny, 77–92. Ann Arbor: Department of Near Eastern Studies, University of Michigan.

Ryding, Karin. 1995. "Discourse Competence in TAFL: Skill Levels and Choice of Language Variety in the Arabic Classroom." In *The Teaching of Arabic as a Foreign Language: Issues and Directions*, edited by Mahmoud Al-Batal, 223–32. Provo, UT: American Association of Teachers of Arabic.

Younes, Munther. 1995. "An Integrated Curriculum for Elementary Arabic." In *The Teaching of Arabic as a Foreign Language: Issues and Directions*, edited by Mahmoud Al-Batal, 233–56. Provo, UT: American Association of Teachers of Arabic.

———. 2006. "Integrating the Colloquial with Fuṣḥā in the Arabic-as-a-Foreign-Language Classroom." In the *Handbook for Arabic Language Teaching Professionals in the 21st Century*, edited by Kassem M. Wahba, Zeinab A. Taha, and Liz England, 157. Mahwah, NJ: Lawrence Erlbaum.

Younes, Munther, Makda Weatherspoon, and Maha Foster. 2014. ᶜ*Arabiyyat al-Naas: An Introductory Course in Arabic*, Part 1. London: Routledge.

Notes

1. The Middle States Commission on Higher Education accredits West Point.
2. The standard educational program at West Point is eight semesters.
3. The first two semesters of foreign language study at West Point are considered part of the core curriculum and do not count toward a major in foreign languages.
4. One of the authors of the study is a career military officer with both operational and academic experience in the Middle East. Conversations with numerous officer-instructors assigned to the department from 2005 to 2013 confirmed the author's belief that proficiency in colloquial forms of the language is critical to linguistic success in the region.
5. Because this dataset (and many similar datasets consisting of ordinal rating scale data) contains numerous outliers and is not normal in its distribution, nonparametric statistical testing (Wilcoxon Rank-Sum and Mann–Whitney U) were used to compare the MSA-only (control) group's scores to those of the experimental group receiving instruction in MSA plus the dialect.
6. Robert Grissom and John Kim (2012) suggest an effect size statistic for nonparametric comparisons of independent samples, which divides the Mann–Whitney U score by the product of the two sample sizes. This calculation is similar to a Cohen's d calculation and can be interpreted similarly.
7. The number of cadets taking the DLPT after integration is smaller because the number of Arabic majors is limited to one graduating class (2015), those who have completed all their Arabic studies since integration.
8. While Munther Younes (2006) argues that educators should not be concerned about confusing students with presentations of *al-fuṣḥā* and colloquial at the same time, that argument should not extend to presenting *al-fuṣḥā* with more than one dialect at the same time.

PART 4

Learners' and Teachers' Voices and Perspectives

13

Integrating Colloquial Arabic in the Classroom

A Study of Students' and Teachers' Attitudes and Effects

MARTIN ISLEEM

Bucknell University

THE CALL TO INTEGRATE Colloquial Arabic (CA) with Modern Standard Arabic (MSA) within the Arabic as a foreign language (AFL) curriculum has been the focus of a number of scholarly works in the last two decades (Al-Batal and Belnap 2006; Donista-Schmidt, Inbar, and Shohamy 2004; Isleem 2015; Palmer 2007, 2008; Shiri 2013; Wahba 2006; Younes 2010). This call deviates from the prevailing ideology that prioritizes the teaching of MSA over CA in that it emphasizes the needs and goals of the students.[1]

Nevertheless, there are many convincing reasons to adopt the integration approach within the AFL curriculum. Presenting MSA and CA together to students of Arabic bestows a sincere linguistic reality in which both registers coexist and complement each other in Arabic native speakers' daily lives and linguistic repertoires. CA is used as the primary means of communication among native speakers of Arabic while the use of MSA is limited, to a large extent, to religious sermons, official media, textbooks, and written literature. However, recent studies show that CA has become more prominent in sociolinguistic spaces and communication, for example, in written communications that previously were exclusively restricted to MSA. These sociolinguistic changes are attributed to globalization and technology, the use of advanced electronic communication, and local linguistic market dynamics (Haeri 1997; Isleem 2015; Warschauer, El-Said, and Zohry 2007).

Another reason to support the integration of CA in the AFL curriculum is because there are now more students interested in the study of the contemporary Arab world and culture as a result of the tragic events of September 11, 2001, in the United States as well as the rise of political Islam and the ongoing political instability in the Middle East and North Africa. Many universities and colleges, particularly in the United States, have shifted their focus from Classical Arabic studies to the contemporary social, cultural, and political realities of Arabic-speaking countries (Younes 2010). In addition to this trend, many schools in the United States have adopted the new Arabic textbooks *Al-Kitaab fii Taᶜallum al-ᶜArabiyya* (Brustad, Al-Batal, and al-Tonsi 2011, 2013) and *ᶜArabiyyat al-Naas* (Younes and al-Masri 2014; Younes and Chami 2014; Younes, Weatherspoon, and Foster 2014), which officially integrate CA materials within the Arabic curriculum.

Recent studies conducted in the United States have shown that the learning needs and goals of students of Arabic play a major role in substantiating the importance of integrating CA (Belnap 1987; Isleem 2015; Palmer 2007, 2008; Shiri 2013). These studies point out that the students' primary reason for studying Arabic is to travel and to be able to interact with native speakers in their native language, spoken Arabic (Kunz and Belnap 2001; Husseinali 2006; Palmer 2007; Younes 2010). Student attitudes and learning motivations are the focus of more recent studies in the field of teaching Arabic as a foreign language (TAFL). These studies report that students of Arabic hold more positive learning motivations toward CA than MSA (Donista-Schmidt, Inbar, and Shohamy 2004) and tend to develop a more negative attitude toward MSA as they continue taking Arabic classes (Isleem 2015).

The importance of students' attitudes stems from the notion that attitude is a supporting factor in motivating learning, so motivated students tend to evaluate the learning situation more positively (Gardner 2001). While attitude is not a sufficient factor in predicting students' achievement, motivation does seem to have a causal relationship with achievement, particularly integrative motivation that "reflects a genuine interest in learning the second language in order to come closer to the other community" (Gardner 2001, 5). Robert Gardner (1985) suggested that integrative motivation is a stronger indicator of second-language achievement than instrumental motivation, in which the student seeks to achieve a practical goal such as course credit or a job promotion as a result of learning a second language (Gardner 1985).

While studies on students' needs, goals, and motivations seem to have become more prevalent among AFL scholars in the United States, the study of Arabic teachers' status, motivations, and roles remains limited. An important study of the profiles and attitudes of Arabic teachers is that of Mahmoud Abdalla and Mahmoud Al-Batal (2011–12). This study provides comprehensive demographic, institutional, and programmatic profiles of college-level teachers of Arabic in the United States. Regarding integrating CA, the study indicates that the majority of the teachers surveyed (over 65 percent) agree that training in a dialect should start in the beginning classes of Arabic, but in existing Arabic curricula, the instruction of dialect in the first years of Arabic is very limited (Abdalla and Al-Batal 2011–12, 16).

The current study seeks to expand the understanding of attitude and motivation behind the learning and teaching of AFL and to provide empirical evidence in support of the integration of CA within the Arabic curriculum. The present study examines two areas related to colloquial integration: attitudes of college-level students and teachers from schools in the United States and other countries toward MSA and CA. Although data on teachers' perceptions and their effect on students' motivation and achievement is still meager (Dörnyei and Ushioda 2013), there is ample evidence to suggest a direct association in that teachers themselves may influence a student's learning experience (Donista-Schmidt, Inbar, and Shohamy 2004).

Methodology

Two attitude questionnaires were developed and designed by the researcher of this study. The questionnaires were offered to each group to measure the attitudes of the students and teachers who learn and teach AFL.

Participants and Data Collection

The student participants in this study are college-level students from the United States, Europe, and American study-abroad programs. Any student who was enrolled in one semester of Arabic was eligible to participate in this study. The teacher participants in this study are teachers of AFL, including both native and nonnative speakers of Arabic.

The students' survey was voluntarily self-administered and electronically distributed through a mailing list of directors of Arabic programs and Arabic teachers in the United States. The teachers' survey was electronically distributed through the Arabic-L listserv for Arabic instructors, sponsored by Brigham Young University.[2]

It is important to note that, although the students' survey contained two sections related to learning motivations and outcome expectations, the findings of these two sections are not discussed in this study because they are not directly related to the integration of the CA within the Arabic curriculum. Moreover, there were a number of challenges in collecting the data caused by the way the questionnaires were distributed and the ethical research policies of universities. Due to policies concerning research on human subjects, the researcher was not able to match obtained students' data to their corresponding-ing teachers at the same time. Second, although the students' survey was very successful in terms of its scope and representation of the various universities and colleges in the United States, there was significant lack of representation of schools from other countries. Regarding the teachers' survey, the number of teachers from schools in the United States is three times greater than that of schools in other countries; therefore, teachers from US schools are better represented in this study.

Students' Survey Layout

The students' questionnaire is composed of thirty-five items.[3] The Arabic instructors' questionnaire consists of thirty-four items.[4] The students' survey contains seven sections, the first consisting of nine items having to do with the participants' demographic and learning background, such as school name, gender, and how many semesters of Arabic the student has taken. Other items in this section ask whether Arabic is the native language of at least one of the student's parents and whether the student's major is related to Arabic language, literature, or linguistics.

The second section consists of two questions inquiring about the student's opinion as to how CA is being integrated in Arabic classes as well as the amount of time the students feel should be devoted to CA in their classrooms. The third and fourth sections aim to elicit students' attitudes toward the intrinsic value of learning both MSA and CA. There are a total of fifteen questions in these two sections. The questions were randomly mixed and the response to each question was assigned a number on a scale of 0 to 10, 0 indicating "strongly disagree" and 10 indicating "strongly agree."

The fifth section consists of three questions designed to elicit information about the instrumental motivations of students. The sixth section consists of three questions designed to reveal the integrative motivation of the students. The responses of section five and six were distributed on a scale of 0 to 10, with 0 indicating "not at all likely" and 10 indicating "extremely likely." The seventh section, the last section of the survey, is composed of five items and is designed to elicit students' outcome expectations in the process of learning AFL. The responses were distributed on a scale of 0 to 10, with 0 meaning minimal expectations were met and 10 indicating that all of their expectations were met.

Teachers' Survey Layout

The teachers' survey is composed of five sections. The first section is designed to elicit the demographic, teaching, and learning background of the teachers, for example, gender, education, and specialization. This section includes questions regarding formal training in teaching Arabic and experience in teaching different Arabic language proficiency levels.

The second section of the teachers' survey includes two questions inquiring as to whether the teachers are required to integrate CA or not and, if not, whether they incorporate it on their own. The second question asks how much time the teachers devote to CA in the different proficiency levels. In the third section of the teachers' survey, there are four statements that measure the attitudes of the teachers toward integrating CA in class. The fourth and fifth sections measure the teachers' attitude toward MSA and CA in various contexts such as in which language should the students communicate in Arabic classes, which method would help students acquire the most knowledge, and the appropriateness of MSA versus CA. The responses to the statements in the third, fourth, and fifth sections were distributed on a scale of 0 to 10, 0 indicating "not at all likely" or "extremely disagree" and 10 indicating "extremely likely" or "strongly agree."

Results

One hundred and forty-one students took the students' survey. The participating students are from twenty-two colleges and universities.[5] The vast majority of the participating students (93.6 percent; $n = 132$) attend American universities and colleges in the United States, and the rest (6.4 percent) attend college-level schools outside of the United States, such as New York University Abu Dhabi, Münster University, and Universität Bayreuth. Nearly 60 percent ($n = 84$) are female and 40 percent ($n = 57$) are male. The survey reveals that students who are nonnative speakers of Arabic but who were brought up by Arabic-speaking parents find the Arabic language very appealing. About 11 percent ($n = 15$) of the participants reported that at least one of their parents is a native speaker of Arabic. More than half of the students, 55 percent ($n = 78$) are majoring in Middle Eastern studies, Arabic language, or Arabic literature. These findings support the notion that there is a growing interest in the Arabic language and culture as well as in the Middle East in general among students in the United States. A large number of the students, 81 percent ($n = 114$), study the *Al-Kitaab fii Ta*ᶜ*allum al-*ᶜ*Arabiyya* textbook series, 15 percent ($n = 21$) study the ᶜ*Arabiyyat al-Naas* textbook series, and about 4 percent use different textbooks. The adoption by most of the schools of the *Al-Kitaab fii Ta*ᶜ*allum al-*ᶜ*Arabiyya* and the ᶜ*Arabiyyat al-Naas* textbooks is an important move on the part of Arabic programs toward integrating CA within the Arabic curriculum since the teaching philosophy of these textbooks strongly promotes the integration approach. The majority of the participants have studied Arabic for up to two years; 36 percent ($n = 68$), only one year or less; 32 percent, two years; 17 percent, up to three years; and about 14 percent, more than three years. Moreover, the survey shows that the students' firsthand experience of Arabic language and culture—meaning visiting or studying in one of the Arabic-speaking countries—is limited. Only one-third ($n = 48$) of the students report that they have visited the Arab world as travelers, only a fourth ($n = 34$) have participated in an Arabic study-abroad program, and 5 percent of those are part of the Flagship and CASA programs.

Regarding the teachers' backgrounds, 59 teachers took the survey. Nearly 54.23 percent ($n = 32$) of them are females and 45.77 percent ($n = 27$) are males. The survey shows that the number of teachers who are nonnative speakers of Arabic is relatively high. Thirty-four of the participants, 57.6 percent ($n = 34$), are native speakers of Arabic, and 42.4 percent ($n = 25$) identify themselves as nonnative speakers of Arabic. These findings are consistent with Abdalla and Al-Batal's (2011–12) findings that indicate a growing number of Arabic teachers who are nonnative speakers of Arabic (Abdalla and Al-Batal 2011–12, 4). Forty-six of the participants teach in thirty-four American universities and colleges, and fifteen teach in twelve non-American universities and colleges.[6] Regarding experience in teaching Arabic, figure 13.1 shows that 44.07 percent ($n = 26$) of the teachers began teaching Arabic within the last eight years, 25.42 percent ($n = 15$) have been teaching for nine to twelve years, and the remaining 30.51 percent ($n = 18$) have more than twelve years of experience in teaching Arabic. In other words, about 70 percent of the Arabic teachers have been recruited in the last twelve years in response to the increased demand for Arabic teachers in the United States.

The survey reveals that the participants are highly educated; about 45.77 percent ($n = 27$) hold PhD degrees and 49.15 percent ($n = 29$) hold master's degrees. Nearly 39 percent ($n = 23$) of participants report specializing in TAFL while nearly 34 percent report specializing in linguistics, 22 percent in Arabic literature or Islamic studies, and 25 percent specialize in other majors. A significant number of the participants (64.5 percent, $n = 38$) report that they have received training in a formal Arabic teacher-training program. While these findings indicate that the participants are professionals and that some have done formal Arabic teacher-training, they also show that the majority of teachers surveyed (61 percent) are specialized in majors that are traditionally associated with Arabic literature, Islamic studies, and linguistics but not language pedagogy.

Most teachers report that they teach Arabic language classes, while less than half of them state that they also teach classes such as Arabic literature,

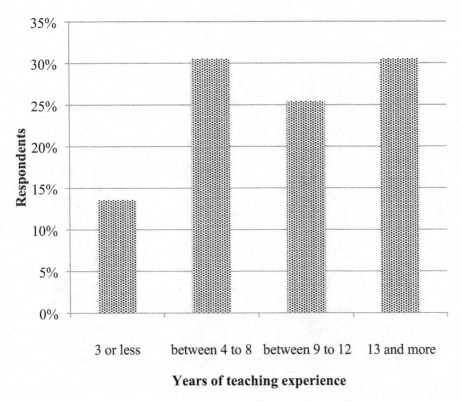

Figure 13.1 Percentage of respondents across years of teaching experience in Arabic

media, and culture. The vast majority of the teachers, 81.4 percent, report that they teach beginning Arabic classes, and 86.4 percent report that they teach intermediate classes. Nearly 55.9 percent also teach advanced Arabic classes, and 44.1 percent teach Arabic topic classes.

Students' Responses to the Integration of CA

The students were asked to respond to two questions about the way CA was incorporated in their current Arabic class and how much time they would have preferred to be devoted to CA. Figure 13.2 shows that about 41 percent (n = 58) of the students believe that MSA is the focal language or the only language taught in their Arabic classes. Nearly 31 percent (n = 44) indicate that both MSA and CA are presented equally in their current Arabic classes, and only 27 percent said that CA is the main language taught in the class.

Although the students believe that MSA receives more time than CA in general, these results indicate a remarkable and positive change toward

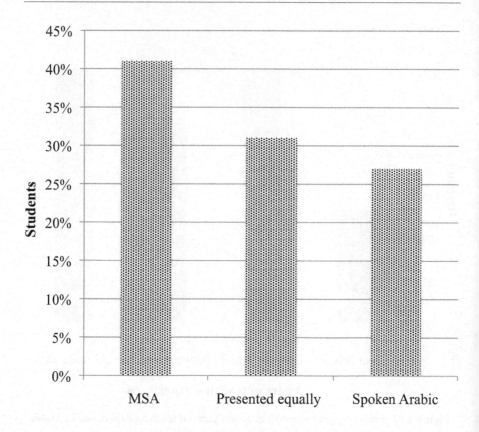

Focal language in Arabic classrooms

Figure 13.2 Students' opinions on the focal language in Arabic classrooms

integrating CA in the Arabic curriculum and breaking away from focusing only on MSA.

To further understand the students' opinions of how CA is incorporated within their Arabic classes, figure 13.3 illustrates cross-tabulation between students' opinions of how language is taught in their Arabic classes and the number of semesters of Arabic they have studied. Figure 13.3 indicates that students of first-year Arabic believe that CA is presented very well at this level. However, students who have studied more than two semesters believe that MSA is more dominant and that it represents the focus of the Arabic classes. One of the explanations behind the difference in the opinions of first-year students and those in higher levels on the integration of CA is that the activities in first-year Arabic tend to focus on speaking skills while upper-

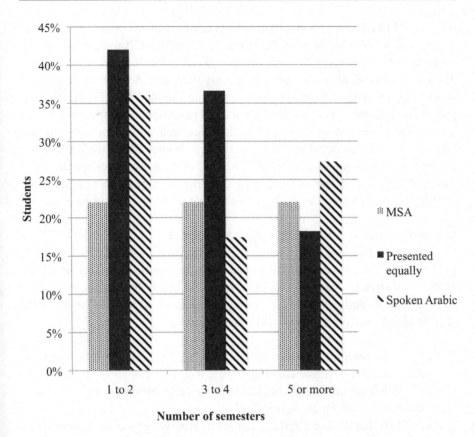

Figure 13.3 Students' opinions on the focal language across number of semesters

level classes include more reading and writing, activities that tend to focus more on MSA. Moreover, it is more likely that first-year students with no previous exposure to Arabic language do not have sufficient knowledge of the diglossic state of Arabic as do students who have been taking Arabic more than one year. Therefore, any type of speaking performance in first-year classes, whether in colloquial or MSA, would likely be considered by some students to be spoken language production yet is not an indication of official integration of CA.

Students' Responses to Time Devoted to CA
Our survey results reveal that the students' preferences regarding the time that should be devoted to Arabic does not match the actual time devoted to this variety in their current Arabic classes: 14.90 percent of the students stated that

they would like to see CA incorporated in their classes for up to 30 percent of the class time; 26.24 percent of the students would like CA to be integrated in 30 percent to 50 percent of class time; 31.91 percent of them would like to designate 50 percent to 70 percent of class time to CA; and 26.95 percent would like more than 80 percent of class time devoted to CA.[7] Half of the participants would like to see 50 percent to 90 percent of class time devoted to CA. Students' responses show clearly that their goals are to develop knowledge in CA and enhance their speaking skills, however, these needs and goals do not necessarily match the Arabic teachers' and programs' goals. This gap calls for a change in the existing Arabic curricula in order to provide more time for CA and respond to the needs and goals of Arabic language students.

Students' Intrinsic Attitudes toward MSA and CA

Students were asked to express their intrinsic attitudes toward MSA and CA. The students' survey contains fourteen attitude questions, seven of which address the students' attitudes toward MSA and seven similar questions that address their attitudes toward CA. In this section, I will refer to such similar attitude questions toward MSA and CA as *pairs*.

> Pair 1: "The learning material in Standard / Colloquial Arabic helps me to better learn the Arabic language."
>
> Pair 2: "Outside the classroom, I always strive to enrich my knowledge of Standard / Colloquial Arabic."
>
> Pair 3: "In this Arabic course, I am motivated when we learn Standard / Colloquial Arabic materials."
>
> Pair 4: "When learning Standard / Colloquial Arabic, the challenges that I face in class motivate me to learn more about this language."
>
> Pair 5: "Even when I do poorly in my Standard / Colloquial Arabic tasks in this course, I try to learn from my mistakes."
>
> Pair 6: "I find that what we are learning in Standard / Colloquial Arabic in this course is interesting."
>
> Pair 7: "I think what I am learning in Standard / Colloquial Arabic in this course is useful for me to know."

In general, students strongly agree with the intrinsic value statements for both MSA and CA. However, as figure 13.4 demonstrates, in the cumulative percentage of the categories "agree" and "strongly agree," there is a noticeably higher agreement among the students regarding the attitude statements toward CA than toward MSA. Examples of this can be seen in pair 3: "In this Arabic course, I am motivated when we learn Standard / Colloquial

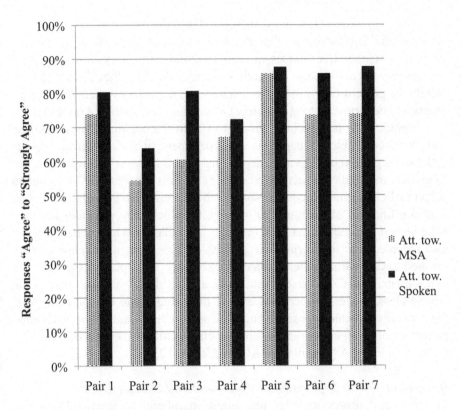

Attitude statements toward MSA and spoken Arabic

Figure 13.4 Total percentage of "agree" and "strongly agree"
with the attitude statements

Arabic materials"; in pair 6: "I find that what we are learning in Standard /
Colloquial Arabic in this course is interesting"; and in pair 7: "I think what
I am learning in Standard / Colloquial Arabic in this course is useful for me
to know."

The comparison between the statements shows that 80.6 percent of students agree or strongly agree that they are motivated to use CA materials,
whereas 60.4 percent of the students agree or strongly agree that they are
motivated to use MSA materials. Moreover, 85.7 percent of the students
agree or strongly agree that CA materials are interesting and useful, whereas
73.6 percent agree or strongly agree that MSA materials are interesting and
useful. These results indicate that, in general, the intrinsic value toward both
MSA and CA is relatively high, but it is clearly higher toward CA.

Teachers' Devoted Time to CA

The teachers' survey reveals that almost 67.2 percent ($n = 39$) of the participants have taught CA courses in their teaching careers. Additionally, 81.4 percent ($n = 48$) of them report that they incorporate CA in their Arabic classes. Nearly 46 percent ($n = 27$) of the teachers are required by their Arabic programs and departments to incorporate CA in some way in their Arabic classes. The average time the teachers devote to CA in the beginning, intermediate, and advanced Arabic language classes is 40.90 percent of class time. It appears that the integration of CA varies depending on the students' proficiency level. Beginner Arabic classes seem to receive the highest exposure to CA (about 46 percent of class time) in comparison to other levels. These results are in line with the findings of the students' survey, in which they reported that they experienced less exposure to CA in upper-level classes. The teachers' survey also revealed that in intermediate classes 41.5 percent of the class time is devoted to CA, while in the advanced classes only 39.23 percent of class time is designated for CA. These results indicate that the higher the level of the Arabic class, the less the teachers expose their students to CA. Nevertheless, these results indicate a positive and welcomed adjustment to the traditional pattern of offering colloquial in separate classes after two years of exclusive instruction in MSA (Abdalla and Al-Batal 2011–12, 16).

Integration versus Separation of Colloquial and Standard Arabic

The teachers' survey includes four questions about the teachers' attitudes toward the integration of CA in Arabic classes: (a) "Colloquial Arabic should not be incorporated along with Standard Arabic in every Arabic class"; (b) "Colloquial Arabic should be avoided as much as possible in advanced level classes"; (c) "Colloquial Arabic should not be incorporated equally as Standard Arabic in every Arabic class"; and (d) "Colloquial Arabic should be taught in classes separate from Standard Arabic."

In general, the concept of separating CA from MSA received relatively high negative scores. For example, the percentage of respondents that agree or strongly agree with question (a) was 13.3 percent with an average score (of five Likert categories) of 3.22 (SD = 3.37), with 0 representing "strongly disagree" and 10 representing "strongly agree." Comparatively, similar results were received for question (d), where the percentage of respondents that agree or strongly agree was 31 percent and with an average score (of five Likert categories) of 3.95 (SD = 3.81), indicating a moderately high negative attitude toward the statement.

Moreover, correlation tests were conducted to examine whether there is a correlation between the average general attitude toward one of the varieties in statements (b) and (d) above. The correlation tests yielded a significantly strong positive relationship between the two statements and the average general attitude toward MSA, statement one: $r = 0.528$, $n = 57$, $p = 0.000$, and statement two: $r = 0.600$, $n = 59$, $p = 0.000$. These results imply that the more positive attitude a teacher holds toward MSA, the stronger his or her belief that CA should be taught separately in general and in advanced Arabic in particular.

Additionally, a series of one-way analysis of variance tests were conducted to compare the effect of the number of years of teaching Arabic on the attitude statements and the integration of colloquial in Arabic classes. An analysis of the variance showed that the effect of the number of years of teaching Arabic was statistically significant in the statement "Colloquial Arabic should be taught in classes separate from Standard Arabic," $F(3, 53) = 4.630$, $p = 0.006$. A post hoc Tukey test showed that teachers who have been teaching AFL for more than nine years and those with between four and eight years of teaching experience differed significantly at $p < 0.05$.[8] Teachers with nine years or more of experience in teaching Arabic are less supportive of integrating colloquial with MSA. The group of teachers who have been teaching Arabic for up to three years was not significantly different from the other two groups. These results show a positive change in the teaching philosophy and practices between the older and newer generations of Arabic teachers. This may be attributed to the fact that newer generations of Arabic teachers have received training in teaching pedagogy that highlights the importance of integrating CA within the Arabic curriculum, while older generations of teachers received their training in programs (in Arab countries or in the United States and Europe) in which teaching beliefs and practices are exclusively oriented toward MSA.

Regarding the statement "Colloquial Arabic should be taught in classes separate from Standard Arabic," the findings revealed difference in attitude between teachers who teach Arabic in American universities and colleges and those who teach outside of the United States. An independent samples t-test showed that teachers who teach in the United States ($M = 3.41, 3.66$) agreed less with the statement in comparison with teachers from other countries ($M = 5.77$, SD $= 3.87$); $t(55) = -2.01$, $p = 0.049$). Although CA is far from being fully incorporated in the Arabic curriculum of American universities and colleges, the integration movement seems to have much wider support in the United States than in other Western universities and colleges. One explanation for this difference may be that, historically, American scholars have been more interested in general linguistics and contemporary languages, whereas European scholars have been more interested in the philology of languages (Versteegh 2014).

Teachers' General Attitudes toward MSA and CA

The teachers' survey contains eight general attitude questions, four of which address attitudes toward MSA and another similar four questions that address attitudes toward CA.[9] In this section, I again refer to similar questions toward MSA and CA as pairs.

Pair 1 (statements 19 and 27): "Students should communicate in Standard / Colloquial Arabic in Arabic classes."

Pair 2 (statements 22 and 30): "Teachers should avoid speaking in their dialect / in Standard Arabic as much as possible in class."

Pair 3 (statements 23 and 31): "It feels more appropriate when I teach in Standard Arabic / Colloquial Arabic."

Pair 4 (statements 24 and 32): "I think Standard / Colloquial Arabic is the appropriate language in any setting."

Each response was placed on a scale of 0 to 10, 0 indicating "not at all likely" or "extremely disagree" and 10 meaning "extremely likely" or "strongly agree."

Comparing the means (M) of the similar pairs of statements revealed that the mean scores of attitude statements toward CA are higher than the mean scores of attitude statements toward MSA in every pair.[10] These are encouraging results toward the integration approach. Presenting Arabic as one language in the classroom requires change in the attitudes and beliefs of the teachers toward the significance of both varieties for the Arabic learners.

Teachers' Attitudes toward the Functions of MSA and CA

The teachers' survey contains four statements regarding the functions of MSA and another four similar statements regarding the functions of CA: pair 1 (statements 25 and 33): "Standard / Colloquial Arabic is the best language to communicate with native speakers of Arabic"; and pair 2 (statements 26 and 34): "Standard / Colloquial Arabic is the key to understanding the Arab culture"; pair 3 (statements 21 and 29): "Students of Arabic can achieve the most when studying Standard / Colloquial Arabic"; pair 4 (statements 20 and 28): "Arabic textbooks should only be presented in Standard / Colloquial Arabic to foreign students." The percentage of the teachers who rated the pairs of statements 6 through 10 on a scale of 0 to 10 is an interesting finding.[11] The majority of the participants, 84.71 percent, agree or strongly agree that CA is the language variety that students should use to communicate with native speakers of Arabic, while only 27.6 percent of the teachers agree or strongly agree that MSA is the best language variety to communicate with native speakers of Arabic. Moreover, 72.4 percent of the teachers agree or strongly agree that CA is the key to accessing the Arabic culture, whereas only 35.5 percent agree or strongly agree that MSA can play the same role. About half of the teachers agree or strongly agree that CA is the vehicle for greatest student achievement, while about a third of the teachers agree or strongly agree that MSA is the means to greater student achievement. However, only 8.6 percent of the teachers agree or strongly agree that CA should be the only language in Arabic textbooks, while 19.3 percent agree or strongly agree that MSA should be the language of the textbooks. These results indicate that the Arabic teachers of this sample are in considerable disagreement with the idea that Arabic textbooks should feature only one of the varieties. Moreover, these results indicate that teachers of Arabic are receptive to the idea that MSA and CA should be presented as one language in Arabic classes. Integrating the two varieties more accurately reflects the linguistic reality of Arabic-speaking countries and is more responsive to students' needs.

Effect of Training in Formal Arabic Teacher Programs
Training in formal Arabic teacher programs, whether through brief workshops or long-term training in TAFL, seems to have a positive effect on teachers' attitudes toward CA as well as on how much time they devote to CA in their classes. Teachers who received training in formal Arabic teacher programs in comparison with those who have not received such training devote more time on average to CA in their classes.[12]

Training in formal Arabic teacher programs was also found to affect teachers' attitudes toward the integration of CA. As figure 13.5 demonstrates, attitude statement scores of "agree" or "strongly agree" toward CA of teachers with formal Arabic teacher training are higher than those of teachers who have not received training.[13] At the same time, the scores of attitude statements for the categories "agree" or "strongly agree" toward MSA of teachers without formal Arabic teacher training programs are higher than those of teachers who have received training.[14] Only in statement 24, "I think Standard Arabic is the appropriate language in any setting," is the difference between the two groups marginal, as figure 13.6 shows.

Differences are also found in attitudes toward MSA between teachers who majored in TAFL and those with other majors.[15] Teachers who majored in TAFL agree less with the attitude statements toward MSA than those with other majors, as figure 13.7 shows.

The positive effect of training in TAFL on teachers' attitudes toward CA indicates a welcome change in the field of TAFL, one that recognizes the importance of colloquial becoming an integral part of the Arabic curriculum.

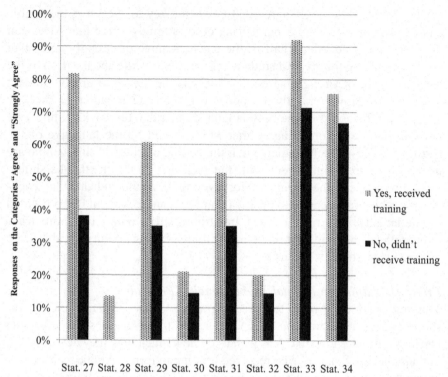

Figure 13.5 Total percentage of "agree" and "strongly agree" with the attitude statements toward spoken Arabic across formal training

Native- and Non–native Speaker Teachers' Attitudes

Another topic explored by this study is the difference between the attitudes of native- and non–native speaker teachers. As shown in figure 13.8, there is a significant difference in attitudes between native and nonnative teachers toward MSA on a scale of 0 to 10, with 0 indicating "strongly disagree" and 10 indicating "strongly agree." The computed average of attitudes toward MSA was statistically tested across native-speaker teachers ($M = 4.544$, SD $= 2.90$) and non–native speaker teachers ($M = 2.578$, SD $= 1.953$), indicating that non–native speaker teachers hold less positive attitudes toward MSA ($t(57) = 2.926, p = 0.005$). The difference in attitudes toward CA between the two groups is relatively very small.

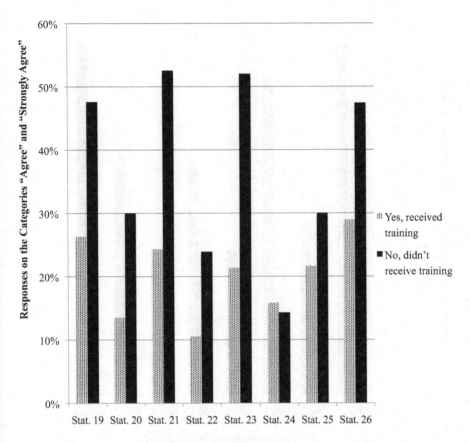

Figure 13.6 Total percentage of "agree" and "strongly agree" with the attitude statements toward MSA across formal training

One explanation for these results is the fact that a large majority of the non–native speaker teachers have lived for long periods of time in Arabic-speaking countries (Abdalla and Al-Batal 2011–12, 5) and have come to realize the importance of CA in the daily and cultural lives of natives and as the major means of communication. Another explanation is that native-speaker teachers, particularly those who have not received training in language pedagogy, tend to adhere to traditional teaching practices that give MSA dominance in the curriculum.

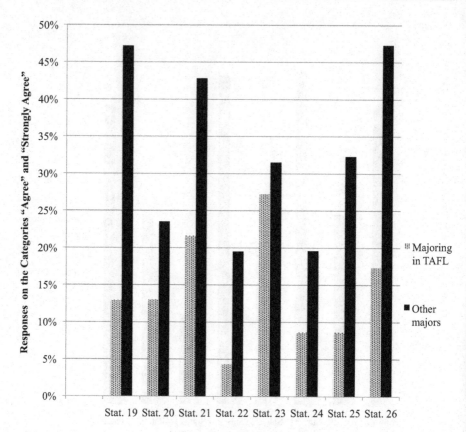

Figure 13.7 Total percentage of "agree" and "strongly agree" with the attitude statements toward MSA across majoring in TAFL

Discussion and Conclusions

The findings of this study suggest that most of the participating teachers and students hold positive intrinsic attitudes toward MSA and CA; however, their attitudes toward colloquial are more positive than their attitudes toward MSA.

The study also reveals that a majority of the teachers and students recognize the importance of mastering the skills necessary for communicating with native speakers while traveling in Arabic-speaking countries. Both teachers and students believe that Arabic language courses should help students to develop skills that enable them to interact with native speakers.

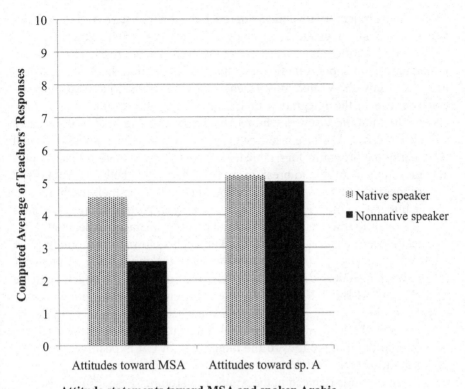

Attitude statements toward MSA and spoken Arabic

Figure 13.8 Average of attitudes toward standard and spoken Arabic
across native- and non-native-speaking teachers

These results are in line with other studies since the 1980s that have focused on the needs and goals of students of Arabic (Belnap 1987; Husseinali 2006; Isleem 2015; Palmer 2008; Shiri 2013).

Regarding integrating CA within the Arabic curriculum, both students and teachers of Arabic strongly believe that colloquial should not be a separate course with its own curriculum. Only 15.3 percent of the teachers agree or strongly agree that CA should not be incorporated with MSA, and 85 percent of the students would like to see colloquial incorporated in the MSA curriculum. However, the teachers' beliefs fall short in implementation and actual classroom practices, as the surveyed teachers of Arabic report devoting only about 41 percent of class time to CA. Students' opinion on how much time should be devoted to colloquial is clearly more than the time teachers actually designate for colloquial. However, these findings present an encouraging picture and a trajectory toward an approach in which the two Arabic varieties are taught as one language, reinforcing all language-learning skills.

Nevertheless, there are three developing factors that are likely to play an important role in supporting the integration of CA within the Arabic curriculum. The study shows that most teachers who are trained in language pedagogy believe in the integration of CA and devote more time to it in their classes. In addition, teachers who received such training hold more positive attitudes toward CA. These results suggest that the growing number of formal Arabic training programs for Arabic teachers will play a major role in encouraging teachers of Arabic to break away from traditional pedagogy and move toward incorporating CA and other colloquial elements in their teaching.

The integration of CA seems to be particularly important to the new generation of qualified nonnative Arabic teachers who themselves learned AFL. The positive attitude of non–native speaker teachers toward incorporating CA is a welcome change particularly since they have the ability to play a mediator role between a student's native culture and the culture of the target language (Abdalla and Al-Batal 2011–12, 5). The engagement of non–native speaker teachers in the teaching process of AFL indicates a growing maturity in the field of TAFL that will encourage more learners to become future teachers.

Although the attitude toward the integration of CA is positive, the study called attention to the fact that, as the level of a student's proficiency increases, integration of CA is reduced in the Arabic classroom. These results raise two major issues: (a) a possible covert teaching ideology that promotes the idea that knowledge of colloquial should not exceed basic and casual conversation since complex discourse and narrative is restricted to MSA; and (b) a lack of resources in colloquial materials for advanced Arabic classes that would expand the functionality and integration of colloquial in topics that exceed basic conversational discourse. To tackle these issues, Arabic teachers and scholars in the field of TAFL need to develop learning and teaching materials that emphasize the integrality of both MSA and CA and make both available to audiences of varying proficiencies.

The study shows that the integration of CA within the Arabic curriculum is no longer a question for debate but is part of a pedagogical vision for Arabic that emphasizes the importance of meeting students' needs and demands in learning AFL. The results of the present study suggest that Arabic programs and teachers of Arabic need to:

(a) Listen closely to the students' needs and adjust the syllabi, materials, and textbooks accordingly;

(b) Integrate CA at every level and devote as much class time to it as is devoted to MSA;

(c) Hire qualified and trained teachers of Arabic and develop formal training programs in the field of TAFL; and

(d) Develop resources and materials in CA that suit various levels of Arabic to overcome the belief that CA is suitable only for lower levels of Arabic proficiency.

These steps will likely lead to liberating Arabic language pedagogy from the traditional teaching methodology that presents an incomplete model of the language and deprives students of the chance to more fully engage with the culture.

The results of this study provide a strong argument in support of integrating dialect instruction alongside MSA. However, due to the limitation of the scope of this study, I suggest conducting a larger scale study to further investigate the role of non–native speaker teachers in enhancing the integration approach. Valuable information could also be obtained by conducting a comparative international study on teachers' and students' attitudes toward the integration of CA in order to shed light on both teaching dynamics and students' needs in various Western universities and colleges.

References

Abdalla, Mahmoud, and Mahmoud Al-Batal. 2011–12. "College-Level Teachers of Arabic in the United States: A Survey of their Professional and Institutional Profiles and Attitudes." *Al-ᶜArabiyya* 44/45: 1–28.

Al-Batal, Mahmoud, and Kirk Belnap. 2006. "The Teaching and Learning of Arabic in the United States: Realities, Needs and Future Directions." In *Handbook for Arabic Language Teaching Professionals in the 21st Century*, edited by Kassem M. Wahba, Zeinab A. Taha, and Liz England, 389–99. Mahwah, NJ: Lawrence Erlbaum.

Belnap, Kirk. 1987. "Who Is Taking Arabic and What on Earth For? A Survey of Students in Arabic Language Programs." *Al-ᶜArabiyya* 20, no. 1–2: 29–42.

Brustad, Kristen, Mahmoud Al-Batal, and Abbas al-Tonsi. 2011. *Al-Kitaab fii Taᶜallum al-ᶜArabiyya: A Textbook for Beginning Arabic*, Part One, 3rd ed. Washington, DC: Georgetown University Press.

———. 2013. *Al-Kitaab fii Taᶜallum al-ᶜArabiyya: A Textbook for Intermediate Arabic*, Part Two, 3rd ed. Washington, DC: Georgetown University Press.

Donista-Schmidt, Smadar, Ofra Inbar, and Elana Shohamy. 2004. "The Effects of Teaching Spoken Arabic on Students' Attitudes and Motivation in Israel." *Modern Language Journal* 88, no. 2: 217–28.

Dörnyei, Zoltán, and Ema Ushioda. 2013. *Teaching and Researching*. Hoboken, NJ: Taylor and Francis. http://public.eblib.com/choice/publicfullrecord.aspx?p=1569920.

Gardner, Robert. 1985. *Social Psychology and Second Language Learning: The Role of Attitudes and Motivation*. London: Edward Arnold.

———. 2001. "Integrative Motivation and Second Language Acquisition." In *Motivation and Second Language Acquisition*, edited by Zoltán Dörnyei, 1–19. Honolulu: National Foreign Language Resource Center.

Haeri, Niloofar. 1997. "The Reproduction of Symbolic Capital: Language, State, and Class in Egypt." *Current Anthropology* 38, no. 5: 795–805.

Husseinali, Ghassan. 2006. "Who Is Studying Arabic and Why? A Survey of Arabic Students' Orientations at a Major University." *Foreign Language Annals* 39, no. 3: 395–412.

Isleem, Martin. 2015. "Developing Attitudes toward Learning Arabic as a Foreign Language among American University and College Students." In *Arabele2012: Teaching and Learning the Arabic Language*, edited by Victoria Aguilar, Luis Pérez Cañada, and Paula Santillán, 81–98. Murcia, Spain: Universidad de Murcia.

Kuntz, Patricia, and Kirk R. Belnap. 2001. "Beliefs about Language Learning Held by Teachers and Their Students at Two Arabic Programs Abroad." *Al-ᶜArabiyya* 34: 91–113.

Palmer, Jeremy. 2007. "Arabic Diglossia: Teaching Only the Standard Variety is a Disservice to Students." *Arizona Working Papers in SLA & Teaching* 14: 111–22.

———. 2008. "Arabic Diglossia: Student Perceptions of Spoken Arabic after Living in the Arabic–Speaking World." *Arizona Working Papers in SLA & Teaching* 15: 81–195.

Shiri, Sonia. 2013. "Learners' Attitudes toward Regional Dialects and Destination Preferences in Study Abroad." *Foreign Language Annals* 46, no. 4: 565–87.

Wahba, Kassem. 2006. "Arabic Language Use and the Educated Language User." In *Handbook for Arabic Language Teaching Professionals in the 21st Century*, edited by Kassem M. Wahba, Zeinab A. Taha, and Liz England, 139–55. Mahwah, NJ: Lawrence Erlbaum.

Versteegh, Kees. 2014. *The Arabic Language*. Edinburgh: Edinburgh University Press.

Warschauer, Mark, Ghada R. El-Said, and Ayman Zohry. 2007. "Language Choice Online: Globalization and Identity in Egypt." In *The Multilingual Internet: Language, Culture, and Communication Online*, edited by Brenda Danet and Susan C. Herring, 303–18. New York: Oxford University Press.

Younes, Munther. 2010. "الفصحى والدارجة وتكامل دوريهما في منهاج اللغة العربية." In *Arabele2009: Teaching and Learning the Arabic Language*, edited by Victoria Aguilar, Luis Pérez Cañada, and Paula Santillán, 63–75. Murcia, Spain: Universidad de Murcia.

Younes, Munther, and Hanada al-Masri. 2014. ᶜ*Arabiyyat al-Naas*, Part 2. London: Routledge.

Younes, Munther, and Yomna Chami. 2014. *ʿArabiyyat al-Naas*, Part 3. London: Routledge.

Younes, Munther, Makda Weatherspoon, and Maha Foster. 2014. *ʿArabiyyat al-Naas*, Part 1. London: Routledge.

Notes

Additional data and examples are freely available to view and download on this book's product page on the Georgetown University Press (GUP) website (www.press .georgetown.edu).

1. MSA is the medium for the official education system, and it is used as a spoken and written medium in the contemporary Arabic media and news channels. However, Classical Arabic is the language of the religious, medieval, and classic texts. The morphology and syntax of MSA and Classical Arabic are similar to a very large extent.

2. The website of the Arabic Linguistic List, http://lists.leeds.ac.uk/mailman/ listinfo/arabic-l.

3. See appendix A on the GUP website.

4. See appendix B on the GUP website.

5. See appendix A on the GUP website.

6. See appendix B on the GUP website.

7. As can be seen in figure W13.1 on the GUP website.

8. The post hoc Tukey test provides additional information on the differences among means of the variable's groups.

9. See appendix B on the GUP website.

10. Demonstrated in figure W13.2 on the GUP website.

11. As demonstrated in figure W13.3 on the GUP website.

12. As figure W13.4, on the GUP website, shows.

13. See statements 27 through 34 in appendix B on the GUP website.

14. See statements 19 through 26 in ibid.

15. See statements 19 through 26 in ibid.

14

Dialect Integration

Students' Perspectives within an Integrated Program

MAHMOUD AL-BATAL AND CHRISTIAN GLAKAS
The University of Texas, Austin

OVER THE PAST TEN YEARS, the Arabic teaching profession in the United States has witnessed two notable developments toward the integration of spoken Arabic, a term that we use here to refer to dialectal Arabic, with Modern Standard Arabic (MSA). The first is the growing interest in incorporating dialect elements in the curriculum alongside MSA from the early stages of instruction. The field seems to be moving from the question of *why* integrate to *how to* integrate. The fact that we currently have two textbook series, *Al-Kitaab fii Ta'allum al-'Arabiyya* by Kristen Brustad, Mahmoud Al-Batal, and Abbas al-Tonsi (2011) and *Arabiyyat Al-Naas* by Munther Younes, Makda Weatherspoon, and Maha Foster (2013) that are based on integration of MSA and dialect is clear testimony to the change that has been taking place in the field.

The second of these developments is the increased attention paid to understanding students' perspectives on their learning experiences, including their attitudes toward the study of Arabic dialects. Such attention is manifested in six recent surveys that provide valuable insights into the attitudes of students.

In the most recent of a series of surveys of US students studying Arabic, Kirk Belnap found significant correlation between the students' desire to learn spoken Arabic and the instructors' attitude toward spoken Arabic. He also notes that 27 percent of students surveyed indicated that their teachers encourage the use of spoken Arabic in class. This, in his opinion, can be taken as a sign of "progress toward a more authentic approach to teaching the speaking skill in Arabic" (2006, 176). In another survey aimed at understanding the profiles and motives of students, Ghassan Husseinali (2006) concludes that it is important for Arabic teachers and programs to acknowledge that colloquial is an integral part of Arabic that cannot be ignored.

Two studies of learners who had studied abroad show strong student support for dialect inclusion. Jeremy Palmer (2008) conducted a survey of students who had studied Arabic for at least two semesters before traveling to the Arabic-speaking world. He reports that the majority of the respondents believe that students should learn spoken Arabic before traveling to the Arabic-speaking world. Eva Hashem-Aramouni (2011) investigated Arabic students' and instructors' perceptions regarding spoken Arabic. The students she interviewed had all traveled to the Arabic-speaking world for language immersion. She concludes that students' exposure to dialects is an important factor in shaping the development of speaking proficiency in both domestic study and study abroad. She suggests a role for explicit instruction in different Arabic dialects and approaches that would enhance learners' motivations and interactions with the spoken varieties of Arabic.

Investigating student attitudes toward the issue of dialect variation, Sonia Shiri (2013) surveyed students' opinions toward learning MSA and different dialects and the factors influencing their attitudes. Her results reveal that respondents are willing to learn multiple dialects in addition to MSA as part of their Arabic language education. Her results also show that students gain a sophisticated sociolinguistic awareness of the role dialects play in communication and culture in the Arab world, and they attribute their newly gained attitudes to learning Arabic in the region. Furthermore, she observes that "once in contact with the target societies, students of Arabic almost unanimously rejected the current exclusive focus on MSA and realized the importance of learning a dialect—any dialect and even multiple dialects—to connect and bond with members of their host community, suggesting that educators and program directors should take their cue from the students on the ground and add, or further strengthen, the dialectal and socio-linguistic aspects of the Arabic curriculum at home" (2013, 584).

Finally, Martin Isleem (in the present volume) reports the results of a survey aimed at analyzing attitudes of Arabic students and teachers toward the dialects and MSA. His results also provide support for the call to integrate spoken Arabic in the curriculum and demonstrate that both students and teachers hold positive attitudes toward the integration of dialect in the curriculum. He notes, however, that teachers—particularly at advanced levels of instruction—do not integrate the dialect as much as the students desire.

This focus on gauging students' attitudes and perspectives on integration is a welcome addition to the debate in the field because it helps bring to the forefront the voices of those whose needs matter the most, the learners of Arabic.

The present chapter aims to bring additional students' voices to the debate on integration by examining their perceptions of its benefit to their overall learning experience in Arabic. The voices represented in this chapter are those of students who studied in the Arabic program at the University of Texas (UT), Austin in 2015. The UT Arabic program started experimenting with integrating a dialect within the Arabic curriculum in 2007 and proceeded to adopt a fully integrated curriculum in 2009. This full integration was motivated by the program's vision of "Arabic as One" and its effort to provide students with the knowledge, tools, and learning strategies they need to successfully engage with Arabic as it is used by its native speakers.

The present study is driven by the following three research questions:

1. What are the students' general perceptions regarding the simultaneous integration of MSA and Arabic dialects in the curriculum?
2. To what extent do students perceive integration to be linguistically beneficial for their learning of Arabic?
3. What, if any, are the nonlinguistic benefits students perceive in integration?

Instrument

This study is based on a survey that was administered to students enrolled in undergraduate-level Arabic courses at UT in April 2015. The survey consisted of thirty-three items: thirty multiple-choice items (including five binary-response items, seven categorical-response items, and eighteen ordinal-response items) and three open-ended response items. The survey items were organized in groups as follows:

1. Background knowledge of Arabic before attending UT (two items)
2. Academic experience at UT (five items)
3. Travel experience in Arabic-speaking countries (three items)
4. Motivations for learning Arabic (two items)
5. Opinions regarding Arabic dialects and their integration with MSA (eleven items)

6. Perceptions of the linguistic benefits of integrating Arabic dialects with MSA (five items)
7. Perceptions of the nonlinguistic benefits of integrating Arabic dialects with MSA (three items)
8. Comments and suggestions (two items)

The analysis presented in this chapter focuses only on students' responses to the items in groups 5–7 listed above because they are the most directly relevant to the scope of the present study.[1] The researchers created the items in group 5 to help answer research question 1, the items in group 6 to answer research question 2, and the items in group 7 to answer research question 3.[2]

Participants and Their Backgrounds

The researchers sent the survey link to all the teachers of the thirteen different sections of Arabic offered at UT in the spring of 2015. Students were invited to take the survey through their Arabic classes. Participation in the survey was voluntary, and 184 UT Arabic students elected to participate. Students were informed on the first page of the survey that it had been approved by the UT Institutional Review Board and that their continuation to the survey questions constituted their consent to participate in the study.

The overwhelming majority of respondents were taking Arabic courses domestically at UT Austin (96 percent), and the remaining 4 percent of respondents were studying abroad with the Arabic Flagship Program "Capstone Year" at the Arab American Language Institute in Morocco. Table 14.1 shows that over half of the respondents were students in first-year Arabic, with the remaining domestic students distributed fairly evenly between second-year, third-year, and upper-level undergraduate content courses. The

Table 14.1 Course levels of all respondents

Course Level	# Respondents	% Respondents
1st Year	96	52
2nd Year	33	18
3rd Year	23*	13
Content Course (in Arabic)	29*	16
Study Abroad / Capstone Year	7	4
Total	184	

* Four students who were in 3rd year were also in a content course.

survey was conducted in April of 2015, near the end of the spring semester, so it should be noted that students who reported being in first-year Arabic courses had nearly completed two intensive semesters (6 weekly contact hours, 15 weeks per semester, for a total of approximately 180 contact hours for the year) of Arabic. For second-year students, the number of contact hours is also 6 hours per week; for third, it is 5 hours, and content courses meet 3 hours per week.

Of the 184 respondents, 25 (14 percent), reported having heard or spoken Arabic in their homes growing up; we will refer to these students as "heritage students" of Arabic. A surprising 99 respondents (54 percent) reported that they had traveled to or lived in an Arabic-speaking country. Table 14.2 shows the Arabic course levels for these students.

Comparing these figures with the data from table 14.1, we see that less than half of all first-year Arabic students reported traveling to an Arabic-speaking country (40/96, or 42 percent), while over 50 percent of students in second-year (19/33, or 58 percent), third-year (13/23, or 57 percent), and content courses (20/25, or 80 percent) reported having done so. While 52 percent of students who traveled to Arabic-speaking countries stayed for three months or less, many students took longer trips, nearly a quarter of them spending more than one year in an Arabic-speaking country.[3] We see that the most common purpose for students' trips was studying abroad. Sizable numbers of students traveled to Arabic-speaking countries for vacations and family visits, while a very small number of students did so in the course of their military service.

Students reported a wide variety of motivations for studying Arabic. Over half of all respondents listed "academic and/or career development" as their main reason for studying Arabic.[4] The next most common reason was "personal fulfillment" (22 percent), with less than 10 percent of respondents citing

Table 14.2 Course level of students who have traveled to or lived in an Arabic-speaking country

Course Level	# Respondents	% Respondents
1st Year	40	40
2nd Year	19	19
3rd Year	13	13
Content Course	20	20
Study Abroad / Capstone Year	7	7
Total	99	

other primary reasons for studying the language. In response to a related question, forty-eight students (26 percent of respondents) reported that they were taking Arabic primarily to fulfill the foreign language requirement of their UT degree program.

Results and Discussion

In this section, we present the individual survey questions and accompanying response data in three broad categories based on the three research questions (RQ) outlined earlier. In each table below, we present the number of responses in each category along with the percentages in parenthesis. Since not every respondent answered every question, the total number of respondents that answered each individual question is reported for each table ($n = x$).

RQ 1: Students' General Perceptions Regarding the Simultaneous Integration of MSA and Arabic Dialects in the Curriculum

While our survey examines several facets of the integration of Arabic dialects with MSA in the UT Arabic program, the principle goal of the survey is to determine the extent to which UT students support this integration as it is currently carried out from day one, compared with the degree to which they think integration should be postponed to a later phase of Arabic study. The current practice of most Arabic programs and the opinion expressed by many teachers of Arabic in the United States is to focus on MSA alone for the first two years, with the expectation that students will develop their knowledge of a dialect either by taking a separate upper-level course in the dialect or by living and studying abroad (see Hashem-Aramouni 2011). Our survey includes several items designed to gauge how students themselves feel about how and when the dialects should be taught. Table 14.3 presents their views on whether the study of dialects should be postponed until they go abroad.

Table 14.3 Students' views on whether the study of dialects should be postponed until students go abroad

To what extent do you agree with the following statement:	Strongly Agree	Agree	Disagree	Strongly Disagree
The study of Arabic dialects should be postponed until students are studying Arabic abroad in an Arabic speaking country.	3 (2%)	8 (4%)	67 (36%)	106 (58%)
$N = 184$				

Student responses in table 14.3 indicate that UT students overwhelmingly support the domestic integration of dialects with MSA as opposed to post-poning the study of dialects until they go abroad. Only 6 percent of respondents selected "agree" or "strongly agree," with 94 percent of respondents selecting "disagree" or "strongly disagree," underscoring the broad support among respondents for introducing the dialects during the domestic study of Arabic. This perspective is consistent with those reported in the studies cited above (Husseinali 2006; Palmer 2008; Hashem-Aramouni 2011; Shiri 2013).

Central to any discussion of Arabic dialects is the variation, actual or per-ceived, between the dialects and MSA. In chapter 1 in the present volume, Al-Batal presents a view of "Arabic as One" that is based on the belief that the dialects and MSA are parts of the same language system and do not con-stitute separate languages. However, there are some who argue that MSA and the dialects represent different languages (see, for example, Kaye 1994; Sala-meh 2011). But how do students feel about this? In order to gauge students' perceptions of the link between the Arabic dialects and MSA, our survey asked students whether they viewed the dialect they were learning as being a "sepa-rate language" from MSA. Table 14.4 shows their answers to this question.

What makes the students' responses here significant is the fact that they are based on real experiences with these varieties of Arabic. Through their study of the vocabulary, roots and patterns, and grammatical structures of Arabic—whether in MSA or the dialects—students are able to notice the com-mon elements that connect these Arabic varieties together. They are also able to see the ways in which MSA and the dialects differ yet continue to be per-ceived as parts of "one Arabic."

Within these responses, we noticed an interesting pattern: students at higher levels of domestic study are less likely to view MSA and their dialect as "sep-arate languages" than students at lower levels of study. This pattern is illus-trated in table 14.5.

We see that the percentage of students who view MSA and their dialect as "separate languages" decreases from 30 percent among first-year students to 24 percent of second-year students to 22 percent of third-year students to 20 percent of students in upper-level content courses. This suggests that, as stu-

Table 14.4 Students' views on the difference between MSA and dialect

Question	Yes	No
Do you view MSA and the dialect you are learning as "separate languages"?	51 (28%)	133 (72%)
N = 184		

Table 14.5 Students' views of differences between MSA and dialect by level

Do you view MSA and the dialect you are learning as "separate languages"? N = 184	Yes	No
Arabic level of respondents	# (% of responses within level of study)	
1st Year	29 (30)	67 (70)
2nd Year	8 (24)	25 (76)
3rd Year	5 (22)	18 (78)
Content Course	5 (20)	20 (80)

dents progress through their integrated Arabic sequence and build their proficiency in the language, they see fewer differences between MSA and the dialects.

Given that less than one-third of respondents viewed their dialect and MSA as separate languages, it might follow that students would feel optimistic about their ability to learn a dialect at the same time as MSA. Table 14.6 shows that this was, in fact, the case: we see that 97 percent of respondents either "agreed" or "strongly agreed" that it is possible to learn an Arabic dialect simultaneously with MSA.

We can now turn our attention to the question of the effect of dialect integration on the learner. One of the main objections that has been raised against integration is that it would cause confusion for students. Al-Batal (1992), Shiri (2013), and Younes (2015) discuss the confusion argument and the difficulty involved in what seems to be learning two different forms to express the same meaning. In the student online forum "Learning and Teaching Arabic" (Palmer 2005), discussion of the relationship between MSA and the dialects often includes the word "confusing." In our survey, we wanted to understand our own students' perceptions regarding this simultaneous exposure; thus, we included three items that were specifically intended to elicit

Table 14.6 Students' belief in possibility of learning MSA and dialect simultaneously

To what extent do you agree with the following statement:	Strongly Agree	Agree	Disagree	Strongly Disagree
Learning a dialect simultaneously with MSA is possible. N = 184	132 (72%)	47 (25%)	3 (2%)	2 (1%)

Table 14.7 Students' belief of effects of learning MSA and dialect simultaneously

To what extent do you agree with the following statement:	Strongly Agree	Agree	Disagree	Strongly Disagree
Learning a dialect simultaneously with MSA is confusing. N = 184	26 (14%)	95 (52%)	56 (30%)	7 (4%)
Learning a dialect simultaneously with MSA is discouraging. N = 184	7 (4%)	26 (14%)	84 (46%)	67 (36%)
Learning a dialect simultaneously with MSA is empowering. N = 184	86 (47%)	83 (45%)	12 (7%)	3 (2%)

their perceptions. Table 14.7 presents the students' response on the effects of dialect integration on them in terms of confusion, discouragement, and empowerment.

This data shows that, not surprisingly, over half of the respondents agree that it is confusing to learn a dialect at the same time as MSA. However, while many students report being confused by dialect integration in the classroom, less than one-fifth of respondents (18 percent) report being discouraged by it. On the contrary, the vast majority of students report that learning a dialect simultaneously with MSA is "empowering" (92 percent). Simply put, while many students acknowledge that it is confusing to learn a dialect at the same time as MSA, their responses on the other two items indicate that they feel able and willing to take up the challenge.

While we do not want to underestimate the feeling of confusion students may experience in an integrated program, we need to keep in mind that confusion is part of any learning process and that teachers can play a major role in managing it. Al-Batal discussed this very issue in 1992: "This confusion is a reflection of what native speakers of Arabic experience when they start their formal study of Arabic. . . . Teachers should be prepared to deal with this confusion and should make it clear to the students that the level of confusion will gradually diminish as they become more proficient in the language" (302).

We should also emphasize that the feeling of confusion is not restricted to students who are learning Arabic in integrated programs or to those trying to speak in any variety of Arabic, including *al-fuṣḥā*. The confusion learners feel about MSA and the dialects is no different from the confusion they feel, for example, when they learn how to conjugate verbs or learn about the different forms of *iʿrāb* inflection or the different verb *awzān* patterns. Confusion constitutes a necessary phase in the learning process, and our challenge as teachers is to seek pedagogical approaches to integration that manage this sense of confusion by reassuring students that it is natural, temporary, and leads to deeper understanding. We should also admit that confusion may sometimes be caused by unrealistic or unclear expectations on the part of the teacher regarding the elements they want the students to learn. Do we want students to learn two different forms for each word, one in MSA and one in dialect? Do we expect students to master them equally, or do we expect full control of one form and partial control of the other? Such expectations need to be made clear to the students from the outset and stated repeatedly in any integrated program. It is crucial for teachers to show flexibility and tolerance of mixing the various MSA/dialect forms. Any successful learning process requires patience and feedback from the teacher to help learners overcome their sense of confusion.

In another survey question, respondents were given the opportunity to pick the best word from a range of options to describe their feelings about learning a dialect simultaneously with MSA. The responses are shown in decreasing order of frequency in table 14.8.

Table 14.8 Students' feelings about learning MSA and a dialect simultaneously

Pick the one best word that represents your feelings about the integration of MSA and an Arabic dialect in your Arabic classes. *N* = 184	Responses # (%)
Realistic	44 (24)
Necessary	28 (15)
Crucial	25 (14)
Rewarding	17 (9)
Stimulating	15 (8)
Challenging	13 (7)
Helpful	11 (6)
Frustrating	8 (4)
Confusing	5 (3)
Difficult	5 (3)
Exciting	5 (3)
Fun	5 (3)
Waste of time	3 (2)

The three most frequently chosen words, "realistic," "necessary," and "crucial," which represent the opinion of over half of all respondents (53 percent), indicate that the challenge of learning a dialect is an inevitable and beneficial part of studying Arabic. The next four most frequently chosen words, "rewarding," "stimulating," "challenging," and "helpful," representing 30 percent of respondents, convey other students' positive feelings associated with dialect integration. Only 13 percent of respondents selected a word that has an overtly negative connotation ("frustrating," "confusing," "difficult," or "waste of time"), while the remaining 6 percent of respondents selected words with different positive connotations ("exciting" or "fun").

One of the defining features of the UT Arabic program is that it exposes students to different Arabic dialects within the program. Students who first enroll in an Arabic class with an Egyptian (*Maṣri*) flavor may find themselves, in a subsequent semester, in a section that has a Levantine (*Shāmi*) flavor. Heritage students and students who have studied abroad also bring different Arabic flavors to our Arabic classes, and these varieties are welcomed in class as part of the program's philosophy of providing exposure to various forms of Arabic. As part of our survey we wanted to explore the students' perspective on this aspect of the program. We asked participants to select the best word—from the same selection of options—to describe their experiences being exposed to *more than one* dialect of Arabic in their classes.[5]

It is important to note the difference between the numbers of students who chose the word "challenging" (21 percent) and those who selected "difficult" (3 percent). In the context of the high numbers of students who chose the words "stimulating" (13 percent) and "rewarding" (11 percent), it seems that the students who selected "challenging" acknowledge the difficulty but also wish to allude to the benefits of exposure to multiple dialects. Only 17 percent of students chose a word with directly negative connotations to describe their feelings about exposure to multiple dialects ("confusing," "frustrating," "difficult," "waste of time"). In contrast, over 60 percent of respondents chose a word with positive connotations, such as "challenging," "stimulating," "rewarding," "fun," "helpful," and "exciting." These results further confirm the results reported by Shiri (2013), who found that 81 percent of the students who participated in her study agreed that learners of Arabic need to learn more than one dialect in order to connect with speakers of Arabic throughout the Arabic-speaking region.

The last question regarding students' perspectives on dialect integration asked participants to indicate the stage in the program at which they think dialects should be introduced. This question was presented only to the twenty-nine students who identified themselves as taking content courses.

Table 14.9 Students' ideas about what level dialect should be incorporated

When do you think Arabic classes should begin incorporating dialects to be taught simultaneously with MSA? N = 29	Responses # (%)
1st year	26 (90)
2nd year	3 (10)
3rd year	0 (0)
With content courses	0 (0)
Not at all	0 (0)

We made the decision to restrict this question to these students only because they had spent more time with the language and were in a position to provide a retroactive view of when dialect should be incorporated in the curriculum. The current practice of many Arabic programs in the United States that focus on instruction in MSA is to offer dialect, if at all, only at the upper levels of instruction after students have taken two or three years of Arabic. As table 14.9 shows, the vast majority of the respondents (90 percent) recommended that dialect be incorporated in the first year. None of these students felt that dialect integration should be postponed beyond second-year Arabic courses.

RQ 2: Perceptions of the Linguistic Benefits of Integrating Arabic Dialects with MSA

The survey questions and response data above clearly demonstrate that most respondents have a generally positive attitude toward learning a dialect simultaneously with MSA. Our second research question pertains to the extent to which students feel that integration is linguistically beneficial to them and helps prepare them for later stages of learning Arabic. We included four questions in the survey aimed at gauging their perceptions in this area. The first question in this group targeted students' perception of the value of integration for building overall proficiency in Arabic. From our surveys, 90 percent of respondents felt that dialect integration was "essential" for their overall Arabic proficiency, further elaborating the view they expressed in the previous question (see table 14.9) in which the vast majority recommended that integration begin in the first year of instruction.[6]

In addition to being essential to overall proficiency in Arabic, students see significant benefit in integration preparing them for upper-level content-based courses. At UT, content-based courses are offered beyond third year after students have reached Advanced proficiency on the ACTFL scale. In addition to reading texts, all content courses involve substantial listening to authentic video programs taken from satellite television and the internet that often involve people speaking in MSA, various Arabic dialects, and a mixture of MSA/dialect within the same program. Of the thirty-six survey participants who were either enrolled in or had previously taken upper-level content courses, over 90 percent of them felt that dialect integration in their first-, second-, and third-year classes had prepared them for those content courses.[7]

We mentioned earlier that one of the characteristics of the UT Arabic program is the opportunity for students to be exposed to and develop knowledge of different Arabic dialects. We wanted to assess the extent to which students felt that their knowledge of one Arabic dialect in the integrated curriculum was helpful to them in learning another dialect. The students who responded to this question either learned the two dialects through their study in the UT integrated program or developed knowledge of one dialect in our program and then learned another during their study abroad. A substantial majority (75 percent) of the 145 students who had studied more than one dialect indicated that knowledge of one dialect helped them when the time came to begin learning another.[8]

The responses to this question in our survey provide support to the findings of Emma Trentman (2011), who concludes that knowledge of Egyptian Arabic does not limit a student to understanding Egyptian Arabic only but also assists them in understanding Levantine varieties and vice versa. They are also congruent with John Weinert's study (2012) in which participants indicate that exposure to multiple Arabic dialects is beneficial to their learning experience despite the increased challenges it engenders. Weinert's participants advocate for incorporating such exposure in elementary and intermediate-level Arabic courses, with the caveat that multiple dialect forms should not be presented with the expectation that students will produce more than one actively. Furthermore, our results are consistent with those reported by Shiri, who reports that 84 percent of her respondents agree (57 percent strongly agree and 27 percent somewhat agree) that learning one Arabic dialect helps them learn other dialects (2013, 576). One obvious implication of this finding is that the choice of dialect is far less important than the decision to integrate any dialect. We return to this implication in the conclusion.

We also wanted to learn about the impact that integration within the domestic program has on preparing students for their study abroad.[9] These results indicate that 91 percent of respondents feel that integrating the dialect within their domestic program in the United States has had a positive impact on preparing them for their study abroad experience. In her survey, Shiri notes that many participants indicate that they had not received adequate linguistic and sociolinguistic preparation at their home institutions prior to study abroad. She notes that "the majority of participants only recognized the importance of dialects once they were engaged in the experience abroad, at that point realizing that dialect was the 'practical' and 'natural' means of communication" (2013, 582). Taken together, these results strongly suggest that Arabic programs in the United States need to do more starting with early stages of instruction to help students develop the sociolinguistic and cultural skills—that necessarily entail dealing with an Arabic dialect—required for proper communication with Arabic speakers.

RQ 3: Perceptions of the Nonlinguistic Benefits of Integrating Dialect with MSA

Our third research question deals with students' perceptions regarding the nonlinguistic benefits of integration. We designed three items in the survey that specifically aim at eliciting these perceptions. One area in which students felt they stood to benefit by studying Arabic dialects is their understanding of Arab culture.[10]

In recent years, many teachers of world languages have been placing increasing emphasis on the importance of learning about the culture of the regions where those languages are spoken (see Byram, Gribkova, and Starkey 2002; Lustig and Koester 2003). The field of Arabic is no exception; many teachers incorporate culturally relevant authentic materials such as literature, music, and dance, among others, into their texts and curricula. The full benefit of these materials would not be attained in a curriculum that favors one variety of Arabic at the expense of others (Stokes 2016). Against this backdrop, it is no surprise that over 95 percent of our survey respondents feel that the integration of a dialect with MSA in the curriculum would help them develop a more thorough understanding of Arab culture. Students see the direct link between comprehension of Arabic dialects and an increased engagement with aspects of Arab culture in which the dialects are featured prominently.

Student responses also indicate that integration could bring them social benefits and help them engage with the language socially outside of the classroom. We found that 96 percent of respondents agreed that dialect integration would improve their social connections with Arabs.[11] The findings of our survey confirm those of Palmer (2008), who surveyed students who were studying in the Arab world and reported that, because of their use of colloquial Arabic, they felt they were more trusted by the people and could easily integrate into the culture.

In section 3 of this study (Participants and Their Backgrounds), we point out that 52 percent of the participants indicate that they were taking Arabic

Table 14.10 Students' perceptions of the effect learning a dialect will have on their career/research

To what extent do you agree with the following statement:	Strongly Agree	Agree	Disagree	Strongly Disagree
Learning a dialect simultaneously with Modern Standard Arabic will help me in my career/ research	114 (62%)	48 (26%)	15 (8%)	7 (4%)
N = 184				

because of career and professional reasons. Given this high level of student interest in Arabic as a career-related skill, it is worthwhile to investigate students' views on the professional benefits of an integrated curriculum. Table 14.10 shows their answers to this question.

These responses show that students plan on using their Arabic skills in their careers and research, and that they believe that learning dialect along with MSA will help them do so. The results in this section show that respondents feel very strongly that they will apply their integrated proficiency in a myriad of ways outside of class, including in their social lives, their academic endeavors, and in their future careers.

Conclusions and Implications

The aim of this chapter has been to bring the voices of the University of Texas at Austin Arabic students to the debate on dialect integration in the Arabic curriculum. The fact that the results of this survey are consistent with those reported by other student surveys on this issue suggests that they are reflective of learners of Arabic in the United States at large. We believe that the results generated by this survey bear significance not only to the UT Arabic program but to the entire Arabic teaching profession as well. In what follows, we discuss the implications of the results of this survey for teaching, material development, and curriculum design in Arabic.

Most of our respondents perceive MSA and the dialects to be components of the same language system rather than distinct entities that need to be separated, as is the practice of many Arabic programs in the United States. When students are presented with a supportive approach that integrates spoken Arabic and MSA, the vast majority of them do perceive Arabic as one language. More importantly, their awareness of the symbiotic relationship between MSA and the dialects appears to grow stronger as they continue their learning of Arabic. Advanced students' responses demonstrate that they prefer a curriculum that integrates a dialect with MSA and presents it as part of their "Arabic" course beginning with the first year of instruction. This preference seems to emanate from the students' experience over time that proficiency in Arabic is best gained when a dialect component is fully integrated from the beginning.

Of particular interest here is the similarity between the students' perception expressed in this survey and that of the teachers as reported by Abdalla and Al-Batal (2011–12) in their survey of Arabic teachers in the United States. In that survey, 65 percent of the teachers surveyed strongly agreed or agreed that a dialect component needs to be incorporated in the curriculum at the early stages of instruction. Yet many of the teachers who hold such beliefs find themselves teaching in Arabic programs that do not allow any dialect presence, especially at the lower levels of instruction. These results strongly suggest a disconnect between what most students—as well as many of their teachers—see as necessary to achieve proficiency in Arabic, on the one hand, and what the prevailing practice is at many Arabic programs in which dialects are absent from the curriculum, on the other.

Most students surveyed here see great value in integrating dialect with MSA because this helps them develop a more comprehensive understanding of the culture. While the current practice of focusing only on MSA helps develop important aspects of cultural understanding, the picture remains incomplete if the dialect component is absent from it. Students are prevented from developing a range of intercultural and pragmatic skills and, consequently, from fully engaging with the culture.

A notable percentage of our respondents expressed the feeling that the integration of a dialect with MSA is confusing to them. However, their responses also showed that they were not discouraged by such integration. Teachers can acknowledge confusion and work to address it and manage it as part of the learning process. Possible confusion can serve as an impetus for the development of better pedagogical approaches and techniques of integration in the classroom as well as realistic, clearly articulated expectations and outcomes for learners.

Most students in upper-level content-based courses indicate that their prior study of the dialect in integrated classes helped prepare them for their content courses. As Arabic programs work to develop more content-based courses at the upper levels, integration of dialect at the lower stages becomes crucial. Most content-based courses that focus on issues related to modern Arab societies and cultures will necessarily involve materials that include spoken Arabic. To leave the dialect out of content-based courses and focus exclusively on

MSA is to deprive learners from important cultural content that they need both to understand the content they are studying and continue to develop their language skills as they move toward higher levels of proficiency in Arabic.

If the ultimate goal of Arabic program administrators and curriculum designers is to offer programs that cater to the needs of their students and reflect their priorities, then they need to reexamine their positions regarding dialect integration. In chapter 1 of this volume, we point out that there are multiple approaches to integration; there is no one model that "fits all." Local program contexts and student goals should be carefully considered when selecting the institutional approach to integration. The key element here is for the Arabic curriculum to include a dialect component that is integrated in some fashion with MSA in the curriculum. The privileging of only one variety cannot be maintained and justified if we truly want to offer our students Arabic that is communicative, authentic, and representative of its cultures. A second important implication of this survey, and one that reinforces conclusions reached by Shiri (2013), is that students are not fixated on the question of which dialect to learn. They are interested in learning *a dialect* as part of their Arabic learning, and many of them welcome exposure to other Arabic dialects within their program. One of the objections raised—usually by teachers and program administrators—against implementing integration is the question "Which dialect to teach?" (Younes 2015). Our results confirm that the field needs to move beyond the question of which dialect to teach because it does not matter; teachers can teach any dialect with which they are comfortable and for which there exist enough materials. All Arabic dialects are important, and all share a symbiotic relationship with MSA, and our students will greatly benefit from integrating *any dialect* in their curriculum. The task of integrating some dialects might prove to be challenging at the beginning due to the lack of adequate materials that would support the integration of some dialects with MSA. Most of the students in this survey said that integrating a dialect with MSA is "possible," "rewarding," and "empowering"; Arabic teachers need to follow the students' lead and believe that the development of these integrated materials is also possible, rewarding, and empowering.

References

Abdalla, Mahmoud, and Mahmoud Al-Batal. 2011–12. "College-Level Teachers of Arabic and Attitudes." *Al-ᶜArabiyya* 44/45: 1–28.

Al-Batal, Mahmoud. 1992. "Diglossia Proficiency: The Need for an Alternative Approach to Teaching." In *The Arabic Language in America*, edited by Aleya Rouchdy, 284–304. Detroit: Wayne State University Press.

Belnap, R. Kirk. 2006. "A Profile of Students of Arabic in US Universities." In *Handbook for Arabic Language Teaching Professionals*, edited by Kassem M. Wahba, Zeinab A. Taha, and Liz England, 169–78. Mahwah, NJ: Lawrence Erlbaum.

Brustad, Kristen, Mahmoud Al-Batal, and Abbas al-Tonsi. 2011. *Al-Kitaab fii Taʿallum al-ʿArabiyya: A Textbook for Beginning Arabic*, Part One, 3rd ed. Washington, DC: Georgetown University Press.

Byram, Michael, Bella Gribkova, and Hugh Starkey. 2002. "Developing the Intercultural Dimension in Language Teaching: A Practical Introduction for Teachers." Strasbourg: Council of Europe.

Hashem-Aramouni, Eva. 2011. "The Impact of Diglossia on Arabic Language Instruction in Higher Education: Attitudes and Experiences of Students and Instructors in the US." PhD diss., California State University of Sacramento. http://www.csus.edu/coe/academics/doctorate/research/dissertations/cohort -2/assets/hashem-aramouni-eva-impact-diglossia-arabic.pdf.

Husseinali, Ghassan. 2006. "Who Is Studying Arabic and Why? A Survey of Arabic Students' Orientations at a Major University." *Foreign Language Annals* 39, no. 3: 395–412.

Kaye, Alan S. 1994. "Formal vs. Informal in Arabic: Diglossia, Triglossia, Tetraglossia, Etc., Polyglossia—Multiglossia Viewed as a Continuum." *Zeitschrift Für Arabische Linguistik* 27: 47–66. http://www.jstor.org/stable/43525622.

Lustig, Myron W., and Jolene Koester. 2003. *Intercultural Competence: Interpersonal Communication across Cultures*. New York: Longman.

Palmer, Jeremy. 2005. "Learning and Teaching Arabic for Students and Teachers of the Arabic Language: For Students and Teachers of Arabic." *Arabic Acquisition* (blog). October 24. http://arabicacquisition.blogspot.com/2005/10/amiyya-vs -fusha-debate-is-on.html.

———. 2008. "Arabic Diglossia: Student Perceptions of Spoken Arabic Living in the Arabic-Speaking World." *Arizona Working Papers in SLA & Teaching* 15: 81–95. http://slat.arizona.edu/sites/default/files/page/awp15palmer.pdf.

Salameh, Franck. 2011. "Does Anyone Speak Arabic?" *Middle East Quarterly* 18, no. 4: 47–60.

Shiri, Sonia. 2013. "Learners' Attitudes toward Regional Dialects and Destination Preferences in Study Abroad." *Foreign Language Annals* 46: 565–87.

Stokes, Corinne. 2016. "A Post-Diglossic Critique of Arabic Language and Culture Pedagogy." PhD diss., University of Texas at Austin.

Trentman, Emma. 2011. "L2 Arabic Dialect Comprehension: Empirical Evidence for the Transfer of Familiar Dialect Knowledge to Unfamiliar Dialects." *L2 Journal* 3: 22–49. http://escholarship.org/uc/item/6qx1381h.

Weinert, John Orbison. 2012. "Dialects in the Arabic Classroom: A Pedagogical Survey of Arabic Language Learners." MA thesis, University of Texas at Austin. https://repositories.lib.utexas.edu/bitstream/handle/2152/ETD-UT-2012 -08-6162/WEINERT-THESIS.pdf.

Younes, Munther. 2015. *The Integrated Approach to Arabic Instruction*. London: Routledge.

Younes, Munther, Makda Weatherspoon, and Maha Foster. 2013. ʿArabiyyat al-Naas, Part 1. London: Routledge.

Notes

Additional data and examples are freely available to view and download on this book's product page on the Georgetown University Press (GUP) website (www.press.georgetown.edu).

1. Student responses to items 1–4 and item 8 as well as the complete raw data for the entire survey (in both Excel and PDF formats) are available in appendices A–E on the GUP website.

2. The entire dataset of student responses generated by the survey are available on the GUP website.

3. Table W14.1, on the GUP website, shows the students' descriptions of the purposes of their trips.

4. See table W14.2, on the GUP website.

5. Table W14.3, on the GUP website, shows their responses.

6. Table W14.4, on the GUP website, shows the result.

7. See table W14.5, on the GUP website.

8. See table W14.6, on the GUP website.

9. Table W14.7, on the GUP website, presents a breakdown of the perceptions of the thirty-six students who indicated that they had experience studying Arabic overseas.

10. As reflected in table W14.8, on the GUP website.

11. See table W14.9, on the GUP website.

15

Integration and Students' Perspectives in a Multidialect Environment

MAI ZAKI AND JEREMY PALMER

American University of Sharjah

THE ISSUE OF TEACHING Arabic in an integrated approach has gained considerable attention in the past decade (Al-Batal and Belnap 2006; Palmer 2008; Younes 2006, 2015). This issue, however, needs more qualitative and quantitative studies. Our research seeks to add to the literature by investigating a curricular model that provides students with exposure to Modern Standard Arabic (MSA) and Colloquial Arabic in a multidialect environment. In this model, students learning Arabic at the American University of Sharjah (AUS), an English-medium university in the United Arab Emirates (UAE), learn both MSA and one colloquial variety of Arabic. Due to the variety of Arabic-speaking expatriate communities in the UAE, there is not one predominately used colloquial variety of Arabic. In addition to the local Emirati dialect, there are sizable Egyptian, Levantine, and other regional varieties commonly used in the UAE. This particular linguistic situation presents its own challenges to an integrated approach.

The integrated approach came as a response to the long-established preference for MSA at the expense of the colloquial varieties in the context of teaching Arabic as a foreign language. Within this approach, the invisible line dividing Standard Arabic and the colloquial disappears, and the focus becomes how to teach a learner to use both varieties appropriately. Kassem Wahba (2006, 139) explains that selecting only one variety of Arabic to teach would "seriously prejudice the ability of the nonnative learner to communicate effectively in an Arabic-speaking community." Similarly, Karin Ryding (2006) warns that teaching learners to talk about daily functions in *al-fuṣḥā* creates a gap in their communicative competence and prevents them from achieving their full potential in language proficiency. In the same vein, this study supports the integrated approach in teaching, with a focus on the students' perceptions, expectations, and reflections on the experience of learning MSA and a colloquial variety simultaneously.

This study investigates three main research questions:

1. Are students enthusiastic about learning MSA and at least one colloquial variety of Arabic in the same course?
2. Do students feel that learning MSA and at least one colloquial variety of Arabic in the same course was beneficial? Were students concerned about being confused with two varieties in the same course?
3. Do students feel that studying Arabic (MSA or colloquial) enhanced their learning of Arab culture?

These questions raise important issues at the heart of the integrated approach in Arabic teaching. The study emphasizes students' perceptions and expectations with the aim of reaching a better understanding of students' needs. Another important aspect of the study is to assess the impact of an integrated approach on learning about Arab culture. With the increasing demand of students wanting to study Arabic in order to "know and talk to" the people, it would be of value to assess how well an integrated approach can satisfy this need.

Results indicate that students are generally enthusiastic about learning both MSA and a colloquial variety of Arabic at the beginning of the semester. Students also feel, for the most part, that learning both varieties would be beneficial. Nearly half of them, however, think that studying both varieties in the same course would be confusing. Interestingly, at the end of the semester, most students report that they plan to continue to study both varieties. However, when students are asked more specifically about details relating to their opinion about learning MSA and a dialect, results indicate quite diverse ideologies. Although most of them feel that learning both varieties in the same course helps with their Arabic overall, many of them believe that MSA should be learned first and then a dialect. Finally, results also show that more than half of the students believe that studying both MSA and a dialect has a positive impact on their learning about the culture. Negative opinions also provide an interesting perspective on the relation between Arabic and culture in the context of this study.

This chapter is organized as follows: The first section presents a brief review of literature, followed by the background and scope of the study in light of the linguistic situation in the UAE in general and at AUS in particular. The second section discusses the methodology and research design, including issues such as participants, length of study, surveys, and so on. The third section presents the qualitative and quantitative analysis of the data and the results. The fourth section is a discussion of the results followed by comments about limitations and recommendations for further research. Finally, the last section concludes the chapter.

Literature Review

One crucial factor in the discussion of which variety of Arabic to teach should be students' needs; that is, what do students want to learn? Answering this question is probably the motivation for what is now known as "the integrated approach" in teaching Arabic (Younes 1990, 2006, 2015). The dominance of the higher written variety of Arabic at the expense of the spoken dialects in Arabic programs is evident, as Jeremy Palmer (2008, 85) argues, that "Arabic programs in the United States ignore the spoken varieties of Arabic," and Christopher Horn (2015, 101) states that Colloquial Arabic "has historically never been given much importance or recognition." But the situation is now changing; with the growing numbers of students in the Western world wanting to learn Arabic, combined with a shift in students' needs, it is no longer enough to idolize MSA while disregarding any other variety. Most of the earlier generations were only interested in learning Classical or Standard Arabic for academic reasons, while others were only interested in learning a colloquial variety to communicate with native speakers orally. But in recent years, research (Belnap 2006; Husseinali 2006; Palmer 2008; Wahba 2006) has shown that the needs of students of Arabic have changed. In fact, all the surveys in these studies show that the main motivation for studying Arabic is to communicate with native speakers.

According to Munther Younes (2006), the integrated approach is built on the assumption that learners study Arabic in order to achieve proficiency in all language skills (listening, speaking, writing, and reading). This cannot be done if you are teaching al-fuṣḥā only or al-ᶜāmmiyya only. Of course, the integrated approach can also face numerous challenges, as this study shows. Issues such as learners' confusion, which dialect to choose, and how comfortable teachers can be teaching a dialect not their own all need to be considered. However, these challenges are seen as practical hurdles that can be overcome in a well-designed program. In the next section, we introduce our study, which attempts to integrate the colloquial in an environment that is already rich in colloquial varieties of Arabic.

Background and Scope of the Study

In this study, we present the results of an integrated model adopted in teaching Arabic to nonnative speakers at the undergraduate level at AUS. The sociolinguistic situation in the UAE is rather interesting for several reasons. First, according to IndexMundi, around 80 percent of the total population in the UAE are foreigners. Of those, the South Asian population (Bangladesh, Pakistan, India) make up around half while the rest consist of other Arab nationalities and Westerners.[1] This results in a situation where, on the one hand, the local Emirati dialect is a minority in its own country while, on the other hand, there is a plethora of other Arabic dialects being used all the time. The large foreign population in the UAE also means that generations of immigrants have been born in and live in the country. The non-Arabic-speaking immigrants who are long-term residents in the UAE normally have some formal Arabic study in schools as it is compulsory by law to teach Arabic for nonnative speakers. However, in recent years there has been much media attention commenting on the poor status of Arabic teaching in general in the UAE. Numerous articles in leading Emirati newspapers, both in English and in Arabic, discuss the "negligence" in Arabic teaching and the need to raise the standards of both Arabic curricula and teachers.

AUS is a microcosm of the broad sociolinguistic status quo in the UAE. According to the latest figures from the AUS website, the population of students in the spring of 2015 reflect the multicultural and multilinguistic environment within the university.[2] The top four categories of students are from Arab countries, with Emiratis at the top of the list (16 percent), followed by Egyptians (13 percent), Jordanians (11 percent), and Syrians (8 percent). Together with other nationalities, including Palestinian, Saudi Arabian, and Lebanese, this means that there is an abundance of different Arabic dialects on campus. The biggest non-Arabic-speaking nationalities among AUS students are Indian (7 percent) and Pakistani (6 percent). These groups form the basis for many of the heritage students enrolled in different Arabic for nonnatives courses at the university. Zeinab Ibrahim and Jehan Allam (2006, 443) identify four types of heritage students, among them, "Moslems who came from many other non-Arab countries and were exposed to only one variety of Arabic through their learning of the Qur'an or aspects of religion." In our study, we have found that these students, most of whom have lived in the UAE for some time, have a high degree of awareness of the diglossic nature of Arabic. This does not come as a surprise since, for most of them, their relationship with Arabic prior to taking our courses is shaped by their study of Islam. They can easily compare Qur'anic Arabic with the Arabic they hear around them in the streets or in the university.

However, heritage students in this sense are but one segment of the student population in our Arabic as a foreign language classes. The other big segment of students is exchange students who come from various backgrounds. It is not uncommon in one class of Arabic with twenty students to have fifteen different nationalities or ethnic backgrounds represented. What is interesting for the purpose of this study is to assess the level of awareness of the diglossic nature of Arabic for this type of student. Therefore, in the pre-survey in this research, all students were asked the following question: "Before enrolling in this course, did you know about Arabic having a formal standard language along with numerous dialects?" Of the forty-four students who completed the pre-survey in the fall of 2014, only ten of them (23 percent) indicated that they were *not* aware of the issue of different varieties of Arabic. In the spring of 2015, only fifteen of the sixty-two pre-survey responses were negative (24 percent). Thus, it is apparent that most students, including non-Arab exchange students, were aware of the Arabic sociolinguistic situation before enrolling. These results do not, however, indicate that students expected to study more than one variety of Arabic after enrolling.

Methodology

This study started in the academic year 2014–15, covering two semesters: fall 2014 and spring 2015. The study consisted of three main elements: (a) pre- and post-surveys, (b) journal assignments, and (c) colloquial activities. Students completed pre- and post-surveys that asked about their linguistic and cultural experiences learning Arabic in the proposed model. Students kept a weekly (later changed to monthly) journal that asked about specific instances of language usage and cultural insights. Test/quiz questions and homework activities required students to master course materials in both MSA and a colloquial dialect.

Model 1: Fall 2014

This model employed the integrated approach in three classes representing two levels of Arabic: two classes of Elementary Arabic 1 and one class of Elementary Arabic 2. In all our Arabic foreign language classes, the textbook used for instruction is the *Al-Kitaab* series (Brustad, Al-Batal, and Al-Tonsi 2011, 2013), including the *Alif Baa* book (Brustad, Al-Batal, and Al-Tonsi 2010), which is used in the beginning of Elementary Arabic 1 class. This textbook series includes dialect material for two specific colloquial varieties, Egyptian and Shāmi (Levantine), alongside MSA. This allowed us in the first model of this study to give the students a choice in learning a specific dialect. However, for the sake of relevance to the locality of the AUS in the UAE, we also designed the model to include a third option for the students: Emirati Arabic.

The decision to include the Emirati dialect was motivated by the obvious geographical situation in addition to the recognition that many students expressed their desire to learn Arabic in order to "speak with the locals." This decision, however, did not come without challenges. It was important for the study to prepare instructional material for Emirati Arabic to be on par with the Egyptian and Shāmi material already included in the textbook. Since none of the instructors are natives of the Emirati dialect, we had to seek the help of several Emirati students prior to the beginning of the semester and throughout to prepare lists of vocabulary equivalent to the ones in the textbook.[3] This was done through both written feedback (via emails) and personal meetings with the Emirati students to verify pronunciation issues. Once the lists were ready, they were given to students who chose to study the Emirati dialect.[4] In class, students were typically seated in groups according to their chosen dialect to facilitate group work during colloquial activities.

Model 2: Spring 2015

Model 2 employed the integrated approach in three classes representing two levels of Arabic: two classes of Elementary Arabic 1 and one class in Elementary Arabic 2. With the second semester, we made some changes in the model to address some issues raised in the first semester. In the previous model, the practicality of offering three different dialects and maintaining this throughout the semester proved to be challenging. First, preparing the Emirati material for both levels of Elementary Arabic was a time-consuming process, especially given the content and time restrictions. Ideally, hiring a native Emirati teaching assistant would have been a great help, but that could not be achieved due to lack of funds. Throughout the fall semester it became clear that students learning the Egyptian and Shāmi dialects were exposed to more material from the textbook compared to their colleagues who chose the Emirati dialect. A particular challenge was the lack of audiovisual content in the Emirati dialect. Second, the classroom setting with three different groups of students according to their chosen dialects was also difficult to manage at times. Therefore, model 2 did not allow students a choice of colloquial dialect. In Elementary 1 classes, each teacher assigned one colloquial dialect to the entire class—that is, one class studied Egyptian and the other one studied Shāmi. In the Elementary 2 class, all students studied the Shāmi dialect.

Pre- and Post-Surveys

The surveys represent an important instrument in this study as they allowed us to address our research questions in a rather direct way. Before administering the pre-survey in both semesters, each instructor introduced the students to the adopted model of teaching. The pre-survey was designed to elicit some background information about the students in addition to items that addressed our main research questions within this model. Background information included the students' native language and previous exposure to any Arabic dialects. The post-survey was administered toward the end of the semester. It included items directly related to the research questions as well as other questions related to frequency of use of MSA or a dialect outside the classroom, whether or not learners of Arabic should study a dialect first before learning MSA, and their future plans for learning MSA or a dialect.

In the fall of 2014, 44 students in Elementary Arabic (both levels) completed the pre-survey while only 15 students submitted the post-survey. As for the spring of 2015, a total of 62 students took the pre-survey while 50 students took the post-survey. Thus, in both models a total of 106 students took the pre-survey and 65 took the post-survey. To sum up, the number of students who submitted both pre- and post-surveys was a little more than half (61 percent).

Journal Assignments and Colloquial Activities

Journal assignments were designed to give the students the opportunity to express their opinions regarding our main research questions and to give examples. The journal included questions regarding enthusiasm, benefit, and culture, as discussed in the following section. It also included a question about language usage outside the classroom, whether in MSA or in the dialect. In the fall semester, these journal assignments were assigned on a weekly basis. However, following observation and students' feedback, it was apparent that this was too much work for the students and did not give them enough time to write new examples. Therefore, in the spring semester, we decided to assign the journal assignments on a monthly basis.

There were some variations in how colloquial activities were integrated into each class. However, generally speaking, classes included the following elements:

- Discussion of colloquial vocabulary of each lesson
- Colloquial homework assignments
- Specific colloquial questions in quizzes, midterm exams, and final exams

Discussion of various colloquial assignments and vocabulary as well as questions in quizzes and tests were done both in the written and oral modes by the instructor, in addition to the audiovisual material. A typical classroom activity would involve small groups of students engaging in a specific conversation.[5]

Results

This section presents the results for each research question individually.

Research Question 1: Are students enthusiastic about learning MSA and at least one colloquial variety of Arabic in the same course?

Students' enthusiasm for learning different varieties of Arabic is an important starting point. If students are not enthusiastic about learning a particular variety of Arabic, perhaps they and their teachers should question why it is offered. To investigate enthusiasm during both semesters, students were asked to respond to items on the pre-survey that sought to gauge their enthusiasm for studying both MSA and a dialect of Arabic. At the end of the semester, students were asked to respond to items on a post-survey about their intentions to continue studying MSA and a dialect of Arabic. Results from both are presented below.

Pre-Survey (Enthusiasm)

In the fall 2014 ($N = 44$) and spring 2015 ($N = 62$) pre-surveys, students were asked to select how much they agreed or disagreed with the statements "I am enthusiastic about learning MSA" and "I am enthusiastic about learning my selected dialect" using a Likert scale with options including strongly agree, agree, neutral, disagree, and strongly disagree. The item addressing MSA is presented first, followed by the dialect.

MSA

Results from the fall 2014 pre-survey ($N = 44$) about enthusiasm for studying MSA indicate that 15 students strongly agreed (34 percent), 18 agreed (41 percent), 8 were neutral (18 percent), 2 disagreed (5 percent), and 1 strongly disagreed (2 percent). Most of the students responded in the affirmative, with 75 percent of them expressing strong enthusiasm for studying MSA. As for the pre-survey in the spring of 2015 ($N = 62$), the results concerning agreement about enthusiasm for MSA reveal that 30 students agreed strongly (48 percent), 26 agreed (42 percent), 5 were neutral (8 percent), 1 disagreed (2 percent), and 0 disagreed. Combining strongly agree and agree demonstrates that 90 percent of the students were enthusiastic about studying MSA. Thus, it is apparent that most of the students in both semesters were enthusiastic about learning MSA.

Dialect
Students were asked about their enthusiasm for learning a dialect using the same Likert scale. In the fall of 2014 ($N = 44$), the results show that 17 strongly agreed (39 percent), 19 agreed (43 percent), 8 were neutral (18 percent), and 0 disagreed. Combining the strongly agree and agree responses reveals that 82 percent of the fall 2014 students were enthusiastic about learning a dialect. Enthusiasm for studying a dialect on the pre-survey in the spring of 2015 ($N = 62$) reveals that 27 students strongly agreed (44 percent), 23 agreed (37 percent), 12 were neutral (19 percent), and 0 disagreed. Combining the strongly agree and agree responses shows that 81 percent of the spring 2015 students were enthusiastic about studying a dialect.

Our survey of students in these semesters reveals that almost all of the 106 students who completed the pre-survey were enthusiastic about learning both MSA and a dialect. In fact, no students indicated disagreement with the statement about enthusiasm for learning a dialect. Very few students disagreed with the statement about enthusiasm for learning MSA. The results from the post-survey about intentions to continue with MSA, with dialect, or with both are presented next.[6]

Post-Survey: Continuing with Arabic
In the fall 2014 ($N = 15$) and spring 2015 ($N = 50$) post-surveys, students were asked to indicate how much they agreed or disagreed with the statements "I plan to continue learning MSA" and "I plan to continue learning a dialect of Arabic" using a five-option Likert scale, as explained above. The item related to MSA is presented first, followed by the one related to the dialect.

MSA
Responses in the fall 2014 ($N = 15$) post-survey about plans to continue studying MSA revealed that 5 students strongly agreed (33 percent), 10 agreed (66 percent), and none had neutral responses or disagreements. Thus, everyone in the fall 2014 semester expressed interest in continuing with MSA. In the spring of 2015 ($N = 50$), students responded to the same items on the post-survey. Results about continuing with MSA revealed that 21 students strongly agreed (42 percent), 20 agreed (40 percent), 6 were neutral (12 percent), and 3 disagreed (6 percent). Adding the strongly agree and agree

responses shows that 82 percent of the students expressed interest in continuing their study of MSA.

Dialect
As for continuing with the study of dialect, results from the fall of 2014 (N = 15) show that 6 students strongly agreed (40 percent), 6 agreed (40 percent), 2 were neutral (13 percent), and 1 strongly disagreed (7 percent). These results indicate that 80 percent of the students showed interest in continuing with a dialect.

In the spring of 2015 (N = 50) the results indicate that 14 students strongly agreed (28 percent), 20 agreed (40 percent), 12 were neutral (24 percent), 2 disagreed (4 percent), and 2 strongly disagreed (4 percent) about continuing to study the dialect. Thus, the majority of the students (68 percent) indicated interest in continuing to study a dialect.[7]

Interestingly, the post-survey results indicate about the same results as the pre-survey in relation to enthusiasm for MSA and studying a dialect. However, the post-survey results reveal that several students are not interested in continuing to study a dialect. Due to restrictions on length and scope of this article, brief comments about these students' post-survey responses are presented. One student reported that he mixed up the vocabulary of the varieties and wished he could have studied Emirati Arabic (not possible in spring 2015). A second student expressed confusion resulting from learning more than one variety and said that this was too much to handle in one class—especially at the beginner level. Another student wanted to focus on MSA and expressed regret that in spring 2015 she could not choose the dialect that suited her (another student expressed similar regret).

Research Question 2: Do students feel that learning MSA and at least one colloquial variety of Arabic in the same course was beneficial? Were students concerned about being confused with two varieties in the same course?

Benefit
Students were asked in the pre- and post-surveys for their thoughts about learning the two varieties of Arabic in the same course. Before sharing results from the post-surveys, it is helpful to investigate what the students thought about potential benefit at the beginning of the semester. Accordingly, this section first investigates student responses from the pre-survey about the potential benefit of studying MSA and a dialect in the same course. In addition,

and since the research question also deals with potential confusion, results from the post-surveys and journals are presented.

In the pre-survey, students responded to the following item using the same Likert scale as above: "Choose how much you agree or disagree with the following statement: I think learning MSA and a dialect at the same time will be beneficial." There were 106 students total in the fall 2014 and spring 2015 semesters who responded to this question. Out of these responses, 28 students strongly agreed (26 percent), 45 agreed (43 percent), 30 were neutral (28 percent), 3 disagreed (3 percent), and 0 strongly disagreed.[8]

Further below, we present results from post-surveys that highlight how the students felt about this issue at the end of the semester. However, before discussing the post-survey results we want to address an important topic that is frequently mentioned in academic conferences about dialect integration. The topic in question is that of possible student confusion when faced with two different varieties of Arabic within the same course.

Confusion

Because some of our students have voiced concerns about confusion resulting from dealing with more than one variety of Arabic in the same curriculum, we wanted to gauge the extent of this concern (for a more thorough discussion of this issue, see Younes 2015).

In the pre-survey, students responded to the following item using the same Likert scale as above: "Choose how much you agree or disagree with the following statement: I think learning MSA and a dialect at the same time will be confusing." Results ($N = 106$) indicate that 6 students strongly agreed (6 percent), 37 students agreed (35 percent), 37 students were neutral (35 percent), 20 students disagreed (19 percent), and 6 students strongly disagreed (6 percent). The survey results depict the students' responses from both the fall 2014 and spring 2015 semesters about potential confusion of studying MSA and a dialect in the same course, showing that more students felt that studying both MSA and a dialect in the same course would be confusing. Ignoring the neutral responses, 43 students (41 percent) indicated a level of agreement with the statement about confusion while 26 students (25 percent) disagreed to some degree. Considering the neutral responses with those who disagreed, however, does show that 63 students (59 percent) are not actively concerned about confusion.[9]

Results from the Post-Survey

At the end of the semester, students were asked about learning the different varieties of Arabic in the same course. The questions were formed to elicit the students' opinions about various issues, such as whether they believe it would be better to learn one of the two varieties before the other and whether they believed that learning both varieties of Arabic (MSA and a dialect) in the same course led to better Arabic learning experience overall. We focus here on the results for the latter issue as it directly relates to the research question. In the post-survey, students responded to this item: "Choose how much you agree or disagree with the following statement: Studying MSA along with my selected dialect in the same course helped me learn Arabic better overall." Responses from both the fall 2014 and spring 2015 ($N = 65$) semesters reveal that 2 students strongly disagreed (3 percent), 9 disagreed (14 percent), 15 were neutral (23 percent), 27 agreed (42 percent), and 12 strongly agreed (18 percent).[10]

Interestingly, these results show that the majority of the students believed that learning both MSA and a dialect in the same course was beneficial to their overall Arabic. The 39 of the 65 students who agreed or strongly agreed represent 60 percent of the total respondents. This may have something to do with the background of this particular student group, which, as mentioned earlier, was well aware of the diglossic situation of Arabic.

Research Question 3: Do students feel that studying Arabic (MSA or colloquial) enhanced their learning of Arab culture?

For many students, foreign and heritage alike, the experience of learning Arabic is not complete without gaining insights into the culture of the people, especially while learning in an Arabic-speaking country. In the following, we present results from the post-survey that deal with this aspect.

In the post-survey, students responded to the following item: "Choose how much you agree or disagree with the following statement: Studying MSA along with my selected dialect in the same course helped me better understand Arab culture." Results from both semesters ($N = 65$) reveal that 4 students disagreed strongly (6 percent), 5 disagreed (8 percent), 21 were neutral (32 percent), 28 agreed (43 percent), and 7 strongly agreed (11 percent).[11] It is not surprising that most students agreed with this statement; however, nearly a third of them were neutral. In order to better understand the students' perspective, the statistical data alone is not enough. Therefore, in a later section we discuss some qualitative comments from the journal assignments that shed more light on the result that 54 percent of the students thought this integrated model of teaching helped them to understand aspects of Arab culture.

In the journal assignments, two questions concerned this issue, while keeping MSA and the colloquial dialect distinct in their relationship with culture. The questions were as follows:

1. Do you feel that studying MSA this week helped you learn about Arab culture? If yes, how? Please share specific examples.
2. Do you feel that studying the dialect this month helped you learn about Arab culture? If yes, how? Please share specific examples.

The questions are formulated in a way to encourage students to share their personal opinions as well as specific examples. For the first question, the results show that the cultural aspects the students benefited from fell into two groups:

1. Cultural elements within the language (e.g., linguistic structures, the root-pattern system, varieties of Arabic)
2. Cultural elements outside the language (e.g., issues related to news, education, death, Islam)

For the second question, the students expressed the view that cultural elements in the dialects highlight for them cultural differences in the Arab world. However, the results from the journal assignments also show that not all students agree that learning either MSA or the dialect had any bearing on learning about the culture. These results are discussed in more detail in the later sections.

Discussion

This section discusses the results relevant to each research question individually.

Research Q1

The first research question reveals that at the beginning of the semester (pre-survey) all students were enthusiastic about learning a dialect. In fact, no students disagreed at all. The vast majority of the students were also enthusiastic about learning MSA, with very minimal disagreement ($n = 4$ out of $N = 106$).

At the end of the semester (post-survey) students remained enthusiastic about continuing to learn MSA and a dialect. Out of the 65 respondents, only 3 disagreed with the statement about continuing to learn MSA. As for the dialect, only 5 students out of 65 disagreed. Thus, this question suggests that, overall, students were enthusiastic about learning both varieties of Arabic at the beginning of the semester *and* they were interested in continuing to study both varieties. This might reflect their awareness of the diglossic nature of Arabic. However, when investigating more nuanced items about learning MSA and a dialect, results are not always so optimistic. The next research question reveals more details about student ideological opinions pertaining to learning both varieties in the same course.

Research Q2

As mentioned earlier, 69 percent of the students agree that learning both MSA and a dialect in the same course would be beneficial and thus were mostly optimistic about the prospect of studying more than one variety of Arabic. Interestingly, however, 41 percent feel that learning both varieties would be confusing. Thus, it is safe to say that most of the students looked forward to the opportunity to learn two varieties although nearly half were also concerned about possible confusion.

At the end of the semester, some students seemed to have lost a bit of their optimism about learning both MSA and a dialect in the same course. Asked whether they thought learning both varieties together in the same course helped them to learn Arabic better overall, responses reveal that 60 percent of the total respondents agree. However, this is still a big percentage, and the result might be attributed to the particular student population in these courses, in which many come from predominantly Islamic countries. In such countries, the more formal variety of Arabic is highly revered and emotionally connected with the Qur'an and, therefore, deemed necessary to learn.

To elaborate, out of the 106 submissions of the pre-survey, 54 of them were from students outside North America and Europe (51 percent). The remaining countries, obviously, make up the additional 52 (49 percent). However, there were only 37 students (35 percent) from North America. Thus, it is possible that, since the remaining 69 students were from outside the United States—with the largest group from Pakistan (19 percent)—the results of this particular research may differ from those reported in other chapters in the present volume.

Although religion was not queried in this research, it is probable that many of the students from outside North America and Europe are Muslim, and their reasons for studying Arabic may be closer in line with programs that offer more focus on MSA. When talking about learning Arabic in the Arab/Islamic world, it is common to hear that MSA is the expected variety for various religious and nationalistic reasons. The close ties between *al-fuṣḥā* and both Islam and Arab nationalism have been extensively discussed in the literature, and it proves true at least for a big part of the student population in this study. However, for the other group of students who come from North America and other countries, learning a dialect would be equally important to them as learning MSA is to Muslim students. This is reflected in the results of both the pre- and post-surveys, where no less than 60 percent of all students were content with the idea of learning both MSA and a dialect. Nevertheless, the results of this research question have implications for the design of any integrated model of teaching Arabic. We particularly argue that programs with many heritage students or students from Islamic countries should conduct a needs analysis before assuming that teaching a dialect will be welcomed.

Research Q3

As mentioned in the previous section, a little more than half of the students report that learning Arabic has had a positive impact on their understanding of the culture. A more illuminating source, however, are the journal entries, which provided more insights into the students' perspectives. There are two factors to be considered while looking at these entries: first, the less time in class dedicated to the dialect compared to MSA and, second, the variation noticed among students in their understanding of the concept of "culture."

For the first question, regarding MSA helping in learning about the culture, many students consider the close relationship between Arabic and its culture to be reflected in certain linguistic aspects within the language itself. Among the examples mentioned were the root system, politeness, forms of address, and levels of formality/informality. According to a number of students, while learning about the roots of words, "there is often a cultural element to be explored," and, to these students, such a systematic structure of roots and patterns reveals a lot about the grammar, literature, and culture of the language. The politeness aspect and its reflection on forms of address in Arabic was also mentioned frequently as a typical cultural element. One student finds the forms of address when conducting a dialogue in Standard Arabic to be "very representative of the Arab culture in the sense of respect given while addressing someone." Also, culture is represented in the students' heightened awareness of the different levels of formality in Arabic. Some comments show that students have learned to differentiate between suitable social contexts for the two varieties of Arabic (MSA and the dialect). Moreover, they have come to appreciate that this is an acquired skill that is not only linguistically appropriate but culturally appreciated. Other students learned about the culture in the contexts of news, education, death, Islam, and other fields. A combination of textbook-based discussions and life in an Arabic-speaking country makes certain cultural aspects stand out for students. One student specifically noted that "MSA is the medium used for news, books, street names, etc. All of these form an integral part of Arab culture."

As for the second question, which asked the students if learning the dialect helped them in learning about the culture, many students commented on the fact that learning a variety of Colloquial Arabic highlights the differences, linguistic and cultural, between the different dialects. One student explains that "dialect learning is especially useful for gaining cultural perspectives." Common observations are that students are more aware of the different dialects they are hearing on and off campus and more able to identify them. Students also mentioned understanding Arabic songs and some dialect-specific idiomatic expressions as a bonus from learning a dialect. On the other hand, comparing the dialect and MSA in terms of the cultural component, one student notes that "some of the words of the dialect vocab are shortened versions of MSA vocab, but are often more complex than their MSA counterparts" because of the layer of cultural complexity added to the dialects. Even further, one student comments that "the culture of a place is not defined by MSA anymore. Arab culture is way too varied now!" This particular comment highlights the multicultural and multidialectal situation in the UAE generally and the AUS specifically as reflected in its varied Arab student population.

To summarize, this research question was designed to elicit students' views on the impact of learning Arabic, in both its standard and colloquial varieties, on gaining a better understanding of the culture. Some students think that learning MSA was most beneficial for learning about cultural aspects, while others favor the dialects. Linguistic aspects of MSA such as the root system, politeness, and degrees of formality and informality were all mentioned as having a cultural side. In addition, students consider the fact that learning MSA gives access to Arabic media and the news to be a positive cultural byproduct of learning MSA. However, probably one of the greatest cultural gains that came from the students' experience with the dialects is that it taught them to "fit in the culture" and to recognize culturally appropriate situations for the two varieties.

Limitations of the Present Study

With such a large-scale project, there were some challenges in both design and implementation. Concerning design, there were obvious limitations when it comes to our integration models adopted in this study. The dialect portion of this research is not as well developed as the MSA one. This is partially due to the nature of the textbooks themselves as having more developed MSA material. The teachers did expand the dialect materials, but due to time constraints and shortage of support, such endeavors were limited in scope. Furthermore, the nature of Arabic in the UAE is such that there is no one dominant colloquial variety of Arabic. Since the host nationals, Emiratis, are a small minority in their own country, and Emirati Arabic learning materials are scarce, it is difficult to adopt an integrated approach based solely on MSA and Emirati Arabic. There are efforts from various language institutes and researchers to develop materials in Emirati and Gulf Arabic, but these are still limited. Besides, many Arab students on campus from other countries do not speak Gulf Arabic. In the fall semester, Emirati material on par with the range of vocabulary and grammar offered in the textbooks was developed with the help of Emirati students, but the lack of resources prevented the continuation of this model. The Emirati material, albeit limited, provided this study with an opportunity to test the two models of integration.

On a more practical level, there were some challenges in implementation. For example, on a few occasions students entered survey or journal information late. The researchers tried to avoid this problem, but students' busy schedules (or forgetfulness?) sometimes warranted permission for late submissions. In the process of analyzing the data, the researchers also found a few examples of students who submitted the same survey or journal more than once. In such cases, the earliest version was used for this research. The change in the frequency of the journals (from weekly to monthly), which was implemented in the second semester, came as a response to the students' feedback in the fall of 2014 regarding workload and other course commitments.

Conclusion and Future Research

In closing, the researchers feel that an integrated approach in teaching Arabic has great value and should be the path for the future, considering the changes in student needs that have been taking place in the past decade or two. Students of Arabic are eager to, and indeed capable of, grasping the whole rich and complex context of the Arabic language: One student would read a political analysis written in a newspaper in MSA and then talk about it in the local dialect with a friend. Even in a country like the UAE, with its many dialects of Arabic, learning the sociolinguistic reality of Arabic from the beginning helps students to cope with their situation.

While this study does not address the nature of the integration process itself, the authors highlight the fact that successful integration in the classroom greatly contributes to removing the separation wall between MSA and the dialect. This is especially important in an Arabic-speaking country where learners note that native speakers automatically change from MSA to the colloquial or vice versa, according to the situation. Other issues that this study attempts to address in the design of an integrated approach include how to deal with confusion between the two varieties, how to develop or create a balanced curriculum that does not favor MSA for historic reasons regardless of students' needs, and how not to underestimate the power of both MSA and the dialects in reflecting various cultural aspects of the language.

There is a great potential for future research on this topic, with a few suggested improvements. For example, we note that the dialect materials in the textbooks are not equally presented when compared to MSA. Thus, we undertook the task of creating additional dialect materials, not just for Emirati dialect in the fall 2014 semester but also for the Egyptian and Shāmi dialects. However, for the purpose of implementing a fully integrated model of instruction, more attention needs to be paid to the development of robust curricula of Arabic dialects to be integrated with MSA.

References

Al-Batal, Mahmoud, and Kirk Belnap. 2006. "The Teaching and Learning of Arabic in the United States: Realities, Needs and Future Directions." In *Handbook for Arabic Language Teaching Professionals in the 21st Century*, edited by Kassem M. Wahba, Zeinab A. Taha, and Liz England, 389–99. Mahwah, NJ: Lawrence Erlbaum.

Belnap, Kirk. 2006. "A Profile of Students of Arabic in US Universities." In *Handbook for Arabic Language Teaching Professionals in the 21st Century*, edited by Kassem M. Wahba, Zeinab A. Taha, and Liz England, 169–78. Mahwah, NJ: Lawrence Erlbaum.

Brustad, Kristen, Mahmoud Al-Batal, and Abbas Al-Tonsi. 2010. *Alif Baa: Introduction to Arabic Letters and Sounds*, 3rd ed. Washington, DC: Georgetown University Press.

———. 2011. *Al-Kitaab fi Taᶜallum al-ᶜArabiyya: A Textbook for Beginning Arabic*, Part One, 3rd ed. Washington, DC: Georgetown University Press.

———. 2013. *Al-Kitaab fi Taᶜallum al-ᶜArabiyya: A Textbook for Intermediate Arabic*, Part Two, 3rd ed. Washington, DC: Georgetown University Press.

Horn, Christopher. 2015. "Diglossia in the Arab World." *Open Journal of Modern Linguistics* 5: 100–104.

Husseinali, Ghassan. 2006. "Who Is Studying Arabic and Why? A Survey of Arabic Students' Orientations at a Major University." *Foreign Language Annals* 39, no. 3: 395–412.

Ibrahim, Zeinab, and Jehan Allam. 2006. "Arabic Learners and Heritage Students Redefined: Present and Future." In *Handbook for Arabic Language Teaching Professionals in the 21st Century*, edited by Kassem M. Wahba, Zeinab A. Taha, and Liz England, 437–46. Mahwah, NJ: Lawrence Erlbaum.

Palmer. Jeremy. 2008. "Arabic Diglossia: Student Perceptions of Spoken Arabic after Living in the Arabic-Speaking World." *Arizona Working Papers in SLAT* 15: 81–95.

Ryding, Karin. 2006. "Teaching Arabic in the United States." In *Handbook for Arabic Language Teaching Professionals in the 21st Century*, edited by Kassem M.

Wahba, Zeinab A. Taha, and Liz England, 13–20. Mahwah, NJ: Lawrence Erlbaum.

Wahba, Kassem. 2006. "Arabic Language Use and the Educated Language User." In *Handbook for Arabic Language Teaching Professionals in the 21st Century*, edited by Kassem M. Wahba, Zeinab A. Taha, and Liz England, 139–55. Mahwah, NJ: Lawrence Erlbaum.

Younes, Munther. 1990. "An Integrated Approach to Teaching Arabic as a Foreign Language." *Al-ᶜArabiyya* 23, no. 1–2: 105–22.

———. 2006. "Integrating the Colloquial with *Fusha* in the Arabic as a Foreign Language Classroom." In *Handbook for Arabic Language Teaching Professionals in the 21st Century*, edited by Kassem M. Wahba, Zeinab A. Taha, and Liz England, 157–66. Mahwah, NJ: Lawrence Erlbaum.

———. 2015. *The Integrated Approach to Arabic Instruction*. Oxon, UK: Routledge.

Notes

Additional data and examples are freely available to view and download on this book's product page on the Georgetown University Press (GUP) website (www.press .georgetown.edu).

1. "United Arab Emirates Ethnic Groups," IndexMundi, October 8, 2016, http:// www.indexmundi.com/united_arab_emirates/ethnic_groups.html.

2. American University of Sharjah Fast Facts Fall 2016, http://www.aus.edu /info/200129/why_aus/434/fast_facts.

3. The authors would like to thank the AUS Emirati students who volunteered to help in the preparation of the Emirati dialect material in the fall of 2014.

4. See figure W15.1 on the GUP website for an example.

5. See FigureW15.2 on the GUP website for an example.

6. On the GUP website, we present figures depicting the results: figure W15.3 presents results for the fall 2014 pre-survey, figure W15.4 presents results for the spring 2015 pre-survey, and figure W15.5 shows the combined results of the pre-survey items about enthusiasm for learning MSA and a dialect together for both semesters.

7. Figures on the GUP website illustrate these results. Figure W15.6 and figure W15.7 depict the post-survey results about continuing with MSA and a dialect for fall 2014 and spring 2015. Figure W15.8 shows the combined results of the post-survey items about enthusiasm for learning MSA and a dialect together for both semesters.

8. Figure W15.9 on the GUP website presents the students' responses and indicates that most of the students felt that studying both MSA and a dialect in the same course would be beneficial.

9. See figure W15.10 on the GUP website.

10. Figure W15.11 on the GUP website demonstrates these results.

11. Figure W15.12 on the GUP website shows these results.

16

Teachers' Voices

Analysis of Teachers' Speech and Teachers'
Perspectives in Integrated Arabic Classrooms

CAROLINE NAJOUR
University of North Texas

CODE-SWITCHING between Modern Standard Arabic (MSA) and dialect is an inherent part of the communicative competence of speakers of Arabic who are constantly moving along an MSA-dialect continuum (Blanc 1960; Badawi 1973; Meiseles 1980; Al-Batal 1995; Holes 2004). Haim Blanc, who distinguishes five levels along this continuum, writes, "Once one gets beyond homespun conversation in relaxed colloquial within a single dialect, it is the exception rather than the rule to find any sustained segment of discourse in a single one of the style varieties alluded to. Speakers tend to pass from one to the other, sometimes within a single sentence" (1960, 85). The issue this chapter seeks to address is how the speech of instructors in an integrated classroom moves along the MSA-dialect continuum, replicating the authentic use of the Arabic language by a native speaker. The present study is the first to examine the nature of instructors' speech in integrated Arabic classrooms.

Two surveys of Arabic-language instructors in US colleges have paved the way toward a better understanding of the profiles, attitudes, beliefs, and dispositions of Arabic-language teachers. The first study is Kirk Belnap's (1995) survey, which provides a picture of the institutional setting of teaching Arabic in the United States, including the types of instructors in the teaching of Arabic as a foreign language (TAFL) field, their training, and their priorities. The second study is by Mahmoud Abdalla and Mahmoud Al-Batal (2011–12), conducted almost fifteen years later, which surveyed approximately 50 percent of all college instructors of Arabic in the United States, describing their profiles, needs, and perspectives. My study here expands on their work and helps further unveil the attitudes of Arabic foreign language (AFL) instructors by focusing on instructors who have taught or are currently teaching Arabic courses that integrate both MSA and a dialect. My purpose is to understand what drives them to adopt the integrated approach (IA), how they resolve some of its challenges, how they integrate MSA and a dialect in their teacher talk, and what some characteristics of their dialect registers are.

The instructors interviewed in this study list several main arguments in support of the IA. It is beyond the scope of this study to reproduce all the arguments in favor of integration as they have been discussed as far back as 1990 (Younes 1990, 1995, 2015; Al-Batal 1992; Al-Batal and Belnap 2006). Rather, my purpose is to share the personal perspectives of teachers integrating dialects with MSA in their programs regarding the prominent arguments in support of the IA. Fifteen instructors list replicating the authentic use of Arabic by its native speakers as one of the main arguments in favor of the IA. According to these instructors, novice and intermediate functions are not reproduced in MSA in the Arabic-speaking world, and there is no reason to choose a register for class activities that is different from the one a native speaker would use. Eight instructors emphasize the importance of conveying the oneness of the Arabic language as another significant argument in support of integration. They argue that teaching MSA and dialect in different classes would send students the false message that the varieties are two distinct languages; it would create an artificial division that does not exist in the real world of Arabic. Moreover, eight surveyed instructors raise the issue of sociolinguistic competence, emphasizing that dialect is particularly relevant to teaching culture. The change in learner profiles is also a reason that integration is a more appropriate approach to teaching Arabic, according to seven instructors;[1] integration addresses the needs of today's students, who are interested in overall proficiency in Arabic and in interacting with native speakers. Two instructors mention pressure from students as one of the main factors that motivated their adoption of an integrated curriculum. Four instructors maintain that the IA enables students to reach fluency faster. For instance, with the IA, students can begin to form sentences within the first couple of weeks since they do not have to wait to learn complex MSA constructions such as المضارع المنصوب, the subjunctive mood.[2]

Participants and Methods

The present study is based on an empirical examination of the speech of instructors in Arabic-language classrooms at the University of Texas at Austin (UT) and on interviews with twenty integrative instructors of AFL; fifteen of the instructors currently teach in the United States, while five others have taught or are currently teaching in Australia, Europe, and the Middle East.

Data collected from one hundred hours of recorded or observed AFL classes have been analyzed to discover prominent characteristics regarding integration between MSA and dialect in the instructors' speech. Class sessions of twelve Arabic-language instructors at UT were recorded or observed between August 2012 and April 2015. The present study includes first-, second-, and third-year Arabic-language classes as well as three content-based courses, which are upper-division classes taught in Arabic for students who have completed three years of UT language courses or their equivalent.[3] In addition to data gathered from classes that have been observed or audio recorded specifically for this research, my study is based on previously video-taped classes that are currently available on the Arabic program website of the University of Texas at Austin (2012).[4] Twenty instructors of AFL were interviewed between October 2014 and September 2015 in order to examine their perspectives on the IA and the way they were implementing it in their classes.[5]

Analysis of Instructors' Speech in Integrated Arabic Classrooms

This section delineates the most prominent features related to teacher talk observed after analyzing the discourse of twelve instructors of Arabic at UT. Data reveal that instructors spend time discussing the linguistic situation in class and that they succeed in integrating a dialect that is not their own. It also shows that several variables, such as the content being discussed and the proficiency level of the class, play a role in how teacher talk moves along the MSA/dialect continuum; the most important factor, however, seems to be the instructor's preference. Code-switching between MSA and dialect is an integral part of the speech of instructors as educated speakers of Arabic; the last part of this section reveals the most prominent triggers of code-switching in instructors' speech.

Linguistic Reality in Integrated Classrooms

In class, instructors who implement integration discuss the linguistic situation of the Arabic language and spend time explaining the appropriate use of each register and highlighting the similarities and the logic behind the differences between MSA and dialect. Here, instructor A discusses with his advanced students, who were required to watch an episode of an Arabic TV series, the coexistence of multiple dialects as a new reality that speakers of the Arabic language often encounter, especially when watching certain TV programs:[6]

١. الآن هناك اسلوب جديد او طريقة جديدة في المسلسلات، انو في المسلسل يكون هناك اكثر من لهجة، في نفس المسلسل. حتلاحظوا فيه ناس عم يتكلّموا بالمصري، وناس عم يتكلّموا باللبناني او بالسوري . . . عملية المزيج اللغوي . . . ماذا يعني هذا لنا، يعني كمتعلمين للغة العربية؟ . . .

In Intensive Arabic II, instructor B highlights the similarities between MSA and dialect after watching a video in MSA:

٢. هو شو قال لـ"امس؟" []7البارحة. شايفين الشامي قريب . . . البارحة قريب من امبارح. صح؟ الفصحى والعامية مش بعيدين جداً.

Instructors also tend to reference, even if briefly, other dialects in class, such as when instructor C states:

٣. "فرح" بالعامية المصرية ما هيك؟، هو "عرس" بالعامية الشامية.

Or when instructor D explains the meaning of حيف "injustice" in MSA and then proceeds to discuss its different connotation in certain dialects:

٤. في اللهجات الشامية، في القرى وعند البدو تستخدم "يا حيف" للتعبير عن الأسى.

Successful Integration of a Different Dialect
Two instructors were observed teaching the same lesson in different classes, one that integrated MSA with Egyptian dialect and the other with Levantine. Analysis reveals that the instructors succeeded in shifting dialects. Here is a sample of Instructor E's speech during the morning session:

٥. ممكن دلوقت إحنا حنكون في مجموعات مع زميل مختلف؟ عايزين نتكلم شوية عن المأكولات اللي بحثنا عنها في الإنترنيت.

A few hours later, she addressed a class integrating Levantine with MSA:

٦. ممكن هلّق نكون في مجموعات من اثنين؟ لازم نحكي عن المعلومات اللي بحثنا عنها في الإنترنيت.

Despite making the effort to speak in the dialect integrated in the class, there is evidence that some instructors do not feel the need to completely censor their native dialect. For example, traces of instructor E's native Levantine dialect remain while teaching a class integrating Egyptian when using dialectal interrogative particles such a ليش؟ "why?" and شو؟ "what?" and in inconsistent phonological shifts when pronouncing the *jīm* phoneme.[8] Students do not seem surprised or confused in such instances. When she asked students in the Levantine dialect "شو نوع هاي الكلمة؟" "What type of word is this?" they answered اسم فاعل "active participle," and the discussion moved along.

Code-Switching Variables

Data analysis reveals that code-switching is governed by three main factors: (1) the proficiency level of the class, (2) the subject matter being discussed, and (3) the instructor's personal style and preference. Analysis suggests that instructors' personal preferences are the most influential factor in determining the instructor's code choices.

Level of Proficiency

My study reveals an overwhelming predominance of dialect in instructors' speech in first-year Arabic courses. Moreover, MSA is rarely maintained for over a sentence at the novice levels. As the proficiency level advances, the material discussed moves to the less concrete, resulting in increased usage of MSA with code-switches to Educated Spoken Arabic (ESA).[9]

Among thirty hours of intensive Arabic I and II courses analyzed, there were three Arabic II (second semester, Intermediate-Low level), seventy-five-minute sessions taught at different times during the day by three different instructors, all of whom taught the same listening text (drill 17, lesson 11, *Al-Kitaab* Part 1; Brustad, Al-Batal, and al-Tonsi 2011). The Arabic speech of instructor F was exclusively in dialect, whereas instructors G and H both integrated a few MSA sentences in the span of the session (fourteen sentences in the case of instructor G and six sentences with instructor H). A comparison of the register of the speech of two other instructors in a fifty-minute lesson covering a vocabulary activation and a root and pattern exercise (in lesson 10 in *Al-Kitaab* Part 1) corroborates the previous data that elementary Arabic instructors' discourse is either exclusively or predominantly in dialect: Instructor I's Arabic discourse was exclusively in dialect, and instructor J uttered only six sentences in MSA.

Shifts by the instructors to MSA at the beginners' levels happen at the level of a sentence; rarely do any of the observed instructors use more than two consecutive sentences in MSA. Instructor G does not sustain MSA for longer than a sentence in his Arabic Intensive II class; shifts to MSA are highlighted in bold here and throughout the chapter:

7. شو قال؟ اوكي، فهو عندو مشكلة، صح؟ اوكي، كويس، شو كمان؟ . . . تفضّلي. اوكي **فمسألة مثلاً "الذهاب الى المول"** والشوبنغ. شنو الشوبنغ؟

However, the following excerpt from the speech of the same instructor when teaching an advanced content-level class is mostly in MSA despite one code-switch to dialect (underlined in the excerpt below and throughout the chapter).

8. هل نستطيع ان نضيف شيء <u>كمان ع اساس نخلّي الأسلوب عربي اكتر</u>؟ مع الفعل المضارع، بعد اي نتيجة او شرط او ربط شيئين ببعضهما البعض؟ [ ] "فيلاحظ"، بالظبط! هذا قد يكون افضل.

The tendency to use MSA for large intervals of instructor speech at the higher levels is further illustrated in the sections below.

Subject Matter
The subject being discussed in class is another important factor in determining the instructor's choice of register, especially, but not only, in content courses, which are courses taught in Arabic for students at the advanced level of proficiency. Data collected from a content course with the title "Arab Political Speeches" revealed that instructor D's discourse is largely in MSA with occasional code-switches to dialect in order to discuss the dialect connotation of a specific MSA word, give classroom-management instructions, and ask short questions. On the other hand, the speech of instructor C in a course examining contemporary popular poetry, rap, and hip-hop is predominantly in the dialect register, whether ESA or plain vernacular, with spontaneous moves to MSA.

Instructor's Personal Preference/Style
When it comes to implementing integration, instructors included in this study fall into two major categories:

1. Some instructors' speech is consistently in dialect:
   They might read aloud words or sentences written in MSA for the purpose of grammatical analysis or for reading comprehension questions, for instance; however, their speech in follow up questions or discussions takes place solely in the dialect variety. Instruc-

tor K reads a quote from an article written in MSA that the students were required to read prior to class and proceeds to ask the questions in the Egyptian dialect:

9. "كثافة السكان تزداد،" بيتكلّم عن ايه هنا؟ ايه هو اللي بيزداد؟

In another session on grammar, the instructor's speech is also entirely in dialect, except for when she names the MSA relative pronouns, which are the grammatical features being examined:[10]

10. عندنا كمان اسم موصول مختلف شوية عن دا، هو "ما" و "من." "من" للأشخاص ولّا للأشياء؟

2. Other instructors' speech moves spontaneously to and from MSA: Those instructors shift back and forth between MSA and dialect, sometimes within the same sentence. Instructor E starts in MSA but goes through several code-switches when explaining an activity:

11. نريد اولاً ان نقرأ هذه الأسئلة، وبعد هيك حنشوف الفيديو، وبعدين حنتناقش حول هذه الأسئلة، لكن اولاً اقرأوا هذه الأسئلة منشان تركّزوا على الأجوبة من الفيديو، يللا، عندكم دقيقتين، اقرأوا الأسئلة.

Data analysis reveals the instructor's preference and style to be the guiding factor regarding how dialect and MSA are integrated in teacher talk. For instance, while two interviewed instructors consider translation to be a topic that would require the use of a formal register and indicate that their speech when teaching a course on translation would be predominantly in MSA, my observations of a content course with the title "Professional Translation in Arabic" reveals that instructor G uses the dialect in his class. Here, the instructor uses the dialect as he encourages a student to use a more formal word in her translation:

12. "لمّا" شوي عامية، صح؟ شو الكلمة اللي هي اكثر فصاحةً بهالسياق؟

Hence it appears that the instructor's personal style outweighs both the level of proficiency of the class and the subject matter being discussed in determining integration in teacher talk. This finding corroborates Reem Bassiouney's (2006) conclusion in her study *Functions of Code-Switching in Egypt*, which examines the speaker, the audience, and the subject matter as factors that are at play when code-switching occurs in public discourse in Egypt. She concludes that the speaker rather than the subject matter is the most important variable when it comes to code-switching.

Prominent Triggers for Code-Switching

Code-switching is a prominent feature of the discourse of teachers in integrated classrooms. In this part, I survey prominent triggers to code-switching in their speech.

Questions

By far the most prominent trigger of code-switching to dialect or to MSA takes place when asking questions. It is not the case, however, that every question leads to a code-switch. Question words at the beginners' level are the predominant triggers to short, one-sentence code-switches to MSA. In fact, all six code-switches to MSA in one of instructor J's Arabic II classes were introduced by an MSA question word. Here is one example:

13.دا ترجمة من الإنجليزي . . . في اللغة العربية، هل بنقول "اكثر من الناس"، ولّا "أكتر؟"] ["اكثر الناس"، شكراً جميل جداً . . . اوكي، صورة جديدة يا شباب. اوكي، **ماذا عن الجامع؟** ممكن نقول إيه هنا؟

The instructor starts her first question with the MSA interrogation particle هل but continues the question in dialect. She shifts briefly to MSA with her second question and then shifts back to dialect by repeating almost the same question in dialect.

In the following example, instructor E starts with MSA but shifts to dialect when prompting students to give more examples:

14. اذن هم يطلبون ان تكون اللغة موجودة. **شو كمان غير اللغة؟** عادةً في رأس السنة الميلادية او رأس السنة الهجرية، ماذا يوجد من الحكومة؟

Notice that the second question does not prompt another code-switch. Although asking questions is the most widely observed trigger to code-switch, not all questions lead to change of register.

Repetition

Another prominent trigger to code-switch happens through repetition. Many repetitions happen with questions as seen above in example 13 and as the following sample from instructor D reveals:

١٥. لاحظوا هذه العمامة، ما لون هذه العمامة؟ **شو لونها؟** عندما يرتدي رجل الدين الشيعي العمامة[السوداء]، هذا يعني انه من الأسياد.

Repetition does not, however, take place exclusively with questions, as the following example from the speech of instructor E shows:

١٦. بدي اسمع نهاية القصة وبعدين ممكن في مجموعة كبيرة **سنتكلّم عن القصة**. بس شو نهاية القصة؟[ ] حرية وما فيه داعي للمظاهرة . **هو لا يريد المظاهرة**. خلص، الحمدلله يا رب، فيه حريّة.

While the first shift happens with the future clause, the second shift to MSA is almost a reiteration of what the instructor had just said in dialect. In the following example, instructor A repeats exactly what he had said in a different register:

١٧. وعندنا الإعلام المرئي، يعني الذي نراه، <u>اللي منشوفه</u>.

Transitions

Another noticeable phenomenon is that transitioning to a new activity is often a space where code-switching takes place, specifically when instructions are being given. In the following excerpt, instructor B briefly shifts twice to MSA when she gives instructions explaining the activity, and again we see here that MSA is not maintained for long intervals of speech at the beginner's level:

١٨. نحن تكلّمنا كتير عن شو فهمنا، **الآن عندكم ثلاث او أربع دقائق مع الزميل**. أنا بدّي اعرف هذه الكلمة . . . **ممكن نعمل الآن الأسئلة**، شو الأشياء اللي ما نعرفها؟

Here is an excerpt from the speech of instructor E as she transitions to a new activity:

١٩. فيه عندنا بالأوراق بالـpdf، عندنا مجموعة من الأسئلة . . . في صفحة ستة مع التمرين رقم تلاتة . . . بدنا **نغيّر المجموعات**، لو سمحتم نريد أن نغيّر المجموعات، ونريد أن **نتكلّم ونتناقش حول هذه الأسئلة الموجودة في صفحة** ستة تمرين تلاتة. تمام؟ . . . بدنا نغيّر المجموعات.

The instructor shifts to MSA to give instructions about the new activity and shifts back to dialect when giving the page number.

Discussion of Important Topics

The move to a topic that is considered important often triggers code-switch to MSA. In this excerpt, instructor L is wrapping up a grammar activity in dialect, and she shifts register to MSA to discuss the importance of land in Palestinian culture, a topic that is typically considered to be both important and abstract.

20. هو في المعنى، مش في الشكل، فلازم نفكّر في المعنى، صح؟ اوكي يا شباب، . . . امبارح كان يوم مهم في الثقافة الفلسطينية، يوم ثلاثين مارس، ويوم ثلاثين مارس يُعرف بماذا؟ يوم الأرض، يوم مهم جداً جداً. طبعاً الفلسطينيون يحتفلون كل سنة بالأرض.

A few minutes earlier, the instructor had brought up the same topic when talking with one student, and again the importance of the topic leads to a spontaneous shift in register to MSA:

21. انتِ بتعرفي في هادا، سناء؟ يوم الأرض، هذا شيء كبير في الثقافة الفلسطينية.

Contact with MSA

Contact with MSA in a listening or reading text is another possible trigger for shifts to MSA. Here instructor E, who had been speaking in dialect, shifts to MSA as she encourages students to look at the text to find answers:

22. وبالنسبة للأرض؟ هذا موجود في الفقرة الأولى، في نهاية الفقرة الأولى تقريباً.

After watching a video in MSA, indicated by the use of empty brackets, instructor B adopts that register to ask a few questions before shifting back to dialect:

23. رح نشوف هذا الفيديو [ ]هم يتكلّمون بأي عربية هنا؟ يتكلّمون الفصحى؟ يتكلّمون الشامي؟ ماذا يتكلّمون؟[ ] يتكلّمون الفصحى، جميل جداً! هل إحنا سمعنا كلمات؟ ما سمعنا بكرا، صح؟ شو قال؟

Writing

My observations also reveal that, while instructors might sometimes write on the board in dialect, writing on the board is still predominantly associated with MSA; thus, writing is another trigger for code-switch to the formal register. Instructor H says and writes students' main points on the board in MSA, but all his other speech remains in dialect. Quotation marks signal sentences the instructor writes on the board.[11]

٢٤. بالنسبة ليكم، شنو بعض المشاكل اللي ممكن تكون بين المرأة والرجل في امريكا؟ [ ]
اوكي فـ"**هم مشغولين**." زوين. مشكل آخر، يا ياسر [ ] ... فـ"**هم ما عندهم**" كيف نقول؟
فلوس هيك أو كلمة أخرى يا محمّد. [ ] "مال،" ممتاز! فـ"**ما عندهم مال**، " ما عندهم فلوس.
مشكلة. لماذا ما عندهمش فلوس؟

Example 7, above, is an example from the speech of instructor G, working on the same listening text. He also shifts to MSA when saying aloud words he is writing on the board.[12]

Negation, Relative Pronouns, and the Particle of Existence
Negation, relative pronouns, and the particle of existence فيه "there is" are also triggers for code-switching. While negation and the particle of existence usually trigger shifts to dialect, relative pronouns initiate a code-switch to MSA or to dialect. When a student wonders about the grammatical function of a word, instructor L responds:

٢٥. اذا كان يبدو مصدر، فهو مصدر، هذا <u>مش ممكن يكون صفة</u>، يا داريل. <u>مش ممكن يكون</u>
<u>صفة</u>، هو مصدر، هذا وزن مصدر، هو دائماً مصدر ودائماً اسم.

The instructor, who is focusing on a written sentence for grammatical analysis, starts with MSA, switches to dialect when using the negative, and then returns to MSA for the rest of her explanation. Similarly, instructor G shifts to dialect with the negative; here the particle of existence فيه is negated:

٢٦. من يريد أن يقول لنا ما هو الفرق أو الـ difference بين المرفوع والمنصوب؟ يعني أنا
ممكن اتكلّم كثيراً، <u>ما فيش مشكلة</u>.

In the following example, the particle of existence initiates the code-switch to dialect:

٢٧. لماذا التاء؟ <u>فيه تاء؟ بس</u> هل أنا ألفظ التاء المربوطة؟ [ ]<u>ما فيه اضافة</u>، جميل!

In the example below, instructor C begins with dialect, moves spontaneously to MSA with the relative pronoun التي, and then moves back to dialect at the end of the relative clauses; his first relative clause does not lead to a change of register:

٢٨. شو فيه بعض الأشياء اللي ممكن نقارنها؟ وبدنا نربطها بالوضع السياسي طبعاً بالعالم
العربي والربيع العربي، الثورة ضد النظام، **الثورة التي تأتي من العشوائيات في القاهرة**
والثورة التي تأتي ايضاً من المناطق الريفية في سوريا. بدنا نقوم بالجمع بين الأنماط
الموسيقية وسياقهن الاجتماعي.

(2) overloading their cognitive resources. Eighteen out of the twenty instructors interviewed said that they are not troubled when students mix registers since it does not impede communication. Rather, they insist that mixing is expected in the early stages of learning and that this "confusion" is part of the learning process since the ability to code-switch appropriately is a skill that requires time.

Instructors also acknowledge that learning both varieties might place an extra burden on students, but this also reflects the reality of the Arabic language. Hence, many instructors assert that it is the instructor's task to manage this burden. They list the following strategies to mitigate the risks of student overload:

1. Modify teacher expectations of students so that they are fair, and tolerate a certain degree of mixing if and when it arises. Students' anxieties are minimized when they are not overwhelmed by the fear of mixing MSA and dialect. "We alleviate the confusion if we don't obsess about it," assures instructor 8.[15]

2. Spend time in class, especially during the first semester, discussing the diglossic nature of Arabic and raising students' awareness about the appropriate use of every variety. Highlighting the similarities between both and discussing the logic behind the differences equips students with tools to predict future instances of differences among varieties. This approach helps students in their learning of both MSA and dialect.

Implementing Integration in Instructors' Speech

Interviews with instructors corroborate the results of my data analysis, which suggests that there are two models for integration in the teachers' talk in class. Three interviewed instructors contend that replicating the authentic use of Arabic by its native speakers in the classroom requires that writing and reading take place in MSA while class discussion should be in dialect. This approach is supported by Munther Younes (2015), who advocates a program where "conversation and discussion take place in ʿĀmmiyya and reading and writing take place in FuṢḥā" (34).

Other instructors are wary of a rigid distinction between MSA as the variety used for the written and dialect as the spoken variety. According to these instructors, such a clear-cut dichotomy does not exist in the speech of educated native speakers who mix between MSA and dialect in many contexts. Thus, the speech of these instructors, similar to that of educated speakers of Arabic, features a coexistence between MSA and dialect and spontaneous movements back and forth between both varieties. When discussing their choice of register, these instructors often mention the words "I tend" and "I might," revealing a large degree of spontaneity in their choice of variety. Instructors' rich integrated speech allows them to speak in a way that feels comfortable and natural and reflects real-life use of the language by its speakers. To instructors who do not maintain an oral versus written divide, the choice of register is often driven by level expectations and tasks. The speech of the instructor in first-year Arabic, for instance, will be largely in dialect because the level expectations for this class is for students to learn to perform communicative tasks carried out by native speakers in the spoken variety. Still, even at the beginners' level, instructor 14 emphasizes that students should be aware of the coexistence of both varieties. Therefore, she creates oral tasks that invite the use of MSA, such as modeling a formal TV interview. At more advanced levels, those instructors agree that the nature of the material and tasks invite more MSA use.

Interviews with instructors also emphasize the role of subject matter in the instructor's choice of register. Instructor 19 maintains that when discussing a literary text, she tended to use more MSA whereas her discussion of youth culture took place predominantly in dialect. Instructor 15 lists a graduate seminar on modern Arab thought, and instructors 4 and 20 list Arabic media as examples of courses in which their discourse was predominantly in MSA. Still, they all acknowledge that code-switching between MSA and dialect would occur continuously in these courses.

Characteristics of Instructors' Dialect Speech
Interviews with instructors reveal that teacher talk in dialect is not a close replica of a specific regional dialect; rather, a process of "leveling" takes place where instructors suppress the idiosyncrasies of their specific dialect in favor of speech that is more widely understood.[16] The interviews suggest that these instructors, especially when teaching beginners, made various phonological and lexical accommodations in their teacher talk. Instructor 20, for instance, suppresses the *imāla* or "deflection," a prominent phonological feature in her Lebanese dialect, in order to remain closer to the phonological characteristics of MSA. In a similar vein, instructors 1 and 6 sometimes revert to pronouncing the /q/ as it is pronounced in MSA instead of the /ʔ/ used in the Levantine and Egyptian dialects to make it easier for students to recognize certain words.[17] Instructors make lexical accommodations as well. To lessen the burden of requiring students to memorize more words, instructors 9, 10, and 20 all mention opting for words that are closer to MSA when several choices of words are available. A few of the examples instructors

provided are opting to use the verb "*yibda*" instead of "*yballish*" ("to begin") and the verb "*ya'mil*" rather than "*ysāwī*" ("to do"). Instructors 6, 9, 10, 12, 18, and 20 all emphasize that instructors must make conscious choices in the dialect they use in the classroom with the aim of choosing vocabulary that is widely spoken in the Arab world and avoiding regionalism and local words in their teacher talk. Instructor 12 mentions opting to use the word "*kwayyis*" rather than "*mlīḥ*," ("good"), and instructor 6 avoids using the Syrian negation particle "*mū*" in favor of the more widely used "*mish*." Six instructors felt less compelled to make such adjustments to their use of dialect when teaching advanced classes.

Interdialectal Situation in the Arab World Reflected in TAFL Classroom

The changing linguistic situation in the Arab world where speakers of Arabic are exposed to materials from a variety of dialects, such as when watching television, is reflected in TAFL instructors' attitudes and practices. Nineteen instructors were willing to integrate MSA with a dialect other than their own and felt comfortable doing so at the beginner's level.[18] In fact, instructor 15 goes further by asserting, "It is the responsibility of every Arabic teacher to have the ability to teach a dialect other than his or her own." Nine instructors go beyond the ability to teach another dialect and express confidence that they can learn to teach a beginners' class, which integrates MSA with *any* Arabic dialect, if they have access to the right resources, support, and material.[19] The high percentage of instructors willing to teach a class integrating a dialect that is not their own is consistent with the results of the survey conducted by Abdalla and Al-Batal (2011–12), in which 60 percent of instructors asserted being comfortable teaching in another dialect at the beginner's level. Our data suggests that the percentage is even higher among instructors in integrated programs.

Interviews with instructors reveal the emergence of classrooms that boast the coexistence of several dialects, a situation that mirrors interdialectal conversations taking place whenever native speakers of different dialects converse. Seven of the interviewed instructors had students who came from previous classes and integrated a different dialect, and all of the instructors enthusiastically report successful transitions despite students' initial concern. They assert that their experiences reveal that when instructors allow students to keep speaking in the dialects they are comfortable with, students transition smoothly to a class that integrates a different dialect.

Instructors used a variety of strategies to provide a supportive learning environment that celebrates dialectal diversity and makes students feel comfortable using the dialect they had previously learned. Instructors mention several accommodations, such as when Egyptian instructor 5 sometimes pronounces her *jīm* as they do in the Levant (phonetic accommodation) or when instructor 8 of Egyptian dialect sometimes uses Levantine interrogative particles such as شو؟ "what?" (lexical accommodation) as a nod to the Levantine speakers in their classes. By making adjustments to their own classroom speech, instructors encourage students to feel free to keep using the dialect they consider their own. Instructor 15 makes an effort to include in his speech words from the other dialects; his aim is not only to send students the message that those words—and, hence, the other dialects they speak—are part of Arabic and do belong in the classroom but also to celebrate linguistic diversity within Arabic.

Conclusion

The instructors whose interviews or classroom speech were analyzed for the present study did not seek to "protect" their students from the diglossic reality of the Arabic language; rather, they took responsibility for creating a supportive environment in which both registers could be learned. To minimize possible student frustration arising from learning both varieties simultaneously, instructors accepted confusion as part of the learning process and tolerated awkward MSA and dialect mixtures in students' output, especially at the beginning levels. Rather than fixating on unnatural mixtures, instructors emphasized communication since they realized that the skill to code-switch appropriately would take time and would require long-term fine-tuning.

The integrated classroom exposes students to more than one register and sometimes to more than one dialect. Such exposure seems to desensitize students to register, enabling them to focus on the meaning instead of being distracted by the register. During my observation of classes, students not only managed to keep up with instructors' code-switching, they also displayed no sign of confusion when an instructor used a dialect that is not theirs. Students of the Levantine dialect were not taken aback, for instance, when traces of their instructor's Gulf dialect sometimes emerged. When the instructor occasionally adopted phonetic features of his Gulf dialect or made non-Levantine lexical choices, the students remained engaged and answered his questions without reluctance.

Results from the present study also reveal that the coexistence between MSA and dialect—a feature of all integrated classrooms—varies depending on several factors. Most importantly, topics covered in more advanced classes invite the increased use of MSA, while teacher talk at the beginner levels is predominantly in the spoken variety. The preference and style of the teacher, however, remains the most important variable when it comes to how dialect is integrated in the classroom.

Spontaneous shifts to and from MSA give instructors the flexibility to be comfortable as speakers of Arabic and allow them also to code-switch in ways that feel natural. Instructors do not feel the need to censor code-switches. Hence, their spontaneously integrated speech mirrors the authentic use of the Arabic language by its native speakers and is reflective of what the students will encounter when they are in contact with Arabic outside the confines of the classroom.

References

Abdalla, Mahmoud, and Mahmoud Al-Batal. 2011–12. "College-Level Teachers of Arabic in the United States: A Survey of Their Professional and Institutional Profiles and Attitudes." *Al-ᶜArabīyya* 44/45: 1–28.

Al-Batal, Mahmoud. 1992. "Diglossia Proficiency: The Need for an Alternative Approach to Teaching." In *The Arabic Language in America*, edited by Aleya Rouchdy, 284–304. Detroit: Wayne State University Press.

———. 1995. "Issues in the Teaching of the Productive Skills in Arabic." In *The Teaching of Arabic as a Foreign Language: Issues and Directions*, edited by Mahmoud Al-Batal, 115–33. Provo, UT: American Association of Teachers of Arabic.

Al-Batal, Mahmoud, and R. Kirk Belnap. 2006. "The Teaching and Learning of Arabic in the United States: Realities, Needs, and Future Directions." In *Handbook for Arabic Language Teaching Professionals in the 21ˢᵗ Century*, edited by Kassem M. Wahba, Zeinab A. Taha, and Liz England, 389–99. Mahwah, NJ: Lawrence Erlbaum.

American Council on the Teaching of Foreign Languages (ACTFL). 2012. "ACTFL Proficiency Guidelines 2012." American Council on the Teaching of Foreign Languages. http://www.actfl.org/publications/guidelines-and-manuals/actfl -proficiency-guidelines-2012.

Badawi, El-Said. 1973. *Mustawayāt al-ᶜArabīyya al muᶜāṣira fī Miṣr.* Cairo: Dār al-Maᶜārif.

Bassiouney, Reem. 2006. *Functions of Code-Switching in Egypt: Evidence from Monologues.* Leiden: Brill.

———. 2009. *Arabic Sociolinguistics: Topics in Diglossia, Gender, Identity, and Politics.* Washington, DC: Georgetown University Press.

Belnap, R. Kirk. 1987. "Who Is Taking Arabic and What on Earth for? A Survey of Students in Arabic Language Programs." *Al-ᶜArabīyya* 20, no. 1–2: 29–42.

———. 1995. "The Institutional Setting of Arabic Language Teaching: A Survey of Program Coordinators and Teachers of Arabic in U.S. Institutions of Higher Learning." In *The Teaching of Arabic as a Foreign Language: Issues and Directions*, edited by Mahmoud Al-Batal, 35–77. Provo, UT: American Association of Teachers of Arabic.

————. 2006. "A Profile of Students of Arabic in U.S. Universities." In *Handbook for Arabic Language Teaching Professionals in the 21st Century*, edited by Kassem M. Wahba, Zeinab A. Taha, and Liz England, 169–78. Mahwah, NJ: Lawrence Erlbaum.

Blanc, Haim. 1960. "Style Variations in Spoken Arabic: A Sample of Interdialectal Educated Conversation." *Contributions to Arabic Linguistics*, edited by Charles Ferguson, 80–156. Cambridge, MA: Harvard University Press.

Brustad, Kristen, Mahmoud Al-Batal, and Abbas al-Tonsi. 2011. *Al-Kitaab fii Taᶜallum al-ᶜArabiyya: A Textbook for Beginning Arabic*, Part One, 3rd ed. Washington, DC: Georgetown University Press.

Holes, Clive. 2004. *Modern Arabic Structures, Functions, and Varieties*. Washington, DC: Georgetown University Press.

Meiseles, Gustav. 1980. "Educated Spoken Arabic and the Arabic Language Continuum." *Archivum Linguisticum* 11, no. 2: 118–48.

University of Texas at Austin's Arabic Program. 2012. "Arabic Language Teaching Videos: Year One." University of Texas at Austin. http://universityoftexasarabic.com/.

Younes, Munther. 1990. "An Integrated Approach to Teaching Arabic as a Foreign Language." *Al-ᶜArabiyya* 23, no. 1–2: 105–22.

————. 1995. "An Integrated Curriculum for Elementary Arabic." In *The Teaching of Arabic as a Foreign Language: Issues and Directions*, edited by Mahmoud Al-Batal, 233–55. Provo, UT: American Association of Teachers of Arabic.

————. 2015. *The Integrated Approach to Arabic Instruction*. New York: Routledge.

Notes

Additional data and examples are freely available to view and download on this book's product page on the Georgetown University Press (GUP) website (www.press.georgetown.edu).

1. For a study of learners' profiles, see Belnap (1987, 2006).
2. A point brought up by instructor 18 during the interviews.
3. At the end of the first year (after two courses, six credit hours each), students are expected to reach a proficiency level of Intermediate-Low to Intermediate-Mid (ACTFL 2012); at the end of the second year (after four courses totaling twenty-four credit hours), Intermediate-Mid to Intermediate-High; and, at the end of the third year (after six courses totaling thirty-four credit hours), students are expected to reach a proficiency level of Advanced-Low.
4. A table that indicates the level(s) taught by each instructor is available in appendix A, on the GUP website.
5. A list of the interview questions is available in appendix B, and a list of the country where each instructor teaches and the courses taught when the interview took place is found in appendix C, both on the website. All of the excerpts of teacher talk are available in a single document, along with English translations, in appendix D, on the GUP website.

6. For this section, I refer to each instructor with a different letter. The instructor whose discourse is analyzed first in this section is referred to as "instructor A" throughout the chapter. You can listen to audio 16.1 on the GUP website. All the listed examples of instructors' speech along with their translations to English are available on the GUP website.

7. Throughout the chapter, unless otherwise noted, I use empty brackets [ ] to signify student speech that has been edited out.

8. In the Cairene dialect, the *jīm* sound is pronounced /g/, as in "rug," while in most of the Levant it is pronounced /ʒ/, as in "pleasure."

9. When discussing the continuum stretching between classical and colloquial Arabic, linguists recognize that dialect is split into several levels (Blanc 1960; Badawi 1973; Meiseles 1980). Following Gustav Meiseles, who identifies only two levels of dialect, I distinguish between ESA, a colloquial language that is very influenced by MSA, and plain vernacular. Meiseles defines ESA as "a vernacular type characterized by the aspirations of its speakers to get rid of local features peculiar to their dialects through a process of koineization and/or borrowings from LA [literary Arabic], especially on the lexical and morphophonemic levels" (1980, 126).

10. Audio samples 16.2 and 16.3 on the GUP website are samples from the same instructor that reflect the consistent use of dialect.

11. Listen to audio sample 16.4 on the GUP website.

12. You can listen to the full excerpt in audio sample 16.5 on the GUP website, which has been partly transcribed in the text shown here.

13. You can listen to audio sample 16.6 on the GUP website.

14. This chapter does not cover all the questions asked during the interviews but, rather, a few points that the author believes to be particularly pertinent to providing a comprehensive overview of the attitudes and practices of integrative instructors. A complete list of the interview questions is presented in appendix B, on the GUP website.

15. In this section, each of the interviewed instructors is referred to with a number. Instructor 1 is the first instructor interviewed.

16. For references on leveling in Arabic dialects, see Blanc (1960), Holes (2004), and Bassiouney (2009).

17. Examining recordings of classes reveals that this phonological accommodation of pronouncing the /q/ is widely used among instructors.

18. Instructor 12 is the only one who chooses not to speak in a nonnative dialect because it feels unnatural and artificial.

19. Instructors list videos, audio recordings, and grammatical and cultural notes as well as help from colleagues who are native speakers of that other dialect as important resources. One instructor expected that she would rely more on MSA when she integrated it with a dialect with which she was not particularly familiar. Another instructor welcomed the challenge on the condition that her workload that semester would be light; she expected to need a month of preparation to immerse herself in the new dialect.

Contributors

Mahmoud Al-Batal is a professor of Arabic in the Department of Arabic and Near Eastern Languages at the American University of Beirut. He is specialized in applied linguistics and teaching Arabic as a foreign language and is coauthor of the *Al-Kitaab* Arabic textbook series published by Georgetown University Press. He has published numerous articles dealing with Arabic language pedagogy and Arabic sociolinguistics and is developer of *Aswaat Arabiyya* "Arabic Voices," a web-based resource for Arabic listening materials.

R. Kirk Belnap is a professor of Arabic at Brigham Young University. From 2002 to 2015 he served as director of the National Middle East Language Resource Center and continues to lead the Project Perseverance team in developing resources to assist learners to become more effective in accomplishing their goals. His research focus is on second-language acquisition. He has directed numerous intensive language programs since 1989, including Arabic summer camps for high school students.

Gregory R. Ebner is the head of the Department of Foreign Languages at the United States Military Academy, West Point. He earned his bachelor of science degree in engineering from West Point and his master's degree in Middle Eastern Studies from the University of Michigan while serving as an Army Foreign Area Officer. He earned his doctorate in Arabic (focusing on teaching Arabic as a foreign language) from the University of Texas.

Jonathan Featherstone is a senior teaching fellow of Arabic at the University of Edinburgh. He has worked as a lecturer of Arabic at the Defense School of Languages in the United Kingdom and at the Foreign and Commonwealth Office where he was a senior lecturer of Arabic. He is a teacher trainer and has designed and delivered numerous intensive courses to postgraduates and school and college teachers of Arabic in the United Kingdom, all using the integrated approach. He is the author of *BBC Talk Arabic*, a beginners' book to the Arabic language.

Manuela E. B. Giolfo was a lecturer in Arabic at Exeter University (UK) 2008–2013. Since 2013, she is a researcher in Arabic language and literature and a lecturer in Arabic and Arabic philology at the University of Genoa (Italy).

She is a supervisor of PhD candidates in Arabic linguistics at Exeter University and Digital Humanities at the University of Genoa. She also teaches Arabic at the International University of Languages & Media in Milan (Italy). She is *chercheuse associée* at IREMAM CNRS Aix-Marseille Université (France) and holds a PhD in Arabic linguistics from the same university.

Christian Glakas is business development director for Black Barn Financial, LLC. He served as assistant director of the Arabic Flagship Program at the University of Texas at Austin from 2012 to January 2017. Before joining the AFP, Mr. Glakas worked at Refugee Services of Texas, where he worked to help Iraqi refugees secure employment. He has advanced proficiency in Arabic and professional experience in the Middle East, having worked with the Business Development Center in Amman, Jordan in 2010.

Elizabeth Huntley is pursuing her PhD in Second Language Studies from Michigan State University. Huntley has taught Arabic at the University of Michigan and at Cornell University. She served as resident coordinator for Middlebury College's School in the Middle East in Egypt. Huntley is also the former director of the STARTALK Arabic Summer Academy of the Boston Public Schools. Her research interests include applied linguistics, curriculum design, and second-language acquisition.

Martin Isleem is director of the Arabic program at Bucknell University. Dr. Isleem's areas of study focus on teaching Arabic as a foreign language and sociolinguistics, particularly the languages of minorities in Israel. His most recent research lies in investigating the attitude of students of Arabic in the United States toward Standard and spoken Arabic, the linguistic landscape in Druze and Circassian towns, and code-switching between Arabic and Hebrew among the Druze community in Israel.

Charles Joukhadar is an Arabic language instructor and coordinator at the University of Arizona. He has a broad experience in material development and teaching Arabic as a foreign language both in the United States and the Middle East. He is also completing his PhD in Arabic linguistics, with a focus on language variation and change in Arabic dialects. His research interests include exploring ways through which technology can enhance the acquisition of Arabic language and culture.

Thomas Leddy-Cecere is a PhD candidate in Arabic linguistics at the University of Texas at Austin (UT). He has received training and experience in Arabic language instruction at Dartmouth College and UT. His research interests include sociophonetics, the synchronic and diachronic outcomes of dialect contact, and grammaticalization studies, and his fieldwork in Arabic, North American English, and other languages has taken him to Egypt, Morocco, and across the United States. His research interests include sociophonetics, the synchronic and diachronic outcomes of dialect contact, and grammaticalization studies, and his fieldwork in Arabic, North American English, and other languages has taken him to Egypt, Morocco, and across the United States.

Caroline Najour is a lecturer and the Arabic program coordinator at the University of North Texas. Her areas of interest include second-language acquisition, teaching Arabic culture, and contemporary Arabic fiction. Her research focuses on feminist and postcolonial theories to examine Western characters at the intersection of colonialism, gender, and modernity in contemporary Arab novels.

Lama Nassif is an assistant professor of Arabic at Williams College, where she teaches courses on Arabic language and linguistics. Her research interests include noticing and attention in second-language development, and the interface between second-language acquisition and second-language pedagogy. She has held teaching and administrative positions at various Syrian and US institutions, and her publications include articles and book reviews in *Language Awareness, Modern Language Journal*, and *Applied Language Learning*.

Jeremy Palmer earned his PhD (2009) from the University of Arizona in second-language acquisition and teaching with a major in pedagogy. Dr. Palmer has taught at several universities in the United States and more recently in the United Arab Emirates. His research revolves around adult learners of foreign and second languages. His interests also include sociolinguistics, teacher training, and immersion program administration. He also enjoys running ultramarathons.

Federico Salvaggio holds a PhD in digital humanities from the University of Genoa (Italy). His doctoral dissertation deals with the application of digital technologies to TAFL to integrate the teaching of Standard Arabic with colloquials in the light of CEFR. He teaches Arabic and computer-assisted Arabic translation at the International University of Languages & Media in Milan (Italy). He was a lecturer in Arabic translation at Cairo University (Egypt) and at the University of Benghazi (Libya). He obtained an MA in Arabic language from the University of Palermo (Italy) with a dissertation on TAFL for religious purposes.

Sonia Shiri is an associate professor and the Middle East Language Programs coordinator at the University of Arizona. She is the director of the Arabic Flagship Program and an affiliated faculty of the Second Language Acquisition and Teaching program. Dr. Shiri's research focuses on language learning in study abroad, computer-assisted language learning, linguistic landscapes, and critical discourse analysis. Prior to Arizona, she taught at UC Berkeley and Oxford, and she served as senior academic director of the Critical Language Scholarship.

Emma Trentman is an assistant professor of Arabic at the University of New Mexico. She received her PhD in Second Language Studies from Michigan State University in 2012. Her research focuses on language and intercultural learning during study abroad and telecollaboration, Arabic dialect acquisition, and Arabic pedagogy. She has published articles in the *Modern Language Journal, Foreign Language Annals, Al-ᶜArabiyya*, the *L2 Journal*, and the EUROSLA monograph series.

Mike Turner is a PhD student in the Department of Middle Eastern Studies at the University of Texas at Austin, where he works on the linguistic history of Arabic and Berber. His research focuses on processes of grammatical change and the effects of language contact. He has taught Arabic at the beginning, intermediate, and advanced levels and is primarily interested in materials development and teaching spoken dialects to second-language learners.

Jeff R. Watson is the chair of Linguistics and Language Acquisition in the Center for Languages, Cultures, and Regional Studies at the United States Military Academy, West Point, New York. He received his MA in teaching foreign languages from the Middlebury Institute of International Studies at Monterey and his PhD in sociocultural theory and second-language acquisition from Bryn Mawr College. In addition to teaching linguistics and Russian at West Point, Dr. Watson pursues applied research on topics pertaining to language, regional expertise, and culture in academic and military contexts.

Munther Younes is Reis Senior Lecturer of Arabic Language and Linguistics and director of the Arabic program at Cornell University. He received his PhD in linguistics from the University of Texas at Austin. He is the coauthor of the three-textbook series *ᶜArabiyyat al-Naas* and the author of *Kalila wa Dimna for Students of Arabic, The Routledge Introduction to Qur'anic Arabic*, and *The Integrated Approach to Arabic Instruction*. His other publications include articles on Arabic linguistics, teaching Arabic as a foreign language, and the language of the Qur'an.

Mai Zaki is an assistant professor in the Department of Arabic and Translation Studies at American University of Sharjah. She obtained her PhD degree in linguistics from Middlesex University, UK, and a certificate in TAFL from SOAS, University of London. She has taught linguistics, translation, and Arabic for nonnative speakers in a number of universities in Egypt, the United Kingdom, and the United Arab Emirates. Her areas of interest in research include Arabic linguistics, pragmatics, corpus-based teaching, and using technology in the TAFL classroom.

Index

Surnames beginning with "al-" are alphabetized by remaining portion of name.
Figures, notes, and tables are indicated by f, n, and t following the page number.

Siegel, Jeff, 159–60, 203
skill development, xiv, 173–234; Colloquial Arabic, 175–98; speaker output, 199–220; written language skills, 221–34. *See also specific skills*
Sobḥ, ᶜAlawiyya, 22n2
social media, 8, 161
sociocommunicative tasks (SCTs), 95
sociolinguistic authenticity, 38
sociolinguistic competence, 114, 123–28, 126*t*
speaker output skill development, 199–220; dialect system interaction stages, 204–17, 217*t*; study methodology, 202–3; study purpose and rationale, 200–201
speech patterns of teachers in IA classrooms, 298–317; characteristics of, 312–13; code-switching triggers, 305–14; code-switching variables, 302–5; contact with MSA, 307; integration of different dialect, 301–2; and interdialectal situation in Arab world, 313–14; and linguistic realities, 300–301; negation, 308–9; and particle of existence, 308–9; proficiency levels, 302–3; questions, 305; relative pronouns, 308–9; repetition, 305–6; student-triggered code-switching, 310; study methodology, 300; transitions, 306; and writing, 307–8
Spoken Colloquial Arabic (SCA), 73–74, 80, 83, 88n4
Stokes, Corinne, 11
student perspectives: arguments for and against integrated approach, 75–78; on Colloquial Arabic in classroom, xv, 237–59, 243–45*f*, 247*f*, 253–55*f*; on dialect choice, 76–77; on dialect integration, xv, 260–78, 263–69*t*, 271*t*, 274*t*; experiences abroad, 81–84; experiences in classroom, 78–81; on learning burden, 75–76; in multidialect environment, 279–97; needs of students, 77–78; preparation for inte-

grated approach learning, 73–89; study methodology, 75
Sudanese dialect, 18–19
systemic functional linguistics (SFL), 115, 117

Tabouret-Keller, Andrée, 203, 209, 210–11, 216
Tāksi (al-Khamīsi), 22n2
teacher perspectives, 298–317; barrier of fear for integrated approach, 59; on Colloquial Arabic in classroom, 237–59, 243–45*f*, 247*f*, 253–55*f*; creativity development, 62–65; deconstructing and reconstructing Arabic, 61; "diglossic gap," 61; empathy with learners, 66–67; fear of handling dialect and MSA simultaneously, 59–60; integrative drills, exercises, and games, 65–66; mini lessons, 67; post-reading activities, 65; preparation for integrated approach teaching, 54–72; pre-reading tasks, 64; reading tasks, 64–65; relationship between dialects and MSA, 61–62
television programs and commercials: and BYU Model, 39; dialect use in, 8–9; in University of New Mexico Model, 119
third-year productions, 188–92, 189*f*
third-year skits, 189*f*, 191–92
Thornbury, Scott, 72n18
Al-Tonsi, Abbas, 260
Trentman, Emma, xiii, 44, 75, 114, 272
Trudgill, Peter, 203, 206, 209, 211
Turner, Mike, xiii, 134

United Kingdom, IA approach in, 56–57. *See also* Edinburgh University Model
United States Military Academy at West Point, xiv; *Alif Baa* used in, 226; Egyptian Colloquial Arabic in, 225; *Al-Kitaab* used in, 222; Levantine Arabic in, 224, 225, 231; Modern Standard Arabic in, 225–26, 231–32; written language skill development at, 221–34

University of Arizona Model, xiii, 16–17, 154–72; diglossia in, 156–57; and Noticing Hypothesis, 156, 159–60; student levels of mixing of two varieties, 163–65, 164*t*; student proficiency levels, 165–67; study methodology, 161–63; teacher strategies, 167–68

University of Michigan Model, xii, 73–89; *ᶜArabiyyat al-Naas* used in, 88n6; dialect choice, 76–77; Egyptian Colloquial Arabic in, 76; experiences abroad, 81–84; experiences in classroom, 78–81; integrated approach rationale in, 75–78; *Al-Kitaab* used in, 74, 78; learning burden in, 75–76; Levantine Arabic in, 76; Modern Standard Arabic in, 73–74, 80, 83; preparation for integrated approach learning, 73–89; Spoken Colloquial Arabic in, 73–74, 80, 83, 88n4; student needs in, 77–78; study methodology, 75; vocabulary in, 76

University of Texas, Austin Model, xiv, 17–18; *Alif Baa* used in, 135, 136, 138, 146–47, 149–50; *ᶜArabiyyat al-Naas* used in, 260; code switching in, xvi, 300; dialect system interaction stages, 204–17, 217*t*; Egyptian Colloquial Arabic in, 17, 141, 148, 199, 204, 206, 207–17, 270; *Al-Kitaab* used in, 17, 134–36, 138, 142–50, 201, 260; Levantine Arabic in, 17, 141, 148, 199, 204, 207–17, 270; Modern Standard Arabic in, 17–18, 141–45, 148, 199, 204, 206, 207–17, 300–301; Moroccan Arabic in, 17, 199, 204, 207–17; speaker output skill development, 199–220; student perspectives on, 260–78; study methodology, 202–3; study purpose and rationale, 200–201; verbs in, 146; vocabulary in, 135, 142–45

Van Dyck, Cornelius, 3
verbs: in Colloquial Arabic, 180, 182; in Cornell University Model, 29; in first-year productions, 182*f*, 183–84; in Levantine Arabic, 186; in second-year productions, 185–86, 185*f*; in third-year productions, 188, 189*f*; in third-year skits, 189*f*, 191; in University of Texas, Austin Model, 146
Versteegh, Kees, 191
virtual learning environments (VLEs), 95
vocabulary: in Cornell University Model, 26, 28–29; Moroccan Arabic, 142–45; in University of Michigan Model, 76; in University of Texas, Austin Model, 135, 142–45

Wahba, Kassem, 279–80
Warnick, Paul, 53n3
Watson, Jeff R., xiv, 12, 221
weather broadcasts, dialect use in, 8
Weatherspoon, Makda, 260
Weinert, John, 272
Western Michigan University Model, 15–16
West Point. *See* United States Military Academy at West Point
Wilmsen, David, 53n3, 53n6, 109
Winford, Donald, 203
World Language Standards, 11
written language skills: in Common European Framework, 101–2; development of, 221–34; and dialect studies, 224–27; study methodology, 227–28

Younes, Munther, xi, 5, 23, 24, 34, 70n2, 100, 113n17, 158, 176, 234n8, 260, 267, 281, 311

Zaki, Mai, xv, 279

CPSIA information can be obtained
at www.ICGtesting.com
Printed in the USA
BVOW03s0907221117
500360BV00014B/4/P

9 781626 165045